P9-CBI-719

MAY 3 1990

CLASSICS OF TLINGIT ORAL LITERATURE

Edited by

Nora Marks Dauenhauer and Richard Dauenhauer

VOLUME 1

Haa Shuká, Our Ancestors: Tlingit Oral Narratives

Haa Shuká, Our Ancestors

TLINGIT ORAL NARRATIVES

Edited by Nora Marks Dauenhauer
and Richard Dauenhauer

UNIVERSITY OF WASHINGTON PRESS
Seattle and London

SEALASKA HERITAGE FOUNDATION
Juneau

Copyright © 1987 by Sealaska Heritage Foundation
Manufactured in the United States of America

All rights reserved. No part of this publication
may be reproduced or transmitted in any form or by
any means, electronic or mechanical, including
photocopy, recording, or any information storage
or retrieval system, without permission in writing
from the publisher.

This book is published with the assistance of
a grant from the Alaska Humanities Forum, a
state-based program of National Endowment for
the Humanities.

Preparation of this volume was made possible in
part by grants from the Division of Research
Programs of the National Endowment for the
Humanities, an independent federal agency, and
by grants from the Alaska State Legislature.

Library of Congress Cataloging-in-Publication Data

Haa shuká, our ancestors.

    (Classics of Tlingit oral literature ; v. 1)
    English and Tlingit.
    Bibliography: p.
    1. Tlingit Indians--Legends. 2. Tlingit Indians--
Religion and mythology. 3. Indians of North America--
Alaska--Legends. 4. Indians of North America--Alaska--
Religion and mythology. 5. Tlingit language--Texts.
I. Dauenhauer, Nora. II. Dauenhauer, Richard.
III. Series.
E99.T6H22 1987   398.2'089970798   87-2164
ISBN 0-295-96494-4 (cloth)
ISBN 0-295-96495-2 (paper)

Cover art by Joanne George

in memory of our ancestors

Tradition...
cannot be inherited,
and if you want it
you must obtain it
by great labour.
            --T. S. Eliot

EDMONDS COMMUNITY COLLEGE LIBRARY

CONTENTS

PREFACE

We are involved in Tlingit oral literature
because we believe it has value, that it is a
treasury of spiritual gifts from which we can
draw in times of need, and that Tlingit people
especially, and especially the youth, may find
comfort and reward in seeing how their
ancestors faced decisions in their lives.

These are not simple children's stories, but
adult literature that addresses the "ambiguities
of the human condition" with which we all must
come to grips: coming of age as adults, alienation,
identity and self concept, conflict of loyalty,
pride and arrogance, separation and loss--and many
other experiences that are part of being human.

We have been most fortunate to have as our
instructors some of the tradition bearers in
this volume. Much of the instruction was very
difficult, and our instinct was often to give
up. But their faith in us helped us to
continue, because they wanted this work to
continue, for their grandchildren. Our hope is
that their words will be appreciated and will
inspire our generation and generations to come,
both Tlingit and non-Tlingit, as they have
inspired us.

We must also say that this collection is not

for everyone, but is for those who wish to
know who they are (whoever they are) and who
the Tlingit people are. Only through stories
and traditions like these do we begin to learn
who we are, no matter who we are.

These stories are Tlingit clan stories.
They belong to all who are Tlingit through
birth or adoption because the Tlingit kinship
system makes isolation of individuals
impossible. Each of us, Tlingit or not, may
have lonely decisions to make, but we do not
stand alone. Tlingit people are connected by
the clan system in operation in these stories.
But all people have a system of some kind. To
readers of all cultures living in an age of
increasing fragmentation, these stories offer
examples of how such connecting systems operate.

So, while these stories are about various
Tlingit clans, and are in the stewardship of
specific clans, they are simultaneously about
all Tlingit people, and about people everywhere.
They are about family, community, and membership.
Each of us is connected, but it is important
for each of to learn how, and act accordingly.

At Sealaska Heritage Foundation, an
organization committed to fostering the culture
and heritage of the Native people of Southeast
Alaska, we have worked intensively for over
three years preparing these texts for
publication. But we have been living and
working with some of these texts for over 15
years. During this time, many of the Tradition
Bearers have passed from this life. Of the
twelve Elders whose work is presented here,
only three are still alive as this goes to
press.

Each death brings the Tlingit language and
the great oral tradition composed and
transmitted in the language closer to
extinction. We work with the sober awareness
that linguists predict the extinction of the
Tlingit language within the next 50 or 60
years. Children no longer speak Tlingit. Few

young parents speak the language; as far as we
know, there are no speakers under the age of
30, and there are only a handful of speakers
under the age of 50.

We have no doubt that many aspects of
Tlingit culture and heritage will endure and
thrive in spoken and written English, but the
Tlingit language itself, and those traditions
which are bound to the language will probably
not survive.

Tlingit is one of the most complicated
languages in the world, and it is unrealistic
to expect it to make a comeback as a spoken
language through classroom teaching--at least
as presently constituted. Still, it is very
realistic to expect that many people in coming
generations will learn to read and appreciate
the ancestral language through study of the
classics of the past, and it is reasonable to
hope that in the meantime families and
communities will work together to cultivate
their traditions, whether in English or
Tlingit, working with their living elders, and
with the documented inheritance of the past.

George Steiner points out in his book *After
Babel* that part of the enduring greatness of
Classical Greek and Hebrew literature is due to
the entrance of literacy at a crucial point in
their histories, so that the oral literature
was able to outlive its original relationship
between composer and audience, and thrive and
have meaning for generations to come. Three
thousand years after the "Golden Age" of their
oral composition, ancient Greek and Hebrew
literature remain alive and powerful, far
beyond their original culture and audience.

The transformation from oral to written form
is not easy. Oral and written literature have
widely differing and often conficting aesthetics
and rules for composition and publication. The
non-literate world view is rich and complicated,
often beyond the comprehension and appreciation
of those steeped in literacy and written

literature. The skills and methods demanded of oral and written composition are often alien to each other, yet the skills from both traditions are required for success in the transfer, and even the greatest success in making the shift is often only partial.

Yet it is also reasonable to hope that, as the words of Tlingit composers reach out into world literature, people around the world can and will respond in meaningful ways to the experiences of Tlingit oral literature.

Elias Canetti, Nobel laureate of 1981, says, "Tribes, sometimes consisting of just a few hundred people, have left us a wealth that we certainly do not merit, for it is our fault that they have died out or are dying before our eyes, eyes that scarcely look. They have preserved their mythical experiences until the very end, and the strange thing is that there is hardly anything that benefits us more, hardly anything that fills us with as much hope as these early incomparable creations.... They have left us an inexhaustible spiritual legacy."

We dedicate this effort to the memories of the Elders who have enriched our lives so much through the spiritual legacy which they embodied and have bequeathed to generations to come. We are proud and at the same time humble to present you with Haa Shuká.

Nora Marks Dauenhauer
Richard Dauenhauer
Juneau, February 1987

ACKNOWLEDGMENTS

The editors wish to acknowledge appreciation for the support of the Sealaska Heritage Foundation Board of Directors: Judson L. Brown (Chair, 1983–86) L. Embert Demmert, A. John Hope, Clarence Jackson, Toni Jones, Esther Littlefield, Robert Martin (chair, 1986–) Conrad Mather, Roy Peratrovich, Sr., Robert Sanderson, Walter Soboleff, Richard Stitt, Ed Thomas, Alfred Widmark, Sr., Ronald Williams, Rosita Worl, Carlton Smith (Corporate Secretary); Administration (David G. Katzeek, President; Gordon Jackson, Vice-President); Language and Cultural Studies Production Staff (Fred White and Rhonda Mann, Research Assistants) and all of our colleagues at the Sealaska Heritage Foundation, who shared our vision of the possibility of using new technology to help document traditional ways. We note especially that Fred White and Rhonda Mann were involved in word processing the manuscript, Rhonda Mann in final type setting of the book, and that the map on page xvii was drawn by Rhonda Mann.

We gratefully acknowlege the following institutions, agencies, organizations, and individuals, whose efforts and support helped make the project possible.

Major funding for this project came from the Alaska State Legislature 1983-87, whose support made it possible to document for posterity these treasures of the oral literature of Alaska that are the heritage of all Alaskans, regardless of ethnicity.

Part of the funding to complete the project is through a Translation Grant from the National Endowment for the Humanities (Grant RL-20533-86.) Some of the materials were collected, and/or earlier versions of some manuscripts were drafted with the support of the National Endowment for the Humanities Translation Grant RL-00160-80-1070 (1980-1981), and as projects of the Alaska Native Language Center, University of Alaska-Fairbanks, during its first year of operation 1972-73. Funds for publication of this volume were provided by a Grant from the Alaska Humanities Forum. Any opinions, conclusions, or findings contained herein do not necessarily represent the view of the National Endowment for the Humanities, or of the other supporting agencies.

We also acknowledge the personal and technical support of our friends and colleagues who helped us pioneer in the development of software and firmware for fluent word processing, screen display, printing, and electronic transmission of Tlingit and other languages with character sets other than English; especially: Dr. James Levin, Interlearn and formerly of University of California-San Diego, now of University of Southern Illinois; Dr. Moshe Cohen, Interlearn and Hebrew University of Jerusalem; Mr. Allan Rogers of Hands-on Training Company, Bonita, California, who helped in the development of an inexpensive foreign language chip for the Apple 2e; and Drs. Ron and Suzanne Scollon, formerly of University of Alaska-Fairbanks, now of Gutenberg Dump, Limited, Haines, Alaska. We thank the Scollons not only for their part in

the computer work that helped make this
possible, but for frequent and valuable
discussions on form and content of the book
as well.

We are happy for this opportunity to thank
our many colleagues in linguistics, anthropology
and literature who have supported our work and
who have encouraged us over the years in so many
ways. Their contributions are reflected in
this series in general and/or in this volume
in particular. Among these are Michael Krauss,
Irene Reed, Frederica de Laguna, Catharine
McClellan, Fannie LeMoine, Robert Rehder,
William and Karen Workman, Kerry Feldman,
O. W. Frost, Margritt Engel, Gary Holthaus,
and H.-Juergen Pinnow.

Special thanks go to Jeff Leer, Constance
Naish, and Gillian Story, not only for their
support over the years, but for their
proofreading and discussion of the linguistic
intricacies of the Tlingit language texts. We
thank Emma Marks and John Marks for their help
in clarifying many of the difficult Tlingit
concepts involved in the narratives.

Some of the Tlingit texts included here were
first drafted in the early 1970's. We want to
acknowledge those who helped with the typing
in the early history of these manuscripts:
Georgina Davis, Vesta Dominicks, Joanne George,
and Janice Gregory. Andrew Hope III was
printer for most of the first editions of
these Tlingit texts. For her administrative
support in the early years we also thank Ms.
Elaine Abraham. For their help in typing
and proofreading in the more recent stages we
thank Carmela Ransom, Elena Topacio, and Susan
Anderson.

We are grateful for the help of the families
and friends of many of the elders, who assisted
us with photographs and in the writing of the
biographies. These people are noted in the
biographies and photo credits.

Any errors of omission or comission as may

be found are, of course, entirely our own as
editors, for which we accept full responsibility
and offer our apologies.

We especially thank the Tlingit elders
themselves for their faith, enthusiasm,
courage, vision, and patience in supporting our
work. It grieves us that so many have passed
away since we first began working with them,
but we are happy that their words will live on,
as well as their names and memory. It is all
of these elders and tradition bearers, known
and unknown, living and departed, to whom this
work is dedicated and for whom it is entitled.

All royalties accruing to the editors from
publication of this book will go to Sealaska
Heritage Foundation and will be used for the
publication of additional books in this series
honoring the works and memories of the Elders.

To all of these people we are happy to say
Gunalchéesh, hó hó!

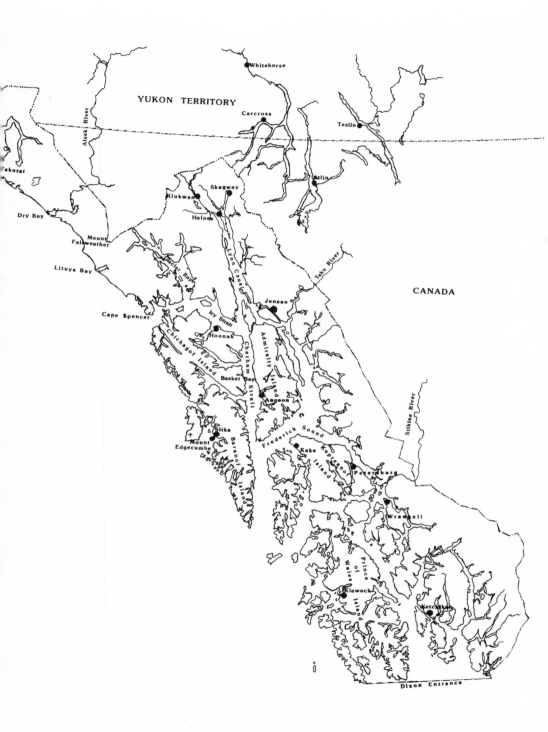

YUKON TERRITORY

Whitehorse

Carcross

Teslin

Atlin

Aiseki River

Yakutat

Skagway

Klukwan

Haines

Dry Bay

Mount
Fairweather

Lituya Bay

Glacier Bay

Lynn Canal

Cape Spencer

Icy Strait

Juneau

Hoonah

Chichagof Island

Chatham Strait

Admiralty Island

Taku River

CANADA

Basket Bay

Angoon

Stikine River

Sitka

Mount
Edgecumbe

Baranof Island

Frederick Sound

Kake

Kupreanof
Island

Petersburg

Wrangell

Prince
of
Wales
Island

Klawock

Ketchikan

Dixon Entrance

Haa Shuká, Our Ancestors

INTRODUCTION

In any works of literature, the general
reader who crosses the boundaries of time,
place or culture will require some introduction. We will start with some background
on the Tlingit people and social structure.
The Tlingit Indians live in Southeast Alaska
from Yakutat to Dixon Entrance, with inland
communities in SW Yukon and NW British
Columbia. A variety of evidence as well as
Tlingit tradition suggest that the Tlingits
migrated to the coast at a very ancient date,
and expanded on the coast from the southern
range of their territory to the north, and
were expanding toward the Copper River at the
time of European contact.

The relationship of Tlingit to other groups
is uncertain. There is great cultural
similarity between Tlingit and other Northwest
Coast groups such as Haida and Tsimshian, but
no obvious linguistic similarity. Tlingit is
clearly not related to Tsimshian, and possible
ancient linguistic relationship to Haida is a
subject of continuing scholarly debate.

On the other hand, Tlingit grammar is
parallel to the grammar of Athabaskan languages
(such as Navajo, for example) but there are

very few obvious similarities in vocabulary. It remains unclear whether the relationship is genetic, or one of languages in contact. But it seems that Tlingit is genetically related to the Athabaskan family of languages, and that the now extinct Eyak language and nearly extinct Tongass dialect of Tlingit provide the "missing link." Still, the origin of much of the Tlingit vocabulary remains a puzzle.

Coastal Tlingits live in a rain forest, and this has shaped their lifestyle and material culture, which, in turn, along with other cultures of the Northwest Coast, have captured the imagination of explorers ever since first contact. These are the people of totem poles, wooden bowls, plank houses, carved ocean going canoes, Chilkat robes, and other well known but often stereotyped and misunderstood cultural features.

The stories in this book are an integral part of this natural and social context. In order to understand and enjoy the stories (as well as Tlingit visual and performing art) the reader must become familiar with the basic concepts of Tlingit social structure.

All of Tlingit social structure is organized in two reciprocating divisions called moieties. Tlingit society is also matrilineal--organized by the mother's line. An individual is born into his or her mother's moiety, clan, and house group. The two moieties are named Raven and Eagle. Raven is sometimes also known as Crow, and Eagle as Wolf. Moieties as such have no political organization or power, but exist for the purposes of exogamy; that is, a person traditionally married into the opposite moiety.

Each moiety consists of many clans. Among the Raven moiety clans mentioned in this book are Lukaax̱.ádi, L'uknax̱.ádi, T'ak̲deintaan, Kiks.ádi, Suk̲tineidí, Tuk̲.weidí, X'atka.aayí, Kak'weidí, and Deisheetaan. Some of the Eagle moiety clans mentioned in this book are Kaagwaantaan, Wooshkeetaan, Chookaneidí,

Shangukeidí, Yanyeidí, Teikweidí, Dakl'aweidí, and Tsaagweidí. Political organization rests at the clan level; clans own crests, names and other property. Clans have traditional leaders, whereas there is no single leader for all the Ravens or Eagles.

In addition to the clan names as listed above, many appear in variant forms for women, such as Chookan sháa, L'uknax sháa, Shanguka sháa, and others. The endings -eidí and -ádi refer to men, and sháa to women.

Each clan traditionally included many house groups, although this genealogical awareness has been largely lost in the recent generations due to changes in physical housing brought about by missionary pressure and other social changes in the 20th century resulting in the rise of single family dwellings and apartments and the demise of traditional community houses. Most simply stated, the house was where people lived, but the concept is far more complex, and much too difficult to explain here.

Due to marriage and living patterns, not all residents of a house were members of the house group, and not all members of a particular group were physical residents of the house. As the population expanded, new houses would be built. As houses grew in population and stature, they often took on the status of independent clans, closely related to the parent clan. This process is important in some of the stories, and is decribed in the notes to the Glacier Bay stories. Various house groups are mentioned in the biographies.

The father's clan is also significant, but difficult to explain. Because the traditional social pattern called for marriage into the opposite moiety, a man's children were traditionally not of his own, but of his wife's moiety and clan. This is a very important concept in Tlingit social structure, visual art and oral literature. While a person is of his or her mother's clan, he or she is also known

as a "child of" the father's clan. The Tlingit
term for this is yádi; the plural is yátx'i.
For example, a man or woman may be Raven
moiety, Kiks.ádi, and Kaagwaantaan yádi. The
term Kaagwaantaan yádi or child of Kaagwaataan
does not mean that a person is of that clan,
but that his or her father is of that clan.
This concept is basic to any serious
understanding of the Tlingit culture in general
and oral literature in particular. For
example, most songs are addressed to members of
the opposite moiety, but according to the
kinship term for child of the father's clan,
which is most often the clan of the composer.

The rest of this introduction is arranged in
6 sections, each of which provides background
to some aspect of the book itself. Sections
of more general importance and appeal are first,
followed by the more technical sections.

Sections I, II, and III (on Format, Oral
Style, and Themes and Concepts) are intended
for all readers; section IV is for readers
interested in translation; and sections V and
VI (on the Tlingit Alphabet and the Nature of
Tlingit Grammar) are for those interested in
the Tlingit language--whether in just trying
to pronounce the names in the stories or in
more technical features of the sounds and
grammar of Tlingit as they bear directly on
this work.

In general, we have tried to take our
examples as much as possible from the first
few narratives in the book, so readers will
see them in context as soon as possible, and
then begin to notice further examples in the
rest of the stories.

I. FORMAT

Oral literature is different from written
literature. It has different "rules" for being
created and passed along to others. But most of

us are so influenced by reading and writing
that we rarely notice how we really talk to
each other and tell stories. Therefore it is
important to explain a few things that make
this book different from other books you may
have read.

These stories were all told in Tlingit, and
recorded on a tape recorder. They were
transcribed (written down) in Tlingit from the
versions on tape. We have tried to write these
stories the way they were told in Tlingit, and
to translate them into English keeping Tlingit
oral style in mind.

At each stage of the recording of oral
literature, something gets lost. Even on
video-tape, it is difficult to capture the
total relationship of the story teller and his
or her audience. With audio tape, all of the
gestures are lost: we no longer know what the
story teller looked like, and how he or she
used facial expressions and hand and arm
motions to tell the story.

When the story is written down, we lose
everything about the voice. We don't know how
the story teller sounds. We can't hear the
change of voice for different characters
speaking. We can't hear the tone of voice to
know if the story teller is joking. We can't
hear the unique voice quality of each elder. We
can't hear how story tellers use their voices--
for example, J.B. Fawcett's different "voices"
for Naatsilanéi, his wife, and the Spirit
Helper, or Susie James' range of voices in the
Glacier Bay History. Quotation marks are a
poor substitute for the marvellous gift of the
human voice.

When the Tlingit text is translated into
English, we lose the original language--the
way the story teller put his or her words
together to create a special and unique
performance of an event that will never be
repeated. (Even if the story is told over and
over, it is never exactly the same, because the

conditions are different, and the audience is
different.)

When the story is read by a person outside
the culture of the story teller, the cultural
context is lost.   Information and assumptions
shared by the composer and original audience
may no longer be shared.   Many things may no
longer be understood.   This applies not only
to persons totally outside the Tlingit
culture, but to younger generations within
Tlingit culture.   In all cultures, and at all
times, there has been a "generation gap."
This is especially true in contemporary Native
American cultures.   The experience and
understanding of a fifteen year old Tlingit,
or even of a fifty year old Tlingit, are not
the same as that of an eighty year old
Tlingit.   Some of the story tellers included
here, if they were still alive, would now be
over 100 years old, and they emphasize that
they are passing on things they learned from
their elders.

Despite this inevitable loss, there are ways
we can try our best to retain or recreate on
the written page as much as we can of the
original performance.

Lines. Readers immediately notice and ask
about the short lines.   We have arranged the
lines on the printed page to show as much as
possible how the stories sound. The lines are
split according to the pauses and punctuated
according to the intonation. The lines reflect
in print the pauses of the story teller.   Where
there is a pause, there is a line turning.
Heavier and longer pauses are marked with
period, comma, or semicolon.   The line
turnings in Tlingit and English attempt to
reflect the pace of the stories as told in
Tlingit. Try reading them out loud. If you
follow the lines, you will soon get a sense of
the speed and rhythm of the story.

Please keep in mind that these are not
"poems" in the popular sense, even though

poetry is what you usually see arranged this
way, whereas most non-poetic writing is
arranged in square or rectangular paragraphs--
such as the one you are reading now. The
short lines at first disturb some readers, who
expect all non-poetry to be arranged in a
square or rectangle, ideally typeset with an
even, flush, right hand margin. Some readers
find the short lines strange at first. But
this arrangement of lines presents no
difficulty to readers familiar with Homer or
other classics of oral literature. This style
of writing oral literature, especially Native
American oral literature, has been used in most
ethnopoetic transcription and translation of
the last fifteen to twenty years. For more on
this, see the books by Dell Hymes and Dennis
Tedlock cited in the bibliography.

Indented, "wrap around," or runover lines
are simply those in which the first line was
getting too long for the width of the page;
that is--everything would have been included
on the same line if the page were wide enough.
In these places the line is continued on the
next line, but indented. Read the indented
lines as continuations of the line above. The
indented lines are not counted separately in
the line numbering--that is, the total line is
counted once, where it first begins flush to
the left margin. Because the line turnings mark
pauses in the narration, a long line or series
of indented lines indicates rapid speech or
speech with fewer pauses, as in line 76 of
"Mosquito" or lines 25-36 and 54-64 of "Basket
Bay History" compared with the slower opening
lines.

Line Numbering. To help in talking or
writing about the narratives, we have numbered
the lines, counting by tens. Keep in mind when
using the notes that the information being
discussed may be in lines numbered slightly
differently in Tlingit and English, due to the
demands of word order in the different languages.

Punctuation follows the intonation and grammatical units of Tlingit or English (depending on the language being written.) A regular, unmarked line turning without punctuation indicates a slight pause. A comma indicates a sustained pause with no pitch drop.   In general, a period indicates a falling sentence contour, followed by a pause.   Periods are used where grammar and intonation together indicate the closing of a major unit.

Some phrases and sentences present special problems.   For example, line 36 of "Mosquito," consists of a single word (actually a noun and definite article) introducing a topic to be elaborated or developed in subsequent lines. We have punctuated it differently in Tlingit and English. In lines 50–55 of "Mosquito" there is a pause and pitch drop in the Tlingit narrative, but there seems to be no word marking a sentence boundary. We have punctuated with periods, even though commas might have been used in both Tlingit and English, so as not to convey what English grammar conventions consider a sentence fragment.   In other places where grammar and intonation "quarrel" (grammatically there could be two sentences, but intonation shows them to be semantically one) we have generally used a semi-colon, although in some places we retain a period to mark the end of a grammatical sentence within a line, but where the story continues without a pause or drop in pitch.

The general pattern marking a sentence boundary is: verb (sometimes noun or other word) at sentence end accompanied by pitch drop, followed by a pause, followed by áwé or some other conjunction indicating transition to a new topic.   The Tlingit pitch contours alone do not match the English sense of a sentence, and where Tlingit grammar indicates subordinate constructions we have sometimes used a comma even though the pitch and pause pattern might suggest or call for a period.

In places where there is a very long pause
between sentences, we have inserted extra
space between the lines. As you read through
the stories, you will notice how each story
teller paces his or her narrative differently.

Different Versions. Three stories are
presented in two versions: "Naatsilanéi" is
told by Willie Marks and J. B. Fawcett; "The
Woman Who Married the Bear" is told by Tom
Peters and Frank Dick, Sr.; and "Glacier Bay
History" is told by Susie James and Amy Marvin.
The Lituya Bay stories may possibly be viewed
as variants of the same historical event, but
we take them as accounts of two different
encounters, although with overlapping themes.

The versions of "Naatsilanéi" show how two
versions may compliment each other because
different tradition bearers focus on different
things. J. B Fawcett tends to emphasize the
setting of the story--where did it happen? --
who did it happen to? --whose ancestors are
these people? Willie Marks raises a different
set of questions: how did it feel? --what was
it like?

Even where the versions are different, such
as "The Woman Who Married the Bear," or where
they even conflict in certain details, such as
the name of the woman who stays behind at
Glacier Bay, it is important to stress that we
do not present one version as "better" or
"worse" than the other, or one version as
"right" and the other "wrong."

Variation is common in oral literature, and
traditions evolve differently in different
places. It is not our intention or desire to
merge different versions into a single
"literary re-write," as has often been done in
the history of oral literature. Our intent
here is to present the tradition bearers as
they present themselves--one specific version
by one specific person composed and published
orally at one place at one moment in time. We

have tried to make the texts as accurate as possible, and retain the style of oral delivery in English translation. We have edited out only false starts or corrections requested by the elders.

Notes. Our focus in this book is on the stories and the story tellers themselves. We have added other information along the way as may be helpful--such as notes, biographies, and photographs. Neither the notes nor the introduction are intended as a rigorous, systematic interpretation, but rather as background commentary. In providing this detail and background, some notes are more technical, and will be of interest and appeal mainly to linguists and students of Tlingit language and literature. Other notes are of more general interest. In all cases, the notes supply a linguistic and cultural background assumed by the story teller. They also point out aspects of the verbal art of the composers.

There is always the problem of how much to include, how much to say about a story. We don't want to "spoil the stories" or in any way lessen the reader's discovery and enjoyment of them. But we do want to supply information that the peers and fellow composers in this generation of tradition bearers would have shared. These are things that the younger Tlingit generations may or may not share to varying degrees, and that non-Tlingits could not be expected to share or understand.

The notes are intended to provide cultural background assumed as shared knowledge by the story teller and his or her original audience; to explain additional points that might be missed by readers not familiar with Tlingit oral literature; to point out interesting features of oral style; to point out grammatical features of interest to students of Tlingit language; and to point out problems in the text.

Each set of notes begins with recording data
and identifies the transcriber and translator.
Where important, the history of the text is
described. The notes include a list of "other
versions" that is by no means exhaustive, but a
starting place. Some of the notes go into
detailed commentary on such topics as marine
mammals, bears, and the history of European and
Tlingit contact, and other notes comment
directly on the story or simply note examples
of things discussed in the introduction.

The notes are aimed at the general reader,
and vary in content and detail from story to
story. We have tried to avoid technical terms
except where it would cause confusion NOT to
use them. The Tlingit grammatical terms are
probably the most technical, but these are
still directed to the beginning and
intermediate student rather than to
linguists. Professional linguists,
anthropologists, folklorists, and specialists
in oral literature will recognize familiar
things and be able to draw their own
observations from the data and commentary.

To help students of the Tlingit language use
this book to read the texts in the original,
many of the language notes contain a brief
grammatical analysis of verbs. Verbs are the
heart of the Tlingit language, and they
present special and often nearly
insurmountable difficulties for beginning and
intermediate students. We hope these notes
will be of some interest to the general reader
as well, and offer some insights into a complex
grammatical system totally different from
languages with which most of us are familiar.

The notes are selective, not exhaustive. We
comment not on every verb, but from time to
time on those that seem most "interesting."
We offer apologies to our colleagues and
students for whatever errors of omission or
comission their efforts may disclose. While
we hope the Tlingit texts themselves may be

definitive, the translations and notes are not intended as the "last word" but as aids to people wanting to learn the language or enjoy its classics in translation.

We urge readers interested in the Tlingit texts to consult our *Beginning Tlingit* for some basic information on the verbs, and to consult the *Tlingit Verb Dictionary* by Naish and Story for more detail. The *Tlingit Verb Dictionary* not only lists the verbs, alphabetized by stem, but includes the best Grammar Sketch of Tlingit available. Although some of the terms we use here are different, this should present no major difficulty. (Most notably, for what Naish and Story call "extensor" we use the traditional Tlingit and Athabaskan term "classifier." What Naish and Story categorize as A and B forms of extensors, we label I and A, according to their vowel pattern.) Our notes are designed specifically to lead students into the Naish and Story dictionary. As students work through the analyses in the notes here, they should be able to use the Naish and Story dictionary on their own to read and enjoy Tlingit texts, and make inroads into the general language.

Biographies are included for all tradition bearers. These amazingly different lives reflect in some small way a part of the complexity of Tlingit life in the 20th century, a period characterized by unprecedented political and economic impact and social change. The generation coming of age in the early 20th century reacted to this change in different ways. Some of the elders in this book ran away to go to school; others ran away from school; some struggled hard to go to Sheldon Jackson School or Chemawa; others rejected them totally. We hope that the biographies will give some sense of the human dimension behind the stories.

To add yet another human dimension, photographs are included for all tradition

bearers. We have tried to include a variety of
photos showing different aspects of Tlingit
life, but we have also limited the selection to
those depicting people actually in the book.
While experiences such as commercial fishing,
cannery work and subsistence life style are
common to all the biographies, photographs are
not equally extant or available for all elders,
so we have relied primarily on the Marks family
pictures to illustrate these activites.

Other Ancestors. Books are always limited
by time to write them and space to include
everything we want. This collection is not
complete. We hope it is just a start. Every
Tlingit clan and house group has its
ancestors, of whom the descendants are
justifiably proud. This book contains by no
means all of the elders or all of the stories--
just the first few with whom it has been our
privilege to work. There are many other
stories by tradition bearers of other groups,
and we hope to include their works in
additional volumes of "Ancestors" at a later
date. In the meantime, different types of
Tlingit oral literature composed by these and
other elders are forthcoming in other volumes
in this series.

II. ORAL SYTLE

Repetition. Readers of Tlingit classics
notice repetition as part of the oral style.
Some readers are bothered by it. Although
repetition is a common feature of oral
composition and story telling all around the
world, it is frowned upon in written
composition, so many readers at first assume
that repetition is a sign of bad style. In
fact, many people, in collecting and writing
down Tlingit oral literature, have taken out
all the repetition and have "re-written" or "re-
told" the stories to make them more acceptable
to people reading books in English (and other
languages.)

While there may be a place for such "retellings," we believe that the story tellers
speak well for themselves orally, and should be
allowed to speak for themselves on the printed
page. We have tried to make the printed page,
in both Tlingit and English, an extension of
the voice of the original story teller. In
reading Tlingit and other oral literature from
around the world, newcomers should begin to
look for, appreciate, and enjoy the different
kinds of repetition. This is one of the things
that makes oral literature oral, and Tlingit
oral literature Tlingit. When you begin to get
a feel for repetition, you will begin to
appreciate the craft of good oral composition
as well as good written composition.

Story tellers use repetition for many
purposes. They use it to emphasize main ideas,
build the story with a sense of rhythm and
balance, or simply give listeners a break
without overloading them with too much new
information at once. They also use it as an aid
to oral composition, to help them "think on
their feet" and shape in their minds what is
coming next.

There are many kinds of repetition used in
oral literature. Words, phrases, lines, and
entire passages can be repeated exactly and
totally, or just partially. On a more complex
level, ideas, themes and general shapes can be
repeated--like when a tailor or dressmaker
uses a particular pattern to make many items of
clothing that may not at first look exactly
alike. This is very common in Homeric epics,
and in Hebrew poetry such as the Psalms, where
an idea is repeated or developed, but with
different words. It is also common in Tlingit
oral literature.

Exact repetition. Sometimes a phrase is
repeated word for word in a sequence of lines:

Tle x'adus.aax̱w;   They tied them off;

tle x̱'adus.aax̱w;   they tied them off;
tle x̱'adus.aax̱w.   they tied them off.
                    Basket Bay 51-53

Tsu ashaawax̱ích.   He struck it again.
Tsu ashaawax̱ích.   He struck it again.
Tsu ashaawax̱ích.   He struck it again.
                    Mosquito 102-104

Sometimes the repeated phrases are separated
from each other by another line or two:

Yá aan tayeedéi,   Underneath the village
....ana.átch,   ..they would go...,
yá aan tayeedéi.   underneath the village.
                    Basket Bay 14-16

Yá x̱áat.   The salmon.
Yá el'kaadáx̱   From the ocean
haa x̱'éi kei x̱'ákch.   they would come up
                              for us to eat.

Yá x̱áat.   The salmon.
A áyá tlax̱ daat yáx̱ sáyá And these how good
   haa x̱'éi yak'éi   they tasted to us,
yá x̱áat.   the salmon.
                    Mosquito 36-41

Repetition with Variation. Sometimes a
phrase is repeated with slight variation.

Yankaadéi yaa kg̱adéinin   When the tide was
   áwé tsá,   finally nearly up
yankaadéi yaa kg̱adéinin, when the tide was
                              nearly up,
                 Basket Bay 65,66

Yú haa aaní áyú,   That land of ours,
yú haa aaní,   that land of ours,
              Basket Bay 1,2

Notice in this sample that the English
translation is exact repetition whereas the
Tlingit original has variation. For more on

this, see section IV, where we explain the
translation of words such as "áyú."

Dialog is often repeated word for word. In
this example, the repeated phrases are separated
by two or three lines, and the second time is
with slight variation.

"Dei éekdáx   "The tiiiide is
    yaawadáaaaaa."   starting uuuuup."
"Eekdáx   "The tiiiide is
    yaawadáaaaaa."   starting uuuuup."
"Dei éekdáx   "The tiiiide is
    yaawadáaaaaa."   starting uuuuup."
                        Basket Bay, 38, 41, 45

Sometimes the variation is in grammar as
well as choice of words. This creates a nice
rhythm.

Ch'áagu aayí   The one of long ago,
    ch'áakw woonaa.   he died long ago.
              Mosquito 13,14

Parallel Structure and Refrains. Such
repetition of both grammar and some but not all
of the words creates phrases that are parallel
in structure and meaning but sometimes not in
exact words. Often these phrases appear as
refrains in the story. Some good examples are
found in Frank Dick Sr.'s delivery.

144. Haaw! wáannée sáyá haadéi anaa.aat
     Now! at one point they were coming in

178. Gwá! wáannée sáyá yeik kukandak'ít'
          tsu.
     Hey! at what point was it they were
          coming down again?

The lines are parallel in structure and
meaning even though all the words are not
the same. (Notice that the verb stems are
different in Tlingit, but the English uses

"coming" for both verbs.) The passages are
used as a refrain to mark a transition from
one scene to another in the story.

Another example of a refrain is in the story
teller's emphasis that the girl was not harmed
by the bear. Words to the effect that "she
was alright," or "there was nothing wrong," or
"she didn't notice any difference" appear in
5 parallel phrases within 34 lines.

> 88. Hél wáa sá utí.
>   There wasn't anything different.

> 91. Hél tsu wáa sá utí.
>   There wasn't even anything different.

> 99. Hél wáa sá uteeyí.
>   Because there wasn't anything
>   different.

> 119. Tlél tsu wáa sá du toowú utí.
>   She still didn't feel any different.

> 121. Hél tsu wáa sá utí.
>   There wasn't even anything different.

The repetition creates a rhythm of sound and
meaning that builds tension and excitement in
the story.

Terrace. Many story tellers use repetition
to build their stories like a terrace or like
steps, building a second line or phrase on
words in the line or phrase before.

> Yées yadák'wx xat sitee.
> Tle ch'u yées yadák'wx xat sateeyídáx
> s'eenáa yaakw ax jee yéi wootee.

> I was a young man.
> From the time I was a young man,
> I had a seine boat.
>   Mosquito 15-17

As you read the stories, look (and listen)
for the different kinds of repetition. This
is a big building block of oral tradition
around the world.

Code Switching is a technical term that
means changing languages or otherwise changing
the way we speak, depending on the situation.
It is very common in bilingual communities for
a person to use words from one language while
speaking another. Sometimes a story teller will
use English words or phrases in the story.
This is usually done for some kind of emphasis,
sometimes for humor or to establish detachment
or "aesthetic distance" from the story--but not
because they don't know the Tlingit word.
Sometimes the whole sentence switches to English.

> I had
> nineteen hundred and six model,
>   Mosquito 18,19

Sometimes the grammar will be Tlingit and
some of the words English.

> tle shóogoonax come out-x yaa nastéeni.
> (from when they first came out.)
>   Mosquito 20

Sometimes the code switching is a form of
repetition, where something said in Tlingit is
repeated in English.

> Tle akawliwál'.
> He wrecked the boat.
>   Mosquito 25, 26

Not all code switching is between Tlingit
and English. In lines 106-109 and again in
line 165 of his telling of "Naatsilanéi,"
Willie Marks counts in Chinese, bringing all
of his linguistic resources to bear in his
narration!

III. SOME THEMES AND CONCEPTS

The accounts of clan ancestors presented in this book include a range of themes and styles that can be enjoyed in private reading or in world literature classes.

The narratives can be studied thematically. For example, stories of migration and exploration open and close the book, beginning with Robert Zuboff's account of the migration of the Basket Bay People to the coast, and ending with Tlingit oral traditions of first encounters with French and Russian explorers at Lituya Bay. These accounts, told here by Charlie White, Jennie White, and George Betts are interesting to historians because they are oral histories that document the same events as the written records of the voyages of La Pérouse (1786) and of Izmailov and Bocharov (1788.) The written and oral accounts record the Tlingits and Europeans encountering each other for the first time. While the voyage of La Pérouse is well known to American historians, the written and oral records of Russian exploration remain little known.

The stories between the Tlingit migration to the coast and the arrival of the Europeans are about the ancestors of various clans, whose adventures resulted in certain covenants with the spirit world, the establishment of certain social institutions, and the right to claim and use certain land, names, heraldic designs, and other prerogatives called in Tlingit at.óow.

These central narratives in the book are arranged in general order of difficulty, beginning with those less complicated thematically, and culminating with the very rich, intricate, and profound stories about Bears and Glacier Bay. Coincidentally, this arrangement of the narratives also very roughly follows the approximate age of the stories as nearly as can be determined. For example, the events at Glacier Bay and Lituya Bay are much later in time than the migration to the coast and the stories of southern origin such as "Naatsilanéi," "Strong Man," and "Kaats'."

The story of Kaax'achgóok told by A. P. Johnson describes the famous voyage of this ancestor of the Kiks.ádi clan, who, like Odysseus, was swept out to sea by a storm, but skillfully navigated his crew back home, where he then must deal with how life had changed during his absence.

In contrast to the compassion of Kaax'achgóok, three stories of revenge are Robert Zuboff's story of the origin of Mosquito from the ashes of the cremated Cannibal Giant, and the two versions of Naatsilanéi and the origin of Killer Whale told by Willie Marks and J. B. Fawcett. Among other things, these stories comment on the ambiguity of revenge--on the one hand sweet and satisfying, and on the other hand exacting a terrible human price on the person who becomes obsessed with it.

There are two stories that focus on themes of pride and arrogance, appearance and reality. Frank Johnson tells the well known story of the "Strong Man," which explores the difference between true strength and apparent strength. Willie Marks tells the story of how Kaakex'wtí brought copper to the coast, but was mistakenly rejected by his own clan. These stories warn us that things may not be as they seem, and that our pride can often blind us to reality--usually at a great cost.

Stories probing the depths of alienation and self-concept are "The Woman Who Married the Bear" told in versions by Tom Peters and Frank Dick, Sr., and the story of Kaats', who is the man who married a bear. These stories explore the delicate and ambiguous relationship of humans and bears, and of the individual to his

or her society. These stories are also about
conflict of loyalty and the difficult choices
we are often called upon to make.

While the Bear stories are also about the
dilemmas of conflict of loyalty, nowhere in the
collection is this theme, and the related theme
of duty, more important than in the Glacier Bay
History, told in two versions, one by Susie
James and one by Amy Marvin. In these powerful
accounts, the individual must make the
difficult choice between her own physical
survival, and the physical and spiritual
survival of her people.

Journeys are important in all the accounts
in the book. The collection begins with a
clan migration to the coast and ends with the
arrival of Europeans in Southeast Alaska--
voyages that would change the course of
Tlingit life and culture forever. Men like
Ḵaax̱'achgóok and Ḵaakex'wtí go on extended
journeys to other places and return with
fabulous wealth. Others, such as Naatsilanéi,
Kaats', the boy who kills the Cannibal Giant,
and the Woman Who Married the Bear go on
spiritual journeys through time and space and
encounter other forms of life. Some men, like
the "Strong Man," go on a spiritual journey to
self realization without ever leaving home.
Some set off on journeys to eternal life, such
as the woman who elects to stay behind in
Glacier Bay and become one with the spirit of
the ice.

Many stories in this volume are about the
encounters of ancestors with the spirits of
other forms of life, such as Bear, Killer
Whale, and Ice. The experiences range from
encounters with spirit helpers who come to
humans, sojourns by humans among other forms
of life, (such as marriages with bears), and
ultimately giving up human life to merge with
the spirit world for all eternity.

Some of these experiences involve journeys,
sometimes even "out of life" experiences where

people travel to the spirit world and return.
We see some of this in Naatsilanéi and the bear
stories. These journeys are dangerous and most
often costly in terms of human life. Most of
the stories show how difficult the return
voyage is. This theme or "archetype" of the
journey is widely discussed in comparative
literature, mythology, and religion, for
example in Joseph Campbell's *Hero With A
Thousand Faces*. Most often "you can't go home
again." The sacrifice of the ancestors is very
great indeed.

Often these "close enounters" result from
violation of a taboo, usually involving lack of
self control and lack of respect for the
spirits of other forms of life. Many of the
stories emphasize the "cosmic connection" of
human action and experience--how we behave in
the physical world has significance in the
spiritual world. Both of these worlds are
equally real, but the reality is difficult to
express.

Part of the experience and its expression in
literature often includes metamorphosis or
"shape shifting." Mountains seem like logs,
time is warped, animals appear as humans, and
humans as animals. There is a marvellous image
in Tom Peters' story of the woman carrying a
back pack that transforms into a brown bear
with a hump among the bushes.

In terms of modern physics, things are
relative. Relativity is a difficult concept
to convey, and various devices are used to
express it, most often a literal putting on or
off of a bear skin. Part of the problem is
how to express spiritual reality in physical
terms. Another part of the problem is of human
perception--optically and culturally seeing
and interpreting what we see. Things are not
only relative, but our perception of reality
is often insufficient at best and deceptive at
worst.

At.óow. Some important Tlingit terms and

concepts need to be introduced here. The single
most important concept in the entire book is
at.óow. The word means, literally, "an owned or
purchased thing." The concepts of "thing,"
"owned," and "purchased" are equally important.

The "thing" may be land (geographic features
such as a mountain, a landmark, an historical
site, a place such as Glacier Bay) a heavenly
body (the sun, the dipper, the milky way) a
spirit, a name, an artistic design, or a range
of other "things." It can be an image from
oral literature such as an episode from the
Raven cycle on a tunic, hat, robe or blanket;
it can be a story or song about an event in
the life of an ancestor. Ancestors themselves
can be at.óow--Kaasteen, Kaats', Duktootl'.

The "purchase" may be with money or trade,
as collateral on an unpaid debt, or through
personal action. Most of the accounts of
ancestors in this collection are important to
the Tlingit people because the stories recall
the actions of their ancestors whose deeds
purchased certain things for their
descendants. Most often, and most seriously,
the purchase is through human life. Thus the
name of Kaasteen, the land of Glacier Bay, the
story and the songs, and the visual image of
the Woman in the Ice are the property or at.óow
of the Chookaneidí clan. These at.óow were
purchased with the life of an ancestor.

In Tlingit tradition, the law is that a
person pays for a life he or she has taken with
his or her own, or someone else may substitute
a life or make payment. Hence, if an animal
takes the life of a person, its image may be
taken by relatives in payment, and the
descendants then own this life taken in
payment.

The pattern is the same for other stories in
the book and for all of Tlingit oral
literature: an event happens in the life of an
ancestor or progenitor, some aspect or a
combination of aspects of the event becomes a

"thing"--an at.óow--the ancestor, the design,
the spirit of the animal, the song, the story,
etc., and the land where it happened is
important in the spiritual and social life of
the people. This is the single most important
concept in Tlingit culture and is reflected in
all aspects of the social structure, oral
literature, visual arts, and ceremonial life.

   An event, person, place or thing doesn't
automatically receive instant status as at.óow.
The design is usually executed on a piece of
art. A specific piece of art or regalia
usually comes into existence when an individual
or clan commissions an artist of the opposite
moiety to create it. It is then "brought out"
at a feast and given a name. It is paid for
by the person who commissioned it. Often
other members of the clan or house group will
help pay for it by contributing to the cost of
materials or the artist's fee. The art object
or regalia will always feature an at.óow of
the clan, such as a frog, bear, mountain, a
person such as Strong Man tearing the sea lion
in half, etc.

   When the individual owner dies, the at.óow
is referred to by a special term: l s'aatí át,
a "masterless thing," an object with no owner.
The object may then go to the next of kin in
the same clan, or to a person who has made
contributions to the livelihood of the owner,
has contributed monetary support for funeral
expenses, or who has given moral and spiritual
support to the owner. In most cases this
support would come from a clan leader who then
claims the estate of the deceased. If there
is no one to take it, then the l s'aatí át
goes into communal ownership. It goes into
the clan collection and becomes a clan-owned
object. When there is no one to claim them,
these at.óow are sometimes displayed on a
table, or held in hand by designated people.
They are often central images in the oratory.

   At other times, members of a clan may pay

for at.óow to be made for the leader of the
clan. This object will become a community
owned at.óow with a steward designated to care
for it. For example, the Lukaax̱.ádi Raven
House collection is a consolidation of at.óow
from many house groups and deceased individuals
now kept as a single collection with one
steward.

In other words, while new art objects always
depict already existing clan heraldic designs,
the new objects themselves are not automatically
at.óow, but may become so. For example, vests
of felt or moosehide, hats and headbands and
felt button blankets depicting at.óow are common
in Tlingit communities. These are called "ash
koolyát kanaa.ádi--play clothes." Once an owner
of such a piece decides it is important enough,
he or she will "bring it out" in memory of a
deceased relative at a feast and give it a name.
It is then usually put on someone by a member of
the opposite moiety according to genealogy. Once
this is done, the piece itself becomes an at.óow
in its own right. It has been "paid for."

Rules for the use of at.óow are very
complex. Obviously, members of the owning clan
use their own at.óow, although this is also
regulated by custom according to the nature of
the at.óow and the seriousness of the occasion.
For example, a beaded pendant or silver jewelry
with clan crests are worn more casually in
daily dress than a Chilkat robe. But, under
certain conditions, non-owners may use the
at.óow of another clan, although they may not
claim them as their own. For example,
relatives of the opposite moiety may hunt,
fish, or pick berries with permission on
another clan's land.

Because the most complicated examples happen
in the context of feasting, and become
important in the images of public speaking, a
complete description of who can use another
group's at.óow and under what conditions is not
included here but will be explained in detail

with examples in the introduction to the volume
in this series on Tlingit oratory. What is
relevant to this collection is that stories can
be told by anybody, so that all people will
know who they are and who everybody else is.
But, under the traditional laws of Tlingit
"oral copyright," it is very important to
identify whose story is being told and why.
The stories must be told with accuracy and
respect. If a particular story is the at.óow
of a given clan, it is important to note this
somewhere in the telling. This is usually done
either by direct statement or implied through
genealogical reference.

This latitude in telling stories is
permitted because familiarity with the songs
and stories of all clans is basic to traditional
Tlingit education. Stories contain not only
practical physical and spiritual "survival skills,"
but social "survival skills" as well. This
knowledge teaches a person to recognize and
interpret the heraldic designs of other clans,
provides "raw material" to be transformed into
images, metaphors and similes in public
speaking, and instills appreciation and respect
for the ancestors, traditions, and at.óow of
relatives and other members of the community.

Two other terms are now ready for
introduction: shagóon and shuká, both of which
mean "ancestor," but with slightly differing
ranges of meaning. Shagóon can be an immediate
parent and also human ancestors more distant
in time. Shuká, which is used in the title of
this book, also means "ancestor," but in a
more general way. The concept is two
directional. It means, most literally,
"ahead." It refers to that which has gone
before us in time--predecessors, those born
ahead of us who are now behind us. It also
refers to that which lies ahead, in the
future. There is a common expression in
Tlingit, "we don't know our 'shuká'--our
'future.'" The term shuká includes both at.óow

and shagóon. It includes all types of at.óow
as well as all human ancestors. Therefore, the
term "shuká" embraces the narratives
themselves, the at.óow and ancestors within
them, and the ancestors who told them.

These concepts are difficult to define,
partly because the terms overlap but are not
synonymous. In general, "shuká" is most often
used for the images or heraldic designs, and
at.óow for the material thing or object made
with the design. L s'aatí át refers to at.óow
left behind by a deceased ancestor. The terms
are sometimes used more loosely, sometimes even
more precisely. For example, an at.óow owned
by an ancestor (shagóon) may also be called
shagóon, especially if it is the grandparents',
the father's father's emblem. This use is
connected to the concept of "outer container"
mentioned in the narratives by J. B. Fawcett.

A few examples may be helpful. The Raven
design is a shuká of all Raven moiety clans.
If a wooden Raven hat is made by a specific
person or clan, brought out at a feast and paid
for, it becomes at.óow. In the Glacier Bay
History, the woman is a shagóon of the
Chookaneidí clan. She is also shuká and at.óow
on specific art objects. Moreover, Glacier
Bay, the glacier, and the icebergs are also
at.óow because the woman paid for them with her
life. In fact, icebergs are called "Chookan
sháa" (Chookaneidí woman) for this reason. The
songs and story are the property or at.óow of
the Chookaneidí clan.

Likewise, Kaats' paid for the bear design
with his life, and it is an emblem of the
Teikweidí. Kaats' is also shuká, and he is
shagóon to the grandchildren of Teikweidí. In
the same way, Kaax'achgóok is a shuká of the
Kiks.ádi; he is biological shagóon of the clan.
The song and story are at.óow of the Kiks.ádi,
and the at.óow may referred to as shagóon by
the grandchildren of the clan.

IV. TRANSLATION

We have tried for translation and not
paraphrase. These are not "retellings" in
English, but attempts to retain as much of the
style and flavor of the original without being
awkward, unclear, and unnatural in English.
After all, these are in good Tlingit, and good
in Tlingit, so they should end up in good
English and be good in English. Needless to
say, one cannot translate word for word and
make much sense. Therefore, we would like to
comment on a few places where the Tlingit and
English may seem different, and where careful
readers may notice discrepancies.

Order of Lines. Elders often comment that
English and Tlingit are "backwards" or the
reverse of each other. Thus, a person
comparing the Tlingit and English texts here
will find many many passages in which we have
reversed the order of the lines. For example,
if the Tlingit is 1, 2, 3, 4, the English will
be 4, 3, 2, 1.

Sometimes this reverse order is simple,
obvious, and clear. At other times the
contrast runs much deeper and presents serious
problems in communication. Not only are
obvious things like nouns and verbs the
opposite of each other in Tlingit and English,
but information is often presented in different
order in the two languages, so that listeners
are puzzled at each other's meaning. Where
the "rules" for such ordering of words, lines,
or information are in conflict, we have had to
compensate in translation. Sometimes the
notes will refer to different lines in Tlingit
and English because the exact word in question
is in a different place in each language.

We have tried to translate with the line as
the basic unit, so as to keep a sense of rhythm
and style of oral performance. Sometimes the
grammatical and informational demands of
English require that the order of English lines

be different from, often the reverse order of,
the Tlingit original. Information that comes
last in a Tlingit sentence often needs to be
first in English. For example, lines 10 and
11 of "Basket Bay History" are in the opposite
order in English translation.

Using the terms suggested by Eugene Nida
(1964) here are the lines in the original
Tlingit text, a literal transfer (word for
word or unit for unit translation), a minimal
transfer (adapted to meet the minimal
requirements of English grammar), and a
literary transfer (an acceptable literary
translation with more attention to English
style.)

> 10. tléinax̱ yateeyi aa k̲áa áyú,
> 11. kanduk̲éich.

> 10. one/only human-number being
>   thing man that yonder one
>   it was
> 11. on the surface along they
>   send occasionally would

> 10. Only one man
> 11. they would send.

> 10. They would send
> 11. one man as guard.

All of this points out that one cannot
translate "word for word." The main thing is
to keep the sense. We have tried to do this,
while keeping some feeling for the oral style
of the original and the composer's choice of
words and synonyms. We have tried to keep as
close to the original Tlingit as possible
without the loss of meaning, power, and beauty
that can result from keeping too close. We
have tried to reject the two extremes of highly
literal and unduly free translation, and stay
within an acceptable range of what Beekman and

Callow (1974) call modified literal and
idiomatic types of translation. In some cases,
as in this example, we have added extra words
in English to convey the sense of the Tlingit.

Thus, we have not "re-told" or "re-written"
or "paraphrased," but first let the elders
speak for themselves in Tlingit, and then
tried to make the English translation cor-
respond and re-create the style and meaning of
the Tlingit original. In the final analysis,
of course, a person who wants to savor the
Tlingit original will have to read the texts in
Tlingit. We hope that for many readers, the
English translation will provide easier entry
into the rich oral style of the originals. For
most readers, who will not attempt to read the
Tlingit texts, we hope that our efforts do
justice to the artistry of the composers.

Nouns and Pronouns. In some cases, we
have used nouns in translation where Tlingit
has pronouns. For example, where Tlingit has
"he" we have often used the name of the
character. We have done this for greater
clarity in English. Likewise, we have often
inserted "he said" to mark dialog, where in
the Tlingit text some other word marks the
dialog, or where in the performance speech is
indicated by gesture, tone of voice, or change
of voice.

Áyú. Some Tlingit words have two
functions. Words such as áyá, áwé, áyú can be
translated as "this is," or "it is," or "that
is." But they can also function to mark the
beginning or end of a phrase, in which case
they are not translated. For example:

> Aas áyú.
> It was a tree.
> > Basket Bay 23.

Here, the word áyú is translated "it was."
More literally, it is "that over yonder is."
See below for discussion of translation of

verb tenses in English. The main point in the
example is that here the Tlingit word "áyú" can
be translated with an English verb.

In other places, the word cannot be
translated in the same way. For example in the
opening lines of "Basket Bay History," given
first in the original text and in a literal
translation.

> Yú haa aaní áyú
> yú haa aaní
> Kák'w áyú yóo duwasáakw;
> Dleit Káa x'éinax ku.aa,
> Basket Bay.

> That our land that is
> that our land,
> Little Basket that is thusly people call it;
> White Man mouth-through however,
> Basket Bay.

In such cases, it seems better to understand
"áyú" as a phrase boundary marker, like a
spoken comma or period. Rather than to
translate the meaning of the word into English,
it seems better to translate the function of
the word into English. Here is a literary
translation:

> That land of ours,
> that land of ours
> is called Kák'w;
> but in English
> Basket Bay.

It could also be translated

> That was our land,
> our land,
> Kák'w is what they call it,
> but in English
> Basket Bay.

Line 21 of "Basket Bay History" is another
typical example:

Dzeit áyú áa wduwax̲út'.
A ladder was adzed there.

Literally the line is

Ladder that is was adzed there.

The word "áyú" functions to set off the word
"dzeit" and mark the boundary of that part of
the phrase.

One of the most difficult things in
translating Tlingit is to know when to
translate words like "áyú" literally, and when
not to translate them. The most frequent
words in this group are áyá, áwé, and áyú. The
fourth member, áhé, meaning "this thing sort
of next to me," is less common in story
telling.

Awé. The word "áwé" works the same way.
For example in the opening lines of "Mosquito,"
the word "áwé" makes up lines 1 and 6, and half
of 10. It also appears in the middle of line
4. It is awkward to translate into English.
The word is used to signal the start of a
phrase, something like a capital letter in
written composition. Literally, it means
"that is" or "it is." A literal translation
of the opening lines is very cumbersome in
English:

That is
in that boat of mine,
"Guide" it was called,
in it that is I used to go around
seining.

To translate "áwé" literally rather than
according to its function (or alternative
meaning) gives a false impression that Tlingit
is somehow awkward. The word could be left out

completely, or translated as "then" or "well,
then," or "well."

The word "áyá" presents the same problem in
translation, and is as common as "áwé" and
"áyú." Because it works the same way it is
not necessary to discuss it here.

Aaa. The Tlingit word "aaa" appears often
in the narratives. It means "yes," and we have
translated it as such. The main point is that
it is not like the English sound "uh" or "uhh,"
that comes when a person is trying to think of
what to say next.

Transitions. Transitions are extremely
difficult to translate smoothly into English.
The most common transitions are "tle," "aagáa,"
and "ḵu.aa." We have not always been
consistant in our translation of these words,
but have tried to select what seemed the best
choice for the situation.

Tle means "then." It is used much more
frequently in Tlingit than in English, and we
have often omitted it in translation.

Aagaa has a variety of possible
translations including: then, at that time, at
one point, this is when, this was when, that's
when, that was when. Sometimes we have
translated it as a "when...then" construction.

Ḵu.aa often easily equates to English
"but," "therefore," or "however." In addition,
it sometimes signals new information or the
introduction of a new topic or character,
without implying any contrast. In these cases,
it is much more difficult to translate and we
often simply omit it. Perhaps it is more like
"moreover" in English. Examples from
Ḵaax̱'achgóok include lines 274 and 379
(contrast, as in English, and translated as
"but" or "however") line 277 (new
information; transition or shift of topic,
translated as "and") lines 173 and 373 (new
information or topic, not translated.)

Another transition phrase difficult to
translate is "wáa nanéi sáwé," which we have

usually translated as "after a while," "a while
after this," or "at what point was it?"

Other Words. There are many "little
words" in both English and Tlingit that change
the meaning of a sentence, but are difficult to
find a good match for in the other language.
The following are some examples, and how we
most often translate them.

ásíwé	wasn't it?
gwál, gwál yé	probably
gíwé (gíyá, gíyú)	maybe, perhaps
gwá wé gé	I guess
ḵach	it really was; "here"
	it turned out to be

These are our translations as a general
rule, but we have varied with the sense of each
phrase. Some story tellers have a style of
inserting such words disclaiming any creativity
on their own, but emphasizing that this is the
way they heard it, and didn't make it up. This
can often look in English as if the story
teller isn't sure of his or her material, but
it is very common in oral literature. Willie
Marks does this as part of his style, as in

> Naatsilanéi yóo gíwé duwasaakw.
> Naatsilanéi was what they say
>   his name was.

or

> Naatsilanéi was maybe/perhaps
>   what they called him.

This is an oral literary device to create
aesthetic distance, among other things.

Verb tense. Translation of verb tense is
often a problem. English verbs are based on
time. Each English verb conveys some information about the time of the action relative
to the present. For example:

I eat seafood.
I am eating seafood.
I ate.
I have eaten.
I had eaten....
I would have eaten....

And so on. This can become very complicated
in English, with sentences such as

The boat would have been being painted,
had we gotten to the paint store on time.

We can "violate" this pattern of time in some
writing, by what is called the "historical
present."

Now Abraham Lincoln decided
to go to the theater.

or

Now the Confederate army
is advancing on Gettysburg.

It seems to us that English prefers past
tenses in more formal story telling ("There
once was a man who lived in....") and present
in more informal and anecdotal narratives
("Well, there's this guy, who goes into a
bar...." or "So there I am, waiting for...."
or, "Yesterday I am in the store and this
person tells me..."
Whereas English grammar is characterized by
concern with time, Tlingit is not. In English,
it is impossible to use a verb without
conveying some sense of time. Tlingit verbs
convey other information--is the action
frequent or habitual, now and then; is the
focus on the action or the object of the verb?
is the focus on the completion or start of an
action? Therefore, some information conveyed

in Tlingit is lost in English, and decisions
have to be made regarding time in the English
verbs that do not exist in Tlingit.

Some of this is "built into" the grammars of
English and Tlingit. For example, "I see" and
"I know" are both "past tense" in Tlingit,
which focuses on the acquisition of the visual
image or the knowledge which is prerequisite to
being able to make a statement about it. In
this case, one almost automatically translates
the Tlingit perfective into an English present.

In other cases, we have translated many
imperfective ("present tense") and progressive
verbs in the Tlingit narration as past tense in
English, keeping with the appropriate
conventions of story telling. For example,

> He went.
> Now he went.
> Now it was fall.

where Tlingit literally may have

> He is going.
> He goes.
> Now it is fall.

Persons reading the Tlingit texts will notice
this throughout.

V. THE TLINGIT ALPHABET

You will soon notice that (like certain
plays such as Macbeth, Julius Caesar, King
Lear, Richard III) some narratives in this book
are known only or primarily by the name of the
main character. Names like Kaax'achgóok,
Kaakex'wtí, Kaats' and Naatsilanéi are not easy
to pronounce without some experience in Tlingit
language. We have tried to use commonly
accepted English titles whenever possible, such
as Dukt'ootl' in Tlingit and The Strong Man
in English, but this is not always possible.

<u>Kaax</u>'achgóok is always and only <u>Kaax</u>'achgóok,
and this name contains sounds common in Tlingit
but not found in English, German, Spanish,
Japanese, or any of the commonly studied
languages of Europe, Asia, and Africa. To help
in pronunciation of these and other names in
the stories, and for readers desiring to work
with the Tlingit texts, some discussion of the
writing system used here is in order.

Tlingit was first written for scholarly use
and community literacy in the first half of
the 19th century by the Russian Bishop
Innocent (Veniaminov), who devised a Cyrillic
alphabet adapted to the sounds of Tlingit.
The Orthodox Church encouraged the use of and
fostered popular literacy in Tlingit and other
Native languages of Alaska through translation,
bilingual education in its schools, and some
publication of books. In contrast, schooling
in the American period discouraged and even
suppressed the use of Alaska Native
languages. Scientific work in the 20th century
has used technical alphabets. The popular
literacy movement was resumed primarily
through the efforts of linguists Constance
Naish and Gillian Story in the 1960's.

The popular alphabet for writing Tlingit
used in this book was designed by Constance
Naish and Gillian Story of the Summer Institute
of Linguistics / Wycliffe Bible Translators in
the 1960's. This has become the "official"
system of writing Tlingit for a range of
community uses, and has been used in all
publications since 1972 by Alaska Native
Language Center, Sheldon Jackson College,
Tlingit Readers, Inc., Sealaska Heritage
Foundation, various school districts and
community programs, and, of course, by Naish
and Story. The system is phonemically accurate
and can be used for writing all dialects of
Tlingit. The original writing system was
revised in 1972, and all books published in
Tlingit in Alaska and Canada for the last 15

years, including the Naish and Story
dictionaries are in the revised orthography.
For more on this see our *Tlingit Spelling
Book* and *Beginning Tlingit.*

Naish and Story began their work on Tlingit
in 1959. Working mostly in the 1960's and
mostly in Angoon, they confirmed the Franz Boas
and Louis Shotridge analysis of Tlingit
phonology published in 1917, and went on to
make important contributions that would form
the basis of following generations of Tlingit
scholarship.

Their work includes scientific research,
especially their MA Theses (1966) on
morphology (Story) and syntax (Naish); design
and teaching of a popular alphabet; religious
publications, including hymns and Bible
Stories, and especially the Gospel of John;
educational publications, especially the
Tlingit Noun Dictionary and *Tlingit Verb
Dictionary* which includes an extremely
valuable "Grammar Sketch."

Constance Naish and Gillian Story have since
left the Tlingit field to work with Athapaskan
languages in Northwest Territories, Canada, but
their work and fond memories endure in
Southeast Alaska. To paraphrase Scripture,
"remembrance of them is from generation to
generation". They also go on linguistic record
as well as into folk tradition as being among
the handful of non-Tlingits who have learned to
speak the language. They are fondly
remembered, most often by their Tlingit names
Naatstláa (Constance Naish) and Shaachooká
(Gillian Story.)

Naish and Story were assisted in their work
by Native speakers of Tlingit, especially
George Betts and Robert Zuboff of Angoon. These
elders devoted many hours to the work,
dictating traditional texts and assisting in
translation. In tribute to and in memory of
these tradition bearers, Constance Naish and
Gillian Story have transcribed and contributed

a text by George Betts and Robert Zuboff each
to this collection.

Complexity. The Tlingit alphabet often
appears overwhelming at first glance. This
reflects the complexity of the Tlingit language
itself, which is one of the most difficult in
the world. There are two major problems in
writing Tlingit: Tlingit is a tone language,
and Tlingit has 24 sounds not found in
English.

The first serious effort to write Tlingit
was in the 1830's by the Russian priest Fr John
Veniaminov (later elevated as Bishop Innocent,
Metropolitan Innocent, and finally canonized as
St. Innocent) who noted the problem of how to
spell the various "k" and "x" sounds. The
"problem," of course, has not gone away, and
various writers have addressed it in different
ways over the years. There is always the
suggestion and temptation to simplify the
alphabet by getting rid of the "hard" letters
and making it easier to read, but that simply
sweeps the difficulties under the carpet, and
denies the complexity and beauty of the Tlingit
language.

Vowels. Tlingit has 8 vowels: 4 short and
4 long, in paired sets:

a	aa
e	ei
i	ee
u	oo

The short vowels are written with one letter
and (with English and Tlingit examples) are:

a	was	tás	(thread)
e	ten	té	(stone)
i	hit	hít	(house)
u	push	gút	(dime)

The long vowels are written with two letters
and (with English and Tlingit examples) are:

aa	Saab (Swedish car; rhymes with "sob")	taan (sea lion)
ei	vein	kakéin (wool, yarn)
ee	seek	séek (belt)
oo	moon	dóosh (cat)

Consonants. Unlike the vowels, which are best and most easily illustrated with English counterparts, many Tlingit consonants have no English equivalents or approximations. The chart on the following page shows the Tlingit consonants. Linguists will be able to identify the value of the letters from their positions on the "grid." For the general reader, descriptions of the main features of the Tlingit sound system are probably more useful.

Voicing. All Tlingit consonants are voiceless, except for n. Dialect exceptions are described in the notes. Thus, the letters such as d, g, and others on the top row do not stand for voiced consonants, as in English, but are plain or unaspirated, meaning that the sounds are not accompanied by a puff of air.

Aspirated is a term referring to the puff of air. The second row across the chart is more or less like English. The t's and k's in English "top" and "tan," "kin" and "cool" are aspirated. They are pronounced with a puff of air. But the t's and k's in English "stop," "stan," "skin" and "school" are plain (unaspirated) and have no puff of air. These unaspirated sounds are the d's, g's and other sounds of the first row in Tlingit.

For the general reader, it is ok to pronounce the top row voiced as you would in English. It will give you an accent in your Tlingit, but that is going to be unavoidable for many years or possibly forever. You will be understood with the voiced consonants.

Tone. Tlingit has phonemic tone. This means that in Tlingit, as in Chinese, the

TECHNICAL SOUND CHART

FRONT OF MOUTH   BACK OF MOUTH

			dental	lateral	alveolar	alveo palatal	velar	velar rounded	uvular	uvular rounded	glottal
S T O P S		Plain	d	dl	dz	j	g	gw	g̲	g̲w	.
		Aspirated	t	tl	ts	ch	k	kw	k̲	k̲w	
		Glottalized ("pinched")	t'	tl'	ts'	ch'	k'	k'w	k̲'	k̲'w	
FRICATIVES		Aspirated		l	s	sh	x	xw	x̲	x̲w	h
		Glottalized		l'	s'		x'	x'w	x̲'	x̲'w	
SONANTS		Nasal	n								
		Semivowels					y	w			

difference between words depends on tone. High
tone is marked by an acute accent over the
vowel or first vowel of a sequence of two
letters. Low tone is unmarked.

sháa	women
shaa	mountain
x̲áat	fish
x̲aat	root

Technically, tone falls on the stem of the
word and is high or low. Any suffix following
the stem becomes the opposite tone of the
stem.

du x̲áadi	his fish
du x̲aadí	its root

In the practical orthography, it is more
practical and equally accurate to write high
tone wherever it appears or is heard, rather
than to mark both high and low tone on the
stem.

Stolen Tone. Sometimes tone is "stolen"
by a word that follows.

woogoot	he went
woogoodí	that he went
woogoodi yé	the place that he went

Tone (as well as vowel length and other
features) changes according to the grammar of
what a person wants to say:

Yaa nagút.	He/she/it is going.
Woogoot.	He/she/it went.
Gug̲ag̲óot.	He/she/it will go.

Héen tudaná.	We are drinking water.
Héen wutudináa.	We drank water.
Héen gax̲tudanaa.	We will drink water.

Cháayoo toolóok.	We are sipping tea.

Cháayoo wutuwalúk.   We sipped tea.
Cháayoo ga<u>x</u>toolóok.   We will sip tea.

Underlines. Tlingit has a series of "back in the throat" or "gutteral" sounds not found in English. These consonants are marked with an underline: <u>K</u> <u>k</u> <u>X</u> <u>x</u> <u>G</u> <u>g</u>.

gooch	hill	ka	on the surface
<u>g</u>ooch	wolf	<u>k</u>a	and

<u>k</u>óok	box	xát'aa	sled
kóo<u>k</u>	cellar; hole	<u>x</u>át'aa	whip

The <u>x</u> sound is very common in Tlingit, and appears in words dealing with "I," "me," and "my." The <u>k</u> and <u>g</u> appear in most future forms ("I am going to" do something).

W for Rounding. Some sounds in Tlingit can be made with the lips rounded. These sounds are written with the letter "w" following the consonant being rounded.

yaak	mussel
yaakw	boat

náakw	medicine
náa<u>k</u>w	devilfish; octopus

Apostrophe. Tlingit has a series of glottalized or "pinched" consonants not found in English and many other languages. Glottalized or "pinched" consonants are made with mouth air left over after the air supply from the lungs has been cut off. These sounds are written with an apostrophe: t' tl' ts' ch' k' k'w <u>k</u>' <u>k</u>'w.

tá	he/she/it is sleeping
t'á	king salmon

du káak	his/her maternal uncle

```
du káak'   his/her forehead

tléik'      no
du tl'eik   his/her finger

ch'áak'    eagle
```

Almost all Alaska Native languages have the
uvular or "back in the mouth" (or "gutteral")
sounds, and all of the Indian languages (but
not the Eskimo-Aleut family) have some series
of glottalized stops (k' t' etc.) but Tlingit
is unique among Alaska Native languages because
it also has a series of sounds technically
known as glottalized fricatives. This is the
5th row of the chart: l' s' x' x'w x' x'w.

```
séek   belt            tíx   flea
s'eek  black bear      tíx'  rope

       yéil   Raven
       yéil'  elderberry
```

One other letter needs comment here. The
period or . in the middle of a word marks a
glottal stop or "catch-in-the-breath." In
English, this sound marks the contrast between

```
uh-huh   (yes)
uh-uh    (no)
```

and many English speakers have this sound
where a "t" is dropped:

```
Bea'ls   for   Beatles
bo'l     for   bottle.
```

In Tlingit this sound is very common and
often marks the difference between words.

```
yaa kunaséin    it is close
yaa kunas.éin   it is growing
```

yei nas.héin   it is floating down
yaa anashéin   it is barking along.

In the story by Susie James, the verb "to be
close" appears in lines 96 and 234, and the
verb "to grow" several times in lines 90-102.

Some of the Tlingit sounds are shared with
English, but in different positions in the
word. For example, the -kw sound is found in
the English "quick," but is never the last
sound in an English word. On the other hand,
ts, tl, dl, and dz often appear at the end of
English words such as cats, little, cattle,
cradle, and adze, but are never the first sound
of an English word.

It is important to remember that the letters
x and x̲ do not represent anything like the
English -ks, but are like the German ich and
ach sounds. Also, remember that the L is
voiceless, like the Welsh or Yupik -ll-, and
unlike the English L, which is pronounced with
the vocal chords. To make the Tlingit L, place
your tongue as for an English L, but just
exhale through your mouth without vibrating
your vocal chords. By the way, the word spelled
"Tlingit" in English (and most commonly
pronounced "Klink-it," as opposed to "Tuh-ling-
git") is spelled "Lingít" in Tlingit, and the
first sound is a voiceless L.

Names. Because the Tlingit names are both
prominent and important (and unavoidable, even
in English translation) it is useful to give a
few special hints that will hopefully give
some confidence to the general reader facing
the unfamiliar names for the first time. It
takes most learners years to begin to master
the sounds of Tlingit, but in the meantime,
many sounds can be approximated.

For example, Kaats' is similar to English
"cots." Just forget the glottalized ts' for
now in such names as Kaats', Dukt'ootl' and
G̲alwéit'. Try to make the voiceless L in
Naatsilanéi and G̲alwéit', but for now just

substitute the English g for g̲.

For K̲aakex'wtí and K̲aax̲'achgóok, just
substitute an English k for ALL the different
k and x sounds. You will be reading Tlingit
with an accent, like a person saying "zee
vindow" for "the window," but you will be
understood in general and you will probably
enjoy trying. It is also very important to
try, because, from the Tlingit point of view,
the names are probably the most important part
of the story.

All of these phonological features combine
with each other and with a very difficult
grammatical system to make Tlingit among the
most complex languages in the world, and one of
the most difficult for people to learn to speak
if they do not grow up speaking it from
childhood. Tlingit is not a simple language to
learn. It is difficult, but not impossible,
and any effort is certainly worth while.
Readers who wish to make the effort to learn
this orthography should be able to pronounce
the Tlingit words in a way that is
understandable to a Native speaker.

VI. THE NATURE OF TLINGIT GRAMMAR

Fixed Variation. Tlingit words and
phrases are organized around a stem. Stems
have one underlying form (by which we list them
in a dictionary) but can and do appear in a
variety of forms. For example, the stem -.oon
meaning "shoot." Its simplist form is the
imperative or command form:

            ún   shoot! shoot it!

The stem can appear in noun form:

        óonaa   rifle; shooting instrument

and it can appear in a range of verb forms:

```
a.únt          he is shooting at it
na.únt         shoot it (over and over)
akₑwa.óon      he will shoot it
wutuwa.ún      we shot it
```

English does something different, yet similar in its system of roots and stems. For example the consonant and vowel variation in bath-bathe, grass-graze, and nose-nuzzle-nasal-nozzle. Another example is the g-l-d theme shared by the words gold, gild, gilt, glitter, and even yellow, where an Old English g changed to y. Another interesting example is the d-r-p theme in drip, drop, droop, drape.

In English, as in Tlingit, stems, by definition, can be added to ("droopy" or "drooping" for example) and they can change in many other ways so an entire range of different but related words can be created, such as dribble, dropped, and drapery.

In English, unlike Tlingit, nouns and verbs overlap in form and can often be told apart only by their position in the sentence.

> Don't shoot.
> The king had a good shoot.
> He's a good shot.
> He got shot.
> He got a shot at it.
> This is a shooting range.
> He is shooting.
> This bird is shot.
> This is bird shot.
> He is a drip.
> Don't drip the paint.
> It's a drop in the bucket.
> Don't drop the bucket.

For all kinds of sentences like these, the Tlingit phrase is built up around a stem. Whereas English has a string of separate words that stand alone, Tlingit has a string of parts of words that do not stand alone. The

Tlingit verb stem is at the end or toward the
end of the word; it almost always has one or
more prefixes (it can have up to 12) and is
commonly suffixed as well--with a string of up
to three suffixes. For more on this, please
see our *Beginning Tlingit* and the *Tlingit
Verb Dictionary* by Naish and Story. Many of
the notes in this book illustrate the stem and
affixes in tabular form.

The stem and other parts change form, but
the variation is fixed. It follows a regular
pattern. Some examples have been mentioned
above in the discussion of tone.

Yaa nagút.	He/she/it is walking along.
Woogoot.	He/she/it went.
Gugagóot.	He/she/it will go.
Héen tudaná.	We're drinking water.
Héen wutudináa.	We were drinking water.
Héen gax̲tudanaa.	We will drink water.
Yaa ntudanein...	We're starting to drink.
Yaa ntudaneiní...	When we begin to drink...
Cháayoo toolóok.	We will sip tea.
Cháayoo wutuwalúk.	We were sipping tea.

Notice how the stem can be long or short,
high or low tone, and sometimes even change
its set of vowels in these stems for go,
drink, and sip.

-gút	-ná	-lóok
-goot	-náa	-lúk
-góot	-naa	
	-nein	

Likewise, the subject pronoun can be long or
short, depending on whether it falls next to
the stem or not:

    -tu-
    -too-

The classifier can have the vowel i or a,

depending on the tense or aspect of the verb:

> -di-
> -da-

The classifier can even be in its "zero" form and not show up at all, or it can be a "ya" that has changed to a "wa" because it follows the vowel "u." All of this variation is regular and follows fixed rules.

And, of course, specific prefixes and suffixes can be added to indicate "tense", mode, and aspect.

> -wu-   perfective
> -ga<u>x</u>-   future.

Here are some examples of fixed variation from lines 90, 92-94, 77, 78, and 114 of <u>K</u>aakex'wtí.

> shaawahík   it was full (main clause)
> shahéek   it was full (subordinate clause)
>
> dulxést   (hooligans) were being trapped
> yeelxeisí   if you trap; if you had trapped
>
> aksaxéi<u>x</u>   they would dump
> akawlixéis'i át   the dumped thing

Notice the variation in stem, prefixes, and suffixes. All of this variation is fixed variation and makes a difference in meaning. English does something similar to show tense in some verbs: drink-drank-drunk; buy-bought; drive-drove-driven.

Free Variation. In contrast to fixed variation, there are places in Tlingit grammar where free variation occurs. Free variation means that different forms can be used with no change in meaning. It doesn't make any difference, for example, if the vowel is long or short. Pronunciation may vary from community to community, from speaker to

speaker within a community, or from time to
time within the speech of a single speaker.
The choice may depend on the situation, or be
totally random.

For example, in the Tlingit possessive
suffix system there is fixed variation between
the choice of the suffix -i or the suffix -u.
Words ending in any form of x, k, or k̲ preceded by oo or u take the possessive suffix -u.

x'úx'	book
ax̲ x'úx'u	my book
at doogú	its skin

Words ending in most other consonants
preceded by all other vowels take the
possessive suffix -i.

héen	water; river
ax̲ héeni	my water; my river
aan	land
ax̲ aaní	my land

Tone is fixed and is opposite of the stem tone.

Within this fixed system, a second kind of
variation is free. The vowel of the possessive
suffix can be long or short, depending totally
on the speaker.

ax̲ héeni	or	ax̲ héenee
ax̲ x'úx'u	or	ax̲ x'úx'oo.

These are in free variation. We have
standardized the spelling short, but both long
and short vowels are heard.

In a sequence of suffixes the same pattern
of free variation exists:

ax̲ aaníx'	in my land
ax̲ aanéex'	in my land
ax̲ aanídei	to my land
ax̲ aanéedei	to my land
ax̲ aaníde	to my land

a<u>x</u> aanéede   to my land.

For some speakers, the second suffix seems to have a lengthening affect on the first. Thus some speakers may say

a<u>x</u> aaní   my land
a<u>x</u> aanéedei   to my land.

In any case, the vowel length here makes no difference in meaning and is in free variation. With the exception of the contingent suffix noted below, suffix vowel length in Tlingit is in free variation. Suffix vowel tone is fixed and predictably opposite the tone of the stem.

Particles and Demonstratives. Some particles are in free variation. (These are hard to translate out of context.)

de   and   dei
tle   and   tlei.

The demonstratives are also in free variation.

wé - wéi   that there
yá - yáa   this here
yú - yóo   that yonder
hé - héi   this (adjacent)

Likewise the phrase markers based on these:

áwé - áwéi   that is
áyá - áyáa   this is
áyú - áyóo   that is
áhé - áhéi   this is

The long vowel forms in this system have the same form as, but should not be confused with some of the adverbial and locative forms:

yóo   bound adverb ("thus")
áyóo   locative ("in it")

Standardization. As this book goes to press, some minor points of Tlingit writing are still being resolved. The values of all the letters, and the writing of all fixed variation have been agreed on for 15 or 20 years, but the writing of some of the free variation is still being discussed. We have standardized most of the free variant forms to short vowel spellings. We have done this for a number of reasons. It is convenient to standardize, and there are fewer letters to type. But most important of all, over the years, as more Tlingit speakers became involved in literacy and using the Naish-Story writing system, many of these writers preferred to write the vowel suffixes and demonstratives short.

Because Tlingit scholars and writers are still in the process of standardizing spelling of some free variant forms, some inconsistancy remains in the writing of long vowels, especially in sets of suffixes, and in some decessives, but these make no difference in meaning.

Other standardization is still being worked out as well, especially in writing personal and place names. A general pattern we have tried to follow is to separate words having separate tones, and join words where there is only one tone over the combined form.

Finally, word division in writing of some "compound words" as one word or two, especially where glottal stops are involved, is still being resolved; for example

        goona<u>x</u>.áwu   or
        goona<u>x</u> áwu

We apologize for this aspect of work in progress, and for whatever inconsistancies may be found in the texts.

Tricky Forms. Especially tricky in proofreading are the words tsu and tsú, and the contingent and decessive endings with -ín.

Tsú   enclitic, meaning "also" and
        modifying the noun phrase before it.

Tsu   particle, meaning "again" and "also"
        and modifying the verb

For example

Xát áwé tsú kkwagóot.   I will go too.
Xát áwé tsu kkwagóot.   I will go again.

The decessive is fairly common and appears
as a main verb in the main clause. The
decessive suffix (conveying a sense of action
over a limited period of time) has variation in
both pitch and length. The pitch is in fixed
variation and is opposite of the stem; the
vowel length is is free variation.

woogoot   he went
woogoodín / woogoodéen   he used to go
gugagóodin / gugagóodeen   he will go
                                 (for a while)

Compare the imperfective form "at éen" in
line 8 of Kaats' with the decessive in line 7.

        8. Daa sáyú aan has at éen?
    What did they harvest with?

        7. at eenéen   used to harvest

Other examples from the texts are:

B. Bay 153.   haa wusdagéen
                we separated and migrated

T. Peters 187.   daxkustéeyin
                 there used to be

T. Peters 188.   daxduhéixwayin
                 they used to be trained
                 in medicine

Kaats' 5. wu.aadéen used to go

In contrast, the contingent (meaning
"whenever") is always in a subordinate clause
with an obligatory short high suffix: -ín.
The contingent is relatively uncommon in the
texts. Its form is characterized by the
conjugation prefix -ga-, the aspect prefix,
and the progressive stem. It usually patterns
with a main verb in the occasional or
decessive. For example, "Whenever he went to
Hoonah he would go hunting." Notice the
required short vowel and the acceptable
sequence of high stem and high suffix, in
contrast to the decessive (which would have to
be opposite of each other.)

yaa kgagúdín   whenever he went (on foot)
kungatínín   whenever he travelled
agaaxsatínín   whenever he sees it

Editorial Errors. The above discussion of
fixed and free variation applies to what might
be called "legitimate" variation in
pronunciation and spelling. It is important
to distinguish such "legitimate" variation
both in oral literature and in the Tlingit
sound and grammar systems from errors deriving
from an inability to hear and transcribe.
   Specifically, many different spellings of
Tlingit names and words are to be found in
popular books. Some of these are early
attempts to spell Tlingit with a writing system
lacking many of the letters needed to do it.
Other examples are simply of words incorrectly
heard. For example, one published version of
the "Glacier Bay History" gives the name of
the woman as "Shaw-whad-seet." The writer, a
non-Tlingit, could not hear the difference
between a glottalized k' and t. The name is
Shaawatséek'.

Often editors who are not familiar with any of the languages involved do not understand what is being spelled. For example, one popular book on totem poles has the name of the hero of the Strong Man story as "Kagaasi." What the editor failed to see is that the name was first transcribed in Russian and used the "g" to represent what English writers would spell with an "h." By this same writing convention, such names as Hitler and Himmler are transliterated as Gitler and Gimmler. Thus, an editor who does not know Tlingit or Russian, seeing "Kagaasi" and "Kaháas'i" can erronously assume that there are two different names. The same problem has occured in modern editors using transliterations of Russian transcriptions of the word for raven (yéil in this orthography, "el" in the 19th century Russian convention, which spelling prompted one editor to speculate that "el" is a Tlingit divinity etymologically related to Hebrew Elohim or Arabic Allah.) These comments are not intended as a criticism of earlier transcriptions of Tlingit, only as a warning that persons comparing and using versions from various sources need to be able to distinguish inaccurate transcriptions and spellings from those which are simply using an alternative but equally accurate transcription system.

Standardization of Dialect. Because the writing system is "phonemic" and not "phonetic," certain phonetic distinctions are standardized in the spelling. In other words, certain "automatic" sound variation can be, but does not need to be, spelled out.

For example, in English, the p's in pin and spin, the t's in top and stop, and the k's in cow, scow, kit and skit are all phonetically distinct, but the different kinds of p, t, and k are not used to contrast meaning in the English sound system, so they can be written with the same letter.

Where something similar happens in Tlingit,

we have standardized the spelling. However, in most places, we have attempted to show regional dialect variation in the spelling. There are some features of individual pronunciation that we have standardized, usually identifying this in the notes.

For example, automatic, non-phonemic labialization is not reflected in most places in the orthography. Thus the clan name Chookaneidí is phonetically "Chookwaneidí," with automatic rounding or labialization of the k following oo, but it is not necessary to spell this. Also, not all speakers have the automatic labialization. So, we have identified places where the sound occurs in the notes.

Likewise, for some older speakers of Tlingit, y and w alternate with each other in certain environments.

a yádi	its child
du wádi	his/her child
ax̲ yéet	my child
du wéet	his/her child

The same pattern is found where some speakers have wux̲ and wax̲ for yux̲ and yax̲ in certain places. Other speakers would have yéet and yádi, yux̲ and yax̲ in all places.

Where the w appears in the text as a variant of y, we have standardized it with commentary in the notes. Historically, this alternation of y and w comes from an older sonorant called "gamma") that has been lost for most speakers in most communities. The "gamma" became w in the environment of u, and y in other places, and is y in most places for most speakers. It is interesting to note the old "gamma" preserved in place names on old maps; for example, modern Yandeistakye near Haines (Yandeist'akyé in Tlingit) begins with "G" on some older maps and records.

The most notable exception to this, and the

most notable exception to the standardization, is in the "y classifier." This routinely appears as wa after u but ya in other places for all speakers, so this is always spelled as a fixed variation pattern, either as ya or wa.

This lengthy and somewhat technical description of variation and standardization is designed to help readers gain a better understanding of the complex patterns at work in Tlingit grammar and therefore increase their skill and enjoyment at working with the Tlingit texts. We hope that some readers will not only enjoy Tlingit literature in English translation, but will use the translations and texts for study and enjoyment of the Tlingit language itself. We have tried to make this book of use in both endeavors, and we apologize for any errors or inconsistancies that careful readers may encounter along the way.

NARRATIVES

Ḵák'w
Shaadaax' x'éidáx sh kalneek

This text is prepared and contributed by
Naatstláa (Constance Naish) and Shaachooká
(Gillian Story) as a memorial to Shaadaax'
(Robert Zuboff) who gave so much help in
their early study of the Tlingit language
upon which the present system of writing
Tlingit is based.

Yú haa aaní áyú,
yú haa aaní,
Ḵák'w áyú yóo duwasáakw;
Dleit Ḵáa x'éinax ku.aa,
Basket Bay.
A áyú, tsaa áyú áa shaduxíshdeen,
yú tl'átk.
Tlax kasiyéiyi yáx áyú yatee yú tl'átk.
Yándei yaa kgaléinin áyú,
tléináx yateeyi aa ḵáa áyú,   10
kanduḵéich.
Yú ḵées' áyú,
kúnáx a ḵáa yan woodáaych.
Yá aan tayeedéi,
téil kagánee káax' áyú ana.átch,
yá aan tayeedéi.
Yá Tus'ḵoowú eexayáak,

62

Basket Bay History
told by Robert Zuboff

That land of ours,
that land of ours
is called Ḵák'w;
but in English
Basket Bay.
You know, they used to club seals,
at that place.
That place is kind of strange.
When the tide was almost out
they would send
one man as guard.
People would keep
a watch on the tide.
They would go underneath the village
in a grotto, by the light of sapwood,
underneath the village.
Down the bay from Shark's Cave,

10

yá Kaakáakw, a shakana<u>x</u>.aaná<u>x</u> áyú,
a shakana<u>x</u>.aaná<u>x</u> áyú yoo aya.átk,
yá aan tayeedéi.   20
Dzeit áyú áa wduwa<u>x</u>út',
aatlein;
aas áyú.
Áyú dzeit<u>x</u> wududliyé<u>x</u>.
Ana<u>x</u> áyá yaa a<u>g</u>a.átjeen yóo aan tayeedéi,
téilx' <u>k</u>aa jee yéi nateech; aadéi akdulgánch.
A káax' áyá shadu<u>x</u>ísht yá tsaa,
yá aan tayeex'.
Ldakát yéidei át áyá át woodaháaych yá diyée.
A áyá yá <u>k</u>ées' latíni <u>k</u>u.aa áyá <u>k</u>u<u>g</u>asteech;   30
tléiná<u>x</u> áyú yú ée<u>g</u>i yan aa uhaanch.
Tléiná<u>x</u> áyú yú hít káx' aa <u>g</u>anúkch.
Nás'gi aa áwé <u>k</u>u.aa, áa ya<u>x</u> haan áwé Kaakáakw
       shakée;
daax'oon aa áwé,
ch'u tle wé wool <u>x</u>'éi ya<u>x</u> haan.
Ch'u tle ée<u>k</u>dá<u>x</u> yaa wunadéini teen áwé,
kei at'aa.í<u>x</u>'ch,
"Dei ée<u>k</u>dá<u>x</u> yaawadáaaaaa."
Ch'u tle yóo hít kát aa,
aa <u>x</u>'éit was <u>g</u>adutéenín,   40
"Ee<u>k</u>dá<u>x</u> yaawadáaaaaa."
Yéi áyú has du <u>x</u>oo<u>x</u> yaa <u>g</u>a<u>x</u>íxch.
Ch'u tle yá hóoch'i aayích áyá, ana<u>x</u>....
aan yá woolná<u>x</u> áyá yéi yaa ya<u>x</u>da<u>g</u>íchch,
"Dei ée<u>k</u>dá<u>x</u> yaawadáaaaaa."
A káax' áyá,
yá <u>k</u>aa jáa<u>g</u>adi,
yá a leikachóo<u>x</u>'uná<u>x</u> áyá kíndei shadu<u>x</u>óot',
yá tsaa yoowú.
Ana<u>x</u> áyá du.úxs'.   50
Tle <u>x</u>'adus.aa<u>x</u>w;
tle <u>x</u>'adus.aa<u>x</u>w;
tle <u>x</u>'adus.aa<u>x</u>w.
Tla<u>x</u> kúná<u>x</u> áyú yasátk yú haa yee.
Oowayáa, yaa shanats'ít'i yá<u>x</u> áyú nateech
     aadéi yasatgi yé.
Ch'u tle <u>x</u>'éi<u>x</u> dushadi yá<u>x</u> áyá yoo yaneek,
yá haa yee.
Ch'u tle tla<u>x</u> kúná<u>x</u> áyú yéi jidunéi nooch,

to the head north of Kaak̲áakw,
to the head north of this they would cross over
to go under the village.   20
A ladder was adzed there
a huge one;
it was a tree.
This is what was made into a ladder.
This is what they came down on to go underneath
        the village.
Sapwood torches were held; they would be lighted.
By the light of this they clubbed seals,
underneath the village.
Many different kinds of animals would gather
        down there.
And you know, there would be tide watchers.   30
One would stand out on the beach.
One would sit on the top of a house.
The third one would stand at the arch of Kaak̲áakw;
the fourth one
would stand right at the mouth of the hole.
As soon as the tide started coming up
he would cry out,
"The tiiiiiide is starting uuuuuuup."
As if it were put in his mouth
the one sitting on top of the house repeated   40
"The tiiiiiide is starting uuuuuuup."
This was how they passed the word.
The very last man
would thrust his head down the hole with the words,
"The tiiiiiide is starting uuuuuuup."
Accordingly,
men would pull up the seal stomachs
through the throats
of their kills.
They would blow them up through the throat.   50
They tied them off;
they tied them off;
they tied them off.
The tide comes in under us very quickly,
like filling a container to the brim
        is how quick it is.
It's like cutting off any escape
under us.

yá ḵaa jáaḡadi daax'.
Ch'u tle yándei yaa yéi ndusneení teen áwé,
    ḵundakél'ch áwé,   60
tláakw áwé;
kíndei yóo dzeit kát áwé ḵaa lugookch
    kaḡít tú áyá;
áwé ch'a wé téil káax' áyá át ḵaa lunagúḵch.
Ch'u tle áyá a náḵ neil oo.aatch
    yá ḵaa jáaḡadi.
Yankaadéi yaa kḡadéinin áwé tsá,
yankaadéi yaa kḡadéinin,
aaḡáa áwé yá ḵaa yakaanáx̱ áwé,
yá Goon X'aak'ú yayeenáx̱ áwé
    kíndei anasgooḵ nooch,
yá ḵaa jáaḡadi.   70
Áyá, yéi áyá.
Ch'u tle ch'as yaakw a káa daak ḵúx̱ji nooch.
Yéi áyá dutláakw,
a daat át,
yá Ḵák'w, aadáx̱ haa ádix̱ siteeyi yé,
aadáx̱ haa ádix̱ siteeyi yé.
Naaléi,
dei ch'áakw áyá,
dei ch'áakw,
aadáx̱ haa dutlaagú;
ách haa dudlisáakw,   80
Ḵak'weidí.
Shóogooná̱x̱,
aadéi yóo at kawdiyayi yé,
yá Lingít,
shayadiheni aa yéi sh kalneek
yá ixkéenax̱ áyá,
haat haa wsidáḵ,
yá ixkée.
A áyá shayadiheni aa,
    Shtax'héen yíknáx̱ yaa wsidaaḵ,
Shtax'héen yíknáx̱.   90
Yá ax̱ éesh hás has dutlakw nooch,
yá Shtax'héen yíknax̱, yaa has wusdaagí.
Tléix' yateeyi yé áyú áx',
yá héen,
sít' tayeedéi naadaa.
Ax' áyá wududlis'ít yá x̱aanás'.

They would work very hard,
on this kill of theirs.
No sooner would they finish the last one   60
          than they would run
quickly;
they would run up the ladder in the dark;
only by the light of the sapwood
          would they run up.
They would even go home from their kill.
When the tide was finally nearly up,
when the tide was nearly up,
was when out from the village, in the bay,
in front of Spring Water Point
their kills would pop up out of the water.
You know, this is the way it was.   70
Then they would just get them by boat.
This is how the history is told,
about
Basket Bay, from the time it's been ours,
from the time it's been ours,
ages.
It was long ago,
it's been long,
since the histories have been told of us;
we are named for it,   80
Kak'weidí.
For the things that happened
to the Tlingits
in the beginning,
many say
we migrated here
through the south,
the south.
And, you know, there are many
          who migrated down the Stikine River,
down the Stikine River.   90
The story of my fathers is always told,
of when they migrated down the Stikine.
At one place, there,
in the river,
the river flowed under a glacier.
This is where they tied a raft together.
They put the elderly women on it.

A káx' áyá yéi has wuduwa.oo
    yá shaanáx'w sáani.
Awastí yóo aa wduwasáakw ḵa Ḵoowasíkx,
yá shaanáx'w sáani.
Hás áyá shóogoonáx yá sít' tayeedéi
    daak has wuduwagúk.   100
A tayeenáx has g̱alháash áwé héinax.aadéi
kei has at kaawashée.
Yá sít' tayeenáx has wulhaashí áyá
át has shukawdlixúx.
A káax' áyá,
x̱aanás' yéi wdudzinee.
A kaadéi aa woo.aat.
A tayeenáx áyá yá sít' tayeenáx áyá ḵuwlihaash,
yá íxdei.
Tsu shayadiheni aa ḵu.aa áyá   110
áa akawdlix̱éetl',
yá sít' tayeedéi wulhaash.
Ách áyá a kát aa uwa.át,
yá sít' kát aa uwa.át.
A áyá Jilḵáatnáx yeiḵ uwa.át
    yá ax̱ éesh hás x̱oonx'i,
yá Dakl'aweidí.
Jilḵáat aax has wusitee.
Yá sít' kát awu.aadí áyá a kaax̱ saa áyá,
Sit'ká á,
Sit'ká, yóo ḵuduwasáakw,   120
yá Jilḵáatnáx yeiḵ uwa.adi aa.
Yá uháan,
yá Deisheetaanx haa sateeyí,
ch'a yaadachóon áyá,
yéi has akanéek,
yá ixkéenáx áyá,
yá ixkéenáx.
Goot'aanáx sá kwshé yeiḵ wutuwa.át uháan.
Goot'á sá kwshé anax yeiḵ wutuwa.át.
Aadáx áyá tsá, yá nándei,   130
yá nándei,
g̱unayéi ḵuwtuwashée.
Shayadiheni yé kawduwa.aakw.
Shayadiheni yé aanx wududliyéx̱.
Wé gaaw áwé,
yá Xutsnoowú yax̱'áak,

One's name was Awasti and the other Koowasíkx,
these elderly women.
They are the first ones who were pushed under   100
        the glacier.
Having drifted under it and through to the
        other side,
they started singing.
Floating under the glacier
gave them their song.
Based on this
a raft was made.
Some went on it.
Under it, under the glacier, they floated,
down the river.
But many of them   110
were afraid
to float under the glacier.
This is why they started over it,
some started over the glacier.
These are the ones who came down the Chilkat,
        the relatives of my fathers,
the Dakl'aweidi.
They became the Chilkats.
The name that came from those
        who went over the glacier
is Sit'ká indeed,
those who came down through Chilkat,   120
are named Sit'ká.
Those of us
who are Deisheetaan,
still
tell it like this,
as coming from the South,
from the south.
I wonder where we came out, those of us.
I wonder where we came out.
From there we finally went northward,   130
northward,
we began searching.
They tried many places.
Villages were founded in many places.
At that time
across from Brown Bear Fort,

yax̱ ilt'éex',
t'éex' kát aa uwa.át,
wé gaaw áwé,
aag̱áa daak ḵuwligas'i yé.   140
Ha! shayadiheni aa yá haa x̱oonx'í,
yá Deisheetaan,
yá dáaḵ káx' yéi aa dax̱yatee.
Ch'u ch'áagudáx̱,
áa yéi has yatee.
Shayadihéin,
yá Nahóowu, áa yéi yatee,
ḵa yá ax̱ saayí,
Shaadaax' tsú áa yéi yatee,
yá dáaḵ ká.   150
A áyá a daa yoo tux̱atángi áyá, hás,
ch'u ch'áagudáx̱ áa yéi s teeyí,
has du een gé yá woochdáx̱ haa wusdaag̱éen.
Yéi áyá a daa yoo tux̱atangi nooch.
Ach yá éil' kát haa kawdiyáa,
uháan ḵu.aa.
Ch'a yéi áyá x̱'akkwanáaḵ,
yá sh kalneek.

when it froze,
they walked over ice
at that time,
at the point when they moved across.   140
Well! There are many who are our relatives,
these Deisheetaan,
some are living in the Interior.
Since long ago,
they have been living there.
They are many,
Nahóowu lives there
and this namesake of mine.
Shaadaax' is also there,
in the Interior.   150
You know, thinking about them,
if they've been living there a long time,
maybe we separated and migrated from them.
This is what I'm thinking about them.
This is why we
gathered here on the coast.
This is where I will end
this story.

Táax'aa
Shaadaax' x'éidáx sh kalneek

Awé
wé ax yaagú yíkt
"Guide" yóo dusáagun,
a yíkt áwé át naxakúxch.
Asgeiwú.

Awé,
yéi xat duwasáakw
Lingít x'éináx
Shaadaax'.
Awé yá   10
yá ax saayínax áwé
áwé xat wooxoox Geetwéin.
Ch'áagu aayí
ch'áakw woonaa.
Yées yadák'wx xat sitee.
Tle ch'u yées yadák'wx xat sateeyídax
s'eenáa yaakw ax jee yéi wootee.
I had
nineteen hundred and six model,
tle shóogunáx come outx yaa nastéeni.   20
Awé wé
déix ax jeex' sitee wé yaakw tlénx'.
Yá hóoch'i aayí áwé
ax yéet jeet xwasitée.

Mosquito
told by Robert Zuboff

It was
in this boat of mine,
it was called "Guide,"
I would travel around in it,
seining.

Well,
my name
in Tlingit
is Shaadaax'.
It was
because of my name
Geetwéin called me over.   10
The one of long ago,
he died long ago.
I was a young man.
From the time I was a young man
I had a seine boat.
I had
a nineteen hundred and six model,
from when they first came out.   20
I had
two of these big boats.
The last one
I gave to my son.
But he wrecked it.

Tle akawliwál'.
He wrecked the boat,
wé a yíkt át naxakúxji aa kúnáx.
Awé yá ax saayí askóo áwé
yéi xat yawsikaa:
"Ax tuwáx' áyá sigóo i een kunáax daak
      kaxwaneegí   30
yá i saayí."
Yú dakká áyá
áx' yéi haa wooteex.
Tlax áyá woot'éex'
haa kusteeyí áx'.
Yá xáat.
Yá el'kaadáx
haa x'éi kei x'ákch.
Yá xáat.
A áyá tlax daat yáx sáyá haa x'éi yak'éi   40
yá xáat.
Kúnax
yat'éex'
kustí yóo dakká.
Wáa t'éex'i sáyú
ch'á á wooch isxá
aantkeení.
Kusaxa kwáan kudzitee
wé gaaw.
A áwé   50
a daa yoo x'atula.atgi nooch,
yá el'kaadéi haa wulgáas'i.
A daa yoo x'atula.átgi nuch.
Ch'u a daa yóo x'atula.átgi áyá.
Yá
tléix' yateeyi aa
yá family áyá has du x'axan.ádi áyá
yaa kunak'éin.
Ayá tléinax yateeyi aa áyá
tle aawal'óon,   60
oogaajaagi átgaa.
Tléil yeik wugoodí áyá yáa
du yinaadéi aa du kéek' du eegáa koowashee.
Tle hú áyá tsú tléil
tléil yeik woogoot.
L yeik ugóot áyá

He wrecked the boat,
the same one I used to go around in.
Then, knowing what my name was,
Geetwéin said to me:
"I would like very much to explain to you   30
this name of yours."
We were living there
in the Interior.
Our life there
was so hard.
The salmon.
From the ocean
they would come up for us to eat.
The salmon.
And these how good they tasted to us,   40
the salmon.
It was very
hard
to live in the Interior.
It was so hard
the people
ate each other.
There were cannibals
at that time.
That was   50
what we would tell about
when we migrated to the coast.
What we would tell about.
What we would still tell about.
There was
this one
family whose food
was getting scarce.
Then one of them
went hunting   60
for something he could kill.
When he didn't come back down
his younger brother went to search for him.
Then he
didn't come back down either.
When he didn't come back down
the youngest one,
maybe he was seventeen years old,

yá kík'i aa,
gwál jinkaat táakw ka daxadooshú,
gwal jinkaat táakw ka nas'gadooshóox gí ustí
yá kík'i aa,   70
ch'a yaa nasgáx áyá du hunxu hásgaa yaa
          kunashéen.
Ayá dáak yá shaa x'áak
áa kaháa áyá awsiteeni káa áyá.
Ch'u tle áyu awsikóo
kusaxa kwáanx sateeyí.
Ash xándei yaa nagút. Tléil aadéi awoonaxdihaani
          yé a nák. Ch'u tle wdudlit'ix'ee át yáx
          áyú. Akoolxéitl' áyú yéi ash wusinei.
Tle ash xándei yaa nagúdi áwé tlé ash
          shaawaxích áwé
kusaxa kwáanch áwé shaawaxích.
Wudzigeet,
áa wdzigeet.   80
Wáa sá du toowú yak'éi wé kusaxa kwáan.
Aadáx awsitaa wé yadák'w
tle gwéil tóodei,
gwéil tóodei.
Tle aawayaa
du aanídei
du hídi át la.aa yéidei.
Gáan áwé
gáan x'awoolx' áwé kaax yéi awdzinei
wé du yáanayi.   90
A yeedéi
du hídi yeedéi neil uwagút wé kusaxa kwáan.
Wé yadák'w ku.aa áwé
wé yáanaa tóowu.
Awé akoo.aakw áwé a tóodáx kei wugoodí.
Alk'óots yáa tíx'
tíx'x'i sáani xaat ách daa wdudzi.axu wé yáanaa.
A tóodax kei góot áwé
du jéet wujixín wé kusaxa kwáan x'ús'i.
A yayeex kei uwahán gáannax.á.   100
Ch'u tle gáannax.áa yúx yaa yanas.éini teen áwé
          ashaawaxích.
Tsu ashaawaxích.
Tsu ashaawaxích.
Tsu ashaawaxích.

maybe eighteen years old,
the youngest one,   70
was crying as he kept on searching for his
        older brothers.
Inland between the mountains
when he reached there he saw it was the man.
He immediately knew
it was a cannibal.
It was coming toward him. He couldn't run from
        it. He was like a frozen thing. It was
        fear that did this to him.
When it came near him it struck him on the head,
the cannibal struck him on the head.
He fell,
he fell there.   80
How good the cannibal felt.
It picked him up from there, that young man
and put him into a sack
into a sack.
Then it packed him on its back
to its territory
to where its house was standing.
Outside
out by the entrance it removed
its pack.   90
The cannibal went inside
inside its home.
But the young man
was inside the pack.
He was trying to get out of it.
He broke those ties,
small strings of spruce roots tying the pack.
When he came out
he got the cannibal's club.
He waited where it was going to come out.   100
As it stuck its head out, he struck it.
He struck it again.
He struck it again.
He struck it again.
He said,
"I know I killed this cannibal.
But it did a painful thing to me.
It killed two of my older brothers.

Yéi x'ayaká
"Xwasikóo áyá xwajaagí yáa kusaxa kwáan.
Ha néekw déin ku.aa yá xat wusinei.
Ax húnxu hás áyá dáxnáx aawaják.
Wáa sgí s'é gé xwsinei gé tsu tsu
    néekw déin naganeiyít xá.
Yak'éi shákdeí   110
du yeet aaxwa.aagi kei xwsagaaní."
A yáx áwé
shóot ada.áak,
tle a kát aawaxút'
wé x'aan kát aawaxút'
wé kusaxa kwáan.
Tle ch'as a kél't'i áa yéi teeyí áwé
tléil a daax' yankáx toodashátx.
"Wáa sgí s'é gé xwsinei wé kusaxa kwáan
    kél't'i gé?"
Ayá ch'a l a daa yankáx toodashátxi áwé
    awli.óox,   120
wé kusaxa kwáan kél't'i áwé awli.óox.
Kaawayíx' yóo woonei áwé,
táax'aax wusitee.
Ach áwé táax'aa
kuwustáax'i,
ch'u tle koodzi yáx áwé yóo kusineik; ch'u
    kusaxa kwáanx áwé sitee yeisú.
L yoo awoodlákwgu ku.aa áwé
du tuwáa sigóo yá kaa sheiyí kaa tóotx kei
    akawujeilí.
Yéi áwé wootee.
Dikée Aankáawu yá Lingit'aaní   130
awliyéx.
Kúnax haa wsixán,
haa yá Lingit'aaní ka.ádi.
Ch'a á áyá ch'a yá Lingit'aaních áyá wliyéx
yá táax'aa.
Ach áyá yéi
a daat sh kalneek
kudzitee, áa yéi haa teeyi áyá Téslin,
Téslin.
Yá áa tlein tuwán áyá   140
yá
Caribou Cross

What more can I do to make it feel more pain?
Maybe it will be better   110
if I build a fire under him, and burn him up."
So just like that
when he built a fire,
he pulled him into it,
he pulled the cannibal
into the fire.
When only the ashes were left,
when he couldn't make up his mind, he thought,
"What more can I do to the cannibal's ashes?"
And while he couldn't make up his mind, he   120
        blew on it,
he blew on the cannibal's ashes.
They went into the air,
they became mosquitos.
That's why mosquitos
when they bite someone,
hurt you bad, they're still the cannibal;
        even today.
When it can't do this
it tries to take all the blood from a person.
That's what happened.
The Lord above created   130
this world.
He loved us very much,
us in this world.
Mosquitos
were created by the world.
That is why
there is a story
about it, when we were living in Teslin,
Teslin.
It's beside the big lake.   140
The place
is called
Caribou Cross,
the place where animals cross.
Right near it is called Teslin.
There are many people there,
we are many.
We are still there.
They speak our language.

yóo duwasáakw yáa
yá at gutu.ádi ana<u>x</u> naa.aadi yé.
A <u>x</u>ánk' áyá yéi duwasáakw Téslin.
A<u>y</u>á shayadihéin,
haa shayadihéin.
Ax' ch'a yeisú áa yéi haa yatee.
Haa <u>x</u>'éiná<u>x</u> yoo has <u>x</u>'ali.átk.
Yéi áyá yándei shuk<u>g</u>watáan.   150
Yáa yeedát
yá at yátx'i teen
sh kak<u>k</u>walnéek
Dleit <u>K</u>áa <u>x</u>'éiná<u>x</u>.

This is how I'll end it.   150
And now
I will tell stories
to the children
in English.

Kaax'achgóok
Ixt'ík' Eesh x'éidáx sh kalneek

Yá Sheet'kaadáx aa
Kiks.ádi
ldakát yéidei áyá yoo haa kaawanéi.
Xáat Kwáanix haa wsitee,
Aak'wtaatseen.
Kooshdaa Kwáani xoox' tsú yéi aa wootee,
Kaakáa.
Haa xoodáx tsú daak aa wlis'ís,
Kaax'achgóok.
Yoo kdujeek nuch áyá aadóo sá yoo x'atángi.   10
Ax éesh
Tak'xoo.
L.aanteech du kéilk'.
Ax léelk'w
Kaak'wáji
ka tsu ax léelk'u tlein
Kaat'aláa
ax éesh niyaanáx.
Daax'oon áyá téeyin ax saayí
ax yáa wduwasayi saax'w.   20
Dleit káach tle tlél átx ulyeix.
Ixt'ík' Eesh,
Woolshook.
Yáat'aa kwá ax léelk'u hásch áyá ax yáa uwasayi
        saa áyá.

Kaax'achgóok
told by Andrew P. Johnson

To those of us Kiks.ádi
from Sitka,
many things happened.
We became salmon people,
Aak'wtaatseen.
One of us also stayed with Kooshdaa Kwáani,
Kaakáa.
And one of us sailed out,
Kaax'achgóok.
People usually wonder who is talking.   10
My father
was Tak'xoo.
He was the nephew of L.aanteech.
My grandfather
was Kaak'wáji
and my great grandfather
Kaat'aláa,
on my father's side.
I have four names,
names given to me.   20
A white man would not use them.
Ixt'ik' Eesh,
Woolshook.
This one though was given to me by my
        grandparents.

Shaayeexáak
ka Wasdéik.
Yá ax tlaakáak hás
has du sh kalneegí áyá yee een kakkwalaneek,
Kaax'achgóok daak wuls'eesí.
Sheet'ká yóo wduwasayi yé   30
yá Lingít aaní áwé
Sheet'ká.
Yáa yeedát yéi duwasáagu yé
Old Sitka.
A ku.aa wé tlél Sheet'ká áwé.
Gajaahéen yóo áwé wduwasáa,
yá haanaanáx aadéi aa tliyaadéi kwás
        Walachéix'i.
A digiygéix' áwé s awulyeixín wé Noow Tlein, yá
        Anóoshich.
Ayá yeedát Old Sitka yóo duwasáakw Dleit Káach.
Ch'a át áyá haa kundayeijín taakw.eetíx'.   40
Wáa nganein sáwé
yá Ch'al'geiyita.aan
áa yéi haa nateech.
A ítnáx áwé
tsu wéit kawtushitán Shaaseiyi.aan.
Taakw.eetít kugahéinín
x'óon áyá yan usdáaych.
Ldakát yá x'áat'x'i xoox' yéi nateech.
Ayá kadulshakxi nuch
woosáani tin.   50
Daxyeekaadéi yú téeyin yú woosáani.
Yá kátdei kdusxatxi át
at kadzaasí,
wáa wdukaayí sá kwshí wé?
At s'aan.aaxw dzaas yóo dusáaych.
Gaadlaani yé yís aa á.
Ka tsu at shaxishdi dzaas
l gwaadlaani yé yís aa.
Dáxnáx áyú wooch káa aawasháa
Kaax'achgóok.   60
Yanwát
ka yées shaawát.
Kalshákx áyá akooshtánin.
Tlél kei jeexíxch.
At s'aatíx áyú sitee.

Shaayeexáak
and Wasdéik.
This story I will tell you
is of my mother's maternal uncles,
when Kaax'achgook sailed out.
The place named Sitka   30
was a Tlingit village,
Sitka.
It is the place now called
Old Sitka.
But that place is not Sitka.
They called it Gajaahéen.
It is the one on this side; on the other side
        is Walach'éix'i.
In between Noow Tlein was built by the Russians.
Now it is called Old Sitka by the white folks.
We only used to travel around in spring.   40
Once in a while
we lived there
in Ch'al'geiyita.aan.
After this
we frequented Shaaseiyi.aan.
When spring came
fur seals would drift in on the tide.
They would be throughout all these islands.
This is what people used to tire out and kill
with spears.   50
They used two different kinds of spears.
How long
were the thongs
that were tied to the spear point?
They were called at s'aan.aaxw dzaas.
They were for a deep place.
And the thongs that battered the head
for a shallow place.
Kaax'achgóok
had two wives.   60
An older woman
and a younger woman.
He frequently went hunting sea mammals.
He never lost out.
He was a master hunter.
Well, I wonder what happened to him.

Ha ch'a wáa ku.aa sá kwshí yá yoo kaawanéi?
Tsu daak kóox áwé s'ootaat
é! desgwach awoostákxaa.
De yaa jindaxwétl.
Yá x'óon át shasatin yéidei áwé gunéi s uwakúx   70
du keilk'i hás teen.
A xoodéi áwé kadagáax wé x'óon yádi.
A tóodei áwé kaa seiwa.áx
"Ihi!
Ihi! Sh eelk'átl'!
Kaax'achgóok át nakuxji yé áyá,
Kaax'achgóok."
Du keilk'i hás áwé yéi ayawsikaa
"yándei déi,
yándei déi!"   80
Gunéi s uwakúx tle.
Aan eegayáakt has kóox
tle héeni wugoodí áwé,
shakáadeix áwé sitee,
tlék'gaa áwé a shakaadáx yéi adaané
du woosáani gootl; tle akal'íx't.
Héendei aléet.
Ldakát yax ayalal'éex' áwé tsá
dákdei gunayéi uwagút.
Tlax wáa sáyú x'egaa adanoogún yú x'óon dleeyí   90
yá yées aa du shát.
Ach áwé tlax yéi
yan ooxeechch kalshákx.
Xáanaa áwé at gadus.ée;   at duxá.
Yú k'wátl yóo tuwasáagu át
kákw áwé
k'idéin wuduwa.agi aa kákw.
Yawdagaat'aayi té áwé a kaadéi dugich nuch; áwé
          ul.úkch tle.
A kát adush.utlxi nuch; dleey tsú a kát dustéix
          yú.á.
Ahé shaawát áwé agawdzi.ée; agawdzitáa wé x'óon
          dleeyí.   100
S'íx' kaadéi áwé yéi adaané.
Awé yées aa du shát wé Kaax'achgóok du shát áwé
          du s'íx'i tle át aawatán.
"Taxhéenak'u a kát yilaxwén."
Tle yáadei áwé yóo wdudzinei du s'íx'i.

When he went out again in the morning,
drat! he began missing his target.
His arms were tiring.
With his sisters' sons   70
he started for the place where the fur seals
        were floating in a cluster.
He heard the sound of a fur seal pup crying.
Among the cries he heard a human voice:
"Don't!
Don't! Hush!
This is the place where Kaax'achgóok hunts,
Kaax'achgóok."
He said to his maternal nephews,
"Let's go in now,
let's go in now!"
Then they started going.   80
When they reached the beach of their village,
as he stepped out into the water,
he was a bow man,
one by one he took his spears
from the bow; then he broke them one by one.
He threw them into the sea.
When he had broken them all then
he started up.
How his young wife   90
loved eating fur seal meat.
That was why
he worked so hard at tiring fur seals out.
One evening people were cooking; they were
        eating.
These things we call cooking pots
were baskets,
tightly woven baskets.
Heated stones were thrown into them; it would
        boil.
People would boil salmon in these;
        meat was also boiled in them, it's said.
This one woman cooked some; she boiled some   100
        seal meat.
She spooned it in a dish.
The young wife of his, this wife of Kaax'achgóok,
        slid her dish along side of it.
"Couldn't you spoon some broth on this?"

Áhé tlax eeshandéin
du toowú awsinei
yá Káax'achgóok ku.a.
Tle yan at duxáa áwé yéi ayawsikaa du
        shatx'iyán, "Já'
ax kaaniyán xoodéi nay.á.
Yéi s yanaysaká,   110
'Woosáani eetínáx áyá yatee Káax'achgóok
woosáani eetínáx.'"
Neil has áat áwé has du ítx áwé yaa yéi ndusnein
tlax wáa dagaak'éiyi aa woosáanx'i sáwé
du kaaniyán jeedáx át á.
S'ootaat áwé yaax has woo.aat.
Gunéi s uwakúx.
A xoot áwé s wookoox.
Tlax du waakgáa wooteeyi aa áwé aawaták.
At s'aan.aaxw dzaas á, a káa yéi yatee.   120
Tlél áyú yíndei aan wultsees wé x'óon ku.a.
Héen xukáx áwé yaa nashk'én dákdei yinaadéi.
Yá Ch'al'geiyita.aan
yakáa yéi dagaateeyi x'áat'
deikéenax.áa s kaháa áwé
ch'a yeisú yaa nashk'én has du shukáx.
Ch'a a ítx yaa s nakúxu
k'eeljáa tlein has du kát agoowashát.
Tup!
At wushtóogu yáx áwé woonei.   130
Tle tláakw áwé kúxdei s ayawdli.át yándei.
"Yee gu.aa yáx x'wán, ax keilk'i hás,
yee gu.aa yáx x'wán.
Tlax yíndei naytsóow yee axáayi."
E'! tláakw áwé aduxáa.
Kaa x'anawóos'ch.
"Ch'a yeisú a shukaadéi ge yaa ntookúx?"
"Tléik'!
Tléik'! de tliyéix' áyá yéi haa yatee."
"Tláakw!   140
Tláakw ayxáa!"
Wáa nanée sáwé yéi yawdudzikaa.
"Ha de kúxdei áyá yaa haa nalhásh." De
        xáanaadéi yaa kunahéin.
Ch'a yeisú ayawditee.
Wáa wdaxweidlí sáyá kik'i.aa

They pushed her dish to the side.
This made
Kaax'achgóok
feel pitiful.
As soon as they finished eating he told his
        wives, "Ja',
go to my brothers-in-law.
Say to them,
'Kaax'achgóok is in need of spears,   110
in need of spears.'"
When his wives came home men were carrying
        behind them
some very nice spears
from his brothers-in-law.
At dawn they went aboard.
They started going.
They came among the fur seals.
He speared the one he thought was nice.
The point that tangles around the animal was   120
        on his spear.
But the fur seal didn't dive down with the spear.
It was jumping on the surface heading for the
        open sea.
When they were on the outside of the islands
off Ch'al'geiyita.aan
when they were outside of them,
it was still jumping on the surface ahead of them.
While they were chasing it,
a strong wind storm overtook them.
Tup!
It was as swift as a gun shot.   130
They quickly turned back towards land.
"Be brave, my nephews
be brave.
Push your paddles way down."
Oh, they paddled fast.
He would ask them,
"Is the boat still moving ahead?"
"No!
No!" "We're not moving now."
"Hurry!   140
Hurry! Paddle!"
In a while they said to him

du kéilk'.
Yaakwdéi aawataan du axáayi.
Jilkáatdáx áyú du.óow noojín yá tsálk.
Tsálgi x'óow
á áwé   150
átx dulyeixín.
Yan sh wudzitáa shanáa wdis'ít.
Ldakát yaakwdéi kawdaxduwayísh kaa axáax'u.
Yándei sh dul.aat.
Kaa ítnáx áwé tsá yaakwdéi aawataan
du axáayi, Kaax'achgóok.
Gunéi s wulis'ís.
Kayikduwa.áxch k'eeljáa tlein.
Teet.
Hél has kool.áxch   160
a t'éiknáx.
Tlax x'oon aa yagiyee shunaxéex sáwé
ch'a yeisú axéx'w.
Tle aadéi sh wududli.ús. "Ch'a gaa déi,
ch'a gaa déi yéi kunganei."
S'ootaat áwé.
Kaax'achgóokch kayik.uwa.áx.
Hé', goodáx aantkeení sáhé?   Tlax yéi daléich.
Ldakát áwé duléich yéi.
Aa sá kwshí yóo gé tlax yéi daléich?   170
Ldaagéinax áwé shanáadáx daak awdiyísh
        du x'óowu.
Yatx awdligén.
Yánt áwé yoo liháshk has du yaagú ku.a.
Analgéin áwé gwál l'awx'áat'i tlein gwáa yóo gé?
        Tlax ligéi yú x'áat' tlein.
A kaanáx áwé kawdi.áa kayaanx'í.
Ch'u tle wdzik'ík' áyú yú át ku.a;   k'ineilx'ú
a káa kaawa.aa.
Yóo kaa yayík ku.a
xach wéi át ásgíwé
x'óon   180
taan
yáxwch'.
Ldakát yá héen táanáx kudaxdziteeyi át áwé
á kát kéen.
Ashawsikéi du keilk'i hás.
"Shaydaké!

"We're drifting backward now." It was toward dusk.
The wind still kept on blowing.
How tired was his younger
nephew.
He pulled his paddle into the boat.
They usually bought those ground squirrels from
        Chilkat.
Ground squirrel robes
were the ones used   150
in those days.
He lay back, wrapping the robe around his head.
All of them pulled their paddles aboard.
They began lying down.
Kaax'achgook was the last one
to pull his paddle aboard.
The wind began to carry them.
They could hear the loud sound of the storm wind.
Waves.
They were deaf   160
to anything else but the wind.
When many days went by
they were still asleep.
They had given up. "Let's just let it happen,
let's just let it happen to us."
It was in the morning.
Kaax'achgóok heard the noises.
My! Where did all the people come from? How they
        yelled!
They were all yelling that way.
Who were they that yelled that way?   170
From around his head he slowly lowered his robe.
He looked up.
Their boat was floating against the beach.
When he looked around he thought,
        "Isn't that a big sand island?"
        It was very large, that big island.
Grass was growing on it.
It was very dense; bamboo
grew on the island.
But the voices though,
weren't they
fur seal   180
sea lion

Shaydaké! Yan áyá haa wlihásh."
Goo sá kwshí yá át kuwlihásh?
Tlél yawduteen.
Daak has at kajéil   190
aagáa áwé daak wuduwatán has du yaagú;
        at gutóox'
daak has aawatán.
"Dlinkwát x'wán yilatín
yee yaagú, ax keilk'i hás.
Dlinkwát x'wán yilatín." kaa shukoojeis'
Kaax'achgóok.
A góot ágé
wé dáadzi
aan shóox adu.ak át?
Wooch yát yóo shaduwateek.   200
K'át
kát adu.aak
wé gán.
Aa wduwaják wé x'óon
shawduwaxích.
At gadus.ée.
Hél koolk'átl'k.
Yan at duxáa áwé yéi kuyawsikaa
"ch'a tlákw yagiyee x'wán a daa yanay.á.
Yee yaagú dlinkwát yilatín.   210
Aaa.
Tlél wáa sáyú uneigík yóo
ka haa at xaayí sákw tsú.
Aa gaxyilaxwáchs'
wé x'óon doogú
ka wé at dookx'ú.
Wé taan doogú ku.aa wés dzaas sákw áwé.
K'wát' yáx áwé kagaxyisahánt
naxlayát'gix'i
wé dzaasx'."   220
A yáx áwé yéi jiduné.
A xoo aa dleey dut'óos'
dusxook; yándei yaa ndusnein.
Tlél áyá héen a ká
yú x'áat'.
Tlé yíndei kanaltleich wé héen ku.a l'éiw
        tóodei.
Yá k'eeljáach aax wudagaal'ix'i aa kineilx'ú

and sea otter?
Many kinds of sea mammals
were sitting on it.
He woke his nephews.
"Wake up!
Wake up! We've drifted ashore."
Where was it they had drifted?
They didn't recognize it.
When they had carried everything up the beach   190
then they brought their canoe up the beach; they
         brought it up
into some bushes.
"Remember to take good care
of your boat, my maternal nephews.
Remember to take good care of it," Kaax'achgóok
instructed.
Were they without
fire rubbing sticks,
the things you start a fire with?
They're rubbed together.   200
They made
a big
fire.
One fur seal was killed,
clubbed on the head.
They cooked.
They were quiet.
When they finished eating he told them
"Remember to check it frequently.
Remember to take care of your boat.
Yes.   210
Don't let anything happen to it
or the things for our food either.
You'll tan some
of the fur seal skins
and other skins.
But make the sea lions into thongs.
You can cut them in a circular motion
so that those thongs
can be long."
They worked like he said.   220
Some of them barbecued meat
and dried it; they were nearly finished.

        agoowx'ú áwé yax shayawlits'ít'
héen, séew héeni.
A áwé duná.
Tlél tsu héen a kát koodéin wé x'áat' ku.a.   230
Tlákw yéi jiduné tlákw yigiyee.
Xáanaadéi áwé
xáanaadéi yaa kukgahéinín áwé
gáanx' áwé ganúkch.
Katushatánin
yándei wdagaawadi aa
yá gáant keen.
"A.án" yóo toosáakw nooch.
Xach yóo a káx' ásgí yú yan kuwoodáaych
yá kutx.ayanahá,   240
K'óoxdísi
ka wé
Lk'ayáak'w
a ya.eetí.
A káa yan kuwoodáaych goox' sá kawuhaayí
ka yú dís anax kéi xixji yé
ka gagaan anax yéi xixji yé.
A káa yan kuwoodáaych.
A káax' áwé át kuyanagwéijin.
A káax' tsú yéi at daaduné.   250
Awé ooltínch xáanaadéi;
Kaax'achgóok áa ganúkch.
Tle k'át kukawushgéedi áwé tsá yan sh ustáaych;
        nateich.
Desgwach tléix' táakw
desgwach a yáanáx.
Tlél wáa sá yoo wookéik
Kaax'achgóok ku.a.
E'! teesh déin kuwdagaanei.
Goosú kaa aaní?
Goonax áwu sá kwshí?   260
Tlél wuduskú.
Tle kaan naasa.áa
a yanaak.áat'ani
kát tani yáx áwé yatee.
Hél wuduskú goonax.á sá.
Kaax'achgóok ku.aa sgíwé de
a daax yaawa.aa.
Ax' áwé kaa jikaawakáa wé k'ineilx'ú,

There was no water
on this island.
But the water would seep into the sand.
Where the wind storm broke the bamboo, the
        stumps were filled
with water, rain water.
That's what they drank.
There wasn't another drop of water on the   230
        island though.
They worked all the time every day.
Toward evening,
toward evening when it was becoming dusk,
Kaax'achgóok would sit outside.
People who were elders
routinely
sat outside.
We used to call it "a.án."
Here they checked
the stars,
Venus   240
and
the Milky
Way.
They would check where they were now,
and where the moon was rising from
and where the sun was rising from.
They would check.
People used this as a map.
They used it also to work by.
That's what he would look at toward evening.   250
Kaax'achgoók would sit there.
When night fell he finally lay back; he'd sleep.
It was already
more than a year.
But Kaax'achgóok
didn't say much.
My, they would get lonely.
Where was their village?
Where was it?
They didn't know.   260
It was like a container
with the lid
lying on top of them.

yaakw yáx kudayat' aa
déix.   270
A shóodei áwé wduwadúx'
wé at yoowú
x'óon yoowú; l'éiw a tóo yéi daxduwa.óo.
Yá taan yoowú ku.a wés wudaxduwa.úx héen daakeit
        sákw aa.
Wé taan x'adaadzaayí tlax dliyat'gix'i aa
kaa x'usyee.ádi sákw
kaa x'usyee.ádi sákw áwé á ku.a.
Daa dus.aaxw tle.
Há'! desgwach kei jiyanayék yá wdudlixwaji at
        dookx'ú tlax wáa dagaak'éiyi aa sá.
Kaa at xaayí tsú de yan kawdudligáa.   280
Xáanaadéi áwé yéi kuyawsikaa Kaax'achgóok
"Eeti.aa yigiyee
s'ootaatx' áwé gunéi gaxtookóox.
Ch'u yaxté atan kadaxwás'i
gunéi gaxtookóox."
Ch'u s'ootáat áwé l at gooháayi shawduwakée
tle yaakw yíkt kawduwajél.
Yú dikee.ádi káax' áwé yan ayawsitán
Kaax'achgóok wé yaakw.
Eeeeei,   290
k'e aduxáa.
Ch'a aadéi aduxaa yéidei áwé at duxá.
Wé wdudzi.iyi dleey ka wdudzixugu aa
at duxá.
Xáanaadéi áwé shawdudziyaa
wé shayéinaa sákw,
k'ineilx'ú.
At yoowx'ú a shóo wdaxduwadúx'
l'éiw a tóo yéi dagaatee wé at yoowx'ú.
A áwé tle héeni kawdaxdudliyaa,   300
yáanax.á
a yat'ák ka yáanax.á, yíndei
naaliyéidei kawdaxdudliyaa.
Ahé tlél gunéi kuwulhaash taatx'
yá axéx'xu.
Tsu s'ootaatx' áwé tsu gunayéi has ukooxch.
Eeeei!
K'e aduxaa nuch.
Hél k'át héen duná.

Nobody knew where they were.
But Kaax'achgóok
had figured it out already.
He told them to get bamboo,
two,
as long as the boat.   270
To the end they tied
the stomachs
fur seal stomachs; they put sand into them.
But the sea lion stomachs they inflated for
          water containers.
And the sea lion whiskers, the very long ones
were for under their feet,
for under their feet,
They began tying them in bundles.
My! They were piled high,
          those tanned skins, the very nice ones.
They gathered all their preserved food too.   280
Toward evening Kaax'achgóok said to them,
"We will be leaving
first thing in the morning.
We'll start out
while the handle of the big dipper is still
          visible."
When it was early morning,
          while they still couldn't see, they woke
and loaded the boat.
Kaax'achgóok steered the boat
by the stars.
Ohhhh   290
did they paddle.
They ate while they paddled.
The meat they had cooked and the ones they dried
they ate.
Toward evening they anchored with the things
they had made for anchors,
bamboos.
They had tied the stomachs to the end,
the stomachs with the sand inside them.
That was what they lowered into the sea,   300
one on one side
and another on the other side; down
deep they lowered them.

Ch'a ḵaa jeewú ḵwá at yoowx'ú tóo yéi daḡaatee   310
wé héen.
X'oon kux̱éi sáwé
yá éil' káx'.
Tléináx̱ aach áwé t'aayaawaḵaa
"Háa! wé kéidladi x̱áa wé! Haa shukát wulihaash.
Yóodu á!
Aadéi yanal.á!
Tle a káa yan yasatán!"
De yeisdé ḵu.aa wé yaa ḵunahéin.
Ha gwál de táakwdei yinaadéi ḵu.a áyú.   320
De shaa yaadéi de aléet yá dleit.
Desgwach héennáx̱ kei yanax̱ásh
wé kéidladi ḵu.a.
X̱ach L'úx shakée ásgí wé.
Dleitx'i sáani áa yéi yatee.
A áwé kéidladi yóo s aawasáa.
Tlél áyú tlax̱ ḵaa tuwáa ushgú wdusaayí
yá shaax̱ sateeyí.
K'idéin a daa ḵuyana.áa áwé
yéi ḵuyawsiḵaa, "Yá a jiḡeidéi x'wán.   330
Yan yasatán wé yaakw.
Góok,
yíndei naytsóow
yee ax̱áayi. "
E'! tláakw áwé adux̱áa.
Tle a kát ḵaa seiwax'áḵw ḵaa at x̱aayí
ḵa wé héen.
Tláakw adux̱áa.
Yá eechx'i t'éinax̱ áa kóox̱
sú áyú áa wsi.aa   340
a géeknáx̱ áwé yaax̱ shukawdudzitee
ḵa a shakaanáx̱.
Tle a yée yan sh wududli.át.
A yíkt ax̱éx'w.
Wé yaakw yíx' áwé wdudlisáa.
Tle ch'u yeedádidéi ách dudlisáakw
Yakwkalaséiḡákw á
áa s wulsaayích yá yaakw yíx'.
Yan has kóox̱ áwé daak at kawduwajél.
Ḵaa yaagú daak wuduwatán; k'idéin   350
sh daaduné.
Yándei yaa sh nadusnein.

They didn't drift away that night
while they slept.
Each morning they would begin paddling again.
Ohhhh!
how long they would paddle.
They didn't drink much water.
But they had some inside animal stomachs,   310
some water.
How many days they had been going
on the ocean.
One man yelled out
"Hey! That's a seagull there; it's drifting in
        front of us.
There it is!
Steer toward it!
Set your bow on it."
It was already nearly fall.
Perhaps it was toward winter.   320
The mountains were already dusted with snow.
The head of the seagull was beginning to cut
through the ocean.
Here it was the tip of Mt. Edgecumbe.
There was a little snow there.
This was what they were calling a seagull.
They really didn't want to call the mountain
by its name.
After they had recognized it,
he said to them,"Steer the boat   330
into the arm."
Go!
Push your paddles
way down."
My! they paddled fast.
They forgot about their food
and water.
They paddled fast.
When they reached behind the reefs
where kelp grew   340
they pulled some on board at the stern
and at the bow.
Then they lay down in the bottom of their canoe.
They slept inside it.
They rested inside the canoe.

Dushóoch.
K'idéin yan sh dusnéi,
Kaax'achgóok _k_u.aa wé té yát áwé uwagút; áx'
        áwé akat'éi_x_'.
Has du yoo kooneigí áwé
a yáa akatéi_x_' wé té.
Ch'a yeisú áa yéi téeyin du ji.eetí.
(A áyá aadéi ga_x_took_ó_ox ch'a goox' sá.)
K'át yan sh dusnéi   360
aa_g_áa áwé tsu yaakw yí_x_ aawa.aat; _g_unéi
        yakw.uwakú_x_.
Da_x_éitt áwé yatán.
Yeisdéi yaa _k_uk_g_ahéiní_n_; Kiks.átx'i has
        nal_g_ás'ch.
_K_unáadei aa nal_g_ás'ch
_G_eey Tleindéi
_k_a Da_x_éitdei,
_k_a yá héená_x_'w sáanidéi; a _x_oo aa
tle aan_x_ áyú da_x_dzitee
yóo áa yéi _k_unateech yé; _k_aa at _x_ayí
a daa yóo akoo.atgi nuch yé.   370
Yóo yées shaawát
du shát
hú _k_u.aa wé dei wduwasháa.
Du kéilk'ích áwé uwasháa.
Tla_x_ a yáaná_x_ de _g_altíshch
wé shaawát.
Ach áwé yées _k_áa du jeet jiwduwatán.
Tla_x_ sh tóodá_x_ _k_uwdzihaa de.
Wé yanwát du shát _k_u.a ch'a yeisú du tóo_x_
        kaawagaa.
Yá du _x_ándá_x_   380
daak uwa_k_u_x_u aa
ch'a yeisú du tóo_x_
kaawagaa.
_G_áan_x_' áyú _g_anúkch _g_agaan yana_x_ yei anaxíxi.
Tla_x_ k'át sh tóodá_x_ akawdajeilí
du tundatáani aa_g_áa áwé tsá neil ugootch.
Ayá tsu yá át aayí áwé
ch'a aadéi
héen du yadaaná_x_ kaawadaayi yé
ch'a aan áwé át ool_g_einch   390
Yoo Luklihashgi X'aa lutú.

Today it's still called
"canoe rest"
because they rested there in this canoe.
When they got ashore they unloaded their boat.
They brought up their canoe; they cleaned   350
themselves up.
They were dressing up.
They bathed.
When they finished dressing up,
Kaax'achgóok went up to the face of a rock;
          there he carved.
He carved on the rock
what had happened to them.
It was still there recently, the work of
          his hands.
(This is where we will go sometime.)
When they were completely dressed   360
they went aboard again; they began paddling.
The boat headed toward Daxéit.
It was near fall; the Kiks.ádi would move.
Some would move to Kunáa
to Geey Tlein
and Daxéit
and to the small streams; some of the places
were villages
where people camped; they would put up
their food.   370
The young woman,
his wife,
had a husband.
His nephew was her husband.
This woman
was missing Kaax'achgóok so very much.
This is why she was placed with a young man.
She had already recovered.
However, he was still lingering on the mind
          of that older wife of his.
The one who sailed   380
away from her
was still lingering
on her mind.
She would sit outside when the sun was setting.
When she had cried until no tears

Anax daak uwakúx wé yaakw.
Yándei yaa kgakúxún yéeyi áyú ax tlaakáak
ax léelk'w Kaax'achgóok,
daax'oondahéen áyú héendei anatsákch
du axáayi; s'át'nax.aanáx
a xukáa awooyíshch.
A káx' áwé yan woos.áaych du axáayi.
A áwé du shátch
tle yaawatín.   400
Tlax k'idéin yan akooltéen aagáa áwé tsá
        wdihaan.
Neil uwagút.
"Ha! Tlagukwáanx'i xáa yú haadéi yaa nakúx."
Ldakát du daa.itnagóowu
áyá de du shantú.
Aa yax kawdayáax áyú duwajée
hú ku.a.
Ach áwé ch'a sh k'akalgedéin daayaduká.
Wáa nanéi sáwé áa yux aawagoot.
"Ha ch'a a yáx áwé   410
yaakw haadé yaa nakúx."
Yées káax'w áwé át kaawa.át taashukaadéi;
        yan áyú uwaláa.
Tlax taashuká yayát' Daxéit.
Áyá áx aa yaawanák
tle yú ixkéedei.
Shayadihéini aa áwé aadéi woo.aat.
K'idéin yan kadusnóok aagáa áwé tsá
        kei t'aawduwa.íx' yú ixkéede.
"Kaax'achgóo-oo-ook
koowagáa-aa-aak."
Tle haadéi yaa nas.áx.   420
Tle yá aant is.áax áwé át kawduwa.át;
        x'óol' yáx at woonei.
Wé yanwáat du shát ku.aa wé tle tláakw áwé
        at sa.ée.
Tlax yáa
daakw aa at xá sá du tuwáa sagóo noojín
á áwé as.ée
du xúx x'eis.
Wé yées aa du shát ku.a áwé
kadéix' áwé; du yáx' yéi woonei
wé du xúx tsú.

were left, she'd go inside.
It was while she was sitting there again
as her tears
flowed down her face
that she kept looking   390
at the tip of Yoo Luklihashgi X'aa.
The canoe came out of there.
When my mother's maternal uncle came toward shore,
my grandfather Kaax'achgóok,
he would put his paddle in the ocean
four times; then he would pull it across the stern
with his left hand.
He would rest his elbows over his paddle.
This is what his wife
recognized.   400
When she was sure of what she saw she stood up.
She went inside.
"Well! The one long dead is coming."
All his mannerisms
were still on her mind.
But they thought
her mind had snapped.
That was why they kidded her.
After a while someone went out there.
"Hey, it's true,   410
a canoe is coming."
Young men ran down the tide flats; it was low tide.
The tide flat extended way out at Daxéit.
This was where the men stood
all the way down the river.
There were many who went there.
When they were sure, they yelled out the news
       from down the river.
"Kaax'achgóoooooooooook
has returrrrrrned!"
They could hear the news coming up.   420
When the news reached the village people started
       to run down; they became like a whirlpool.
But his older wife quickly began to cook.
Whichever foods
he really used to like
was what she cooked
for her husband to eat.

Yindasháan áwé s kéen.   430
Wáa sá kwshí yándei s kaguxdayáa?
Wáa sáyú tlax yéi sh yáa wdiwútl gadusháat?
Haa, kei ginnadutéen wé yaakw.
Ch'a a yíkt has kéen.
Kaa eegayáakt
gindutée áwé aagáa wé tsá
yei s uwa.át; a yíkdáx daak at kandujél;
        yú x'at'aakx' áwé kei jiyawduwayék
        wé at doogú,
wududlixwaji
ka wé
taan x'adaadzaayí.   440
K'idéin yan at duxáa
yan sh kalnéek
has du yoo kooneigí, yan aklanéek
áa kaa jikaawakaa,
"Yóo x'wán
kaa jixoox yala.át wé...
kaa jixoox yéi yaa gaysané
wé taan x'adaadzaayí.
Wé at doogú."
At áwé x'eiwatán du kéilk'.   450
"Gunalchéesh á
ax kéilk', gunalchéesh
yá i tlaakáak
du yáx yeeyashée.
Gunalchéesh.
Ha, wooch yeeydzixán áyá.
Ch'a yéi déi yan kuxdayaayí.
Ch'a yéi déi ngatee.
Wa.é tsú!
Wa.é tsú!   460
K'idéin x'wán dlinkwát latín
wé ax kéilk'
k'idéin. "
Ldakát kaa jixoox ayakaawajél wé at dookx'ú.
E'! toowú sagú yéi daaduné.
Xaju tóox' ásgí yú de yan awsinéi.
Sh tóox' yan awdzinéi de
yá du tundatáani
ka yá aadé yan kawdiyayi yé.
Áyá kei akaawashée   470

But the young wife of his
was shame-faced; it was on the face
of her husband too.
They sat with their heads down.   430
They wondered, what was going to happen to them?
Why was she so in a hurry to be married?
Now they were pulling up the canoe.
They just sat in the canoe.
When it was brought
up to the village that's when they finally
got off the boat; they brought the things from
          inside the boat; they were piled up by
          the door, those skins
that were tanned
and the
sea lion whiskers.   440
When they had finished eating
when he finished telling the story
when he had finished telling
          of the things that had happened to them,
he told the people,
"Will you
distribute these to the people this way?
Hand the sea lion whiskers
out to the people.
The skins."
He spoke with his sister's son.   450
"Thank you, indeed,
my nephew, thank you,
you wiped the face
of your mother's maternal uncle.
Thank you.
Surely, you care for each other.
Let's just let it be.
Let things remain just the way they are.
You too!
You too!   460
Will you take good care
of my sister's son,
good care."
He handed skins out to all the people.
My! It made people happy.
Hadn't he already made up his mind?

yá du x'asheeyí.
Áhé yáadu á
ax tlaakáak
Kaax'achgóok,
aadéi x'ayakáayi yé á
aadéi x'ayakáayi yé!
Ch'a á ku.aa yás
tlél gaxyi.aax.
Has du kunóogu de yan shuwjixín.
Ách áyá   480
tlél gaxyi.aax.

He had already made up his mind
about his thoughts
and what had happened to him.
He started singing   470
his song.
This is the one here
my mother's maternal uncle
K̲aax̲'achgóok,
the way he said it, indeed,
the way he said it!
But this is the only thing
you won't hear.
What they did is now ended.
This is why   480
you won't hear it.

Naatsilanéi
Kéet Yaanaayi x'éidáx sh kalneek

A dlaak' áwé aawasháa wé k'isáani.

Naatsilanéi
yóo gíwé duwasáakw.

Awé aan sh kalnik nuch wé du kaani yán,
aadéi ashigóogu yé yú sixaagu jáajee.

Awé a yeet has awuwawóok
yóo taan eejí
a kaanáx yei wugoodí.

Ach áwé yan has uwanéi.
"Ha k'e daak xat yayxá!" yóo gíwé x'awooká
        wé káa.   10

Dei du jeewú a
wé sixaagu jáajee.

Ax' áwé daak yawduwaxáa aadéi.

Daak yawduwaxáa.

A daat kóox áwé,
há'! taan

Naatsilanéi
told by Willie Marks

He was married to the sister of those young men.

Naatsilanéi
was what they say his name was.

He would tell stories to his brothers-in-law
about how well he could use those crampon snowshoes.

They didn't think
he could get on
the sea lion rock.

That was why they prepared.
"Well! Let's let you all take me out!"   10
        is maybe what that man said.

He already had
those crampon snowshoes.

They took him out there by boat.

They took him by boat.

When the boat got there--
wow! there were a lot of sea lions

yóo x'áat' ká.

Kei jilashátch
wé teet.
Du tóogaa nanéi áwé yándei   20
é! kei wjik'én.

Ch'u shóogu áx wulixáat'i yé áwé.

Héendei guxshax'éel' yóo áwé duwajée.

Ch'a yéi gíyú s asayahéi; héent wusgeedí
      tlél tsu yéi s aguxsaneix.
Ayá s ash yaawadlaak áyú.
Dikeenaa a shantóodei wjixeex.
A shakéedei yóo gwáa wéi gé.
A xoot wujixíx wé taan.
About four, five atáak áwé

"Ax shóot yikúx déi"   30
yóo yaawakaa.

Ch'a yéi yawukaayí áwé yaakwdéi yéi wdudzinei
      wé axáa.
Wáa sá kwshé wduwanúk?   Southeast gíwé wduwanúk.

Tle yaa nals'ís.

Ch'a altín áwé.
Awé tlax wé s du kéek',
kik'i.aa has du kéek' áwé, du káani.
Hú áwé kadagax tin ash shóodei axáa aawataan.
Axáa gíwé
a shóodei wé du káani.   40
Awé du jeedáx yóot wuduwas'él'.

Tle yéi áwé gunéi wlis'ís tsu yándei.
Tlax naaliyéix' yawuls'eesí áwé tsá kindachóon
      aawakei.
Tle gunayéi uwakúx yándei.
Hú kwá a shakéet aa.

Yaa kagashgéet gíwé shanáa wdis'ít

on the island!

The waves
reached high.
When he thought the time was right--
my! he leaped to the shore.   20

He stuck to the spot there.

They thought he would slip into the sea.

Maybe that's what they wanted; if he fell into
        the sea they wouldn't help him.
But then he outsmarted them.
He ran up to the top.
To the top, I guess.
He ran through the sea lions.
When he had speared about four or five of them

he said,   30
"Bring the boat over now!"

Just as he said that they pulled in their oars.
Which way was the wind blowing? Maybe it was
        blowing southeast.

The wind was taking them.

He could only watch them.
It was their very youngest brother,
the youngest of the brothers, his brother-in-law.
It was he, who while he was crying, grabbed an
        oar to get him.
Maybe he was rowing
to his brother-in-law.   40
But they tore it from his hands.

That was how they started to blow toward shore again.
When they were blown far enough out that's when
        they sat up.
Then they began to row to shore.
But he sat at the top of the island.

wé taan eejí káx'.

Tle héent wulitít yóo gíwé s akanéek.
Wé yánx' ku.aa
tlél has awusneix.   50

Yaa kanashgídi áwé aawa.axi át áwé
        du daxakaadéi wé teet jinastaan tóodei.
"I eegáa áyá yaa nxagút."
Sh yaax daak shuwdi.áx.
S'igeidi x'óow áwé yéi aya.óo.
Tlél daa sá á.
Nobody there.

Daax'oon.aa, nas'gi.aa,
yá daax'oon.aa.
Yá nas'gi.aa l daa sá ooxsatéen áwé
        daax'oon.aa a yís yan uwanéi.
Yá a woolí a wak.eetéenáx áwé altín.   60
"What's going on?" yóo gíwé tuwatee.
Du wakkáax' áwé anax wudihaan, wé teet x'atú wé
        káa tlein.
L ash éet x'eitaanjí áwé yéi ash yawsikaa
        "Goodéi sáwé?"
"Yá eech tayeedéi áwé."

"How I gonna get there?"
yóo yaawakaa.
Tle yá héen áwé yatx ashoowa.áx.
"A tayeedéi nagú!" yóo ash yawsikaa.
Tlél tóo awunoogú áwé tle.
Gwá'!   70
Aan,
hít.
Aa yaa woogoot wé diyée.
Tle neildéi yaa nagúdi áwé awsiteen wé át satáan
        wé káa.
Kát du eedéi sixát
wé harpoon x'eidí áwé.
Wudutaagéen áwé.
Hásch kwá tlél has ooteen,
yóo taan kwáanich yóo lingít jineiyí.

When it began to get dark maybe he wrapped himself
        up, pulling his blanket over his head
on that sea lion rock.

Maybe they were saying he was swept into the sea
        by the waves.
On the mainland though
they couldn't rescue him.   50

It was getting dark when he heard that thing in the
        roar of the waves while he was trying to sleep.
"I'm coming to get you!"
He pushed the wrap from his face.
It was a beaver robe he wore.
There was nothing there.
Nobody there.

The fourth time, the third time,
the fourth time.
The third time when he didn't see anything
        he prepared for the fourth one.
He watched through the hole where the   60
        eyehole was.
Maybe his thoughts were "What's going on?"
It stood up right before his eyes,
        at the lip-edge of the waves, this huge man.
Before it could speak Naatsilanéi asked it, "Where to?"
"Under this rock."

"How am I going to get there?"
he said.
It lifted the edge of the sea like a cloth.
"Go under this," it said to him.
He didn't even feel the sea.
Oh!   70
It's a village,
a house.
He went there, down there.
As he was entering the house, he saw that man
        lying there.
A harpoon point was stuck in him.
It was a harpoon point.
He had been harpooned.

"Wáa sá iga<u>x</u>duhéi?"   80
yóo daayadu<u>k</u>á.   "How much you want?"
Ch'a du toowú áwé yéi woonei.
"A tuwáat<u>x</u> a<u>x</u> aaní woon<u>k</u>aadlaa<u>g</u>i át gwáa?"
"You get it!"
yóo yawdudzikaa.
"Ach iwdudzihéi."
Tle wdudzikóo du toowú hú
waa sá teeyí.
Tle wé gwál ch'a act gíwé yéi adaané.
A <u>x</u>ánt uwagút wé <u>g</u>antas'aatí.   90
A daa yoo koolnúkgu áwé,
aa<u>x</u> yóot awsi<u>x</u>út'
wé s'aa<u>k</u> kát.
Ach áwé yéi at <u>g</u>adudlikóo
"Oodá<u>x</u> kát kawdziteeyi yá<u>x</u> woonei."
Ch'a náaná<u>x</u> shawdinúk.

Ach áwé du jeet kawduwatée wé át,

wé balloon tlein,

speed boat balloon, tlél <u>x</u>wasakú wáa sá <u>k</u>wasaayí.

Gwál de a shakéex' áwé du een kéi aawa.át tsu
        wé eech.   100
"Yáat'át tóo<u>x</u> áwé yei k<u>g</u>eegóot.
Tlél tsu yáat daa yóo tik<u>g</u>eetaan. Ch'u tle yú
        i aaní<u>x</u>' x'wán yan tután.
Okay," yóo yawdudzikaa.
A tóodei woogoot tle.
Gwál du een áwé <u>x</u>'awdudzi.á<u>x</u>w.

Yet,
gee,
saam,
sée,
yóo áwé kei kawduwagí<u>x</u>'.   110
Daax'oondahéen wuduwatúw.
Tle haat agoowashát wé yándei át.
Du een áwé yaa kanals'ís.
Ch'áakw yaa kanals'ísi áwé yéi tuwdisháat, "Tláw'!
Tsu ch'oo shóogu á<u>x</u>' tsú s'é <u>x</u>aan <u>kux</u> aya<u>g</u>adatee?"

But they, the sea lion people,
couldn't see what the human had made.

"How will we pay you?"   80
they asked him. "How much do you want?"
He had only to think,
"Something I could reach my village with."
"You've got it!"
they said to him.
"You will be paid with it."
They could read his mind,
whatever he thought.
Then he probably just put on an act.
He went by the sick man.   90
While he was feeling around him
he pulled the bone spear head
out of him.
That's where the proverb comes from
"he was like the man who had a spear removed."
He sat up without feeling pain.

That's why they gave that thing to him,

that big balloon,

a motorized rubber raft, I don't know what to
         call it.

They probably took him to the surface again,   100
         to the reef.
"Get into this thing.
Don't think of this place again; think only
         of your village.
Okay," they said to him.
Then he went inside of it.
They probably tied it shut with him.

One,
two,
three,
four,
they tossed it up in the air.   110
They moved over the waves the fourth time.

Tóo aawanuk yan yóo latítgi.
Gwál zipper áwé a x'atóowu á.
Héidei shuwduwataan.
"We told you not to think like that," yóo.
"Yáa yeedát ku.aa ch'u tle áx' yan tután.
         Tlél tsu kux teedatánjeek. Right
         place to your home."   120
Tsu kawduwa.aakw tsu.
Gunéi kawlis'ís du een.
Daak latítji áwé gwál
waa sá kwshé a tóodáx kei uwagút.
Gwál wé automatic button gíwé áwu?
Gwá', du aaní t'éiknax.á áyú.
Ayaawatín tle.
He's got a hard feeling
what they do to him.
Ach áwé tle woogoot.   130
Gwál yaa kanashgít áwé de.
Wé du shát niyaadéi,
yá du aaní niyaadéi
yaa anal'ún gíwé?

Yáa yeedádi yáx ágé? Tlél woosh daadéi oogaax.
Wé x'aak'w luká wé té shakée áwé át áa du shát.
Ax' áwé gáax.

A xánt uwagút. "Hey, honey!"
"Oh yeh," yóo áwé yaawakaa.
Aan áwé akawlineek what happened to him.   140
Tle yéi gíyá du éek' hás niyaadéi áa yax wujixín.
A géidei áa yáx wujixín du toowú wé shaawát.
Ach áhé tlé du xúxt wudishée.
"Ax xút'ayi ax jeedéi yéi kgisanéi."
Gwál atxá tsú.
"Be sure lotsa rice."
Yéi áwé ash jeet yéi awsinéi taat gíwé.
Anax yaa has kuxji yé ku.aa gíwé awsikóo,
yá hunting, wé du kaani yán.
Axóot' wé át.   150
Gwál wé taanch áwé áa shukaawajáa aadéi
         kgwasgit yé.
Ach áwé tle yéi adaané wé át.
Wé kéet áwé axóot'.

Then the wind gusted, that southeast wind.
The bubble was blown with him.
After the wind had been blowing for a while he
        thought, "Oops,
what if it blows back there with me again?"
He felt the waves pounding him on the shore.
It probably had a zipper for an opening.
They opened it.
"We told you not to think like that!" they said.
"So now think only of that place! Don't let   120
        your thoughts return! Go right straight
        to your home!"
He tried it again.
The wind began to carry him.
When the waves were pounding it on the beach,
I wonder how he got out.
There was probably an automatic button.
Well, it was on the other side of his village.
He recognized it.
He had bad feelings
about what they had done to him.
That's why he went up right away.   130
It was probably getting dark already.
Maybe he was sneaking
toward this wife of his,
toward this village of his.

Was it like now? People don't cry for each
        other any more.
On that little point, sitting on top of the
        rock was his wife.
She was crying over there.

He went up to her. "Hey, honey!"
"Oh, yeah," she answered.
He told her what had happened to him.   140·
Maybe this is how she turned against her brothers.
The thoughts of that woman turned against them.
That was why she helped her husband.
"Get me my adze."
Probably some food, too.
"Be sure there's lots of rice."
That's how she brought them to him, perhaps

Killer Whale.

I don't know what kinda wood.
Koogéiyi l'oowú áwé yéi adaané.
Yéi awsinei
just the easiest way.
They're ready to go.
Héen táax' yéi aya.óo.   160

Gwál yá taat yeen; yax̱ taat ayawdataayí
        ldakát át
tlél ushk'é.
Midnight.
Aag̱áa áwé akaawanáa g̱íwé,
yet, gee, saam, sée.
Tle héent loowagúk̲ tle wé át.
Tléik'! Diginaanáx̱ áwé kei awsigúk̲.
There's no ghost in there.
A tóotx̱ woohaa tle,
the wood.   170
Ach áwé tsu g̱óot át; ldakát át akoo.aak̲w.
Cha ch'a yá x̱áay áwé tsá
awliyéx̱ hóoch'een yís.
A héent akoonáa áwé tsá
yú héen táax̱ has kawduwax'aak.
Deikéenáx̱ has gadanáak̲ áwé ldakát át has
        du x̱'éiwu.
Ayaawadlaak̲
tsaa,
halibut.
"Ha, haandéi déi!" yóo ayawsikaa.   180
"Yáanáx̱ haadéi kg̱wak̲óox̲ wé yaakw.
Ax' áwé yee jikak̲k̲wakáa."
Gwál yóo áwé adaayaká.
"The youngest one k̲u.aa áwé
you put him safe.
Yaakw wáal'i kaadéi áwé gax̱yilanáash."

All right, s'ootaatx̱ áwé yaa gak̲úx̲ch.

Anax̱ haadéi yaa nak̲úx̲ wé yaakw.
Haahá,
yan awsinéi de.   190

                    during the night.
Maybe he knew where they usually passed
when those brothers-in-law of his hunted.
He adzed out those things.   150
Those sealions had probably instructed him
          on what he should do.
That's why he immediately worked on those things.
They were Killer Whales he adzed.
Killer Whales.

I don't know what kind of wood.
He made them from any old wood.
He made them
just the easiest way.
They were ready to go.
He had them in the water.   160

Probably at midnight; when the night turns over
          all things
are evil.
Midnight.
Maybe that's when he told them to go,
one, two, three, four.
Those creatures immediately ran into the sea.
No! They floated up out there.
There was no spirit in them.
There was no trace of it inside
the wood anymore.   170
That was why he tried a different kind; he tried
          all kinds of things.
Only when he finally carved yellow cedar
he carved for the last time.
When he finally told them to go into the sea
they glided through the sea.
When they stood up out in the water they had
          many things in their jaws.
He got
seal,
halibut.
"Well, come over now!" he said to them.   180
"The boat will pass through here.
I will tell you when to go for them."
That's what he probably said to them.

Gwál aan yóo x'ali.átk tláakw wé fish
wé awliye̲xi.
Du tóog̲aa nak̲óo̲x áwé akaawanáa.
Shhhhhhhhhh.
Awé a daaná̲x wudinaak̲.
Has akaawax̲'ál wé yaakw.
Wé awliye̲xi át áwé yéi k̲uwanóok.
Wé smallest k̲u.aa áwé, a̲x̲áa ash shóodei
    awusháadeen,
hú k̲u.aa áwé yá yaakw wáal'i kát wudzigít.
Agíwé yan awsik̲ú̲x,   200
wé át k'átsk'ooch.
Ach áwé sh kawdlineek, hú k̲u.aa,
yá át k'átsk'u.
Gwál aan akawlineek tsú.
Gwál ash x̲ánná̲x shákdéi; yan uwak̲ú̲x
yá du káank'i.
Awé woogoot neildéi.
Aag̲áa áwé
aan yóo x̲'awli.át tsu wé awliye̲xi fish,
wé du jiyís yaakw akaawax̲'éili.   210
"Next time
tlél tsu yéi gax̲yeesgeet,"
yóo yan ayawsikáa.
"Daa sá gax̲yix̲áa á áyá gax̲yi.een."
Ach áwé lingít tlél wáa sá adaa.uné wé át,
yéi kwdligeyi yéix'.
Aag̲áa áyá hú k̲u.aa yana̲x daak̲ uwagút tle
ch'a áa ng̲waanaawu yéidei gíwé.

"But you put the youngest one
in a safe place.
Throw him on a broken piece of the boat."

All right, they would paddle early in the morning.

The boat was passing through there.
Okay,
he had them ready then.   190
He probably talked all the time to the fish
he had made.
When they were right for him he told them to go.
Shhhhhhhhhhh.
They stood up around the boat.
They crunched the boat between their jaws.
Those things he carved were doing this.
But the smallest one the one who had picked up
        the paddle toward him,
fell on a piece of the boat.
Maybe that was what the young boy   200
paddled to shore.
That's why he, that young boy,
was able to tell about it.
Probably Naatsilanéi told him too.
Probably he came to him, I guess; that little
        brother-in-law of his
reached shore.
He went home.
That's when
Naatsilanéi talked again to those fish he had carved
that had crunched the boat in their jaws.   210
"Next time
you will not do this again,"
is what he told them to remember.
"Whatever you'll eat is what you will kill."
That's why those things don't do any harm to humans,
however large they are.
That's when Naatsilanéi went into the forest,
maybe to wherever he would die.

Naatsilanéi
Tseexwáa x'éidáx sh kalneek

Yá sh kalneek:

yéi duwasáakw yá káa, Naatsilanéi.
Du kaani yán teen áwé daak uwakúx
Taan t'iká.
Ch'a anax Lawáak deikéenax áwu á
has du aaní.
Aadáx áwé daak has uwakúx aadéi.
A áwé
a shóotx yan has uwakúx,
has du káani.   10
Wáa sá kwshé yú aan yéi s jeewanei?
A shayinkáx' áwé yéi yatee;
        ch'as yóo deikéex yaa nakúxu áwé,
"haandéi ax shóode, ax kaani yán!"
yóo áyú x'ayaká.
Kudzitee yú káa du x'éitx áyá kadunéek.
Ách áwé wtusikóo.
Yá uháan haa léelk'u hás áwé.
Yéi áyú s tuwasáakw Tsaagweidíx aa sitee.
Naatsilanéi yóo duwasáakw wé káa ku.aa,
wé tléix' aa.   20
Kúnax tlél aadéi naxwdzigeedi yé koostí.
"Wáa sáyá xat gugatée?"

Naatsilanéi
told by J. B. Fawcett

The story:

the name of this man was Naatsilanéi.
He went out by boat with his brothers-in-law
outside of Taan.
Their village
was just outside of Klawock.
It was from there they went out by boat
        to that place.
And then
they came back
without their brother-in-law.
What had they done with him?   10
He was at the middle of the island.
        When they were already way out on the boat
he said
"Come here and get me, my brothers-in-law."
There was a man from whose lips this is told.
This is how we know it.
They are our ancestors.
This is what we call those who are Tsaagweidí.
That man's name was Naatsilanéi,
the other one.   20
He really didn't know what to do.
"What is going to become of me?"
These thoughts were on his mind.

Yá tí áwé du tóowoo á.
Hel awuskú
x'oon sá wux̱eeyí áx'.
Du éet x̱'awduwatán.
Ḵashde naaléi ásíwé gé aag̱áa a káa
        yéi yateeyi yé wé x'áat'.
"Wáa sáyá eewanei?"
A yát awdlig̱én.
Yées ḵáa áwé,
yées ḵáa.
"Ha ax̱ shóotx̱ áwé yan has uwaḵúx̱."
"Ha has tulatín x̱á.
Wé diginaawú á
anax̱ yan has uwaḵux̱u yé.
Ch'a tliyéi g̱anú x'wán,
tliyéi g̱anú."
Tlél yeiwuyáat'i áwé.
Tsu uwax̱ée ásgé.
Aag̱áa áwé,
ash x̱ánt uwagút.
"Haagú!
Haagú!
Yá át tóodei nagú!
Yá át tóodei nagú!"

Daax'oondahéen yóo a kaanáx̱ ayakaawatée
        yú teet kaanáx̱.
Wé ḵáach ḵu.a,

daax'oon aa,

yáax' áwé tsá a tóodei ash kawanáa.
At yoowú áwé.
Aatlein áyú.
Tlél awuskú.
"Tlél ḵux̱ teedatánjik haandéi x'wán.
Tle yóo yan tután.
Awu á l'éiw."
Ch'a a kat'óodi kaháa áwé áa ḵux̱ tuwdishát.
"A tóonáx̱ daak gú.
Awé, i een kax̱anéek.
Náa, yáat'át i jeex'.
Tlél haandéi ḵux̱ teedatánjik x'wán.

30
40
50
60

He didn't know
how many nights he spent there.
Someone talked to him.
He had probably been there a long time
          on that island.
"What happened to you?"
That was the voice he looked at.
It was a young man,   30
a young man.
"They left without me, you know," Naatsilanei said.
"Well, we watched them, you see," the young man
          said.
"It's right out there
where they came ashore.
Just sit still please,
sit still."
Time went fast.
He stayed another night.
That's when   40
he came to Naatsilanéi.
"Come here!
come here!
Get inside this thing!
Get inside this thing!"

He moved it over the waves four times.
Finally,

on the fourth time,

the man told him to get inside.
It was a stomach.
A large one.   50
He didn't know.
"Please don't think back to here.
Only think about the mainland.
There is a sandy beach."
When he was only half way his thought returned.
"Come out of there.
That's what I told you.
Here, hold this.
Please don't think about here.   60
Hold this."

I jeex' yáat'aa."
A jeet aawatée wéit'át.
Tléil aadóoch sá wuskú.
Wududzikóo ku.aa
daat daax sá sateeyí.
"A tóonáx áyá xáax x'akgeetáan,
a tóonáx."
Tlél yeiwuyáat'i áwé.
Wáa sáyá yan kawlihásh; tóo ayanook.
Aa ash shukaawajáa aadé aguxsanei yé.   70
Neilnáx áwé alshát,
neilnáx.
Aagáa áwé a tóodáx tóot awliyísh.
A tóonáx áwé át x'eiwatán wé ash jeet aawatiyi át.
"De yáadu xát,"
yóo áyú ayawsikaa.
"Ha iduwatéen.
Gu.aax x'wán!
Yéi aa kgisatéen.
Daa sá i tuwaagáa yatee   80
gageeséix."
Wé át tóonáx
yóo áwé yoo x'ayatánk.
Tlél yeiwuyáat'i áwé

du xándei yaa yanagwéin wé yaakw.
Du xándei yaa yanagwéin.
"Daat ku.oo sáyú?"
Hél awuskú.
Lingít áyú
ch'a aan kwá tlél awuskú.   90
Ch'a k'át kadu.aakw.
"Wáa sáyá eewanei?"
"Ha wéidáx áyá yan xat yawduwaxáa."
Hél áyú akooneek aan.
"Wéitx áwé yan xat yawduwaxáa."
Tlél has awuskú.
Du shát kudzitee,
du shát.
Ch'áakw aadéi at téeyi yé;
        dáxnáx áwé yatee du shát.
Hél has awuskú.   100
"Wáa sáyá?"

He gave Naatsilanéi that thing.
No one knew.
But it was known
what it was for.
"Through this you will talk to me,
through this."
It wasn't long when he noticed.
Hey--it had floated to shore; he could feel it.
The man instructed him what he would do with it.   70
He held it from the inside,
from the inside.
Then he pulled it out.
Through this thing he was given he spoke to the man.
"I'm already here!"
he said to him.
"Well, we can see you.
Have courage!
You will see more.
Whatever you desire
just name it."   80
He talked
through this thing.
It wasn't long when

these boats were coming toward him.
They were coming toward him.
"What kind of people were they?"
He didn't know.
They were human
but he didn't know them.
But they tried to talk.   90
"What happened to you?"
"Well, I was brought in from out there."
He wasn't telling what had happened.
"I was brought in from out there."
They didn't know what had happened.
His wives were there,
his wives.
This is the way things were long ago;
        he had two wives.
They didn't know.
"Why was it?"   100
they would ask about him; they would weep.

has anawóos'ch; has g̱axsatée nooch.
"Tlél wutusakú.
Du een áwé daak jiwsitán wé x'áat' kaadáx̱.
Hél du káx̱ kuwtooshee."
Yóo áwé s akanéek wé s du káani.
Hél yeiwuyáat'i áyá,
ash x̱ánt uwagút wé ḵáa.
"Haagú.
Iyatéen gé héit'át?"   110
Daa sákwshí yú gí, yóo?
"I atx̱aayí áhé.
I atx̱aayí áhé.
Héidu á."
Du eeg̱áa áyú woosoo.
Du eeg̱áa woosoo.
Wé át kawdliyeeji át.
Ldakát ḵáach áwé wsikóo.
Ḵín yóo duwasáagu át.
Lingít áwé.   120
Lingít.

Aag̱áa áwé,
"Wéidu i atx̱aayí"
áa shukdujeis'.
"Héidu i hídi.
Aadéi kg̱eegóot.
Tléil a x̱'awoolnáx̱ áx̱ eegoodík x'wán.
Tliyaanax̱ áwu i shát.
Wé tléix' aa,
aadéi shugax̱dugóot."   130
Yóo áwé ash daayaká.
Wáa nanéi sáwé át ḵoowaháa,
ḵúx̱dei
yóo wdaneiyí wé taat.
Taat yeen
ḵeix'éidei ḵuwuhaayí áwé,
"Haakw déi,"
yóo ash yawsiḵaa.
Tlax̱ tlél áwé unalé
du x̱'usyeex'.   140
"Yáadu á,
Yáadu á.
Iyatéen ágé wéit'át?

"We don't know.
A wave carried him out from the island.
We couldn't find him."
This is how they told about their brother-in-law.
It wasn't long
when that man came to him.
"Come here.
Do you see that?"   110
I wonder what it was.
"That's your food.
That's your food.
It's over here."
It was his help.
It was help.
Those beings that fly.
Many people know them.
The things called Brant.
It was human.   120
Human.

That's when
Brant pointed them out to him.
"That's your food.
Your house is over here.
You will go to it.
Don't enter through the door.
Your wife will be on the other side.
One of them
will be brought there."   130
That's what he said to him.
At one point it was time
when the night
comes to a halt.
When half of the night
was becoming dawn
Brant said to him,
"Come now."
It didn't seem far
for him to walk.   140
"Here it is,
here it is.
Do you see that thing?
Pick it up!

Aax̱ gasataan!
Anax̱ keix̱ latsaaḵ!
Awu i shát!"
Hél yeiwuyáat'i áwé.
A jeex' át uwashée.
"X̱át áyá,   150
x̱át áyá."
"Wa.é k.wé? X̱át áyá".
"Wáa sá eewanei?"
"Haa ax̱ shóotx̱ áyá yan has uwaḵúx̱ x̱á."
Du jishagóoni
ch'u ch'áagutx̱ áwé ḵudzitee,
aan at dulyex̱ át,
du x̱út'ayi,
ḵa wé aan at layex̱ át.
Dáaknáx̱ áwé ash jeet yéi awsinéi
a gúkshináx̱,   160
yóot'át aadé ash shukaawajayi yáx̱
dáaknáx̱
wé du aaní áa yéi yateeyi yé.
Du atx̱aayí yagéi
du eeg̱áa woosoowu át.
Atx̱ áwé áa yéi yatee.
Ax̱' áwé.
"K'e aadéi anax̱dulg̱einí."
Tléil has awuskú yá áa yéi yateeyi yé.
Aaa.   170
At natí,
al'óoni áwé,
yaa s naḵux̱.
"I een kakkwanéek."
Wé át áwé ash éet x̱'eiwatán
        we du eeg̱áa woosoowu át.
"I een kakkwanéek.
Yáadei,
yáadei s gug̱akóox̱.
Keijínináx̱ a yée s gug̱atée,
hás."   180
Yóo áwé ash daayaká
"Keijínináx̱."
Wé kéet
áx̱' áwé awliyéx̱.
Ch'a ldakát át áwé alyéix̱.

Stick it up through there!
Your wife is there!"
It wasn't but a moment.
He took it from Brant.
"It's me,
it's me," Naatsilanéi said.   150
"Is that you? It's me," she said.
"What happened to you?"
"Well, they went home without me."
His tools
have been in existence for a long time,
the things people make things with,
his adze,
and the things he makes things with.
She gave them to him through the forest side
through the corner,   160
the way the helper instructed him
through the forest side
in that place where he lived.
His food was plentiful
from his helper.
From then he lived there.
It was there.
"Let's look over there," the others said.
They didn't know where he was living.
Yes.   170
They were hunting.
Hunters
were going by boat.
"I will tell you."
It was that being that talked to him,
      that being that was helping him.
"I will tell you.
Here,
they will come here.
There will be five of them in there.
Those are the ones."   180
That is what the helper told him.
"Five of them."
It was there he carved
the Killer Whales.
He carved all kinds of materials.
People don't tell it the same way.

Tlél woosh x'ayáx koodulneek.
Loon awliyéx.
Laax tsu awliyéx.
Woosh gunayáade át; daa sá yan
     wulihásh áwé alyéix.
Kéet yáx áwé akaxáshx tle.   190
Aadóoch sáyú kaawach'áak'w?
Wé du eegáa woosoowu át ásíwéi gé?
Awé wé xáay áwé tsá.
Ach áwé ch'u yáa yakyee
kéet
a taayí ganaltáa wduteeyí
tle yóo xáay yáx du.áxji nuch a katáx'jayi.
Sure-x sitee
yáat'aa yá sh kalneek.
Hél ch'a koogéiyi sh kalneek áyá.   200
Haa saax'ú kudzitee.
Has du tóonáx kuwdziteeyi ku.oo shayadihéin.
Ch'u yá yakyeedéi.
Ch'u yá yakyeedéi.
Hásch has akawsitíy
kéet.
Naatsilanéich áyú kawsitíy.
Wáa nanéi sáwé a kaax kuwduwa.áx
"Wéidu á.
Wéidu á."   210
Daa sá aagáa
yoo akuwakéik.
A yayeidí áwé kudzitee; yaakw yayeidí yáx áwé yatee.
Aadéi shukawduwajayi yáx
wé kéet.
A yayeidí
káx áwé akunanáach.
"Yú át áwé ax tuwáa sigoo,"
yóo áwé yanakéich.
Cháatl,   220
daa sá,
tsaa.
Ach áwé tsaa alijáakwch'án kéet
yá yakyeedéi.

Wáa nanéi sáwé át koowaháa.
"Aaa.

He carved bark.
He carved red cedar.
Different kinds of material; whatever
      had drifted ashore is what he carved.
He'd cut them like Killer Whales.   190
Who was the one that carved them?
It was the helper, wasn't it?
It was finally yellow cedar.
That is why even till today
when Killer Whale
fat is put in a flame
the crackling of it is just like yellow cedar.
This one is true,
this story.
This is not a story without value.   200
We have our names.
From them there are many people.
Even till today.
Even till today.
They were the ones who carved
Killer Whales.
It was Naatsilanéi who carved them.
At one point people heard
"There they are.
There they are".   210
For whatever he needed
he would send out the Killer Whales.
There was a cradle for them like cradles for boats.
That's how he instructed
the Killer Whales.
He would tell them
to get on their cradles.
"This is what I want,"
is what he would say.
"Halibut,   220
what else,
seal."
That's why Killer Whale is the killer of seals
till today.

At one point its turn came.
"Yes.

De wéidu á,
wéidu á."
Aagáa áwé át x'eiwatán
wé du jigayéix át,   230
"Yee gu.aa yáx x'wán.
Wé kik'i aa
ku.a x'wán tlél wáa sá yoo ysaneigík,
wé kik'i aa,"
yóo áwé yaawakaa.
Wáa nanée sáwé
a kaax kuwduwa.áx, "Wéidu á.
Góok!
Góok! Ax jigidagú!
Gu.aa yáx x'wán!   240
Wé kik'i aa ku.a x'wán gaysaneix,"
yóo áwé yaawakaa.
Ash daadéi kawdigaax
yú x'áat' káx'
du nák yaa yakwgakóox.
Ach áwé.

A yáx áwé, hóoch' wé yaakw.
Wóoshdáx has awsigáat.
Kéet áwé.
Wé kik'i aa ku.a áwé yaakw kígi kát áwé
       s akawlixít.   250
Dáagi s ashoowahoo aan.
Dáagi s ashoowahoo.
Ash daadé kawdagaaxích áwé.
Awé wdudzikóo wé kéet a daasheeyí.
X'alitseen.
Yá haa niyaanax.á aa kwa wéináx áwé kei
       shukawsixíx T'aakóonáx.
Ch'u shugu a daasheeyí kéet.
"Yan wulihashi kéet"
yóo áwé shukdulxúxs'.
Aaa.   260
Ldakát káach áyá wsikóo.
Ach áwé kuwa.áxch,
wé át.
Kéet
kuwa.áxch.

It's right there already,
it's right there."
That's when he told them,
those things he had carved,   230
"Be brave.
But the younger one,
please don't do anything
to the younger one,"
he said.
At one point
he heard "There they are!
Go!
Go fight them!
Be brave!   240
But please save that younger one,"
he said.
The younger one had cried for him
on the island
when they left without him.
That's why.

Just like that, the boat was no more.
The killer whales
cracked it in half.
But the younger one was pushed onto a half of the
          boat.
                                                               250
They swam it to the beach with him.
They swam it to the beach.
Because he cried for him.
People know the Killer Whale song.
It is valued.
It's the one from our side but the strands
          surfaced over there from Taku.
It is the same song for Killer Whale,
"Drifted ashore Killer Whale"
are the words to it.
Yes.
                                                               260
Everybody knows this.
This is why those things
can hear people.
The Killer Whale
can hear people.
They can sit on land.

Dáagi s g̲akeech wéit'át.
Ch'u yeedátdei
whale killer yóo duwasáakw dleit k̲áach ku.a.
Uháanch ku.a yei tuwasáakw k̲únáx̲ wé tléix' aa.
Tlél áyú a goosh á.   270
Tlax̲ tlél du gooshí á.
K̲únáx̲ a sháade háni ásíyú gé?
Hú áwé k̲únáx̲
x'áan s'aatíx̲ k̲aa x̲oox' wusitee.
Has du saax'ú...?
Tlax̲ k̲útx̲ yéi kaawayáat' yá sh kalneek.
Aaá. Tléil a tóo yéi haa wutee.
Yá haa shagóonx̲'ich ku.a yá kalanik noojín,
has du daakeitx̲'íx̲ sateeyích.
Ayá ch'a a x̲oo aa áyá wtusikóo de.   280
Tlax̲ k̲útx̲ yéi kooyáat'
tlaagú áyá.
Deikeelunáak yóo áwé duwasáakw.
Lawáak t'ikáwu á
wé noow.
Wé deikée ku.a
wé x'áat' áwé.
Deikéet satéen wé x'áat'.
A káx' áwé yéi yan at kawdiyáa.

Even till today
it's called "Killer Whale" by the Whitemen.
But we have a name for the other one.
It didn't have a dorsal fin.   270
It really didn't have a dorsal fin.
It is surely the real leader isn't it?
It was he
who was the meanest one among them.
Their names....?
This story was told too long ago.
Yes; we weren't in it.
But our ancestors used to tell it,
because they were their outer containers.
We only know some of them.   280
This is too ancient
of a story.
It is called Deikeelunáak.
That fort
is outside of Klawock.
Out there
is an island.
That island lies way out.
It was on it that this happened.

Dukt'ootl'
Taakw K'wát'i x'éidáx sh kalneek

Yóo wé
Henyaa áwé
yéi duwasáakw áwé du.úxx'un.
Taakw.aaní.
Awé tlél tlax
wooch een yan kaxwla.aax wáanáx sáwé
kóox ayawdutltseen.
Gwál tlax ch'áagu sh kalneegí, ách áwé tlél
óonaa koostí ka tlél gayéis'.
Awé tle yéi xwajée nuch wé taan áwé aax has
        jiwtnúk wé atxá sákw.   10
Awé tléináx káa áwé.
Galwéit' yóo duwasáakw.
Naa sháadei hánix sitee.
Yáa du kéilk' ku.aa wé
a xoo aach yéi sáakw nuch kooskáawu yáx yatee.
        Tlél daa.itkooshgóok.
Tle k'idéin ku.oo tóonáx kuwudzitee.
Awé
ch'ul keena.éiji áwé tle héendei ana.átch.
Wé du káak yaa kaa shugagútch.
Sagú yáx kaa yayík du.axji nuch héendei yáa   20
        ana.ádi.
Awé hú ku.a tlél kaa yáa ulk'eiyéech áwé,
ch'a góot héeni yoo uwagút.
Yan awuxéix'u áwé héendei nagútch.

138

Strong Man
told by Frank G. Johnson

It is
called
Henyaa; people used to live there.
It was a winter village.
But I didn't
understand altogether why
people trained for strength.
Maybe this is an ancient story which is why
there are no guns or no metal.
I sometimes think it was the sea lions they
       wanted to kill for food.   10
There was one man.
His name was Galwéit'.
He was the leader of his nation.
But his sister's son was what
some people would call being like a misfit. He
       was awkward.
But he was born from good people.
Then
before daybreak they would go to the sea water.
That mother's brother of his would lead them on.
Their voices would happy sound when they went to
       the sea.   20
But because the men didn't respect him,
he went to the sea alone.
When people went to sleep he would go to the sea.

(F.J.: Shall I tell it just the way they
      tell it?)
(N.D.: Uh huh.)
Awé tle ch'u tle du kaanáx wuteeyéedei áwé
      héeni ganúkch.
Daak gagúdin áwé
wé x'aan yakoolkís'ch.
Yá gan.eetí kwás woot'áaych.   30
Awé gat'aat áwé tle
yá gan.eetéet akoollóox'ch.
Awé a kasáyjayi áwé ash ult'áaych
wé gan.eetéenáx.
Ch'éix'w du daa yéi nateech wé gandaa teixéech.
Awé tlél du daat kaa tooshtí.
Tléináx yateeyi aa du káak shát áwé eeshandéin
      ash daa tuwatee.
Awé yá atxá du x'éidei
du x'éix ateex nuch.
Wé du xúx wakshóot aan tée nuch kwá.
Awé wáa yeikunayáat' sáwé   40
ch'u tle akwdahu nuch hú kwá wé
tléinax héent aayí
wé kus.áat' jeet,
wé tle du x'éináx kei xixji nuch.
Wáa nanée sáwé
tsu hú ch'u héent aayí áwé
yá du t'áanáx du éet x'awduwatán.
"Haat hú" yóo áwé ash yawskaa wé káa.
At awtlgín.
S'eek x'óow áwé atx'óo wé káa.   50
Tlél yéi koolgé.
Awé tle yéi ash yawskaa
"I eegáa áya xat woosoo.
Latseen áyá xat.
Yéi xat duwasáakw Latseen."
Awé yéi ash yawskaa, "Ha
xaan kuklahá."
Awé tle aadéi ash daayaka yáx áwé.
Tlél tsu wáa sá awusnei.
Awé tle   60
tlé yéi ash yawskaa,
"Wéix' yan háan."
Awé tle wé

(F.J.: Shall I tell it just the way they tell it?)
(N.D.: Uh huh.)
He would sit in the water until it overpowered him.
When he came up
the fire would be out.
But where the fire had been would be warm.
Because he wanted to warm up   30
he would urinate right on where the fire had been.
The steam from this would warm him,
from where the fire had been.
Grime would collect on his body because he slept
          by the fire.
No one paid attention to him.
But one of his mother's brother's wives would
          feel sorry for him.
She would give him
food.
But she didn't want her husband to see her do it.
Then after a period of time   40
he would cry out in pain
when he sat alone in the water
from the cold.
It would come out of his mouth.
At one point
while he was sitting in the water again
someone spoke to him from the beach.
"Wade over here," the man said to him.
He looked over there.
The man wore a black bear skin cape.
He wasn't too tall.   50
Then he said to him,
"I'm your good luck.
I'm Strength.
I'm called Strength."
Then Strength said to him, "Now
defeat me."
Then he did as he told him.
He didn't even scratch him.
And then
Strength said to him,   60
"Stand right there."
Then Strength
began to scrub him with yellow seaweed

tayeidí áwé ách ash daa la.ús'kw
yá du s'aag̱ix'áak,
ldakát yá du s'aag̱ix'áak. Nas'gadooshú dutiw
     nuch k̲aa s'aag̲í.
Yá yéi kulyat' aa g̲íwé.
Ldakát yá du s'aag̱ix'áak. Ach áwé al.ís'kw
     wé tayeidí.
Awé tle yéi ash yawsk̲aa "Ha
tsu héenx̱ g̲agú."   70
Tsu héenx̱ woogoot. Tsu ch'u yéi ash yawsk̲aa.
Tsu ch'u wáa sáwé tle yan ash ux̱eechch.
Yáax' áwé tsu,
tsu ch'u yéi ash daa woo.óos'.
Tsu héendei ash kaawanáa.
Daax'oon.aa yéi ash nasnée áwé
tlél yan ash wux̱eech.
Awé tle yéi ash yawsk̲aa "Yan x̲at eex̲éech tsu.
De déi áwé,"
yóo ash yawsk̲aa.   80
Tle ch'as yéi yaa yanak̲éini tóox̱ áwé tle
     a eetéex̱ yaa wutlg̱én.
Ch'as kaxwaan áwé áx̱ yaa anasgúk
     wé héen át háni yé.
Tléináx̱ áwé tle yan wutltsín.
Yóot k̲wá át
ách has wooch skwéiy yéi shkalneek nuch.
Asyádi áwé.
Yá aan kat'ootnáx̱ naashóo.
Aanka.aasí tle yéi wtwasáa ch'a wé k̲u.oowúch.
K̲a
yá sheey oowayayi át   90
yá aas k'éet lukatán.
A k̲u.aa wé Aanloowú yóo wtwasáa.
Ch'a g̲óot yéidei tsú dusáakw nuch.
I'll tell it what it is after this.
Awé át ash kaawanáa.
"Wé Aanloowú x'wán daak x̲óot'.
Héen táax̱ yitaaní tle tsu a tóodei kg̲eegóok̲.
Awé wé asyádi tsu
a x'aannáx̱ gag̲isax'áa tle a k'éedei."
Awé ch'a aadéi ash daayaka yáx̱. Awé tle   100
a x'aannáx̱ yéi anasx'éin tle.
A x̲aadéet awsx'áa.

on his joints,
on all his joints. People count them as eight bones.
Perhaps they are all the long limbs.
On all his joints. So he scrubbed him with
        yellow seaweed.
Then Strength said to him, "Now
go into the water again."
He went into the water again. He told him to   70
        defeat him again.
Without trying, Strength would throw him down.
And here again,
soon he scrubbed him again the same way.
He sent him to the water again.
When he did this the fourth time
Strength didn't throw him down.
Strength said to him, "You have thrown me down now.
That's enough,"
he said to him.   80
As soon as he said that, Strength disappeared.
Only patches of frost floated where Strength
        had stood in the water.
He gained strength all alone.
They say
there was a thing by which they tested each other.
It was a young tree.
It stood in the middle of the village, it
was called "Village Tree" by those people.
And
this thing that was like a large branch   90
stuck out at the base of the tree.
It was called the Village Nose.
It is also called by another name.
I'll tell what it is after this.
Strength told him to go to it.
"Pull the Village Nose out.
Immerse it in water then push it back again.
The young tree too--
split it from the tip down to the base."
He did just as he told him; he began   100
splitting from the top down.
He split it down to the roots.
Only after this he returned home again.
When people awoke, his maternal uncle

Aagáa áwé tsá tsu neildéi woogoot.
Shadukéi áwé du káak
yaa kaa shunagút tsu.
De ch'a litseen yóo áwé du káak.
Latsins'aatéex sitee.
Tle yaa nagúdi áwé tsu akaawa.aakw wé aan loowú.
Tle aax tóot aawaxút'.
Kaa yayík wutwa.áx.   110
Yáax' áwé tle wé asyádi tsu, tle wé yaa
        anasx'éini tle a xaadít awsx'áa.
Yéi ku.aa wé ash yawskaa wé káa
"tsu ch'u eetiyáx x'wán kux yanasteeyán wé aas tsú."
Xóon tú áwu.
Awé tsu eetiyáx a.oowúch áwé,
ách áwé du káakch yéi aawajee ch'u kawushgéedich
hóoch aawax'áa wé at.
Awé ák' awtwahín a yáx wultseení.
Tle at wutwaxoon.
Taan aaní yóo duwasáakw.   120
Tle ch'a yá neech áwé.
Yá yeedát áa yéi yatee tle lishóowu yáx yatee.
Awé wé gaaw kwá hé tlél aas áa yéi utéeyin yóo
        akanik nuch.
Awé taan áa gakéech.
Tlax yá a shakéex' áwé
ganúkch tlax wé aa tlein.
Noowkakáawu yóo
ch'a lingítch áwé yéi uwasáa wé taan tlein tle
tlax ligéiyi aa tlein.
Awé du een át wutxooní wé du káak   130
táakw áwé yú.á.
Tle hú tsú
xwaasdáa s'éil'k'i
gáach s'éil'k'i gíwé yeik oonasgút.
Dé ch'a hóoch' áwé a káa teix át áwé.
Awé tle yawtwatsák.
Tle du shóodáx deikéex dultsaagí áwé tle yá
yaakw géegit uwashée.
Yéi akanéek tle aax akawltéix'.
Tle dáagi koon aawayeesh. Aagáa áwé tsaa a
        yíx woogoot.   140
A áwé ch'u yeedát a yáx at gat.lkóo nuch,
        "ch'a wé sheen x'ayee áwé áx woogoot."

was leading the men again.
His maternal uncle was very strong.
He was a Master of Strength.
As he walked up to it he tried pulling the
          village nose.
He pulled it right out.
You could hear the people cheer.   110
Here then when he began splitting the young
          tree too he split it down to the roots.
But Strength had told the nephew,
"Put the tree back the way it was again."
It was during a north wind.
Because he had put it back the way it was,
his maternal uncle thought, because it was
          still dark,
that he had split it.
People believed he was strong enough.
They began to get ready.
The place is called sea lion land.   120
It's on the mainland.
Now it's steep.
But at that time they say there weren't any
          trees there.
That's where the sea lions usually sat.
At the very top
the very large one would sit.
The large sea lion was called by the Tlingits
"Man on the Fort"
a very large one.
When people were preparing to go with his
          maternal uncle
they say it was winter.   130
But he
carried a ragged rug on his shoulder,
maybe a ragged cloth.
Those were all he slept on.
They didn't want him to go.
When they were pushing away from him
he reached for the stern of the boat.
They say he twisted it off.
Then he pulled it up on the beach with the men
          in it. That's when he stepped in.
Even till now there is a proverb from this,   140

Awé yaa yakwnakúxu áwé
kaskooxóox sitee hú kwá.
Ch'a kunaaléi aadéi yaa yakwnakux yé.
At yakwkóox áwé tle
tle héeni woogoot wé du káak.
Wáa latseení sáyá taan yátx'i yóo ayagwáldi tle
tle a een ch'a du jín tin.
Daak nagút ch'a x'oon sáwé
aawaják tle wé taan.   150
Awé tlax wé a shakéet
aa aa áwé du tóoch wulichéesh áa kei uwagút.
Yá a geen áwé akaawa.aakw. Wóoshdáx a tl'eik
        akgwas'éil' tle wé taan.
Tle du sakáa yéi nanúgu áwé du geen kindei yóo
        awusnei áwé
wé taan ku.aa
tle yóo dikindei kei ash uwaxích.
Yindasháan áwé tsá wé tayakáash káa yan
        shaawagás'. Tle hóoch'.
Tle shakaawawál'.
Eeshandéin kaa tuwatee wé
has du sháadei háni aadéi wooteeyi yé.   160
Ach áwé wé káa ku.aa
Atkaháas'i yóo wtwasáa
wé l ushnéek'ich
áwé tle wudiháan.
Awé tle yéi x'adutee,
"Aadóoch sá daak uwaxút' yá Aanloowú?
Xáach xáa wé daak xwaaxút'.
Aadóoch sá aawax'áa yá aas
yá Aanka.aasí?
Xáach xáa wé."   170
Awé tle yaa nagúdi áwé tle yaakw yíx daak nagút.
Yá yaxak'áawu
a t'éit kawlyáas' tle du xées'dei l'éex'.
Awé
kei wushk'éini áwé
taakw laakásgi yóo toosáakw nuch aa kutstee.
Awé yá téix' yáa teeyí
kax'il'k nuch.
Tle kei wchk'én ch'a aan tlél x'uskawushx'éel'.
Tle kei nagút.   180
Wé taan yatx'i át kin yé kwa wé íkdei gakéech.

"He just went as a bailer."
Then, when they were paddling along,
he was a bailer.
It was kind of far where they were paddling to.
When they got there
his maternal uncle stepped off the boat.
He was so strong when he punched the cub
        sea lions
he killed them with his bare hands.
How many sea lions he killed
as he was going up!
But he wanted to get at the one   150
sitting at the top of the island.
He tried the flippers. He tried to rip it apart
        by the flippers.
But as he was sitting down on its neck the sea lion
raised its flipper
and tossed him up in the air.
He fell head first on a rock. Then he was gone.
His head was fractured.
People felt grief
about what happened to their leader.
But that's why that man,   160
he was named Atkaháas'i
because he didn't keep himself clean,
stood up.
They imitate him saying,
"Who do you think pulled out the Village Nose?
It was I who pulled it out.
Who do you think split this tree,
the Village Tree?
It was I."
                                                          170
Then as he went, he went up walking through the boat.
The thwarts broke
as his shins hit them.
As
he jumped up out of the boat
there was what we call winter seaweed.
When it's on the rocks
they're slippery.
But when he jumped on them he didn't even slip.
He kept on going up.
                                                          180
The place where young sea lions sit is closer

Ch'a wáa sáwé ayagwált
tle ya̠x yaa ayanaljá̠k.
Tle yóo kíndei woogoot wé du káak aawajá̠gi
taan tlein
a ginkáa wchka̠ak.
Ch'a g̠ígaa kíndei yóo ya̠x ash siné. Tléik'!
Tle yá a geen
tle yáa yá woosh tkán yóo awusneiyí
      áwé wóoshdá̠x akaawas'éil'.
Tle aawajá̠k.   190
Aag̠áa áwé tsá yá át ḵin aa taan a x̠oot jiwtgút.
         Tle hóoch'!
A g̠óotx̠ yaa analyéx̠.
Yéi áwé kawdutlneek.
A̠yá dleewkwát
ash daat yawstaag̠i aa
du káak shátch áwé
du jeet uwatée wé át
dáa.
A̠wé aadéi héeni kḵwagoodí áwé tsá
du sha̠xaawú   200
a tóox' a ká̠x wutch'ín yóo toosáakw nuch.
A̠wé gandaadá̠x t'ooch' áwé tle ách yawtlxwáts.
(You know that soot.)
Aan áwé tsá héeni woogoot.
A̠ch áwé tle wé ch'a yéi nateech wé du káak
wé ash daat yawstag̠i aa yéi kdunik nuch
yanwáadi aa du káak shát áwé
tle tóot ajeewatán.
De ch'a yéi at téeyin ch'áakw.
Yá ḵaa káak nag̠anéin   210
tle wé a shát áwé
aa̠x kei duteejéen.
Wé yées shaawátx̠ siteeyi aa ḵwá tlél a daat
         tooshtí tle.
A̠wé tlél wut.skóowun wáa sá dusáagu,
tle wé du káak saayí áwé du saayéex̠ wustee
         G̠alwéit'.
Wé du shát saayí tsú tlél
tlél wut.skóowun a x̠oo aach.
A̠wé yá woonaawu a̠x éeshch
ḵu.aa wé
awsikóo.   220

to the sea.
However lightly he was punching
he was killing them there.
Then he went up to jump on the flippers
of the huge sea lion
that had killed his uncle.
It tried to lift him upward. No!
Then he took it by the flippers
and ripped it in half.
Then killed it.   190
That's when he finally began killing his way
         through the sea lions sitting there. Then
         there were no more.
He kept on slaughtering them.
That's how they tell of him.
The one
that cared for him,
his maternal uncle's wife,
was the one who had given him that thing,
the ermine.
When he was going into the water toward the sea lion
he tied it to his hair
as what we call "ch'éen."   200
The charcoal from the fire was what he blackened
         his face with.
(You know that soot.)
With this he finally went ashore.
That was why, when his maternal uncle died
it is said, the nephew asked for the hand
of the one who cared for him,
the one who was older.
It was really that way long ago.
When a maternal uncle died
the wife   210
was claimed by the nephew.
But he didn't even notice the young one.
People didn't know what his name was,
so his name became Galwéit', his maternal
         uncle's name.
His wife's name too
was not known either by some.
But
my father who is dead

Yéi akanéek has du x̱ooní áwé
áx̱ satéeyin wé shaawát. Shangukeidí.
      Shangukasháa.
Yei twasáakw Seitéew.
Át̲x̱ áwé shayadiheni yéix' tlél wut.skú.
Hásch ḵwá du éenáx̱
ḵa s du shangóonnáx̱ kawuhaayích áwé awuskóowun.
Yéi áyá yan shoowatán wé shkalneek.

knew.

He said the woman

was their relative. Shangukeidí. A Shangukeidí
      woman.

Her name was Seitéew.

People in many places don't know her name.

But because of them

and because this came from their ancestors,

he knew.

This is where this story ends.

Kaakex'wtí
Kéet Yaanaayí x'éidáx sh kalneek

Kaakex'wtí áyá kakkwalaneek yeedát.
Yá Gathéeni yóo duwasáagu yé áwé
áa yéi kuteexéen yú deikée Yant'iká.
Nagukyadaa t'áak áwé yéi duwasáakw Gathéeni.
A áyá ch'áagu káawu áwé yéi yateeyi yé.
Aa yéi teexéen
yá war
jínák áwé; yú safe place-x' yéi s teexéen.
Yú lidzéeyi yé; yéi áwé kuduwa.óo.

Ayá   10
taatx' áwé du.eenín tsaa
kaa atxaayí sákw.
Ach áwé
wookoox.
Du at'eegí tsú du een.
Digiygéidei áwé tsu kustée nuch.
Wáa sá kwshé du ée kaawaháa wé digiygéidei
        ka wé at'eegí?
Has iltsís
wé anax naakwaani yé t'áat.
Du jeewú wé tsaagál'.   20
Gwál has aa woo.een.
Yaa keiga.áa gíwé
kúxdei déi.
Daa sá du yáx woodakeench? Ayá du ée lidzée,

152

Kaakex'wtí
told by Willie Marks

Now, I will tell of Kaakex'wtí.
This place called Gathéeni
is where people lived, out there along the ocean.
On the mainland from Cape Spencer the place
            is called Gathéeni.
It was this kind of a place ancient people lived in.
They used to live there
away from
war parties; they lived in a safe place.
A difficult place; this was how people lived.

Seals
were killed at night   10
for people to eat.
That's why
he went.
His paddlers were also with him
also the one who sits midship in the canoe.
I wonder how the midsection man was related to him,
            and to the one who paddled.
They were anchored
where the seals swam by at night.
He had a spear.
Perhaps they killed some.   20
Maybe it was getting light,

du yadaat wudikeen.
Tsu yéi kunoogú áwé du axáayi áwé yóo awsinei.
A yát áwé wdikín.
Awé yaakw yée wdzigeet.
Daatx' sáyá dulyaakw? Ksiyidéin kaaxát.
Awé wáa sá kwshé? Gwál héent aawaxích wé át   30
wé bird.
(Yeisú a xánt yéi xat daayaduká.)
Aandéi gunayéi s uwakúx.

Ch'u yéi gunéi s kóox; ch'u l yeiwuyáat'i áwé
káx daak shaawaxíx du digiygéidei
a digiygéit aa aa.
Tlax yaa kunaséini gíwé du aaní
du at'eegí
káx daak shaawaxíx tsu.
Tle táach áwé kujákx.   40
Tle yoo kuwanáakw gíwé tle.
Du yataayí áwé ashaawaxích
wé káa.
Tle aant ayaawaxáa
gwál aan eegayáax' gwál éex' áwé
"wáa sá woonei ax yikkáawu?"
Wáa sáyá tléil aadóo sá?
Tléil tsu Lingít yéi oostínch
wé aan.
Tle tleix áwé axéx'w.   50
Aa daak góot,

hóoch'. Kutx shoowaxeex,
yóo yú one city áwé yéi woonei.

A áwé gwál yanax akawsihéit' yá du xoonx'í.
Aagáa wé tsá gunayéi uwagút.
Gaatáa,
ch'áakw kustéeyin; gaatáa yóo duwasáagu át
du jeewú.
Gwál yaa
atuwáatx   60
at nagwaa.eeni át tsú; du jeewú á.

Wáa sá kwshé yoo kaawagút? Yá Tsalxaan
t'éináx gíwé yaa wugoot.

time to return.
What was it that kept flying past his face? It
        bothered him
when it flew to his face.
When it did this again he waved his paddle.
It flew into the paddle.
It dropped in the canoe.
What did he compare it to? It was grotesque.
Then what? Perhaps he threw that thing in
        the sea,
that bird.   30
(I have been reprimanded just recently.)
They began paddling to the village.

They had just begun to paddle; they had not
        been going long
when his midsection paddler keeled over,
the one sitting in the midsection.
Maybe when they were nearing their village
his stern man
keeled over also.
People would fall asleep.
Maybe people were dying then.   40
That man
had clubbed his sleep.
When he brought his dead crew to the village
perhaps to the beach of the village perhaps
        he was yelling
"What's happened to my crew?"
Why was there no one?
He didn't see a single human
at the village.
People were sleeping forever.
When he went up from the beach,   50

they were gone. They had all died.
This happened to the one village.

Perhaps he buried these relatives of his.
Only then he began walking.
Traps
were around long ago. He had
those things called traps.

Ei.i.i.i.i.i!
Yaa nagút.
Gwál tlax, gwál x'oon dís sá shoowaxeex
      aagáa yaa nagut yé.
Aagaa áyá a káx woogoot

yú át áwé
kaa x'us.eetí,
héen yaax.   70
Wáa sáyá kaawahayi
yéixk' áyá yáat la.áa héen táak?

Tle woosh dookx' yéi duwa.óo.
Tlax tliyaa aa yeet áwé aa satáan.
Tléix' saakk' áwé a yeet satáan.
Kaa x'us.eetí a daa yéi dagaatee.
Tle awsikóo wé saak áwé dulxést
(Tléix' yeelxeisí, how much each you get?)
Awsikóo lingít áwé a káx woogoot.
Ach áwé tle yéi awsinei,   80
yá wuháan áa yéi yateeyi yéix' yéi daadune át
wé saak aan yéi daadune át
aan du.een át.
T'éetx á
yóo duwasáakw,
awlis'ít.

Aagáa wé
yanax ax'awsitaan
yú deikée héen táanáx.
Tlax du toowóoch shahéek áwé   90
áa daak uwahóo.
Shaawahík.

Tle wé yéix xánx' áwé yax aksaxéix.
Tle tliyaa aa tsú a xánx' yax aksaxéix.
Tle a tóodei yoo sixíxk wé yéixk' ku.a,
tle yéi áwé adaané.
Yaa keina.éini áwé
aawa.áx kaa sé.
Aax kut wujixeex.
Weh-weh-weh-weh-weh.   100
Daak ana.át.

Probably
he also had some of those things
he might hunt with.   60

Which way did he go? Maybe he came down
behind Mt. Fairweather.
He walked.
Faaaaaaaaaar!
Probably many many months passed during his walk.
That's when he came on them,

those things,
a man's footprints
along a river bank.
What are these little dead falls   70
doing here, sitting there in the water?

They were placed close to one other.
Inside the farthest one
lay one little hooligan.
Some footprints were around them.
He knew that hooligans were being trapped.
(If you trap one, how many will it feed?)
He knew he had come on humans.
That's why he made it,
the thing they make in our land,   80
those things used to catch hooligans,
the thing that is used to kill them.
He wove
the one that is called
a trap, indeed.

That's when
he hooked it down
out there in the river.
When he thought it was very full
he waded out there.   90
It was full.

Then he dumped them by the traps.
Again by the ones beyond them he'd dump some.
Until the traps disappeared
that's how he did it.

Awsiteen
wé Gunanaa.
Duwatéen wé du x'us.eetí.
Ayá tléil goohâa wooyík teen yoo x'adudli.átk;
        tléil goohâa s du eedéi.
Awé tléik',
tléil show off-x sh wustee.
Kux yawdi.át tsu.
Gwál wáa sá kwshé yéi kaawayáat'; gwál uwaxée tsu.
Aagâa áwé tsu kaa sé aawa.áx.   110

Wéix yaa ana.át tsu
wududzikóo lingít áwé áwu; át uwagút.
Wé át, wé át aadéi koogeyi yé; aatlein atxá áyú,
wé aadéi akawlixéis'i át.
Ach áwé du eedéi sh tugáa kunaxdateet áwé
duxoox.
Shaawát gwáa wé gé oon yaa ana.át?
Du jiyís shaawát áwé.

Ch'a yéi yoo x'adudli.átk.
Gwál tle du een duch'éx't.   120
"Yáadu i shát sákw," yóo.
Aagâa áwé tsá wé aas gutóonáx yóot uwagút.
Tle du een kadukaa,
"It's all yours."
Koon yóot uwa.át neildéi.

Ch'u yéi wé áa yéi wootee; x'oon táakw x'áanáx
        sá kwshé a xoo yéi wootee?
Tle yátx'
du yátx'i.
Ch'a yák'wdei áwé
(yá aadéi yanakéich yé kwá yaa kuxwligát.)   130
De yatx kawdligéi
gwál sixteen
fifteen years áyú yéi duwasáakw Lingítch
yatx kawdligéi.
De kúxdei asgí wé tuditee.
K'é éeknáx akunga.aagú?

(A géit kaxwliník.)

When day was breaking
he heard people's voices.
He ran away from there to hide.
Weh-weh-weh-weh-weh.
People were coming out.   100

He saw
the Athabaskans.
They could see his footprints.
It was easy to see they were trying to talk to
        him; it was easy to see.
No!
He didn't show himself.
They left again.
Perhaps for long; perhaps for just one night.
That's when he heard people's voices again.   110

They were coming again,
they knew a human was there; one had come.
How many the hooligans were; there was a lot of food,
the hooligans he dumped there.
Because they wanted to show their gratitude to him
they called him.
Wasn't that a woman they had brought along?
It was a woman for him.

Perhaps they tried to talk to him.
Perhaps they pointed her out to him.
"Here is a wife for you," they said.   120
Only then did he finally come out of the forest.
They motioned to him in sign language
"She's all yours."
He left to go home with them.

That's how he remained there; for how many years
        did he live among them?
Then there were children,
his children.
All of a sudden --
(but I forgot what he would say.)
They were already fully grown,   130
perhaps over sixteen
fifteen years; that's what Tlingits call

Tléináx áwé woogoot s'é
aadáx
yá kúxdei niyaadéi.   140
Eeknáx áwé awsikóo yú anax haat uwagudi yé
        yú dáaknáx
yú shaa t'éináx.
Ach áwé éeknax.aanáx awsikóo áx yaa kgwagudi.

Ei.i.i.i.i.i! Yéi yaa nagút.
Yú Lituya Bay.
A kaanáx gíwé xaanás' yéi awsinei.
Haanaanax.á áwé yéi duwasáakw
yá south niyaanax á
Nagootk'í á.
Gwáa!   150
Lingít du géidei yaa nagút.

A daasheeyí kudzitee
yá du géidei yaa nagúdi
tléil ku.aa wé xwsakú.
A yáanaa yéi koowáat'.
Tlax du xángaa yaa kagooseí áwé du toowúch
        kindachóon yawdzi.aa.
Gwáa,
té gwáa wé gé.
Ach áwé yéi wduwasáa ch'u yáa yagiyeedéi
Nagootk'í.   160
Tle ách wududlisáa.

Kux wudigút tle
tsu.

Aagáa gwál wáa sá kwshé yéi kaawayáat' neilx'.
Gwál tsu dís shuwdagaaxeex.
Yáax' áwé woosh kaadéi yéi awsinei gíwé wé a
        xoot uwagudi
wé tináa,
daa sá kwshé tsú aan,
á áwé du yátx'ich gagayaayít áwé.
Yan has née áwé   170
gunéi has uwa.át
éeknáx.

already fully grown.
I guess he wanted to go back.
Why not try along the shore line?

(I told it wrong.)
First he left there
alone
toward the way back.
He knew how he had come along the shore line   140
        through the forest
from behind the mountain.
That's why he knew how he would go along the beach.

F a r r r r r ! How long he walked.
Lituya Bay.
Perhaps he made a raft to cross it.
On the near side of it
this south side of it
is what is called Nagootk'í.
Hey!
                                                  150
A Tlingit was coming toward Kaakex'wtí.

There is a song for this,
the one who was coming toward him,
but I don't know it.
His pack was very tall.
When he was closer to him he thought
        he lifted his head.
Hey!
It was a rock.
That's why it's called even till today
"The Little Walker."
                                                  160
It was given that name then.

He went back
again.

Then perhaps he stayed long at home.
Perhaps a month went by.
Maybe here he collected those coppers
he came upon,
whatever else with them
all his children could pack.

Yaa s na.át.

A shákdéi wé T'aayx'aa gíwé áa daak has uwa.át.
Goot'á ḵwa sá kwshíwé?
Ch'a yeisú aadáx daak yakw.uwakúx.
We x'aan ch'á yeisú x'aanx sitee wé gán.

Awé áa daak has uwa.át wé aan
tsu aan.
Chookaneidí áwé naakéedei ḵuwa.óo.   180
A niyaadéi ḵuwa.óo Kaagwaantaan.
Ya Kaagwaantaan ḵu.aa áwé s du íxt'i ḵudzitee.
A áwé át at shuwootéeych at sheeyí.
Tl'anaxéedáḵwt áwé ooltaanch.
Yéi áwé ash waaǥée yatee.
Yá Tl'anaxéedáḵw ḵu.aa áyá Auke Bay-dáx áyá
        ḵuwdzitee.
A yakǥwahéiyagu yáx áwé ash tuwáa yatee; ha
        aadóoch sá wsiteen
hú áwé aan ḵáawoox sateexín, wé Tl'anaxéedáḵw.
Yéi áyá at shée nuch yá yéik.
Tl'anaxéedáḵw yaa nagúdi.   190
"Yee gu.aa yáx x'wán," yóo adaayaká du xwáax'u.
Ch'a yák'wde áwé áa daak aawa.át.
Lingít diyáawu.

Aadéi yoo x'adudli.átk; chush x'éináx yoo
        s x'ali.átk.
Áyá Chookaneidí
"háatkées" gíwé áa yux wujixeex.
"Ixinaawú á,
ixinaawú, yee káa at xáshgu ḵu.oo
kóoshdaa ḵáax'w sáani."
Yóo áwé ayawsikaa.   200
Kóoshdaa ḵáax áwé aksanéek.
Tle yéi ayawsikaa du yátx'i
"ixinaadéi haa kdunáa."

Ach áwé yéi at ǥadudlikóo
"chush keekaadáx Gunanaa aa kawdukaayín."
Yá Chookaneidí áwé yéi wdzigeet.
De áwu wé íxt',
wé Kaagwaantaan íxt'.

When they were ready   170
they began walking
along the beach.

They walked.

Maybe they came up there toward the head of
        Dixon Harbor.
But where were they?
People had just left.
The wood was still embers.

That was the settlement they came on
also a settlement.
The Chookaneidí lived uppermost in the bay.   180
Next to them lived the Kaagwaantaan.
The Kaagwaantaan had a shaman.
He was the one who would predict when he sang.
He would compare it to Tl'anaxéedakw.
That is how he looked to him.
Tl'anaxéedakw originated from Auke Bay.
It looked to him like her ghost; well,
        whoever saw
Tl'anaxéedakw would become rich.
This is how those shaman spirits would sing.
The coming of Tl'anaxéedakw.   190
He told his men, "Be brave."
All of a sudden people came out there.
People were across the river.

People were talking there; they were speaking
        their language.
Maybe it was a "hard case"
Chookaneidí who ran out there.
"They're down the bay!
They're down the bay! The people who were
        cutting tongues to get you,
you little land otter people,"
is what he said.
He claimed they were land otter people.   200
So Kaakex'wtí told his children,
"They're telling us to go down the bay."

Aagáa áwé
tsu yéi kuyaawakaa,   210
"Lingít áhé diyáanax.áwu."
Tle du een kawduwaneek wé íxt',
"A áwé,
á áwé."
Has du kaanáx áwé kaa loowagook.
"Gwa'! tináa gwáa wéi gé s du jee."
Aagáa áyá
akawlineek aadéi yoo kawdiyayi yé.
Aagáa gíyás tle yaakwnáx
akaawa.aakw.   220
Aa yoo kuyaawagóo
hé Ikhéeni.
Aagáa áyá yawduwadlákwx' yá eek.
Yáadei ku.aa wé aan káax'ooch.
Aan káax'oo jiyís yéi daa wduwanei.

That's why there's a proverb
about "sending Athabaskans down the opposite bay."
It was a Chookaneidí who did that.
The shaman was already there,
the Kaagwaantaan shaman.
That's when
they told him
"There are some people across the bay."   210
The shaman immediately told them
"They are the ones,
they are the ones."
Then the people ran out to them.
"Hey! They have coppers!"
That is when
he told what happened to him.
Maybe that's when
he tried by boat.   220
Boats went
to the Copper River.
That is where copper was acquired.
But only for the rich people.
It was brought here for the rich people.

Xóotsx X'ayaakuwdligadi Shaawát
Yeilnaawú x'éidáx sh kalneek

Dáxnáx sháa áwé woosh kik'iyán.
Yú áa at wuduwa.eeni yé
dzísk'w áa wduwa.eeni yé
dleeygáa áwé aadéi aawa.aat.
Adax kúxdei neildéi kux du.áat
wé dleey ldakát
wududli.aat.
Aagáa áwé dáxnáx woosh kik'iyán
wé tléikw
wé tléikw xoot áwé s woo.aat.   10

Ha ch'a a xoot has wu.aadí ch'u tle
tle has du nák aawa.aat.
Adax wé kik'i.aa
wé du shátx, "Tláakw déi" yóo áwé adaayaká.
Ash ítx yaa nagút.
Ch'u tle tláakw áwé ka wé
áx ayaawa.adi yéix yaa nagút.

Adax aagáa áwé
wé shatxi.aa
tle wé   20
ch'u kóonáx wé
áwé xóots
yá áx' gándei woogoodi yé

166

The Woman Who Married the Bear
told by Tom Peters

There were two women, sisters.
They went for meat
to the place where animals were killed,
the place where moose were killed.
When they were returning home
the meat was all
packed out.
That's when the two sisters
came on the berries,
they came on the berries.   10

Well, when they came on them, just then
the people left them behind.
Then the younger sister
said, "Hurry now." to her older sister.
She walked behind her.
She went quickly and
along where people had walked.

Then from there
the older sister
walked right through there   20
right through
right where
a brown bear

kóonáx anax kwshéi wé yaa nagút; áwé a káa yan
      kamdliyás'.
A kaax áwé kei mshix'íl' yú.á.
Tle yá du tléigu tle ldakát á du jinák yax
      kamjixín.
Aagáa áwé xóots
gúshé aadéi adaayaka yé? A éet yaká aawatée.
Wé du kéek' kwá tle ash nák woogoot.
Aagáa áwé   30

aagáa áwé ash kagéit uwagút wé káa.
E!
Goodáx káa sáyá yéi yatee?
Yées káa.
Tle ash xándei yaa nagúdi teen áwé yéi adaayaká
"Ax een na.á.
Ax een na.á," yóo adaayaká.
"Tléik' !
Ax éesh
hás xat guxsaháa."   40
"Aadéi gaxtoo.áat.
Ch'u tle, ch'u tleix ax een na.á
yá ax neiléedei
yá ax neiléedei
yú ax neilée áa yéi yateeyi yéidei."
Ts'ás shóogu áwé tlél yéi tootí.
Yá du toowóo gíwé tle gúshé aadéi yoo
        amsineiyi yé.
Yáax' áwé tle aan woo.aat.
Tlél tsu naliyéidei s wu.aadí áwé
xáaw   50
át yatán.
Tle a kanax has yaawa.át.
Ch'a yeisú l unaliyéit has u.aatjí
tsu xáaw tsu át yatán.
Nas'giyeekáx'
a kaanáx has yaawa.át.
Kach shaa ásíyú.
Áwé xáaw yáx du tuwáa yatee wé shaawát.
Ch'u tle, ch'u yaa has na.ádi áwé, ch'u tle
kaa xoot has uwa.át.   60
Ch'u shugu lingít wáa sá nateech; ch'u yéi du
        tuwáa yatee.

had defecated; she stepped on it.
That was what she slipped on, it's said.
And those berries of hers all spilled from her hands.
What was it she said then
to the Brown Bear? She insulted it.
But her sister had already left her.
That's when   30

that's when the man appeared in front of her.
Nice!
Where was this man from?
A young man.
As soon as he came by her he said to her
"Come with me,
come with me," he said to her.
"No!
My parents
will miss me."   40
"We will go there.
Just come, come with me forever,
come home with me,
come home with me
to the place where my home is."
At first she didn't want to go.
Maybe he did something to her mind.
Then she went with him.
They hadn't gone very far
when a log   50
was lying there.
They went over it.
They hadn't been going far
when another log was lying there.
They walked
for three days.
Here they were really mountains.
That's what seemed like logs to the woman.
Then, while they were walking along then
they came on people.   60
They were surely human beings; that's just how
        they seemed to her.
That's when
the one she had gone with said to her,
"Don't look up.

Aagáa áwé
wé aan át woo.aadi aa yéi ash daayaká
"Líl kéi eelgénjeek.
S'ootaat
líl kaa xoot keetées'ik."
Ãhé
de wáa nanéi sgíhé?
"Wáa teeyéech sá kwshéi gé yéi xat daayaká?"
Gúshé du aanikwáani wé shaawát?   70
Du éesh
du tláa
gúshé.
"Wáa teeyích sá kwshé wéi gé yéi xat daayaká?"
          yéi áwé a daa tuwatee.
Aagáa ch'a yeisú s'ootáat
áwé kei mdzigít.
Aágáa áwé
yá x'óow yáx yateeyi át áwé daak aawayísh.
Daa ch'a áa at nagataayí yú neil
xóots.   80

Yáadáx áwé tle
tle kaa gunayáa has uwa.át.
Adax áwé xóots ku.aa ch'a wéidáx áwé yéi
          adaanéi nuch.
Ãwé xáat.
At x'aan
yoo shaaká --
s'aax
tsálk.

Ch'a kóonáx
tléix' táakw.   90
Tléix' táakw yaanáx
aan wooyeix
tléix' taakw.eetée ka yú tléix' táakw.

Aagáa yú táakwdei yaa kugaháa áwé
yan has koowa.óo.
Tlél tsu awuskú tsu ch'a guna.átx sateeyi, du
          toowóoch ku.aa ch'u tle lingít áyá
          yéi yatee.
"Hé keenaa áhé áa kugaxtoo.óo," yóo.

At dawn,
don't look among the people."
But then
at what point was it?
"I wonder why he's saying this to me," she thought.
Weren't they the woman's people?
Weren't they   70
her father
her mother?
"I wonder why he's saying this to me," she thought.
Then, when she woke up
at dawn
that's when
she pushed the blanket-like thing down from her face.
So many animals were asleep inside there,
brown bears.
                                                                 80

From here
they separated from the people.
But from then on, the brown bear
        would hunt just around there.
There were salmon.
Things were drying
on the mountain--
ground squirrel
ground hog.

It was exactly
one year.
She had been gone with him   90
more than a year,
one spring and one winter.

When winter began coming
they had settled in.
She didn't know he was something else either,
        but thought he was a human being.
"We will live up there," he said.
How she liked it!
It seemed to her
like a house made of branches.   100
Nice!
It was very nice.

Wáa sá du tuwáx'.
Chashhít
yáx áwé du tuwáa yatee.   100
E!
tláx wáa ku.aa sá yak'éi.
Hít wáa sá nateech yéi yatee.
Aagáa áwé
yéi ash daayaká
"hé keenaadáx
haaw
haandéi yéi nasné yá haa yeeyís."
Tle aadéi wé woogoot wé shaawát.
Tle amsikóo áwé wéit'átx sateeyi wé xóotsx
        sateeyí wé ash wusineixí.   110
"Líl yú keenaadáx eel'éex'eek wé haaw.
Yú tl'átgi kaax x'wán yéi nasné."

Ch'u tle wé
tle wé haaw al'ix' nóok áwé; tle ch'a wé
        keenaadáx áwé aawal'íx'.
Tle haat amli.át
"Shk'ei.
Yú dikéedáx ágé iyal'íx'?
Áaa,
Shk'ei!"
Aagáa áwé a jeet amli.át.   120
"Hé!
'Yú tl'átgi kaax l'íx',' yóo i daayaxaká.
Haa kakaysikwéy áwé."

Wududzikóo
wé du éesh
ka wé du tláa
ka wé
du koowú áa yéi yateeyi yé.
Duwatéen wé du x'us.eetí wéit'át tin
át wu.aadí.   130
Aagáa ch'a gunayéidei áwé s woo.aat.
Ch'u tle ch'u yéi teeyí ch'u yéi teeyí.
Wáa yeikunayáat' sá kwshéi wé tle dáxnáx at
        yátx'i du jee yéi wootee.
Máa sá lingít
tle yéi dagaatee.

It was the way a house should be.
That's when
he told her
"Bring down some
branches
from up there for our bed."
The woman immediately went up there.
Then she knew what he was, that he was a brown
        bear who had captured her.   110
"Don't break the branches from up there.
Pick them from the ground."

Just then,
then when she broke the branches, she broke them
        from above.
Then she brought them.
"Let me see.
Did you break them from up there?
Yes.
Let me see!"
That's when she gave them to him.
"Drat!   120
I told you 'Pick them from the ground.'
Now you've marked where we live."

It was known
to her father
and to her mother
and others
where the den was.
They could see from her footprints that she had gone
with him.   130
Then they moved to a different place.
Then they stayed there, they stayed there.
She was with him long enough to have two children.
They were just
like people.
Then they moved to a different place.
They settled there.
How the people of our village are
that's how they were.
Everything,   140
there was nothing that they needed,

Tle ch'a gunayéit has uwa.át.
Aa s kuyaawa.óo.
Máa sá nateech ch'a yáa haa aanikwáani
tle yéi áyá yatee.
Ldakát át   140
tlél tsu daa sá a eetéenáx has utí
hít.

Aagáa
keijínináx áyá s yatee
wé du éek' hás.
Aagáa áwé s akaawa.aakw.
Duwatéen wé s du dlaak' x'us.eetí; Duwatéen
wéit'át teen
át wu.aadí.
Ch'u tle mdudzikóo tle a jeedéi yéi teeyí.   150
Aagáa kúxdei kundaháa tlax k'idéin kúxdei
        kundaháa áwé
kayaanée kéi yéi s amsinéi
wé du éek' hás
tle wé keijínináx has teeyí.
Ch'u tle a yís
wé xóots yís áwé kéi s amsinéi.
Tlax x'éigaa kasi.égwaa
yóo kdunéek.
Yisikóo gé yéi duwasaagu át kayaanée?
That's the first one áwé tlél Lingít yisakú.   160
(N. D.) At yayeex' ák.wé yéi yóo kdusneigín?
Yéh, yéh!
Ha yáax' wududzikóo yóodáx áwé haandéi jinahaayín.
Yéi kdunéek ax een.
I don't want to bother that thing.
Tlax x'éigaa strict-x sitee yóo kdunéek.
Awé daasá,
áwé daasá yá dáanaax,
ayís áyá yéi daadunéiyin.
Haa, a tsú a yáx yéi daadunéi.   170
Tle gushéi tle something like crazy yax naneich
        yóo kdunéek.
Awé kéi yéi s amsinéi
adax áwé kayaanée kéi yéi mdusneiyín.
Eight days.
Nas'gidooshú yagiyee x'áanáx

at home.

But that time
there were five of them
the brothers of hers.
That was when they tried.
They could see their sister's footprints; they
          could see
that she had gone
with that thing.
He knew immediately that his life
          was in their hands.   150
When spring returned, when spring finally returned,
the brothers of hers
all five of them,
picked medicine leaves.
They did it just to get him,
just to get the bear.
It is truly sensitive
people say.
Do you know what is called "leaves?"
That's the first Tlingit you didn't know.   160
(N.D.) Is it made to acquire something?
Yeah!   Yeah!
It is known here that they were imported from
          over there.
This was told to us.
I never wanted to try those things.
It is really strictly handled, they say.
They are the ones,
they are the ones
that were made for things like money.
And these too were made correctly.   170
Maybe it was something that made you crazy, they say.
They made medicine,
from then on, medicine was made.
Eight days,
for eight days
in the morning
no
food was eaten
and no water,
water,   180

in the morning
tlél
at duxá
ka tlél héen
héen   180
tlél héen duna.
Aagáa tlax kúnax át koowaháa
springtime
April.
Aagáa wé yeisú they try it.
Adax áwé keitl
daxkustéeyin
daxduhéixwayin.
S'ukkoox'aaxw
yóo duwasáakw wéit   190
wé keitl.
Tlél ch'a tléix' yóo s u.átgin
wé woosh kik'iyán.
Yéi yakyee
yá s'ootaat
wé hunxu.aach
áwé s'é nagútch
yá gooch.
Tsu a eeti.aa
tsu a eeti.aa.   200
Haahá!
Wáa nanéi sáwé kik'.aat koowaháa
wé shaawát wé du éek'.
Awé
wé kúxdei kundaháa
yá gáan áwé áa yux nalnúkch yóo.
Haahá!
K'idéin kúxdei kundaháa.

Aagáa áwé
a kát wakshoowagóo   210
wé át
wé xóots
wé du kaaniyán.
"I éek' hás áwé
ax yís daak has ayamdi.át
He'
Hé!

no water was drunk.
Then spring really returned,
spring time
April.
Now they tried.
Then there used to be
dogs
trained with medicine.
"Chewing Ribs"
was the name
of the dog.   190
Those brothers
didn't go searching just once.
Today
this morning
the eldest
would go
to the hill.
Then the next one
then the next one.
Ah, ha!   200
At one point it was the turn of the youngest
of the woman's brothers.
When spring
returned
she would go outside, groping her way, like this.
Ah, ha!
Spring finally returned.

That's when
the animal,
the brown bear,   210
had a vision
of his brothers-in-law.
"Your brothers
are making medicine against me.
Oh, oh.
Oh, oh.
It seems like it's the youngest who will get me.
Be brave."
That's what he told her, what the one with her   220
told the woman
and her children too,

tle wé kik'.aa jeet xat gugatee yei yáx áwé
        yatee.
I gu.aax x'wán."
Yóo áwé adaayaká wé ash xáni yéi yateeyi aa   220
wé shaawát
wé du yátx'i tsú
dáxnáx.
"I gu.aax x'wán.
Ch'a has du jeet xat natéeni x'wán i gu.aax,
wé i éek' hás has du jeet."
Aagáa wé át wé shaawát ch'u tle hóoch'i aayídei
        gíwé aan yóo x'ala.atgi nuch.
"Eesháan ax éek'.
Líl wáa sás has daa eenéik"
yóo áwé adaayaká nooch.   230
"Wé kik'.aa,
Wé kik'.aa i éek' áwé, hú áwé."
Ayá
adax wé shaawát
ch'u súgaa dágáa yóo oowajée wé shaawát.
Awé té
déix yatee yéi kwdigéi.
Awé at xaayí ch'u tle yá atxá
tle a tóo yaa al.átch
ch'a tlákw.   240
Ch'u tle wé yéi anasnéi áwé,
"Haahá! "
Daa sá yóo héidei dultin át yéi wé du waagí
        yati.
Ha gwáa, át gutu.ádi áwé xóots.
"Haahá!
Haandéi kkwagóot wé i éek'.
Gu.aax x'wán."
Ch'a yeisú
yeisú kee.á yéi wuneiyí teen áwé
wé du toowú neil kamdligás',   250
wé hú.
Yáat
tle yáa neil kawulgáas'i áwé
wéit tle wé s'eenáa wáa sá yateeyi yé.
Wé frashlight yóo duwasáagu yéi gíwé utee.
Tle yóo áwé tle kamdligás'
wé neilnáx.

both of them.
"Be brave.
When I fall into their hands, be brave,
when I fall into your brothers' hands."
At that time the woman would beg the animal
        with all she could.
"Have pity on my brothers.
Don't do anything to them,"
she would say to it.
"The younger one,   230
your younger brother will be the one."
From then
he already knew what the woman
was going to do.
There were two
stones this size.
Each time they ate
she'd roll them secretly
in his food.
When she finished doing that,   240
"There!"
But it seemed to him as if she had done it
        openly.
Surely the bear was an animal of the forest.
"There he is!
Your brother is coming here.
Be brave."
Just as soon,
as soon as it became dawn
his thoughts shot in,
his thoughts.   250
Here,
when they shot inside
they were just like a beam of light,
maybe they were just like a flashlight.
That is how they shot
through the house.
He caught the beams right there.
He snapped them back outside.
These were people's thoughts, it's said.   260
Because of that the black bear
and the brown bear
can see people.

Tle yáax' áwé aawasháat wé át.
Tle gándei ashakaawal'íx'.
Ayá kaa toowú yú.á yéi yatee.   260
They see it.
A tuwáadáx áwé wé s'eek ku.aa
ka wé xóots.
They're pretty hard.
Awé wé á, a koowú tlél
tlél a káx yóo oogútk
áyá kaa toowóo.
Wáa yateeyi káa tle
yóo a neiléet a koowóot kawulgáas'i
ch'u tle gándei ashakool'íxch.   270
That's why they can't found it.
Há'!
Haahá!
Cha ch'a wé yéi asa.áax áwé tsá
wé yéi ash daayakaayí
aagáa áwé tsá
yá gáanax áwé a koowú x'é áwé áa yux woogoot
        wé shaawát.
Yáat
yá du kichyát áwé al.át áwé
áwé té   280
áwé
té du jee yéi yateeyi,
tle yú íkdei
wé shaa yá
wé kukamdlit'ix'i
crust.
Tle yá a kináa yan aawatée,
that thing is rolled down
ka tsu wé tléix'aa aawat'ei.

Awé shaa yáx áwé yaa nagút.   290

Ch'u tle amsikóo tle
wé du keidlí
we du keidlí ash een át woo.aat.
Há'!
Ch'u yaa nagúdi áwé
look like it
at wusineex'i yáx yatee wé dleit ká.

They're pretty hard to find.
That's why he couldn't find it,
why he couldn't find the den,
because of his thoughts.
When a man's thoughts
are shot inside its den,
he snaps them back toward the entrance.   270
That's why they can't find it.
Heh.
Ah, ha.
When she heard this from him,
when he told her those things,
that's when
the woman finally went out to the entrance of
        the den.
Here
she put those stones
between her legs,
those stones   280
she had,
then, toward the beach,
on the side of the mountain,
on the frozen
crust
she rolled them down,
those things rolled down
and he found one.

He walked along the side of the mountain.   290

That dog of his
knew right then,
that dog of his that hunted with him.
Heh!
While it was going along
it acted
as if it got a scent of something on the snow.
It ran around sniffing.
Here it was where the stone had rolled down,
        wasn't it?
Up that way   300
he followed it.
The people of today

Tle yóo áwé át wujixeex.
Kach wé té áwé áx yeik kaawagwadli yé ásíwé;
kíndei   300
ch'a a ítx yaa nagút wé.
Tlél yéi yeedadi aayí
lingít yáx utéeyin áyú ch'áagu aayí.
Tough.
Yáadáx gúshé x'oon kaay sá just one day they run
        over there
Yeedát ku.aa....
Daasá wé?
"Haahá!
Haahá! xat kamlisei i éek'"
yóo áwé adaayaká yú.a.   310
Aagáa áwé yáat
tsaagál'.
Yáat áwé áx kootsúwch
kach yóo a oox ásíyú yéi du tuwáa yatee yú
        shaawát.
Aax
dákdei akayéesh.
Aagáa áwé yeisú x'éigaa
a yáa x'amdigáx'.
"Eesháan ax éek'," yóo.

Ch'a tle yóox áwé kei nagút.   320
Há'!
Ch'a yáak'oodéi áwé keenaadéi samduwa.áx
áwé
wé keitl.
Tlél yá yeedadi keidlí yáx utéeyin.
Has awuskóowun chú tle yá lingít yáx
long time ago.
Há'! gwál yóo éil ká tsú ch'u yéi téeyin
áyú keitl.

Héit   330
tle hé kéenax.á
ch'u tlákw all the time áwé yéi téeyin át
        x'éidei awugoodí.
They can't go straight up.
Tle ch'as wé kéenax.á.
Ch'a daa sá ch'a yá kaa daa.ádi aadéi dugéech.

are not like the ones of long ago.
They were tough.
If they went from here no matter
        how many miles they had to go
        they'd make it in a day.
And now.....
What are they?
"Ah hah!
Ah, ha! your brother's getting close,"
he told her, it is said.   310
Then like when
spears
are hung from rafters
is how his teeth looked to the woman.
He pulled them out
from there.
That is when she really
begged of him,
"Pity my brother," she said.

He was approaching up there.   320
Heh.
Then
suddenly the bear heard the dog barking
from the topside.
It wasn't like a dog of today.
They were as smart as humans
long ago.
Well, probably they were the same on the coast too,
those dogs.

Over there   330
it is always done like this when the entrance
        of a den was approached.
From the upper side.
You can't go straight up.
Only from the upper side.
Whatever, even a piece of clothing, was tossed in.
That is what he did.
He tossed his mitten
into the entrance.
He could only see the paw
inside   340

Ha yéi áwé adaané.
Hé du tsáax'i
a x'awooldéi agéech.
Ch'as yá a jín áwé axsatínch
tle yá neil   340
tle yá du díx'dei.

"I gú.áax x'wán.
Yux yaa kkwagóot
du jiyeex'.
Du een ash kakkwalyát i éek'"
yéi áwé adaayaká yú.á.

Yóo wé yíndei áwé
akaawadóok.
Aagáa áwé áa ash shukaawajáa.
"Du jeet xat natéeni i éek'   350
líl ch'a koogéiyi x'wán yá ax doogú.
Tle s du een kananeek.
Du een kananeek.
Yóo gagaan yanax yéi xixji yé
adasháan x'wán
ax doogú yax has ayagaagaxeech."
Ách áwé ch'u yeedát yéi daaduné.
Ch'u yáat'aa sh kalneekdáx.
Tlél ch'u koogéiyi yóox duxeech.
Tle ch'as yóo a yeex at dultsaak.   360
Tle yóo gagaan anax yéi xixji yé dasháan
yax yéi yaduxíchch
á a x'éidáx.

Yáat'aa a x'awoolt uwagút.
Ch'a a dayéen hán.
Hé'!
Ch'a aan áwé
wé keitl tlél x'eidaxwétlx.
De du jeet wootee wé xóots.
Tle yá a xán áwé át uwagút.   370
Daa sáyú tsu ts'as aadéi wé a koowóo?
Aadéi x'amduwataan.

"Ix'aguxdaxwéitl," yú.á
S'ukkoox'aaxw."

then sweeping behind.

"Be brave,
I will go out
to him.
I will play with your brother "
he said to her, it's said.

The bear lured him
into coming down.
That's when he instructed her.
"When your brother finishes with me   350
don't be careless with my skin.
You tell them right away.
You tell him.
Drape my skin
with the head
toward the setting sun."
That's why it's still done now.
From this very story.
It is never tossed away carelessly.
A pole is placed under it thus.   360
It is hung and pointed
towards the sunset,
from his words.

He came right to the entrance there.
He stood facing it.
Ah ha!
But even at that
his dog didn't tire from barking.
He had already killed the bear.
He went up to it.   370
What else was there in the den?
Someone spoke from inside.

"Your mouth will get tired,
Chewing Ribs?"

He just stood there.
What's more, his sister came out of there,
the one who had been gone
so long.

Ch'a at hán.
Daa sáwé tsú du dlaak' anax yux woogoot
wé de ch'áakw
hél koostéeyin.
Ayaawadlaak.
Tlax wé at yátx'i tsú   380
dáxnáx.
"Adax áyá
yá ax doogú
ch'u tleix x'wán i jee yéi natí,"
yóo áwé ash daayaká.
Aagáa áwé ash ée akoolgúks'
áwé du x'asheeyí.
"Yáat'aa x'wán gashí
yá ax doogú yax yageexíchni"
yóo áwé ash daayaká.   390

     (At this point Tom Peters
     sings two songs. See notes.)

          Part Two

Awé
áwé xóots
áwé kaxwlineegí.
Aagáa
ch'u tle yax wunatee.
Wé du aanikwaani xoox wunadáa.
Aagáa áwé
ch'a wáa sá kustéeyin áyú ch'áakw
ch'u yéi áwé.
Aagáa du jee yéi yatee wé du xúx   400
doogú yéeyi
aadéi ash daayakáayi yé.
Aaa, "gageegoodí x'wán
yá ax doogú
naax nidayeesh."
Aaa; yéi áwé ash daayakáayin.
Adax wé du yátx'i tsú
ch'u tle du t'aakt uwawát.
Aagáa
nagagút   410

He got her.
The children also,   380
the two of them.
"From there
this skin of mine
you will always keep with you,"
is what he had said to her.
That's when he taught her
this song of his.
"You will sing this
when you hang my skin,"
he said to her.   390

        (At this point, Tom Peters
        sings two songs. See Notes.)

            Part Two

It was
the brown bear
that I was telling about.
Then
things were settled.
She became accustomed to her village people.
Then
she lived the way
she had as long ago.
It was then she had her husband's   400
former skin
the way he had told her to do.
Yes. "When you go out
you will put this skin of mine
on your back."
Yes; this is what he once told her.
From then her children
had reached her size.
Then
she would leave them   410
when people would hunt ground squirrels.
She would only go a short way.
How did she get the squirrels?
Only the mound of her pack would be seen

áyá tsálgi xoot anga.át.
Ch'a wéidei áwé nagútch.
Wáa sá kwshé anasneich áwé tsálk?
Ch'u du kagoochk'í yaa gaxíxch neildéi.
Ch'u tléi wé kgwagoodí wé tsá
wé du xúx
doogú yéeyi naát oodayeeshch.
Aaa.
Waa yateeyi yéix' áwé wé tléikw
tléikw xoodéi kgwagoodí.   420
Ch'u tle yá neildáx gunéi wugoodí teen áwé náat
     oodayeeshch.
Tle ch'u shugu xóotsx
áwé nasteech.
Wé du yátx'i tsú.
Yú dikée xéel'i aaniká,
wé tléikw xoo.
Wé shaa yáa daak ugootch.
Wé du yátx'i tsú ash een.
Ha de x'ioondahéen yéi nasgéet sáwé   430
wé du éek' has
wé s du tlaa áyá yei s adaayaká,
"Atlée!
Ax dlaak' s'é yéi yanaská
haa tuwáa sigóo ch'a du een ach katoolyádi."
Aagáa áwé aan akanéek,
"Tléik'!
Tléik'!
Tléil a yísx ustí
yei s xat daaneiyí.
Aaa; tléil ch'u shugu yá ax kustí ax jee   440
     yéi utí.
Áwé
wé ax xúx
du doogú
náat kadayísh
tle tléil yá tlagu tundatáani, ax tóo yéi utéex.
Ách áwé, tléik'!
Ha ch'a yéi yéi xat teeyí.
Ch'a wáa yeikuwáat' sá yee xoo yéi xat gugateé."
Ha ch'a aan áwé,
"Yei s'é yanaská atlée!   450
Ax dlaak',

moving along to her house.
Only when she was ready to go
would she pull on
the skin that was her husband's.
Yes.
At times it would be going after berries,
when she was going to get berries.   420
Just as she was leaving home, as she started
        out, she would pull it on.
She would become
a real bear.
Her children too.
Up there where last year's berries grew
in the berry patch.
She would come out on the mountain.
Her children with her too.
After doing this so many times,
the brothers of hers
asked their mother   430
"Mother!
will you tell my sister
we want to just play a game with her?"
That was when she told her mother
"No!
No!
It is not right
for them to do this to me.
Yes. I am not the same anymore as I used to be.   440
When
I pull on
my husband's
skin
I don't think my old thoughts any more.
This is why. No!
Let me be.
Let me live among you for as long as possible."
But still the brothers asked her
"Mother! please ask   450
our sister
to let us play with her."
How many times
they must have asked this.
Finally she said to them

ch'a du een ash kanax̱toolyát."
De x'oondaheen áyá
yéi yanak̲áa g̲iwé.
Yeisú yéi a daayak̲á.
"Haa, haa, góok!
Gook!
Ax̱ een has ash kung̲alyát."
Tle yéi a daayak̲aayídáx̱ áwé du tláa tle
woogoot.   460
Ch'u tle ch'a yeisú neildáx̱ g̲unéi wugoodí tín áwé
        náat amdiyísh,
wé du x̱úx̱ doogú.
Ch'u shugu xóots wáa sá nateech.
Wé du yátx'i tsú
wé dáx̱náx̱ yateeyi
yá du daa áwé át woo.aat.
Wé keenaa áwé
wé k̲aa kináa áwé wé shaa yát téen
áwé tléik̲w x̱oo.
Aag̲áa áwé áa daak uwa.át.   470
Ha tlél g̲íyá yéi s oojí.
Awé tláak̲
wé chooneit
áwé
loon.
Wé loon áwé a x̱'éidei s aawatsúw.

Adax̱ ch'as wé ash káx̱ woogoodi aa
áwé du éek' tle yóo eetiyádi.
Ha hú áwé
déix̱ yatee du chooneidí.   480
Tle yóo x'éig̲aa tláak̲
áa yéi dag̲aatee.
Awé
choogwéil
yóo duwasáakw áwé.
Awé
wé chooneit a tóo yéi dax̱sitix̱x̱'u át.
Séi yax̱ kadutee.
Awé tle a tóodei amli.aat.
Tléil wé du hunx̱u hás aadéi k̲uwanugu yáx̱ áwé
        adaa.unéi yú.á.   490
Tle ch'a altín áwé.

"Well, okay, let's go!
Let's go!
Let them play with me."
After she said this to her mother
she left.   460
As soon as she left home she pulled on
the skin of her husband.
She looked just like a brown bear.
Her children too
the two of them
went alongside of her.
It was up there
above everyone on the face of the mountain
among the berries.
This is when she came out there.   470
Maybe they didn't believe she would.
The blades
of the arrows
were
pieces of bark.
Pieces of bark were placed on the tip.

Except the blade of the one who found her,
her brother, the youngest one.
It was he,
there were two arrows of his.
They each had   480
a real arrowhead.
There was
what is called
a quiver.
Arrows
are kept inside it.
It's worn around the neck.
He put the arrows inside it.
He didn't do to his sister what his
        older brothers did, it's said.   490
He only watched.
From then his older brothers
stalked her.
The way an animal
is struck with arrows
is how they did it.

Adax áwé du hunxu hás
tle a daadéi áwé s uwa.át.
Wáa sáwé chooneit
tin áwé daa sá dut'úkdi,
yéi áwé.
Tle wé shux'aa aayí
tle wé shux'aa aayí
wé du éet lagáas',
aagáa áwé a sé mduwa.áx.   500
"I itnáx aa."
Yáax' áwé has du xoo ayamdigút.
Tle x'oonínáx sá kwshí hé? Tle tléil tsu daatx
        sá s ustí.
Wé du yátx'i tsú.
Awé yéi nanéi, aagáa áwé s du kéek'
wé déix tláak du jee yei siteeyi
aax kei amsitée.
        (Slap!
            Slap!)
Aawaják
wé du dlaak'.
Ha, that's the end of it.   510

When the first one's arrow,
when the first one's arrow
struck her
was when her cry was heard.   500
"From behind you."
Here's when she turned on them.
How many of them were there? They were helpless
        against her.
And her children too.
When they were dead is when the younger brother,
the one with the two arrowheads,
drew them out.
    (Slap!
      Slap!)
He killed her,
that sister of his.
Now that is the end.   510

Xóotsx X'ayaakuwdligadi Shaawát
Naakil.aan x'éidáx sh kalneek

Xát
xát aadéi
xaan kaduneegi yé
aadéi xaan dutlaagu yé áyá yá
yá sh kalneek.
Yóo
Gunanaa áyá
yá ku.oo
yá dáak ká
Gunanaa.   10
Áyá
hás du daat sh kalneek áyá.
Yáadu á, yáa yagiyee kakkwanéek
jinkaat yaawaxée
yá dís
aadéi xaan kaduneegi yé yáx.
Yóo áyá kadunéek shux'aanáx
yá sh kalneek.
Kúdaxch kuwa.óo yá ku.oo
yá Gunanaa.   20
Aadáx áyá
yá kutaan.
Kutaandéi yaa kunahéin.
Taakw.eetí
yóo áyá wduwasáa; taakw a eetí áyá.

The Woman Who Married the Bear
told by Frank Dick, Sr.

Me.
This is the way
it was told to me,
the way this ancient story
was told to me.
These people,
are Athabaskans,
those living
in the Interior,
Athabaskans.   10
And
this story is about them.
This is it; I will tell it today,
the tenth day
of the month,
the way it was told to me.
This story
is how it was first told.
These Athabaskans
lived really isolated.   20
Next
it was summer.
The season was changing to summer.
Spring
is what they called it; the remains of winter.

A áyá
yaana.eit áyá yaa kana.éin.
Ayá yá shaatk'.
Du éesh,   30
du éesh kéilk' áyá
aan engage-x̲ sitee.
Ash gug̲asháa.
Ayá yana.eitg̲áa aawa.aat.
He', yéi wdudzinee yá yana.eit.
Yáadáx̲ naduyáan.
Ayá ha wáa sáyá
wáa yoo akoo.átgi sáyá
wulik'oots
yá du aayí yá shaatk'.
Ch'u tle   40
yaa ch'u ana.ádi áyá
ch'u ana.ádi áyá
yá xóots
a x̲'us.eetí káa s woo.aat; yeisú áx̲ yaawagút.
Has du shuká
has du shukáx̲ yaa nagút.
Ayá
a eetíx' áyá yán kawdliyás'
yá shaatk'.
Ayá a káx' áyá kéi x̲'uswushix̲'íl'.   50
Ach áyá atx̲ gadaháan ldakát du daa yéi yatee.
Ach áyá yéi ayawsikaa.
"Wáa sá kwshí yáa g̲é
ch'as k̲aa x̲'anaadéi s al'íl' nukch g̲é
tuk̲x̲'ag̲ékákwx'?"
Yá yoo x̲'atánk
aadéi kaawageiyi yé.
De tsu du yeeg̲áa ak̲éen.
Yan sh isnée áwé tsá g̲unéi aawa.át.
X'oon waa sákwshei aax̲ aawa.aat   60
yáax' áwé wulik'oots
wé ách yaa nasyaan át
ayaan dzaasí.
Yóo áyá wduwasáa yá tíx'
ayaan dzaasí.
Ach áyá a yáx̲ at g̲waak̲óo,
"ch'u ayaan dzaasí ng̲wak'oots jeewahaayi át."
Yéi x̲'ayaduk̲á.

And this
Indian celery was growing.
This young woman
was engaged
to her father's nephew   30
her father's sister's child.
He was going to marry her.
And the women went for Indian celery.
Wow! they collected Indian celery.
They were packing them on their backs.
What happened anyway?
After they walked for a long way
the straps broke
on the young woman's pack.
While   40
they were still walking,
while they were still walking
they came upon
bear tracks; it had just gone through there.
Ahead of them,
it went ahead of them.
This
young woman
stepped in the leavings.
And her foot slipped on it.   50
So when she stood up it was all over her.
So then she said this to it,
"Why is it
they always crap in our way
the big basket butt?"
This was all
she said.
Every one was sitting waiting for her again.
They started going again after she cleaned
          herself up.
I wonder how many of them and how they got out
          of there.   60
Here they broke--
the things she was packing with,
Athabaskan thongs.
This is what they called this rawhide:
Athabaskan thongs.
This is why there is a proverb,

Ei.ei.ei.ei. nak'útsch.
Ch'u adaa.us.áxwch   70
deisgwách xáanaa.
Hóoch'
du nák aawa.aat tle.
Aadáx gadaháan aadáx gunéi góot tsu
       adaasa.áxwdáx áyá
gunéi uwagút tsu.
Aagáa du géidei yanagút ch'u shóogu yú du sáni
yú du éesh kéilk'.
Yú aan engage-x siteeyí.
Ch'u shóogu hú áyá du géidei yaanagút.

Haa, ash éet x'eiwatán.   80
Ash éet x'atáan áyá du jeetx awsitee.
Tle awsitee
a jiyís.
Dei sgé yaa s gaa.áat; dei sgé yaa s gaa.áat á.
Tlax wáa yóo s ku.áat de xeewa.át tle.
Ax' áyá uwaxéet has uwa.át, "Gaa déi ch'a yáax'
       has gaxée."
Ach áwé áa s uwaxée.
Hél wáa sá utí.
Lingít áyú du waakx',
ch'u tle lingít, ch'u shóogu lingít.   90
Hél tsu wáa sá utí.
Haaw! wé gán
shóot has awdi.ák.
A gookt has kéen; has at xá.
Gwál wudawú gé
a x'eis.
Yan née yan has at wuxaayí áwé
tayeedéi s woo.aat.
Hél wáa sá uteeyí.
Ch'a lingít ch'u shóogu lingít.   100

Gwál tlax dé keix'akaadéi áwé shákdei.
A dakádeen aa yax uwatáa.
Wé shaawát dakádin áayax uwatáa.
Tle kéi wusgeedí
du toowú yóo woonei.
A x'akwtóot wudlinúk.
Ax' áyá yé

"Even an Athabaskan thong would break."
This is what we say.
Ei.ei.ei.ei, the straps would break.
Toward evening   70
she was still tying the straps.
Gone!
Everyone had left her.
Then she got up and started walking again;
        after she finished tying it
she started walking again.
When he came toward her he was just like her
        paternal uncle,
her father's sister's child,
the one she was engaged to.
He was just like him coming toward her.

So, he spoke to her.   80
After he spoke to her he took the bundle from her.
He packed the bundle
for her.
They went along for so long; they went along
        for so very long.
They walked so long it was now dark.
Now they came to a place to overnight.
        "Let's just spend the night here."
So they spent the night there.
There wasn't anything different.
He was a Tlingit in her eyes,
a human being, a real human.
There wasn't even anything different.   90
Now! With this wood
they built a fire.
They were sitting next to it; they were eating.
Maybe she brought
food for them.
When they were done, when they finished eating,
they went to bed.
Because there wasn't anything different.
Just a human, a real human.   100

It must have been early dawn.
He rolled away from her.
He rolled away from the woman.

tle tóo aawanúk wé xóots.
Adayéen aa yax̱ uwatáa; tsu ch'u shóogu lingítx̱
        sitee.   110
Aag̱áa awé yéi ash daayaká,
"Hél wáa sá i toowú utéek.
Hél wáa sá ik̲kwasanei.
Tle k̲u.aa áyá ik̲kwasháa.
Sh tugéit x̱at yaydzikáa
yáa lingít wakkáax̱'.
Tle l ushk'idéin x̱at yaysik̲áa.
Ách áyá
hél k̲u.aa ik̲kwajaak̲; tle ik̲kwasháa k̲u.aa."
Tlél tsu wáa sá du toowú utí.   120
Ch'u shóogu lingít du wáakx̱'.
Tlél tsu wáa sá utí.
Haa, wáannée sáyá k̲aa x̱oot has uwa.át.

Yeis.
Yeisdéi wáa k̲unáax̱' sá x̱áat héeni yée yéi teex̱.
Aag̱áa áwé
tsá has woo.aat
x̱áat aanídei.

At x'aan
ch'a yáa haa yáx̱
ch'a yáa haa yáx̱ lingít yáx̱.   130
Has at x'áan
du wáakx̱'.
Atx'aan sákw áyú yéi has adaané.
Ayú yá gán
yú du éen sháa
dusgútx̱'.
Tle yú héen táadax̱ shaak̲ áyá yei daaduné
wudlitl'ák̲'.
Awé hú k̲ú.aa áwé
ch'as wusixugu aa áwé aag̱áa k̲ushée wé gán.   140
E! wáa sá gagánch
wé du éen aa has aayí k̲u.aa wé.
ch'a yaadachóon wuduwaxugu yáx̱ áwé nateech.
Haaw! wáannée sáyá háadéi anaa.aat
tle lingít yáx̱.
Haa!
K'e yáa x̱át.

When she awoke
she was startled.
Her fingers felt through his fur.
This is when
she felt it was a bear.
He rolled over to face her; he looked like
        a human being again.
That is when he told her,
"Don't be afraid.   110
I won't hurt you.
I am going to marry you though.
You insulted me
in front of those people.
You cussed at me.
But
I won't kill you; but you will be my wife."
She still didn't feel any different.
He was just like a human being in her eyes.
There wasn't even anything different.   120
Now, at one point, they had come upon the others.

Fall.
Toward fall when salmon come up the streams.
That's when
they started going
to the land of the salmon.

They were drying salmon
just like us,
just like us humans.
To her eyes   130
they were drying salmon.
They were getting salmon for dryfish.
The women with her
were packing
the firewood.
They were getting drift logs right out of the water,
water logged.
But she
was looking only for dry wood.
Wow! How it would burn   140
but the fires of the others,
would look as if they were only steaming.

Xát
neil xwaagút.
Ax kinaak.ádi kaax kei kkwadatée   150
kakkwakéek.
Yéi áyá,
tle neildéi has na.aadí áyá
yá has du kinaak.ádi
kaax kéi has adatéech.
Kawdukéegi gankáx' áwé koodukíkch.
He'!
dáat yáx sá gagánch wé gán.
Du aayí ku.aa áwé tle yakoolkées'ch
wé héenx sateeyí.   160
Wáanáx sá yéi kdayéini?
Ach áwé áa shakawduwajáa yáa du yáx sháach
wudlitl'ak'i aa.
Neildéi na.aadí.
Haaw,
kaa jixan.ádi áwé,
áwé has du jixan.ádi áwé has du ooxú
wéi aatlénx'.
Séitx kéi kdutéech.
T'áa yáx daak has awutéeych.   170
Ch'u tle t'áa áyú yú has du hídi
tle lingít yáx.
Yax daak woodutéeych
dákdei yadul.áat
wé
kaa naa.ádi.

Ch'u yéi, ch'u yéi, tle ch'u yéi áwé tsu.
Gwá! wáannée sáyá yeik kukandak'ít' tsu.
He'!
xáat haa déi yéi daaduné.   180
Táakw niyís at dux'áan.
At x'áan.
At dux'áan.
Uháan haa wáakx' ku.aa s tlél yéi s utí.
Hás axá áyú haa wáakx' ku.aa.
Hásch ku.aa has at x'áan áwé ch'a yá haa yáx.
Gunanaa jiyáx
has at x'áan.

Now! at one point they were coming in
just like humans.
Well.
Take me for example.
Me,
I come inside,
when I take my coat off
I'll shake it.   150
This is how,
as they were coming in
they were taking off
their coats.
When they shook them they would shake them over
          the fire.
Wow!
What did it burn like?
Hers though would keep going out,
being water logged.
Who knows why it was like this!   160
So the other women showed her what to do
with the wet ones,
when they were coming in.
Now,
their weapons,
their weapons are their teeth,
these big ones.
They would remove them from their necks.
They would hang them on the wall.   170
Their home was surely made of wood planks
just like humans.
They would hang them up
set them against the wall
and
their clothes.

They did this over and over again.
Hey, at what point was it they were coming
          down again?
Boy!
they were bringing in fish.   180
Fish were being dried for winter.
Dryfish.
Fish were being dried.

Ldinaxk'iyéidei yan at dux'áan
ldinaxk'iyéidei yan at dux'áan áwé tsá   190
yéi kuyaawakaa.
"Haahá
de at daxwuduwaxoon
táakw aanídei."
K'e uhaan yú
yú at x'aan aanídáx yú táakwx' áa yéi haa teeyí
aadéi kux tuda.aatch haa aaníx'.
Yéi áwé at wuduwaxoon.
He'!
At x'éeshi daat yáx sá yakoogéi   200
has du jee.
Uháanch kwás tlél tooteen
yá has du at x'aaní.

Áwé de
de du kaanáx at wootee
wé yaa na.át
wé kíndei.
Ach áwé yéi ayawsikaa wé du xúx
(wé shaawát x'éigaa
a x'éigaa koowatee)   210
"Ch'a yáat dé."
Ayaawatín
du éek' hás át na.átji yé.
Ayaawatín,
ách áwé á
aanx has axlayeix.

Tláakw kaaxát wéit'át tlein
wé a koowú kahaa.
Du waakx' ku.aa hít áwé,
hít áwé dulyéix.   220
He'!
yan uwanée wé hít.
A yeenáx yéi s uwa.át.
A yeenáx yéi has áat
x'oon áa has uxée sá kwshí wé,
du x'awoolí daak wujixíx
wé naagas'éi.

De has du x'awoolí daak wushxeexí áwé

To our eyes though this is not what they're doing.
To our eyes they're just eating it.
But they were drying the fish though just like us.
They were drying the fish
like Athabaskans.

After they had dried plenty of fish,
after they had dried plenty of fish, then   190
someone said,
"Well,
we're packing up now
to go to our winter land."
Like us, for example;
from our dryfish camp
we go back to our village for the winter.
This is the way they packed up.
Good!
They had
plenty of dryfish at hand.   200
But we don't see
their dryfish.

And now
she was already worn out
walking
up the mountain.
So she said to her husband,
(they did
what this woman said)
"This place will do."   210
She recognized
where her brothers went.
She recognized it,
that was why
she wanted to make it her home.

This huge animal worked fast
digging the den.
But to her eyes it was a house,
it was a house being built.
Wow!   220
The house was finished.
They went in.

yéi ash yawsikaa.
"He!   230
wáa sáyá keeya.óo chxánk'?
Lingít x'usya.áak áyá.
Lingít x'usya.áak áyá iya.óo
chxánk'.
Yú keenaawú
áx kadéix' yé.
Yú taakw kanadá áx kadéix' yé."
Awé ash een aawach'éx'.
Ach áwé aa kei has uwa.át tsu.
Ax' áwé tsá   240
aan awliyéx tsu.
Tle áa yéi s wootee.
Yáax' áwé tsá
taakw.eetí.
Taakw.eetídei áwé.
Daak has ayawdinák wé du éek' hás.
Wududziteen.
Wududziteen xóots x'us.eetí; t'akkáx yawlishóo
        du x'us.eetí.

Awé yéi duwasáagu
yéi dusáagun ch'áagu káawuch   250
"keitl wududzinook."
Gadusnúkch áwé yóo áwé duwasáakw keitl.
Keitl tín aawa.aat.
A áyá yéi wduwasáa.
Keitl tín has woo.aat.
Aawa.aat.
Tle ch'u tle
ch'u tle yú hít yeedáx yux wu.aadí yú du éek'
        hás
yú chooneit yáx áwé neildéi kalgáas'
has du kutéeni   260
wé keitl,
neildéi kalgas'i yáx yú chooneit.
Neildéi kalgas'i yáx áwé yatee.
K'e hé gagaan.
Goot'á sá anax kuyawóoli yeináx neilx kadagáan.
A yáx áwé kuwanóok.
Awé áa kdagútch.
Gándei kúxdei ashakool'íx'ch.

When they had gone in,
when they had spent how many nights there,
this fox
ran out in front of the door.

When it ran out in front of their door
it said to them,
"Hey,
how is this you're living, grandchild?   230
This is a path for people.
You are living in a path for people,
grandchild.
Up above there
is the slide area.
The winter avalanche area."
He pointed it out to them.
So they moved up again.
There finally
he built a den again.   240
This is where they lived.
Here finally
it was spring.
It was toward spring.
Her younger brothers were making medicine.
They saw them.
They saw the bear tracks; her footprints
        were trailing up beside him.

This is what they called,
this is what the men of long ago called   250
"carrying a dog."
They'd carry a dog is what they called it.
They went with dogs.
This is what it was called.
They left with dogs.
They went.
It was when
her brothers left the house
the eyesight
of the dogs   260
was shooting into the den like arrows,
like arrows shooting into the den.
That's how it was shooting into the den.

Tleiyéi yéi nateech.
Yáax' áwé tsu   270
tle ch'u shóogu.
Neil yakoolgeechch
wé keitl ka wé hás
has du kutéeni.
Yóo áwé wuduwasáa
has du kutéeni áwé.
Ch'a wéit'át waakx' áwé yéi yatee
ch'a wé yatseeneit.
Wé xóots waakx' áwé yéi yatee.
Wé káa kutéeni   280
neildéi yakalgéech.
Ax' áwé s gadagútch.
Gándei ool'íx'ch.
Wáanée sáwé du jikaanáx wootee.
Hél ayawudlaak.
Aagáa áwé x'awoolt loowagúk
wé keitl
has du x'awool.
Haahá!

Du kaanáx yaa at gatée áwé wé   290
wéit'át tlein.
Aagáa áwé yéi ayawsikaa
wé du shát.
"I gu.aa yáx x'wán ja'.
De ax kaanáx at wootee.
De ax kaanáx wootee.
Hél kúxde yóo xwsanei."
At k'átsk'u
aawasáa
aadéi akgwasáakw yé.   300
Saa a jeet aawatée
wé du yádi.
Tsu káax sateeyí ka ch'u shaawátx sateeyí
aadéi akgwasáakw yé.
Aagáa áwé tsá áa wdihaan du jixan.ádi.
Haahá!
Hél sh yayeedé akakgwasgaan.
Hél du eedéi.
Ach áwé yéi ayawsikaa wé du xúx.
"Ihí!   310

Take the sun for example.
Through wherever there are holes the beams shine in.
That's how it was happening.
The bear would jump to it.
He would break the arrows back outside.
It would stop for a while.
Then it would start again   270
the same way.
The dogs and
their eyesight
would come piercing into the den.
Their eyesight
is what they called this.
It only looks like this
to the bear.
It's like this in the bear's eyes.
The humans' eyesight   280
was piercing into the den.
He would jump up to it.
He would break it outward.
At one point it overpowered him.
He couldn't handle it.
That's when the dogs
ran up to the entrance,
to their entrance.
Now!

As they were overpowering   290
that big animal,
he told
his wife,
"Be brave, darling.
It's too much for me.
It's too much for me now.
I can't hold them back."
He named
the child
by what it would be called.   300
He gave a name
to each child.
According to whether it was a boy or a girl
he would name them.
Then he stood up for his weapons.

Ihí ja'
ihí!
Yéi x'andulyéich.
Yéi yoo x'adudli.átk.
"Ja', ihí!
I kaani yán át na.atji yé áyá.
Ihí."
Ch'a yéi gwá gushé.
Séitx kéi yéi ajikawdzinéi.
Yax daak yéi ayawsinéi tsu.   320
Yax daak ayaawatée tsu du jixan.ádi.
Aagáa áwé tsá
ch'ú wé neildéi tláakw kadudzixát wé x'awool
wé chooneit.
Awé wé tléix' yateeyi aa áwé neil awaxút' wé
        keitl.
Awé hú ku.aa áwé wé shaawát
tayeedéi awdixeech.
Tayeet as.áa.
Ayaawatín du éek' hás keidlí áyú.

Aagáa áwé yux gugagut nóok yéi ash yawsikaa,   330
"Goosú wéidei i jeet xwaaxích keitl?
Haahí!"
"Tlél keitl áhé tsáax' áhé."
Tsáax' áhé yóo áwé aawasáa aan.
Ach áwé gáant sh wudligás'.

Gáani yux yaa yanas.éini áwé has aawaják.
Tle yóooooooooo
éekdei wooleet.
A ítx kaa loowagook.

Yú éekx' áwé kaa jiyeegáa wootee.   340
Aagáa áwé wé kik'i aa
wé kik'i aa áwé yéi yawdudzikaa,
"Aadéi nagú!
aadéi nagú!

Yux naltl'eet.
Ldakát yá a yee
yux naltl'eet
a yeedáx."

Now!
He was not going to look where he was going.
No, not him.
That is why she said this to her husband,
"Don't,   310
don't, darling,
don't."
That's what they called each other.
That's how couples talk.
"Darling don't,
This is where your brothers-in-law come.
Don't."
Let's leave it at that.
He took his weapons off his neck.
He hung them up on the wall again.   320
He hung up his weapons again.
That was when
these arrows
came fast into the den from the entrance.
He dragged the one dog into the den.
But the woman though
threw it under her.
She had it lying under her.
She recognized it as her brothers' dog.

When the bear was going out he said to her,   330
"Where is the dog I threw in to you?
Give it here."
"It wasn't a dog, it was a glove."
She told him it was a glove.
That's why he dived out.

As the bear was sticking his head out they killed it.
It tumbled aaaáall
the way down the hill.
The dogs ran down after it.

Way down below they were able to handle it.   340
This was when the youngest,
the youngest was told,
"Go up there!
Go up there!

Ch'a áa kéi nagúdi áwé awsiteen
wé chooneit.   350
Wé keitl tsú áwu.
Daawdudzi.áxw.
Wé chooneit l'éex'i yá a x'awoolí
a x'awool goojí
a kát satéen.

"Xát áyá ík'.
Xát áyá.
Tlél ixéixik.
Yee káani áwé.
Du shakwtóot x'áan yaysatí.   360
Du shakwtóot x'áan yaysatí ík'.
I tláa
i tláa yéi s yanaská
ax naa.ádi tín haat has ga.aat."
Ach áwé aadéi woogoot yíndei
akaawaneek.
"Haa káani áwé,
haa káani áwé.
Yéi xát daayaká áx dlaak',
'du shakwtóot x'áan yaysatí   370
yee káani áwé.'"
Háa!
Aadéi nagú!
Yiyják!
Wáa sáyá kuwa.éin yéix'?
Wuduwajági yéix' l gaduxaa?
Aawa.áx.
Ch'a yú dikeedáx.
Yan akawli.áx yú kaa shukaadéi háni áwé.
Yei x'ayaká du x'eis wuduwaják.   380

Ach áwé hú ku.aa wé k'ik'i aa áwé tle dáak
        wujixíx du tláa hás xándei.
Woogoot.
Du tlaa ka du éesh
yéi áwé áa kéi s uwa.át
a naa.ádi tín.
Hél ulgé wé
wé a yádi.
Tle ch'a áa ajeewanák.

Clean it out.
Everything in it
clean out
from inside it."
As he was getting up there he saw
the arrows.   350
The dog was also there.
They were tied up in a bundle.
The broken arrows
were lying at the entrance
on the entrance mound.

"It's me, brother.
It's me.
Don't ever eat that.
He is your brother-in-law.
Put a fire at the fur on his head.   360
Put a fire at the fur on his head, little brother.
Your mother,
tell your mother
to come up here with my clothes."
That is why he went down
and told this.
"It was our brother-in-law,
it was our brother-in-law.
My sister told me,
'Put a fire at the fur on his head,   370
he is your brother-in-law.'"
So!
"Go back up there!
You killed it.
Why shouldn't we, when we've been fasting?
Why not eat what we kill?"
She heard this.
From way up there.
She recognized it was the leader's voice.
He said they killed the bear for him to eat.   380

That's why the youngest brother ran to his parents.
He went.
That's how her mother and father
went up there
with the clothes.

Aan yóo x'awli.át,
wé a kayádi.   390

Xwasakóowun.
Gúnei góot.
Kunáx a kát xat seiwax'ákw
yá a kát gunéi uwagudi shí.
Yá du xúx
a daadáx ashí
yá shí yeik gagóot
wé du xúx
wunaawú,
wudujaagí.   400

Kaldaagéináx áwé tsá
yéi kuyawsikaa
aan yeik ga.áat.
Du x'ayáx wé k'ik'i aa hás.
A tayeet awduwa.ák.
Aawa.aat.
Aagáa áwé tsá koon akaawaneek,"yóodu,
yóodei nay.á.
Yóonáx shatán s'eik"
koon akaawaneek, "yóonáx shatán s'eik   410
s'eek áwé."
Awé aadéi kukaawanáa.
Wuduwaják aax.

A áwé wé
wé kaa shukaadei káa
wé kaa húnxu tlein.
Tlél du tuwáa ushgú du x'éix at wuduteeyí.
Aa kaa jiyawlisík tle.
"Tlél du x'éix at yitéexík.
Ch'á yeeháanch gaxyisakóo wáa sá at gugateeyí   420
du x'éix at yeeyteeyí yáa ax x'akaanáx."
Ach áwé tle du x'éigaa.
Tlé du x'éigaa at wootee.
Hél du x'éix at duteex.
De hóoch'.
De át wudigwáat'.

Tlax wáateeyí sáwé

This child of the bear
was not very big.
So she just left it there.
She was talking
with the cub.

390

I used to know it.
When she started to leave.
I have really forgotten
the song for when she started down.
She was singing
the song about her husband,
when she was coming down,
when her husband
died,
when they killed him.

400

Slowly
she instructed them
while she was walking down with them.
The younger brothers did as she told.
They built a fire under him.
They left.
This is when she told them, "Over there,
go over there.
The smoke rising over there,"
she told them, "The smoke rising over there
is a black bear."

410

That is where she sent them.
They killed the black bear there.

That was
the leader,
the older brother.
He didn't want anyone to feed her.
He kept them from feeding her.
"Don't feed her.
You'll all find out what'll happen
if you feed her against my orders."

420

That was why they obeyed.
They obeyed him.
They didn't feed her anything.
She was a goner.

yóonáx naashóo aas
dúk gíyú,
ch'a yéi aas gwá gíyú,   430
"A k'éedei nagú.
Híl du éex yidasheek.
Ch'á hú
ch'á hú aadéi ngagóot."
Ch'á yéi áwés aadéi wdigwáat'.
At wudigwát' wé aas k'í.
Du chooneidí.
Hél tsú yéi yeekawuyáat'i áwé
anax haat wdikín wé núkt.
Ch'á yáa du kináa wjikaak.   440
Núkt.

Aawat'úk.
Tle yáa du x'aseiyíx' áwé wdzigeet.
S'eek áwé.
S'eekx wusitee.

Áwé tle ch'a yéi
tlákw ch'a yei
wé s'eek
koon yoo akaaníkk
goot'á sá.   450
A káax' áwé aadé anagútch.
Aax at du.een.
Hél du éex idasheek tle ch'a hú
tle ch'á hóoch.
A yáx áwé tlél du éex dushee.
Tle ch'a hóoch.
Tle ch'a yéi teeyí áwé
yax sh yawdzigoodán tle ch'a hú
tle yáax' áwé.
Haaw, yéi áyá shukatán yá sh kalneek.   460
Tle ch'a aadéi yéi kunaaliyéidei áyá xwsikóo.
Tle ch'a hóoch'.

She was only crawling around.

How bad off she was.
There was a tree standing over there
maybe it was a cottonwood,
maybe it was just an ordinary tree,   430
"Walk over to the base of it," they told her.
"Don't help her.
Just her.
Let her walk over herself."
So she just crawled over there.
She crawled to the base of the tree.
Her bow and arrow.
It wasn't very long
when this dusky grouse came flying over.
It landed right above her.   440
A dusky grouse.

She killed it with her arrow.
It dropped right in front of her.
It was a black bear.
It turned into a black bear.

So
from then on
she told only
of where
the black bears were.   450
According to that they went there to hunt.
They would kill them there.
"Don't help her, leave her
by herself."
So they didn't help her.
She helped herself.
Just as she was
it was here
she straightened herself up.
Well, this is how the story ends.   460
This is as far as I know the story.
That's the end.

Kaats'
Tseexwáa x'éidáx sh kalneek

Likoodzi sh kalneek áyá.
Ch'a ldakát át áyá yaa yanaxíx.
Ch'u ch'áagoodáx
yú al'óon
at gutóot aa wu.aadéen
lingít
ka héen xukaanáx aa at eenéen.
"Daa sáyú aan has at een?"
yóo áyá x'ayaduká
a xoo aa ku.oo.   10
X'oon táakw sá shoowaxeex.
Ha aan at du.een át xáa yá kustéeyin.
Lingítch
aadéi s at in yé,
yú heentak ádi tsú
aadéi kéi s ashátji yé
ka yá át woo.aadi át,
yá héen xukaanáx aa
aadéi s a.eeni yé
áwé wdudzikóo   20
ka yú dáakt woo.aadi át xá.
Ha yá káa ku.aa
at natí áyú
keitl.

218

Kaats'
told by J. B. Fawcett

This is a magnificent story.
Many kinds of things happened.
Even from long ago
Tlingits
used to go hunting
in the forest
and harvesting on the sea.
"What did they hunt with?"
is what
some people ask.
How many years have passed.   10
Surely there used to be weapons to hunt with.
Tlingits
knew
how to hunt things,
those sea mammals too,
and how to catch
those animals that walked,
how to harvest
those on the sea
and those that walked inland.   20
There was a man
who went out hunting
with a dog.
Those great inland animals,

A ḵoowóodáx̱ áyú yéi daadunéiyeen
yú daḵka.ádi tlenx'
dligéix'i át.
Keitl teen áwé yéi daadunéi nuch
keitl teen.
Aaḵáa áwé   30
a x̱'éit uwagút.
Du shát ḵudzitee
wé ḵáa
du shát ḵudzitee.
Wáa sáyá?
Ch'u yeisú akoo.aaḡú áyá
ḵáakwx̱ daak uwagúdi yáx̱ áyú yatee.
X̱óots yóo duwasáagu át áwé.
Héidoo áx' yéi at kawdiyaayi yé,
Kichx̱áandáx̱ haandéi kaawaháa.   40
Dakḵá áwé.
Yees Ḡeey yóo áwé duwasáakw Lingítch
dleit ḵáach ḵwá Yes Bay.
Ax' áwé yéi yan at kawdiyáa.
Wé héench áwé; aatlein héen áwé.
Haaw.
Wáa nanéi sáwé?
Ch'u yeisú
ch'u yeisú akoo.aaḡú áwé
ash woosháat.   50
Tle ayawuyeigí áwé.
Tle a x̱'éit áwé uwagút
wé at ḵoowú.
Awé gáaní yux̱ woogoot
wé át.
Aadéi áwé neil ash uwax̱ích.
Ḵaju áwu gíwé gé du shát
wé shéech aa x̱óots.
Wé neilú á.
Ayá a daa áyá aawasháat.   60
Shaawát áwé du waḵshiyeex'.
Tle awusháadi áyá
"Héidu áwé x̱at ḡasneix̱?"
yóo áwé yaawaḵaa
Kaats' ḵu.aa.
Ch'u yeisú x̱'óol' yáx̱ teeyí wé du x̱úx̱ wé gáan
ldakát át ḵoowashée.

large animals,
were taken from their den.
They were taken with the use of dogs,
with the use of dogs.
That's when   30
they came to its entrance.
The man
had a wife,
he had a wife.
Why was it?
After trying for a while
he stepped into a dangerous place.
It was the animal called brown bear.
Over here is where it happened,
it happened on the near side of Ketchikan.   40
It was inland.
Yees Geey is what Tlingits call the place,
but the White People call it Yes Bay.
That's where this happened.
There is a river there too, a large river.
Now,
at what point was it?
While he was trying,
while he was still trying,
it grabbed him.   50
It was while he was aiming at it.
He got right up to the entrance
of its den.
The animal
jumped out.
It tossed him inside.
Its mate was probably in there all along,
that female brown bear.
She was inside.
He grabbed her private parts.   60
She looked like a woman to him.
As he grabbed her
Kaats'
said
"Hey, why don't you help me?"
While her mate was still confused outside
he was searching all over.
While he was searching

Wé atgaa kushée
wé du keitlx'í
du keidlí   70
yanax áwé ash wooxeech.
Ach áyá at kookeidéex sitee,
"Ash tayee
yá a káa yei s kéich."
S du yei.ádi haaw áwé s du yei.ádeex sitee wé át.
A káx áwé loowatsaak.
Ch'áakwx sateeyí áwé
wéináx neil uwagút.
Hít áwé
hít áwé   80
du wakshiyeex'
wé at koowú ásíwéi gé.
"Goosú yáadei neil xwaaxiji lingít"
yóo áwé yaawakaa wé át.
"Tsáax' áwé yáadu á.
Tsáax' áwé yáadu á.
Wé yáanáx neil iyatée,
yáadu á."
A wakkáx wooshee du xúx.
Aadéi sh daa tuwditee   90
yá ash daat jiwuskóox'u
wé shaawát ku.aa
aadéi sh daa tuwditee.
Tlél du tuwáa ushgú akawuneegí.
A wakkáx wooshee du xúx.
Tlél aadéi a nák naxwdzigeedi yé koostí.
Nagútch
gáandei.
Aagáa áwé ash shukoojeis' nuch.
"Tlél wáa sá ikgwatee.
Tlél wáa sá ikgwatee."   100
Wáa nanéi sáyú át koowaháa.
Tléix' dís
tléix' taatx áwé sitee du wakshiyeex'
hú ku.aa
kach tléix' dís áwé.
Tlél koostí
Kaats' ku.aa.
Hóoch'.
Káakwt uwanéi.   110

for those dogs of his,
his dogs,   70
she buried him.
That's why there's a saying
"underneath
the thing they sit on."
Spruce boughs are their beds, the beds of those
          animals.
She lay face down.
After a while
the male bear came in.
It was a house,
it was a house   80
in Kaats' eyes
although it was the den, wasn't it?
"Where is the human I threw in here?"
the animal said.
"It was a mitten, here it is.
It was a mitten, here it is.
That's what you threw in here.
Here it is."
She put her paws over her husband's eyes.
She felt something for Kaats',   90
when he touched her,
the female bear,
she felt something for him.
She didn't want to tell on him.
She put her paws over her husband's eyes.
Kaats' didn't know what he was going to do.
The male bear
would go out.
That's when she would instruct him.
"Nothing will happen to you.   100
Nothing will happen to you."
At one point, the moment came.
In Kaats' eyes though,
for him,
one month was a night,
here it was a month all the while.
But Kaats'
was gone.
He was no more.
He had an accident.   110

Hóoch' áyú.
Tlél wuduskú goosú á.
Kudushee nuch.
Du kéek' hás
tlax kik'i.aa kudzitee
aawasháa.
Du yáx yées shaawát aawasháa
wé kik'i.aa.
Du húnxw ku.aa
at s'aatx'í.   120
Awé yéi yanduskéich "héit'aa ku.aa xáa déi
du húnxu káx kukgwashée."
Duwakeet
wududziteen áyú du x'us.eetí
aáa
jiwánnáx
yá héen yíx kei wlishóo.
Wáa sáyú
yatseeneit x'usyík t'akkáx kei wlishóo
yú kaa x'us.eetí.   130
Aagáa áyá wduwakít
"Atch gíyá wsineix"
yóo x'ayaduká.
Aan yátx'i yéi sh kalneek.
Ch'a aadéi yéi nay.oo x'wán.
X'éigaa sh kalneek áyá
x'éigaa sh kalneek áyá.
Anax wududzikuwu át áyá
du x'éidáx
a áyá.   140
Keitl
tóo akayanook.
Yú neilx' áyú gagaan x'oos áwé oowayáa.
Neildéi
koodagánch neildéi.
Gagaan x'oos áwé oowayáa
wé keitl tundatáani áwé,
wé áa kdahánch,
wé shaawát.

Tlél yóo s a woodlákkw.   150
Goosú á hú?
Ldakát yéit kudushée.

He was no more.
They didn't know where he was.
They would search.
Of his younger brothers
the very youngest one
had a wife.
The youngest
had a wife as young as he.
His older brother
was a master hunter.   120
They would say, "Why doesn't this one
find his older brother?"
People were suspicious,
his footprints were seen
yes,
alongside the bear footprints
they went up alongside the river.
Why
were this man's footprints
going up alongside the brown bear's?   130
That's when people became suspicious,
"Perhaps he was taken by something,"
is what people said.
Noble people said this.
Please excuse this.
This is a true story,
this is a true story.
This is how it's known,
this is
from his lips.   140
The bear would feel the approach
of the dogs.
In the den they seem like sunbeams.
They would shine in,
into the den.
The dogs' thoughts
seem like sunbeams;
the woman
would jump up to reach for them.

They couldn't find him.   150
Where was he?
People searched everywhere.

Tlél du yakaayée koostí
yú kik'i.aa ku.aa
"Héit'aa ku.aa xáa déi."
Wuduziteen áyú du x'us.eetí.
"Héit'aa ku.aa xáa déi du húnxw
du húnxwgaa kukgwashée"
yóo áyu yanduskéich du hunxu hásch
wé kik'i.aa.   160
Du shát
shawatshaan.
Wáa nanéi sáyú át koowaháa.
Du keitlx'í
"At X'éeshee Gwálaa"
yóo ayasáakw tléix' aa du keidlí.
Tleix' aa kwá "Shaayeesxwáa."
Tléix' aa ku.aa
kát xat seiwax'ákw.
Nás'k keitl   170
tle number one
Shaayeesxwáa.
Áwé
wáa nanéi sáwe yéi yaawakaa
"ax téeli yan sané x'wán
áx téelí
kkwagóot
ch'a kukkwashée áwé."
Kach hóoch ku.aa síyú gé a káx kukgwashée du
        húnxw gé?
Woosh woox'áanx' yú x'áan s'aatx'í ku.aa.   180
Wáa nanéi sáwé yéi yaawakaa wé shaawát,
"Haahá.
Iyatéen gé?
Iyatéen gé?"
Ax' áwé ash wakkooká
áa wdihaan
tsu áa kdahánch.
Tléik',
tlél kúxdei yóo udatí
ch'u yéi adaaneiyí áwé x'awoolt loowagúk wé át.   190
Ach áwé yáa yeedát xóots
xóots a koowú yeeysikóo
aan yátx'i daax'oon x'adakít'x
woosh géidei

But the younger brother
wasn't saying anything.
"Why not him?" they were saying.
His footprints were seen.
"Why can't he
find his older brother?"
is what the older brothers said
about their younger brother.   160
His wife
was an old woman.
At one point the moment came.
His dogs,
"At X'éeshee Gwálaa"
is the name of one of his dogs.
The other was "Shaayeesxwáa."
But I forget
the other one.
Three dogs,   170
first class,
Shaayeesxwáa.
Then
at one point the younger brother asked his wife,
"Can you get my shoes ready,
my shoes,
I'll go
to search."
But he was the one who would find his older
        brother, wasn't he?
But the angry men were becoming quarrelsome.   180
At one point the female bear said,
"I see.
Do you see?
Do you see?"
She told him to look there.
She would jump up to grab them,
she would jump up to grab them again.
No,
it wasn't slowing down,
while she was still doing this they tracked to the
        entrance.   190
That's why bears today,
in bear dens, you know,
these noble children make four barriers

aa a yeewú aa.
A anax̱ áwé
x̱'adakÍt'x̱
á anax̱ áwé
yeedát yéi kwdayéin.
Aagáa yú gaaw ḵu.aa   200
ayaawadlaaḵ wé
ch'a yeisú yéi at ḵunoogú áwé x̱'awoolt loowagúḵ
        wé keitl.
Aadéi s yadax̱ún wé at ḵoowú x̱'é.
AyaawatÍn du keitlx̱'Í.
"Ax̱ keidlÍ!"
á áwé
"Gu.aa yáx̱ x̱'wán,"
yóo áwé ash yawsiḵaa.
"I gu.aa yáx̱ x̱'wán."
Tlél aadéi nax̱wdzigeedi yé.   210
Tlél áyú yú óonaa ḵaa jee.
Yú át
chooneit áwé.
Óonaa yáanáx̱ litseen.
Aa x̱wsiteen.
G̱án, yéi wé kwdliyáat'.
Kasiyéi.
Yú ksatán yáax̱' yú at doogú a kadzaasÍ
litseen.
Wé a lú aa ḵwá yéi kwdiyáat'.   220
S'aaḵ.
K'wát' yáx̱ kadiwx̱ás' a shuyatóox̱ dutsaaḵ.
A tóotx̱ yóox̱ xeex.
A tóodei yoo yax̱Íxk yú át.
Tle at katé áwé.
Yéi áwé at eenéen lingÍt.
Ch'u yeisú
a daa yoo jikool.átgi áwé.
    (Slap!)
Tlél aadéi nax̱wdzigeedi yé.
X̱wasikóo du saayÍ.   230
Ch'u tle ḵúnáx̱ áwé x̱'óol' yáx̱
x̱at yatee
yá lidzée.
Lidzée cha shaatk'.
Sometimes tsá

one after the other
on the inside.
Because of what happened
they make barriers,
because of what happened
it's this way today.
But at that time   200
he reached there,
those dogs tracked right to the entrance while she
           was still doing this.
They pointed their noses to the mouth of the den.
He recognized his dogs.
"My dogs!"
he said,
"Be brave,"
he said to them.
"Be brave."
He didn't know what he was going to do.   210
There were no guns.
Those things
were bow and arrow.
They were more powerful than guns.
I saw some.
See, they were this long.
Strange looking.
The bow was curved right here, and strung with hide,
it was strong.
But the points were this long.   220
Bones.
They were round like eggs; they were inserted
           into the end of the point.
It detaches itself.
It attaches itself inside the target.
It was just like a bullet.
That's how Tlingits killed things.
While he was still
trying to get ready
           (Slap!)
Kaats' didn't know what he was going to do.
I knew the brother's name.   230
When I get mixed up,
it's difficult.
It's really difficult, my good woman.

a káa daak tuxwdateení i x'úx' káa yéi kgwatée.
Aak'é yaa koosgé i jeewóo á.
Yak'éi.
Haaw.

240

Awé
yéi ayawsikaa
Shaayeesxwáa
"Yeedát awéigích i x'adaxwétlx ashaa."
Ayalatín du húnxw.
Tléix'.aa tsú ayaawatín.
"I x'adaxwétl déi."
A x'awoolx' yúx yawdzi.aa
du kéek' gwaa wéigé
ash yalatín.
"Tlél wáa sá xat utí   250
xát áyá
x'awugané déi."
Ayalatín du húnxw.
"Yáadu xát!"
"Yáadu xát!"
Tléix' táakw áwé de tléil koostí xá.
Hóoch áwé ayaawadlaak du húnxw.
"Hél keeneegéek x'wán
hél keeneegéek
tsu haadéi kgeegóot.   260
Haadéi kgeegóot."
Du tuwáa sigóowu át a káa yan ayawsikáa
daa sá ash tuwáa sagoowú
yóo éekdáx.
"Hél keeneegéek!"

Yóot loowagúk yú keitlx'.
Wáa sáyú
ch'áakw áyú has du een yoo aya.átk yú kéitl.
Toowú sagú
yo-ho-ho-ho   270
tle kéi s da.átch.
Tle s wududziteen.
Toowú sagú
áyú s duwakeet
"Wáa sáhé tláx s du toowóo sigóo hé keitl."
Tlél du yakaayí koostí.

Sometime
when I think of it, we'll put it down on paper.
You have a good mind.
Good.
Now.

Then   240
Kaats' said
to Shaayeesxwáa,
"If only you'd stop barking."
He stared at his older brother.
Kaats' recognized the other dog too.
"Stop barking now!"
He looked out of the mouth of the den,
why, that was his younger brother,
he stared at him.
"I'm all right,
it's me,   250
tell him to stop barking."
He stared at his older brother.
"Here I am!
Here I am!"
He had been gone for one year, you see.
It was he who found his older brother.
"Please don't tell this,
don't tell,
come back again.
Come back."   260
He asked him to get what he needed,
whatever he needed
from the coast.
"Don't tell."

The dogs ran on home.
Why?
The dogs had gone with them many times before.
They were so happy
yo-ho-ho-ho
they'd jump up on their hind legs.   270
People could see them.
The dogs were so happy
people got suspicious
and said, "Why are these dogs so happy?"

Wé du shát teen akaawaneek x̱á,
"X̱wasiteen ax̱ húnx̱w.
Yan x̱at yawsik̲áa.
I gu.aa yáx̱ x'wán,"   280
yóo adaayak̲á du shát.
"Haadéi k̲wagóot.
Aadéi k̲uk̲wagwaháa."
Kook̲énaa áwé s du jeewú aa.
Ch'áagoodáx̱ áwé wéit'aat k̲udzitee.
Yisik̲óo wéit'át kook̲énaa.
At natí áwé,
de át yaawagás'
tsaa
tsaadáx̱ jidanook áwé ash tuwáa sigóo.   290
Yóo áwé yan ayawsik̲áa du kéek'.
Wé yaakw tsú
du yaagú
"Gax̱tookóox̱.
Héidu á."
Aá ash shukaawajáa anax̱ yeik̲ gugagut yé;
        ch'u yeedát áwu á.
Yóo yú ixk̲ée k̲u.oo yú Teik̲weidí,
gán, haa een has akanéek.
"Yóodu áx' wé yatseeneitch k̲uwsineix̱i yé;
        wéidu á; yáadu á,"
yóodu Ketchikan.   300
Yáadu aa tsú
Yes Bay yóo duwasáakw.
Yees G̲eey yóo duwasáakw; aatlein héen áwé
yú a k̲át kaawadáa
yáadu á á.
X'ax'áan hásch áwé haa een has akanéek.
Teik̲weidí x̱áawé hás áwé yéi s woonei.
Wé shukaadei k̲áa áx' átx̱ wusiteeyi yé áwé.
Aá atoosg̲eiwú.
Haaw   310

áwé at natí
at natí
áwé áx̱ k̲ux̱ yé
has du k̲áa yán k̲oowatée du yátx'í.
Nás'gináx̱ áwé yatee
wé k̲áax'w

He had nothing to say.
He told his wife, you see,
"I saw my older brother.
He instructed me.
Be brave,"
he said to his wife   280
"He will come.
The time will come."
They had a messenger.
They have been around for a long time.
You know what a messenger is.
Kaats' was yearning
to go hunting
for seals,
he wanted to get his hands on seals.   290
This is what he instructed his younger brother.
The boat too,
his boat.
"We will go by boat.
There it is."
Kaats' showed him to where he was coming down;
      it's still there today.
The Teikweidí people down south,
see, they told us about it.
"There's where the brown bear saved a person;
      there it is; here it is,"
Ketchikan is there.
Also this place   300
called Yes Bay.
It's called Yees G̲eey; there's a large river,
the tributary that joins it this way
is here.
X̱'ax'áan and his group were the ones who told us.
They are the Teikweidí whom this happened to.
That's where their ancestor became a thing of value.
We seined there.
Now,   310

this is where they hunted,
they hunted,
where they paddled,
his children were one winter old.
There were three of them,

xóots.
Hás áyá s'ukkasdúkx has sitee yáa yeedát
hás áwé.
Du yátx'í áwé   320
lingít áwé
hú du tuwáatx.
Yóo aantkeenée s wakshiyeex' ku.aa.
Awé át ugootch.
At natí
du kéek'
   (whispered line, inaudible)
Ash shukaawajáa wé du shát
wé xóots
"Yóodu á
áa yéi haa kgwatee yé áwé."   330
Wé xáat
wé xáat héeni
áx' áwé wdudziteen du x'us.eetí áwé.
Kéi wlishóo wé xóots x'us.eetí áwé
yáax kei wlishóo du x'us.eetí.
Ch'a kúnáx yú tléix'.aach áwé tsá wsiteen
k'idéin
aan yaa na.át.
A anax áwé wdudzikóo
ách áwé du eegáa at wootee xá.   340
Yá shaawát áwé mistake yéi awsinei
yá du shát yéeyi.
Tlél yéi ngwaneiyéen ágwá.
Ayá yá shaawát aadéi yaawakaayi yé kúnáx wé du
       shát yéeyi
wé éek aa.
Ash een yak'éi
wé xóots
wé aawashayi aa.
Ash een tuli.aan
du yátx'i du jeewóo de xá   350
ash een tuli.aan.
"Tlél du éex x'eetaanéek x'wán wé i shát,"
yóo ash daayaká.
"Aaá"
yóo yaawakaa.
Tlél áx x'eitaan.
Wéit'aa

male
brown bears.
They are the ones that are called solid rib cage today,
that's them.
They are his children,   320
they are human
because of him.
But to people's eyes, though, they are bears.
He would go there.
His younger brother
hunted.
Kaats' instructed
his brown bear wife,
"There it is,
the place where we will live."   330
The salmon,
the salmon river,
is where her footprints were seen.
The brown bear footprints lead upward,
her footprints lead along here.
Only one person saw them
clearly,
he was walking with her.
That was how they knew.
That's why it seemed proper, you see.   340
It was the woman who made a mistake,
his former wife.
This wouldn't have happened to him, don't you agree?
It was because of what the woman said, his former wife
on the coast.
The brown bear,
the one who was his wife,
was good to him.
She was kind to him,
she already had his children, you see,   350
she was kind to him.
"Please don't speak to your wife,"
she said to him.
"Yes,"
he said.
He wouldn't speak to her.
Those
seals, lots!

wé tsaa, hé'
haat awooskooxch.
(Slap!)
Toowú sagú!   360
yá xóots.
Has du éesh.
Sagú áwé
wé tsaa
asagahéinín dáakdei
a x'eis.
Yáat'aa áwé s du x'eis.
Tlél áwé du tuwáa ushgú
a wanáak
ch'a a wanáak   370
áwé áa yéi yatee.
Awé héen áwé
héen áwé héengaa áwé woogoot Kaats' ku.aa.
Tlél jéalousx ustí wé xóots du yís
ash een tuli.aan.
Ch'al yéi óosh gé wuteeyéen aadéi oosh gé
       ngwateeyi yé dé.
Ch'u tle átx áwé naxwsateeyi át áwé yú.á
       yóo áwé dutláakw xá.
Ach áwé kaa x'aya.áxch wéit'át xóots.

Lingít
lingít kusteeyí.   380
Yóo yagútk.

De tsu s woo.aat
at natí
du kéek' hás.
Hé'
daa sá
gaduwaxaayi át.
Awé héen,
wé héengaa áwé
héen x'é áwé át uwagút; hú ku.aa, Kaats' ku.aa   390
ash yayeet ásíwéi gé wé hán gíwé
wé du shát.
Wé anák ux kéi uwatiyi xá.
Dáxnáx áwé yatee du shát,
dáxnáx.

he would bring in by boat.
        (Slap)
The brown bears   360
were happy!
Their father.
There was joy
when he wanted to bring the seals
to the beach
for them to eat.
These were for them to eat.
He didn't want to
part from them
to live   370
apart from them.
There was a stream,
a stream where Kaats' went for water.
The brown bear wasn't jealous over him,
she was kind to him.
If only things hadn't happened this way,
        how would it have been?
It would have really been something, they say.
        That's how it's told, you see.
This is why the brown bears understand humans.

Humans,
the human way of life.   380
Kaats' would go out.

His younger brothers
had gone out again
to hunt.
Lots!
whatever
was for food.
It was water,
it was for water
that he, Kaats', came to the mouth of the stream,   390
but his human wife
was standing there waiting for him, wasn't she?
The one from before he got lost, you see.
He had two wives,
two.
It was the older one

Yá yanwáat áwé
wé mistake yéi awsinei.
Ch'á aadéi yei kg̲ee.oo
ax̲ sée
yé á.   400
Tle true story áwé.
Wáa sá yak'éi eewóos'i.
A tóonáx̲ k̲iydzitee Teikweidí
x̲wasikóo k'idéin
i éesh,
i léelk'w tsú yé.

Yóot uwagút
héen áyá yaa anas.ín.
Ch'u shóogu du k̲usteeyí.
Ax̲ goot k̲u.aa   410
áx̲ goot k̲u.aa
wé yatseeneit
du shát.
Aadéi óosh gé ng̲wateeyi yé gé
ch'u mistake l yoo oosneigi kát wé shaawát x̲á.
Héen yaa anas.ín.
"Héidú já'!"
yóo ash yawsik̲aa
"De koodzée kwshéi yóo gé yak'wudzix̲aawu át
       awsiteen gé."
(Ch'a aadéi yéi x̲at x̲'akg̲ee.oo.)   420
Yóo áwé ash yawsik̲aa
"Daadzix̲áawu át awsiteen,"
yóo áwé ash daayaká x̲á.
Tlél áx̲ x̲'eitaan.
Ayá yá aadéi ash yawsik̲aayi yéich áwé át x̲'eiwatán.
"Ha dú!
Yeisú shí gé ix̲'akx̲waa.aak̲w héit'aa,"
yóo yaawak̲aa.
Ha.
Hóoch' áwé.   430
Tlél a x̲án
tlél ax̲ ugoot.
Yáatx̲ áwé tle du een át s k̲óox̲; tle at natí
       wé du kéek' hás teen
at natí.
Yóo yanshukát du yátx̲'í

who made the mistake.
Please excuse
this,
my daughter.   400
This is a true story.
How good it is that you're asking about it.
Your birth is from Teikweidí,
I know it well,
your father,
your grandmother too.

He left,
carrying water.
His life was the same as before.
But she'd come to him,   410
but she'd come to him,
that brown bear,
his wife.
How would it have been
if the woman hadn't made the mistake, you see.
He was carrying water.
"Hey there, my dear,"
she said to him,
"Isn't it magnificent to see a tiny face with
        hair on it?"
(Please excuse my language.)   420
This is what she said to him,
"To see a thing with hair on it,"
is what she said to him, you see.
He wouldn't speak to her.
It was because she said this to him that he
        spoke to her.
"You!!
If only I could have coached you on your words, you!"
he said to her.
Now.
That was it.   430
He wasn't with her,
he didn't go there.
From then on, he would go by boat with his
        younger brothers to hunt,
to hunt.
But on the beach

wé xóots ku.aa
de s dligéix'.
"Yiják yee éesh
yiják."

Tsaa,   440
tle anax yeik has lugúkch sagú wéit'át.
Awé yei uwagút áwé yú.á
áwé yá shí ku.aa yaa kuxligát.
Yá haa daakeitx'éech kwá s ashée nuch.
Déix yeekaadéi dushí
aak'é shí áyú
xóots x'asheeyí.
Has aawaják wé s du éesh.
Aagáa áwé áwé altín yú k'atxáan
ka yú goox   450
kookénaa áwé
k'atxáan
s altín.
Yéi áwé kdulneek du x'éidáx.
Du guk.ádi du gúgu yú.á
wé shaawát
du wootsaagáyi; yées káa áwé
at doogú x'óow áwé awdlisík.
Yakawjixít,
ách áwé a yáx has yakashxeet Teikweidí.   460
Wé at yakooxéedayi áwé.
Lingít áwé yú.á.
Hóoch'!
tle agóotx sitee tle wé du xúx.
Has aawaják has du éesh.
Dáakt has uwa.át hás ku.aa.
A xánt hán du xúx
wé át
lingít áwé
s du wakshiyeex'.   470
Ashí wé shí
wé Teikweidéech has ashée nuch.
Kichxáandáx aa
s du dayéen ashí.
Xóots x'asheeyí.
A kát gáax!
A kát gáax.

his bear children
were fully grown.
"Kill your father.
Kill him."

Pleased with the seals,   440
the children would come running down to the beach.
It's said he stepped out of the canoe,
but I have forgotten the song.
But our "outer containers" usually sang it.
It was sung in two ways,
it is a fine song,
the Brown Bear Song.
They killed that father of theirs.
That's when the coward watched
and the slave--   450
he was a messenger--
and the coward
watched.
That's how it's told from his words.
It's said there were earrings on the ears
of the woman,
she had a cane; she was a young person,
she wore an animal skin on her back tied around
        her waist.
She had painted her face,
this is why the Teik̲weidí paint their faces like
        her.   460
It's the animal's face paint.
She was human, they say.
No more!
that husband of hers was mutilated.
They killed their father.
They went back into the forest.
But the animal wife
stood by her husband's body,
she was a human
in their eyes.   470
She sang the cry
sung by the Teik̲weidí.
The one from Ketchikan,
she sang to them.
The Brown Bear Song.

Aadáx has awlik'úts a jíni.
Gaax kíknáx áwé aadéi altsóow yá a daasheeyí
wé du xúx   480
gaax kíknáx.

She cried to it!
She cried to it.
They had torn his arms off.
She joined them back to his body while singing
      this cry
for her husband,
while singing this cry.

480

Sı̱t' Ḵaa Ká̱x Kana.áa
Kaasgéiy x̱'éidá̱x sh kalneek

Ga̲théeni yóo áwé duwasáakw
wé haa aanı̱.
Ga̲théeni,
wé Sı̱t' Eeti Ḡeey.
A áwé á duwa.óo.
Ldaká̱t yéidei x̱áat ḵu.aa áwé á̱x̱ ya.aa.
A ká̱x̱ áwé duwa.óo; wé aanx̱ wududliyé̱x̱.
Ldaká̱t yéidei x̱áat áwu á.
Yak'éiyi x̱áat á̱x̱ ya.aayéen.
Áwé ch'u áa yéi ̲kuteeyée áwé   10
wé hı̱tx̱'.
Tla̲x̱ keijı̱n yaana̲x̱ gı̱wé á̱t uda̲keen
wé hı̱tx̱':
yá Ḵaagwaantaan
ḵa wé Wooshkeetaan
ḵa wé Eechhittaan
ḵa
yá ooháan Chookaneidéex̱ haa sateeyı̱,
ldaká̱t uhaan áwé awu.á.
Aa yéi haa yatee.   20
A áwé
ch'u wáa yóo tukdatángi sá kwshı̱wé
wé shaatk' kwá
wooweidı̱? At t'éit dus.áa.

244

Glacier Bay History
told by Susie James

The name of it is G̲athéeni,
that land of ours.
G̲athéeni,
the bay where the glacier was.
It was where people lived.
Salmon of all kinds ran there.
That's why the people lived there;
        they made it a village.
Many kinds of salmon are there.
Good salmon ran there.
It was while people were still living there,   10
the houses:
maybe as many as five houses stood there,
the houses:
the Kaagwaantaan
and the Wooshkeetaan
and the Eechhittaan
and
us, those of us who are Chookaneidí,
all of us were there.
We were living there.   20
It was then,
what was she thinking, anyway,
that young girl
at the start of her enrichment?
        She was curtained off.

Nás'k táakw áwé at t'éi yéi anúkjeen.
Ach áwé tlax haa shayadahéineen
        yá lingítx ha sateeyí,
yá haa yádi aadéi tulatíni yé.
Tle yá nas'gi aa táakw áwé tsá du xúx sákw jee
        jidunaakch
tle ch'a wé at t'éidáx.
Shaawát yát áwé du een yéi jidunéiyeen.   30
A áwé yéi áwé yéi áwé at t'éit áa; dé déix
        táakw áwé; nas'gi aa táakw áwé a
        kaadéi yaa kunahéin.
De tlél nalé áwé
jigaxdunaagí.
Gaxdushaayí de tlél nalé.
A áwé shux'aa gaadí áwé dux'áan.
Tlé t'éex'
t'éex' tayeet woo.áayjeen gaat;
        yeedát tlél yéi at utí.
A áwé dux'an nuch.
Dusxuk nuch.
A áwé ch'a wáa yoo at koodayáa sá kwshíwé.   40
Wé shaatk' ku.aa du eedée.
Teey áwé anax yóot wuduliyéx,
wé hít k'iyee anax
teey.
A yee áwé áa yéi duwa.óo wé shaatk'.
Tle yóo naakée áwé s tlél goohda yú.a.
A áwé yá shaax' xoonáx áwé duwatini
        sít' áwé yóo naakéeeeeeee;
        yeisú yéi googenk'i át áwé.
Ax wulixáat' yóo naakée.
Tlax wé héen yíkdax tlél duteen; tle yóo
deikéetx áwé tsá duteen nuch.   50
Awsikóo ku.aa yú sít' áa yéi teeyí.
Ach áwé tle akaawagéis
wé sít'
"Sít'!
Geis,
geis."
Wé atx'éeshi aawaxayí, a daa x'éeshi áwé tle
yú keitl jiyáx áwé yá aadéi
        k'astóox; áwé tle ách akoolgéis.
"Sít'.

One was curtained off for three years.
That is why there were very many of us who are
        Tlingit,
because of how we cared for this child of ours.
Only at the end of the third year her hand
        would be given to her husband
straight from her place of isolation.
A female child was handled this way.   30
That was the way it was, the way she sat
        behind a curtain; it had been two years;
        it was the third year approaching.
It was not long
before she would be released.
It was not long before someone would marry her.
There were the first sockeyes they smoked.
The sockeyes
used to run up under the ice, under the ice;
        it's not that way any more.
It was those they smoked.
They usually dried them.
But just what was happening?   40
That girl and her place.
It was an extension made of cedar bark
behind the house,
cedar bark.
That was where the young girl was kept.
It was said you could clearly see up the bay.
Through the mountains there you could see
        the glacier waaaaaay up the bay;
        it was only a tiny piece
It was hanging there up the bay.
It couldn't be seen much from the river;
        it could only
be seen from way out.   50
But she knew the glacier was there.
That is why she called the glacier
like a dog,
"Glacier,
here,
here."
With that dryfish she had eaten,
        the bones from the sides;
The way you call a dog she was spitting on it;
        she called it like a dog with it.

Geis.   60
Geis.
Geis" yu.a.
Gaat daax'éesheech áwé akoolgéis.
Yá teey yee yatx ashoowatán anax áwé.
Awé tle du kéek'ch áwé yéi yawsikaa
"Dú! wáa sá wé tsu x'ayeeká?"
Awé l ax'adaat tooshtí.
Waa nanéi sáwé tle du tláat at'aa oowagút. "Atlée!
Wáa sá wé x'ayaká ax shátx?"
"Wáa sá yú?   70
Jaa! Jaa!" yóo a daa yaká.
"Tlél eet kaax neegí daak duteech."
"Ha lis'éi. I een yan kakaneek aadéi x'ayaka yé?
Sít' áwé akoogéis ax shátx; keitl,
keitl wáa sá kdugéisi ayáx áwé:
tuf! tuf! tuf! tuf! tuf! Aadéi k'astóox wé s'aak
wé gaat s'aagí
tle ách áwé--'sít' geis!
Geis! Geis!
Geis!'   80
gú sá wé tle aadéi kéi awsigíx'."
"L keeneegéek! L keeneegéek!"
tle áx akawligéik wé du sée.
Keena.áa s'ootaat áwé tsá a xánnáx daak uwagút.
"Wáa sá wé tsú x'ayeeká?
Daa sákw sáwé tsú akeegéis?
Yisikóo gé i daa ligaas áya? Tlél yéi kaawahayí
aadéi ax sh x'agaaxdudlishuwu yé.
Wáa sá wé x'ayeeká? Tlél yéi x'ayeekáak."
Aan yóo x'ali.átk.   90
At natéeyi át yanagwéich.
Ch'a yák'wdei áwé yéi sh kawdudlineek
"Wáa sá kaawahayi sít' áyú tlax yéi yaa kana.éin."
Ch'a yóoooooooooooooo
naakéedei duwatini át áwé.
Yeedát ku.aa de wé haanaa yaa
        akunalséin, aadéi yaa kana.en yé
yóo sh kadulneek.
Haa há.
Du téix't uwatée wé shaawát tlé wé kaa tláa.
Tle tláaaaaaaaakw áwé yaa kana.éin.   100
Keitl yaa nashíxi

"Glacier.
Here.
Here.   60
Here," she said.
She called it with the sockeye dryfish.
She lifted the cedar bark from there.
Then her younger sister said to her,
"Hey, why are you saying that?"
She ignored what she said.
At one point the little sister
       went to tell her mother?   "Mother!
Why is my older sister saying that?"
"What's the matter?   70
Sh! Sh!" her mother told her.
"Girls don't bring news from back rooms."
"But wait! Let me tell you first what she's saying.
My older sister's calling the glacier; like a dog,
just like you call a dog:
Ptuh! Ptuh! Ptuh! Ptuh! Ptuh!
       She's spitting on the bone,
the sockeye bone,
and using it to say, 'Glacier! Here!
Here! Here!
Here!'   80
Then she threw it up there."
"Don't tell! Don't tell!"
she warned that daughter of hers.
When dawn came that morning she finally went to her.
"What are you saying those things for now?
What are you calling the glacier for?
Don't you know that you can break a taboo?
       You shouldn't be saying things
about anything like that.
Why were you saying those things?
       Don't you say them again."
She talked to her.   90
Hunters would go up there by boat.
Suddenly people said,
"What's wrong with the glacier? It's growing so much!"
They used to see it w-a-a-a-a-a-y
up the bay.
But now it was near, getting closer,
       the way it was moving,
people said.

kayáanax áyu dulyaakw yóo kdunéek,
        aadéi yaa kana.ein yé.

Ha áyú akoolxéitl' déin koowanéi.
Yá tléix' táakw yándei yaa shagahéek áwé
yéi sh kawdudlineek.
Sít'k'i T'ooch' áwé ch'u ch'áakwdax áa yéi yatee.
Sít'k'i T'ooch' yóo duwasáagu yé.
"De wé Sít'k'i T'ooch' áwé de a tóodei yaa kandayein.
De wé yées aa tóodei de yaa kundayein,"
        yóo áwé sh kadulneek.
"Haa há.   110
Wáa sá yá? Wáa sá yá at gugatée?"
Atóox' ldakát wé Sít' Eeti Geey áwé wshil'úx'.
K'é yóo mínk kawduhéeni tle yéi áyú yatee,
        yóo áyú kdunéek.
Yú diyée
yá l'éiw tóox yaa kana.éin aa, áyú yéi kaaxát.
Yóo yú kíndei dagátch yóo héen takaanáx.
Haat yáx kuwanéekw yóo x'óol' kíndei dagátch.
Wé sít' áx yaa kana.en yé áwé yéi kaaxát.
Yóo míngi yáx kawduwahéen yú s'é.
S'é áyú ch'u tle mínk kawduhéeni yáx yatee wé.   120
Aagáa áwé dawóotl déin koowanei.
Wáa sá yóo? Tlél aadéi kúxdei yóo naxdudzineiyi yé.
Aagáa áwé tle
atshí has awliyéx tle wé
tlagoo káax'u ku.aa.
Naanaa Hít áwé nándei la.áa.
Naanaa Hít.
Wé i aat
gwál yé tlél i een yoo akoolneekk
wé Kaaxwaan.   130
Has du kahídi áwé nándei la.áa.
A neeyaadéi áwé la.áa haa aayí
Xinaa Hít á.
Yóo duwasáakw aagáa
Xinaa Hít á
yóo áwé duwasáakw haa aayí aagáa.
Yáadei áwé
shayadihéin hítx'.
A t'áax áwé tsu aa kdlixwás'.
Shayadahéin wé ku.oo.   140

Oh, no.
It pierced the heart of that woman,
        the mother of the girl.
It was now growing fa-a-a-a-st.   100
They said the way it was moving,
        the way it was growing, was faster
than a running dog.

Then people became afraid.
It was when the year was becoming full
people said.
It was Little Black Glacier that was there from
        long ago.
The place called Little Black Glacier.
"Little Black Glacier is already
        disappearing into the other one.
It is already disappearing into the new one,"
        is what people said.
"Oh, no.   110
What's happening? What's going
        to happen to the people?"
At the same time Glacier Bay was murky.
People said it was like diluted milk.
Down there
the one growing through the sand behaved that way.
It was churning up from the bottom of the bay.
Whirlpools churned over to the surface like the tide.
Where the glacier was moving, it behaved that way.
The clay was like diluted milk,
The clay there was just like diluted milk.   120
This was when people became frightened.
Why was it? Wasn't there any way to stop it?
That was when
they made the songs then,
those people of long ago.
Naanaa Hít stood there,
Naanaa Hít.
Your paternal aunt
Kaaxwaan
has probably told this to you.   130
Their clan house stood up the river.
Next to it stood ours,
Xinaa Hít indeed.
Its name then was

Aagáa áwé tle
du tláa een akanéek
Shaawatséek' een áwé akanéek,
"X'ayaakuwdligadi yáx áwé yatee i dachxán" yóo
        ayawsikaa.
"Yóo sít' áwé akaawagéis.
Awé de yaa haa kunalséin áwé aadéi,
aadéi yaa kana.en yé.
Tle keitl yaa nashíxi yáx áwé akana.éin.
Tle keitl yaa nashíxi yáx.
Tlax tlél tsu aadéi a jeetx at koongaanoogu yé   150
yóo aadéi yaa kana.en yé yú sít'"
yóo áwé adaayaká wé du tláa.
Aagáa áwé hú ku.aa yéi yaawakaa
"Aaa,
tle ch'u kunaliyéix' yándei yaa yeegané tle,
tle ch'u kunaliyéix' yandei yaa yeegané.
Aadéi yee guxdakel' yé.
Yee toowóoch yándei yaa ksané.
Aáa.
Yá ax dachxánk' x'ayaakuwulgáadi   160
xát áwé du eetéex
xát áwé du eetéex.
Yá ax tlaa káak hás hídi ch'a ayeex' yéi xat gugatée.
Ax tlaa káak hás hídi
ch'a ayeex' yéi xat gugatée.
Tlél ayeetx yaakw yídei kkwagoot.
Yá ax dachxánk' kwá yées shaawát áyá.
At yátx'i du jeedáx yéi kukgwastée.
Hú ku.aa du een yaakw yídei gaxyi.áat.
Xát kwá ch'a yá ax káak hás hídi tin
        yóo xat kakgwatée."   170
Tle yóo áwé adaayaká wé du sée.
Aagáa áwé
yéi adaayaká "Dú! Wáa sá tsú x'ayeeká?
Daat yís sáyú ch'a yáax' yéi i ngatéé? Wa.é tsú,
wa.é xáa tsú haa een." "Tléik'
Tlél yee een.
Tlél yee een yáatx kukkwateen.
Aaa!
Yá
ax tlaa káak hás hídi
        ch'a aan yoo xat kakgwatée,"   180

Xinaa Hít, indeed,
that was the name of ours then.
There were many
other houses.
And there was a row of houses behind these too.
There were many people there.   140
That's when
the mother of the girl told her mother,
told Shaawatséek'.
"It seems your granddaughter has
        broken a taboo," she told her.
"She called that glacier.
Now it's nearly on top of us, the way
the way it's growing.
It's growing like a running dog.
It's like a running dog.
There's no way to get away from it   150
the way the glacier has been growing,"
she said to her mother.
That's when her mother said,
"Yes,
then just prepare ahead of time, then,
then just prepare ahead of time.
The place you will escape to:
prepare it in your minds.
Yes!
This little granddaughter of mine
        that broke the taboo,   160
I will take her place,
I will take her place.
I will stay in my mother's maternal uncles' house.
I will simply stay
in my mother's maternal uncle's house.
I will not leave to go to the boats.
But this granddaughter of mine is a young woman.
Children will be born from her.
So you will take her aboard with you.
But whatever happens to my maternal uncles'
        house will happen to me."   170
That's what she said to her daughter.
That's when
she replied, "Hey! What are you saying?
Why should you stay behind? You too,
you'll go with us too." "No!

yóo áwé x'ayaká
Shaawatséek' ku.aa.
Kaasteen ku.aa wé yaakw yíkdei."
(Awé tle yóo áwé shandutlékwch sh kalneegéech.
Xáach aadéi xwasikuwu yé; aadéi
        xa.áxji yé; áyá ayáx kaxlanik
nuch.
Yá yax has yawdlishán ax léelk'u hás
has du káx' ax daa aawadaak,
has du x'éidáx áwé
kaxanéek.)   190
Aagáa áwé
yéi yawakaa hú ku.aa
yú kaa tláa
du xúx teen akanéek
"Yóo áwé x'ayaká ax tláa ka yóo, ka yóo."
Aagáa áwé wé kaa káak ku.aa
shí alyéix.
Shí alyéix.
Akoo.aakw wé shí
alyéixi.   200
Naanaa Hítdei woogoot.
Tle tsu ch'u áx' áwé tle tsu
yéi ayawsikaa
aáa
Kaanaxduwóos'
ch'áagu aayí,
"Shí áyá xlayéix.
Wáa sá kwshí gé i kgwatée wa.é tsú gé
shí ilayéxni?
Tlax ch'as tlax l daa sá haa x'éidei
        koonaxduneek   210
yáadax gunayéi
haa dakél'ni."
"Yak'éi" tle yóo yaawakaa, "yak'é
Daa yóo tuxaatangi át áwé.
Daa yóo tuxaatánk.
Yándei kkwasanéi"
yóo áwé ash yawsikaa.
"A káax' áwé tle
kaydachák.
Kaydachák." Desgwach wé   220
wé Aax'w Xoo t'ikáwu; desgwach.

I am not going with you.
I won't leave here with you.
Yes!
What happens to this,
my mother's maternal uncles' house will happen to
          me,"
is what   180
Shaawatséek' said.
"But Kaasteen will go in the boat."
(It's usually switched by story tellers.
This is the way I know the story,
          the way I heard it; this is how
I tell it.
My maternal grandfathers, those who were already aged
when I first became aware of them,
I'm telling it
from their lips.)
That's when   190
the mother of the girl
said,
telling her husband,
"My mother is saying such and such."
That's when the maternal uncle
was composing a song.
He was composing a song.
He was trying to compose
a song.
He went over to Naanaa Hít.   200
This was where
he said
yes
to Kaanaxduwóos',
the one of long ago,
"I am composing a song.
How would it be if you
compose a song too?
It wouldn't be right if there might
          not be anything heard from us
when we begin   210
our escape from here."
"Fine!" he said. "Good.
That's what I've been thinking about.
I've been thinking about it.
I will compose one,"

De wé Aax̲'w
X̲oo duwasáagu yé de a t'ikáwu áwé
wé sít'.
Aadéi yaa kana.en yé.
Ch'u tle ch'u tle yasatgi át áyu ayaawadlaak̲.
Aadéi yaa kana.en yé yú sít.
Aag̲áa áwé
tle has kawdichák.
Daa sá kwshíwé kducháak   230
wé yaakw yíkdei?
Yaakw yíkdei kawduwa.aak̲w
dulnáax'u yaakw yíkdei.
Ch'u tle wé aan yaká yaa kunaséini wé
wé Aax̲'w X̲oo t'iká,
aag̲áa áwé wé héen k̲u.aa ch'u tle yóo
kíndei shakdakudli yáx̲ k̲uwaneekw.
Aag̲áa áwé k̲aa tóox̲ yei k̲unatéen; aag̲áa áwé
        tle ldkát wé aan áwé át wuduwaxoon tle.
Tle yakwkáa yándei yaa k̲unanein de,
de yakwkáa yándei yaa k̲unanein.   240
Aag̲áa yakwkáa yan k̲unéi áwé
wé hú k̲u.aa tlél du tuwáa ushgú yaakw yíkdei wugoodi
wé k̲aa léelk'w.
"Ax̲ dachx̲ánk' yaakw yíkdei du een nay.á.
Wé Kaasteen yaakw yídei du een nay.á.
X̲át k̲u.aa ch'a yáax̲'
yá ax̲ léelk'w hás hídi ax̲ tlaa káak hás hídi teen
        yóo x̲at kakg̲watée" yóo áwé x̲'ayaká.
Ach áwé tle yaakw yídei du nák̲ g̲unayéi aawa.át.
De shakastíx'i áwé yaakw.
Naanaa Hítnáx̲ aa kéi kawduwashée wé shí.   250

        First Song

Eehee iyaa
eehee yei hei yaa
yei aalaa hei yaahaa
ei hei hayoo oo
aalaa iyaa aa laa

Ax̲ aali
gushei, hei yaa
yei aalaa hei yaa aa

he said to him.
"As soon as I'm done,
you pack.
you pack." Soon   220
it was reaching the outside of Aax'w X̱oo; soon.
The glacier
was outside the place called
Aax'w X̱oo.
How swiftly it was growing.
It was even, even faster than anything.
How swiftly the glacier was growing,
This was when
they packed.
I wonder what they packed   230
into the boats?
Into the boats they worked at
lifting their packs, into the boats.
When it was nearing the front of the village
on the outside of Aax'w X̱oo,
then the water behaved just like
it was churning up in large chunks.
That's when people became frightened;
        That's when the whole village
        began to get ready then.
Then they were getting ready in the boats,
they were getting ready in the boats.   240
Then, when they were ready in the boats
that grandmother
didn't want to go aboard.
"Take my little granddaughter aboard with you.
Take Kaasteen aboard with you.
But I will just stay here.
Whatever happens to my grandparents' house,
        to my mother's maternal uncles' house
        will happen to me," she said.
That is why they began boarding the boats without her.
They were already anchored in the bay.
They began singing the song from Naanaa Hít.   250

        First Song

Eehee iyaa
eehee yei hei yaa
yei aalaa hei yaahaa

yei hei hayoo ooo
aalaa iyaa aa haaa

Ax̲ hidi,
gushei, hei yaa
yei aalaa hei yaahaa
yei hei hayoo ooo
aalaa iyaa aa haaa

Hwee-e-e-e-e-e. G̲aax̲ a.

Second Song
(sung twice)

Ishaan gushei hei
ax̲ aani hee
i shaan gushei, hei
ax̲ aani hee
dinak̲ yaa k̲x̲agoot aa
hee hee hee hee
ahaa haa haa haa
yee hee hee hee
ahaa haa haaa
yee hee yaa hee hee.

Ishaan gushei hei
ax̲ hidi hee
ishaan gushei hei
ax̲ hidi hee
dinak̲ yaa k̲x̲aak̲oox̲, aa
hee hee hee hee
ahaa haa haa haaa
yee hee hee hee
ahaa haa haa
yee hee yaa hee.

G̲aax̲ aa...
G̲aax̲ daa sheeyí áyá.

ei hei hayoo oo
aalaa iyaa aa laa

My land
will I ever....
yei aalaa hei yaa aa
yei hei hayoo ooo
aalaa iyaa aa haaa

My house
will I ever....
yei aalaa hei yaahaa
yei hei hayoo ooo
aalaa iyaa aa haaa

Hwee-e-e-e-e-e. This is a cry.

Second Song
(sung twice)

Won't my land
be pitiful
Won't my land
be pitiful
when I leave on foot?
hee hee hee hee
ahaa haa haa haa
yee hee hee hee
ahaa haa haaa
yee hee yaa hee hee.

Won't my house
be pitiful
won't my house
be pitiful
when I leave by boat?
hee hee hee hee
ahaa haa haa haaa
yee hee hee hee
ahaa haa haa
yee hee yaa hee.

This is a cry.
This is a song for the cry.

Sít' Kaa Káx Kana.áa
Kooteen x'éidáx sh kalneek

Yá yeedát aadéi gunéi sh kak̲kwalnik yé
yá yagiyi.
Haa
shux'áanáx̲,
aadéi yoo haa kudiyeigi yé
yá Glacier Bay.
Aadéi ax̲' yoo haa kawdiyayi yé.
Haa x̲oodáx̲ áyá yá shatkátsk'u
Chookaneidí.
A áyá   10
ts'ítskw áyá
awsiwát.
Yéi duwasáakw
(tlax̲ ch'u short cut áyá oosaaych)
ts'ítskw.
Ts'ats'ée yoo áhé duwasáakw, yá
yei kwdzigéi
héen k̲ukát kanashínch.
A áyá
a k'wát'i áyá tle   20
tle a tóonáx̲ yóot wugoodí áyá;
        tle awsineix̲ yá shaatk'átsk'ooch.
Tle yéi a daayakáa nooch.
Tle a jikgwanaag̲í áwé yaak latséen.
Tle a jikgwanaag̲í áwé tle yéi ayanask̲éich,

260

Glacier Bay History
told by Amy Marvin

Now this is the way I will begin telling the story
today.
Now,
at the beginning
of how things happened to us
at Glacier Bay.
the way things happened to us there.
This little girl was one of us
Chookaneidí.
It was she
who raised   10
the bird.
Its name was
(she would shorten up the name)
ts'ítskw.
Ts'ats'ée was its full name; these
tiny ones
that swim on the sea.
It was when
it came
out of its egg this little girl saved it.   20
She would say to it
as she was letting it go when it got strong,
as she was letting it go she would say to it,

"Tlél naali yéidei yoo i gútgoo_k.
Tlél naali yéidei yoo i gútgoo_k; _kut kéi
    i gu_xlas'ées.
Chookaneidí áyá uháan.
Chookaneidí áyá uháan; _kut kéi i k_kwa_géex'.
Tle ch'ayóok',
tle ch'ayóok, haagú."   30
Yá "Chookaneidí" tle du sháan tóoná_x neil
    yaawdi_gích gíyá yá ts'ats'ée _ku.aa.
Yáax' áwé tle
tle du _xáni ku_xkoodayáaych tle.
Tle yéi áwé tle ash ée_x toowadaa.
A áyá yá
aawdzi_xeet,
á_x'.
Tlákw woosh eetée_x yaa gas_xítch á_x'.
Aa_gáa áyá
tle yéi s _x'ayaká   40
"Chóooooooo-
kaneidí."
Yaakw háa awusteení tle yéi has _xayaká, "Chóoooo-
kaneidí."
Has _k'asa_góo nooch.
Ch'u yeedádidéi yei s _x'ayaká.
A tsú aan haa _x'éi_x akdudliyáakw.
Yéi duwasaakw wé shaatk'átsk'u kwá Shkwá_x'.
Shkwá_x'
yéi áhé duwasáakw.   50
Hú áyá yá ts'ítskw awsiwát.
Haa.
Aadá_x
k'e aadéi haa kandayáayi
aadéi át shushatin yé.

Yáax' áyá
du éet _koowaháa
yá shaatk'.
Yées
yées   60
at t'éit dus.áa.
Yáa yagiyee yéi wduwasáakw teenager.
A_x áyá wsitee yá shaatk'.
Kaasteen.

"Don't go too far.
Don't go too far; you might blow away.
We are Chookaneidí.
We are Chookaneidí; I might lose you
So come back right away,
right away."   30
Maybe it was "Chookaneidí" that stuck
        in the mind of the bird.
Here it would
come back to her then.
This was how it got used to her.
It was this bird
that multiplied
there.
They multiply one generation after another over there.
It was then
they would say   40
"Chooooo-
kaneidí."
When they saw a boat they would say "Choooo-
kaneidí."
They're fun to listen to.
They say this even now.
People don't believe us when we tell this either.
The name of this little girl was Shkwáx̱'.
Shkwáx̱'
was her name.   50
She is the one who raised the bird.
Well,
from there
look at what's been happening to us,
to where this has led us.

Now
the time had come
for this young woman.
Very young
newly   60
put in confinement.
Today she would be called teenager.
This is what this young girl was.
Kaasteen.
This was when

Aagáa áyá
dus.áa.
Tlél yú neil.
Tle yá hit
tóonáx áwé.
Eet kuxdusteech.   70
Yáa yeedadi kusteeyí yáx áyú at yatee.
Tlél yú neilnax.áa kawuhá yú yéi kawdiyayi káa.
Tle yá hít tóonáx áwé
du daakahídi dulyeixch.
Aagáa áwé
kuwduwa.éex'.
Kuwduwa.éex' áwé yoo at kuwateek.
Aadéi áwé tle hóoch'
tle ldakát ku.éex'dei yaa kukandak'ít'.
Yá shaatk' du tláa ku.aa áwé   80
tle ash xánt uwagút.
Gaat yuwaax'éeshi áwé tle ash jeet yéi awsinéi.
"Ná."
Yá shaatk'átsk'u kwá gwál nas'gidooshú táakw
        yá shaatk'átsk'u.
Ayá du tláa du éex tuwsitee tlél du tuwáa ushgú.
Tlél public-déi kaa yátx'i yóo jidul.átgin
aagáa yú gaaw
woosh yáa awudané kát.
Aadéi at téeyi yé.
Tlél kaa yátx'i   90
ch'a baby tsú tlél át yóo koodujélk.
Awé du séek' éex áwé tuwsitee yá shaawát.
A áwe
da.áak.
Du da.aagí daak aawatán.
Da.áak.
Hóoch'! Tlél koodakáatk'.
Awé tle yá shaawátx wusiteeyi aa xándei áwé
        wjixeex yá shaatk'átsk'u ku.aa.
Tle a xánt ishkák.
Axá wé atx'éeshi.   100
Wé Kaasteen.
Alwáal'.
Ch'a yák'udáx áwé yíndei yóo wdzigeet.
Aagáa áwé tle kéi ashoowa.áx.
Tle yáanáx áwé alshát yú.á wé atx'éeshi.

they had her sit.
Not in the house.
But in an extension
of the house.
A room would be made.   70
It was like the bedrooms of today.
Someone who was in this condition would not be
          allowed inside the main house.
They would build a room for her
extending from the main house.
At the same time
there was a feast.
A feast was being held.
Everybody was gone,
everyone had gone to the feast.
But this young girl's mother   80
went to see her.
She gave her some sockeye strips.
"Here."
There was another little girl,
          a little girl maybe 8 years old.
Her mother didn't want to leave her.
People didn't take their children out in public
in those days
because they respected one another.
This is how things were.
People didn't take children   90
even the babies.
This woman didn't want to leave her little girl.
She was weaving
a basket.
She brought her weaving out.
She wove.
They were all gone! It was deserted.
Then the little girl ran in by the one
          who had become a woman.
She sat with her.
Kaasteen   100
was eating the dryfish.
She broke them.
All of a sudden she bent down.
This is when she lifted the edge of her wall.
They say she held the dryfish out with one hand.

Tle yéi áwé áa yaa yawdzi.aa.
Tle aadéi yaa akananik yé áyú
        yú shaatk'átsk'u du tláa een.
"Néi!
Sít'!
Geis, geis, geis, geis, geis.   110
Néi!
Sít'!
Geis, geis, geis, geis, geis, geis.
Néi!
Sít'!
Geis, geis, geis, geis, geis!"
Tle áx áwé ashoowa.aax.
Tle du yáa kut wunei yú shaatk'átsk'u.
Ach áwé tle wdigoot; tle du tlaa xáni daak
        wujixíx.
"Atléi!   120
Waa sáyú x'ayaká?"
'Néi!
Sít'!
Geis geis geis.'
Tle nas'gidahéen yéi yawakaa.
Atléi!
Nas'gidahéen tle yéi yaawakaa."
"Dáa! Júk!
Ldakát yéidei yaa yagakéich,"
tle yóo áwé ayawsikaa du séek'.   130
Yá shaawát áyá wítless-x wusitee.
Yá du séek' teen neilí wukeiyi
        shaawát áyá wítless-x wusitee
du daat
yá Kaasteen daat.
Ach áyá
ch'u shóogu áx yaa ktoonikji yé.
Tlél ch'a yeisú.
Ayá wóosht kawdujeil yá sh kalneek.
Tle aadéi yaa kandulnik yé áyá.
Ax léelk'w,   140
ax tláa,
ax éesh,
tle has wuwáadi áyá kutx has shoowaxeex.
Ach áyá tlél
a wanáakx áyá yaa koonaxlaník ax toowóoch;

Then she bent down that way.
This is how the little girl told it to her mother.
"Hey,
glacier!
Here, here, here, here, here.   110
Hey,
glacier!
Here, here, here, here, here, here."
Hey,
glacier!
here, here, here, here, here.
Then she lowered the wall.
The little girl was surprised by this.
That was why she got up; she ran out by her mother.
"Mom!   120
Why is she saying this?
'Hey,
glacier!
Here, here, here.'
Three times she said this.
Mom!
Three times she said this."
"Don't say that! Go away!
You're always saying things,"
she said to her little daughter.   130
This woman was the witness.
This one who stayed home with her
          little daughter was the witness
about her,
about Kaasteen.
This is why
we tell it the same way.
We didn't just
toss this story together.
This is the way it's told.
My grandmother,   140
my mother,
my father,
were very old when they died.
This is why I don't
deviate when I tell it; I tell it exactly right.
At that time
the ice

_kuná_x ayá_x áyá yaa kana_xlaník.
Aagáa áwé
tlél yú dikéená_x áwé _gunayéi shayawuxaash
yá t'éex'.
Diyéená_x áwé,
diyéená_x áwé _gunayéi yawdig̲ích.   150
Ach áwé tlél wuduskú.
Hél aadóoch sá wuskú.
Tle ch'a yák'wdá_x áwé yá a kát aawa.aadi aa aan
a̲ kat'óott uwagás'.
Wáa sáyá tle kawdzinét yá aan?
Wáa sáyá?
Yoo aan ka.á_x áwé tle wduwajee; tlél yéi _kooshtú.
Tsu a yinaadéi aa,
tsu a yinaadéi aa.
Wáa sáyá tlél tliyéi yéi utee_x.   160
Tle ásíwéi gé, tle tláakw ásíwéi gé woosh
     t'ikaadéi yaa yandag̲ích yá t'éex'.
Ach áwé déi
woosh _xánt wuduwa.át.
"Wáa sáyá at kawdiyaa?
Cha ch'a tléix' dahéen _xaa yá.
Wáa sáyá?
Tléik' á,
tlé yoo aan ka.á gwáa yáa gé?
Tle ch'as a tóodei áyá yaa aa natéen."
Tle tsu tlél yéi _kuwustóo.   170
Tle tsu yéi woonei.
Yáax' áwé tsá déi, yéi yaawakaa wé shaawát,
"Aatlein át áwé! Yú eetkát aa aa áwé.
Yú at_x'éeshi teen akaawageis."
Goot'á sáwé sít' áwu á?
Tlél sít' aadéi duteen.
A áwé a saayí a jeet aawatée yá kaasteench
     _ku.aa; yú "sít'" yóo aawasaa.
Daa sáyú yéi ayasáakw?
Yéi gugéink' áwé á_x wulixáat'i át áwé.
Awé tle saa a jeet aawatée.   180
Ach áwé tle yaa _koosgéix'i _kwá
     tle woosh _xánt wudi.át.
"Oh!
Tlél ásíwé á yá_x yawukaa."
Daa wlig̲aasi káa _xá,

didn't begin advancing from the top.
It began advancing from the bottom,
from the bottom.   150
That was why no one knew.
Not one person knew.
All of a sudden it struck
the middle of the land that people were living on.
Why was the land shaking?
Why was it?
People thought it was an earthquake;
        it didn't bother anyone.
Then another one,
then another one.
Why didn't it quit?   160
Here it was the ice crushing against
        itself and moving in.
That was why
they finally gathered together.
"What's happening?
It should happen just once.
Why is this?
Oh no!
It wasn't an earthquake, was it?
It's becoming stronger."
The people forgot about it again.   170
Then it happened again.
Here this woman finally said
"Oh dear! It's the one sitting in the room.
She called it with dryfish like a dog."
Where was the glacier?
There wasn't a glacier to be seen.
But that was what Kaasteen
        gave a name to; she named it "sít'."
What was it she named this?
There was a little piece stuck there.
That was what she gave a name to.   180
That was why the people who were wise gathered then.
"Oh!
I guess she said a bad thing."
When a person who is ritually unclean, you see,
mistakenly does something,
it turns bad.
That's the reason,

daa sá mistake-déin awsinei,
tlél áyáx utí.
Tle yéi áwé,
tle yéi áwé
tle woosh xángaa wduwa.aat.
Oh, x'ayaakuwdligát ásíwé   190
mistake-déin ásíwé yóot x'awditán a daax'.
Haahá.
Tle woosh kanax áwé kéi kukdak'ít'ch.
Tle woosh kanax áwé kéi kukdak'ít'ch.
Yax at gakú dawóotl yáx yaa at nanein kaa
        aaní áwé; kaa neilí áwé át akéen.
Áwé a káa yaa at kandaxíl'.
Tle tlél yei ushtú wé shaawát ku.a.
Tle gíyáa du tóodei de yaa nagút ch'a tlákw.
Du káx áyú,
du káx áyú yéi yan kawdiyáa yú sít'.   200
Aadéi aawaxooxu yé yáx.
Yáax' áwé yéi kuyaawakaa,
"X'ayaakuwdligát ásíwé.
Góok,
at gaxduxoon dé yáadáx."
Tlél áwé gaa yaa unashtéen.
Ch'u tle yándei yóo aa sixíxk de, wé hít
aadéi kei latsinji yé; yú
        (Slap!)
woosh t'ikaadéi
dagatji yáx kuwanóok.   210
        (Slap!)
Yú t'éex' aadéi, aadéi litseeni yé.
Tle áwé tle wdudzikóo.
Yá t'éex'ch ásíwéi gé yaa kukanashít' gé.
Yaa akanalshít' áwé; yá aan áwé yaa akanalshít'.
Aagáa áwé yéi kuyaawakaa, "Góok!
        Góok! Góok! Góok!
Góok!
Naa gaxlagáas'i dé.
Góok!
Naa gaxlagáas'.
Tlél áyá gaa wushtee.   220
Tlél áyá gaa wushtee."
Aagáa áwé tle yéi kuyaawakaa.
"Góok, at gaxtooxoon.

that's the reason
they gathered together.
Oh, she violated a taboo, didn't she?   190
I guess she mistakenly said things about the ice.
Oh, no.
They kept gathering.
They kept gathering.
They were really troubled by the way
        things were turning out on their land;
        people stayed in their homes.
It was becoming troublesome too.
But the young girl wasn't bothered by this anymore.
Perhaps it was changing her every moment.
It was because of her,
the glacier was doing this because of her.   200
Because of the way she called it over.
Here they said
"I guess she broke a taboo, didn't she?
Quick!
Let's get ready to get out."
Things weren't turning out right.
The house was already falling over on its side
from how strong the ice was getting.
        (Slap!)
It was was behaving
like it was crushing against itself,   210
        (Slap!)
how strong the ice was.
And they knew.
It was the ice pushing the people, wasn't it?
It was pushing; it was pushing the village along.
This was when people said, "Quick!
        Quick! Quick! Quick!
Quick.
Let's move the people.
Quick!
Move the people.
It isn't right.   220
It isn't right."
This was when they said,
"Quick! Let's pack.
Her too.
It's ok to take the one who broke the taboo; it's ok.

Hú tsú,
_gaa yatee wé x'ayaa_kuwdlig̱adi aa; g̱aa yatee
yaax g̱aag̱agoot!
Yaax g̱aag̱agoot."
Woosh daa tuwudzinóokw xá.
Hél aadéi áa jeex̱duwanaag̱i yé; yées shaawát áwé,   230
yées shaatk'.
Aaa, yax at g̱wakú, "at x'aakeidí sákw áwé,
        dus.áa."
Awé yéi yan kawdiyáa.
Aag̱áa áwé tle yéi _kuyaawakaa
"Ha ch'a tlél wáa sá utí yaax wugoodí.
Yaax g̱aag̱agoot."
Ach áwé tle x'awduwawóos', ch'a yóonáx.
"Dé kéi at gax̱duxóon áyá.
Góok,   240
i daa.ádi k'idéin.
K'idéin."
"Tléik',
tlél yaax yéi kkwagoot."
Tláw'!
Tláakw áwé kée yóo x'eiwanei.
" 'Tlél yaax yéi kg̱wagoot,' yú.á
        wé x'ayaa_kuwdlig̱adi aa.
Tlél du tuwáa ushgú yaax wugoodi yú.á."
Haahá!
Tle g̱uneitkanaayéet shuwjix̱ín.
"Wéit'aa du aat aadéi ng̱agoodí
du aat; góok, góok, góok."   250
Héináx̱.á _kwá at wuduwaxoon; x̱'óol' yáx̱ at
        yatee de.
Tle tlákw áyá kawdzinét,
tlákw áwé kawdzinét; adawóotl yáx̱ at yatee de.
Yeedadi aayí óoxjaa yáx̱ g̱íyú.
Tle kulix̱éitlshán aadéi yaa kanax̱at yé.
A sóox áwé.
"Aaa, yóo kawuhaayí, _ka yóo kudayéini kálk'w
ax éek' sée
yóo kudayéini, ha
góok   260
at gaxoon,
at gaxoon!
Eesháan i tláa i éesh eesháan."

Let her come aboard.
Let her come aboard."
People used to cherish each other, you see.
There was no way they could have
          left her there; she was a young woman
a young girl.   230
Yes, like the saying, "they had her sitting for
          seed."
This is when this happened to her.
This was when people said,
"There's nothing wrong with her coming aboard.
Let her come aboard."
That was why they asked her, indirectly,
"People will be getting ready now.
Quick!
Fix your clothes.
Fix them."   240
"No!
I won't go aboard."
Oh no!
Her words spread quickly.
"She said, 'I won't go aboard,'
          the one who broke the taboo.
She said she doesn't want to go aboard."
Oh, no.
Then it came to the opposite groups.
"This paternal aunt of hers should go to her,
her father's sister; Quick, quick, quick."   250
On that side of the village people were packing;
          it was already like a whirlpool.
The village was trembling constantly,
trembling constantly; it was as if
          they were expecting disaster.
Perhaps it was like the storm we just had.
It was very frightening the way things were.
They were trying to beat it.
"Yes, because it is like this, and
          because it is this way, my niece,
my brother's daughter
because things are this way, now,
let's go,   260
pack,
pack!

Du een yoo x̱'adudli.átk.
"Tléik'!
Tléik'!
Tlél yaax̱ yéi kkwagoot.
Tlél yaax̱ yéi kkwagoot.
Ch'a wáa yeikuwáat'dei sáyá
ax̱ yáa yéi kg̱watée yá aadéi yax̱waaḵaayi yé."   270
Tlél oosháaḵ.
"Ch'a wáa yeikuwáat'dei sáyá ax̱ yáa yéi kg̱watée.
Aadéi yax̱waaḵaayi yé; ách áwé
tlél yaax̱ yéi kkwagoot; tlél yéi kg̱watée."
Ách áwé déi du x̱'ayáax̱ kaa taawahaa.
Ach áwé yei ḵuyaawaḵaa
"Góok!
Yáat'át ḵu.aa déi
du x̱ándei.
Hél aadéi ch'a yéi jix̱duwanaag̱i yé.   280
Aaa,
góok!"
Tle gunayéi yaawax̱íx̱.
Daa sáyá yatsáagu yáx̱ yateeyi át áwé,
aan du x̱ándei g̱unayéi aawa.át
du aat hás
ldakát
tle yá uhaan hás teen
du x̱ándei
du atx̱aayí sákw.   290
"Kaasteen x̱'éidei!
Kaasteen x̱'éidei!"
Tle yéi áwé
daa sáyá
ash g̱walit'áayi át.
Yá daa sá dujákx̱i tle dusx̱óok
yá a doogú.
Tle x̱'óowx̱ dax̱dulyéix̱.
Tle á áwé tle; "Kaasteen kaadéi!
(Kaasteen kaadéi!)   300
Kaasteen x̱'éidei!
(Kaasteen x̱'éidei!)
Kaasteen kaadéi!"
Tle yéi áwé.
tle du náḵ ayadu.átx̱ tle.
Haa,

Pity your mother, take pity on your father."
They begged her.
"No!
No!
I won't go aboard.
I won't go aboard.
What I said
will stain my face forever."   270
She didn't deny it.
What I said will stain my face
forever; this is why
I won't go aboard; it won't happen.
That was why they gave up on her.
That was why they said
"Let's go!
But let's take these things
to her.
We can't just leave her this way.   280
Yes.
Let's go!"
It began to happen.
They began going to her
with things that would keep,
her paternal aunts,
all of them,
with all of us,
going to her
with things for her food.   290
"For Kaasteen to eat!
For Kaasteen to eat!"
In this way they brought
whatever
might keep her warm,
the skins
of whatever was killed and dried.
They were made into robes.
These, "For Kaasteen!"
("For Kaasteen!")   300
"For Kaasteen to eat!"
("For Kaasteen to eat!")
"For Kaasteen!"
In this way
they turned then and left her.

ach áwé tle kaa x'éi yéi wootee
tle ch'a wáa yeikuwáat'dei sáyá kaa x'éi yéi yatee
kaa toowú asinóogu káa tle du kaadéi at dujákx.
Cha ch'a a ítdáx tsá kaa toowú
        kei klatseench.   310
Ka "du x'éidei," yóo tsú yoo kuwaakéik.
Cha ch'a du x'éidáx áwé tsá goot aa naa jeex dutee
du x'éit kuxda.oot.
Aagáa áwé du x'éit kooda.óowch
yá kaa toowú asinéegu kaa xooní.
Yú guneitkanaayéech gawdasháadi áwé hóoch tsú
        tle axá.
Ach áyá "koo.éex'" yóo at tuwasáakw.
Koo.éex' ya yagaxíxch
haa toowú neegu sh tóodáx kei xtudateeyít.
Cha ch'a yóo guneitkanaayí jeet wuteeyí   320
yá, daa sá yan wutuwashadi át,
cha ch'a hú du x'éit kuwda.oowú wtusakoowú; cha
        ch'a á áwé tsá haa tuwunáagux yaa ksateech.
Du éenax
yá Kaasteen.
Ka daa sá wtuwajagí át
ha Kaasteen kaadéi
guneitkanaayí jeet wutooteeyí,
cha ch'a a ítdáx tsá haa toowóo kéi latseench.
A náagux áwé sitee, haa tuwunáagu.
Yá aadéi yoo kawdiyayi yé yá Kaasteen; áyá
        kaa ée at wulitúw.   330
Aadáx áwé ldakát du kát kawduwajél.
Aaa.
Yáax' áwé.
Hóoch'.
De yaagú yíndei yaa kukandagéin.
Aagáa áwé du tóox kei at uwaxíx Shaawatséek'.
Aaa.
De woowáat.
Ax yáanáx áwé de woowáat aagáa.
"Likoodzí kwshá!"   340
Gunéi uwagút.
Aaa.
Dé du nák ayaguxda.at aa du xoonx'í áwé át nák
wé a yeex' du nák akgwa.at hídi.
Aagáa áwé tle héidei kéi ashoowaxích.

Now,
this is the reason it became a saying,
it will be a saying forever, for whomever
        is mourned, people relinquish
the ownership of things in their memory.
Only after this do we feel stronger.   310
And "for her to eat," is also said.
Only if the food which is given
        is eaten with another clan
can it go to her.
This is when she will have some,
the relative who is mourned.
When the opposite clan takes a bite
        she will also eat some.
This is the reason we call it "invitation to feast."
A feast is offered
to remove our grief.
Only when we give to the opposite clan   320
whatever we offer,
only when we know it went to her;
        only when this is done does it
        become a balm for our spirits.
Because of her,
Kaasteen.
And whatever we relinquish our ownership to,
for Kaasteen,
when we give them to the opposite clan,
only after this do our spirits become strong.
It's medicine, spiritual medicine.
Because of the things that happened to Kaasteen;
        this is what informed us.   330
When all the things were piled on her.
Yes.
Now.
They were gone.
They were all aboard the canoes.
That was when Shaawatséek' got angry.
Yes.
She was already old.
She was already older than me at the time.
"Isn't it a shame," she said.   340
She started going there.
Yes.

Aaa.
"Yee eetídei ágé yaa kkwadaxéet,
ax éek' hás?
Yaax gaysagú wé Kaasteen kwa.
Yaax gaysagú.   350
Xát kwá du eetéex'.
Tlákw áyá naná
shuxsitee.
Ach áwé xát kwa du eetéex'.
Aaa.
Yaax gaagagoot.
Yaax gaagagoot."
Aagáa áwé tle tsu salagaawdéin yóot x'awditán
        Kaasteen.
"Tlél yaax yéi kkwagoot.
Yéi yaxwaakaa tlél yaax yéi kkwagoot.   360
Ch'a yáa yéi xat gugatée."
Yéi áwé.
Tlél ayawudlaak tsu.
Haa,
hóoch' áwé.
De áx' áwé kaa taawlixaach.
That's the last one áyá
Shaawatséek' du xánt wugoodí.
Ach áwé
du xándáx yóot aawa.át.   370
De gaa áwé kaawagei.
Yax atgwakú
naaléi át wudigadi yé
du aat hás jeedáx
du sani hás jeedáx,
du tlaa hás jeedáx
atxá.
Tléli yú hít shawuheegí yáx áyú du jeet at
        wuduwatée.
Aagáa wé tsáa
yaakwdéi kukawdik'éet'.   380
Aaa.
Tléil tle yóot yawugú du nák.
Wé yaakw yée yan akée áwé
ch'a awsigook.
Tle ch'a yá at gaxoon tóox' ásíwé du sháan tóo
        yéi kuwanéekw wé Kaanaxduwóos' kwá yá shí.

```
The relatives who were going to leave her
        were standing by Kaasteen
in the house they were leaving her in.
This was when Shaawatséek' pushed the door open.
Yes.
"Am I going to bring your next generation,
my brothers?
But take Kaasteen aboard.
Take her aboard.
I will take her place.                                    350
I'm expecting death
at any moment.
So I will take her place.
Yes.
Let her go aboard.
Let her go aboard."
This was when Kaasteen spoke, in a loud voice
"I will not go aboard.
I said, I will not go aboard.
I'm staying here."                                        360
That was it.
Shaawatséek' couldn't persuade her either.
Now,
no more.
They gave up on her.
This was the last try
when Shaawatséek' came for her.
This was why
they left her.
There was enough.                                         370
It measured up.
The food
from her paternal aunts,
from her paternal uncles,
from her mother's people
was piled high.
They were leaving her with almost
        enough to fill the house.
This is when they all finally
went aboard.
Yes.                                                      380
They didn't padddle away just then.
When they were all seated in the canoes
```

Du sháan tóo yéi kuwanéekw.
Awsikóo tsú
du eegáa áa yoo a.átgi.
Ha.
Tléik', áa yan wujikák yú hít yee.   390

Ch'a yá deikéet awusgoogú áwé
tle wdudziteen.
Héidei áa yax wusixíx.
Tle kaa x'éinax yóot uwaxíx
"Héidei áa yax wusixíx!"
Tl'aadéin áwé kei wsixíx s'é,
du een wé hít.
Aaa.
Aagáa wé kaa tláa áwé kadagáax.
Kawdigaax.   400
Yá Kaasteen du tláa áwé kawdigaax.
Aaa.
Tle du x'éidáx áwé
wé sháa tsú kawdzigaax.
Ch'u l ák' has ooheení áwé tle yíndei yei
        yanasx'út',
wé a yeet aa hít
de yíndei áwé.

Naaléi áyú aax duwa.axji yé
yú kaa sé.
Aadéi gaxdusti yé.   410

Hél tsu latseen koostí.
Yaa yeedát áwé tlél,
tlél yá naná.
Daa sáwé héidei wooxeex.
Aagáa ku.aa ch'u t'ukanéiyi
wáa sá wuneiyí ch'u tle yax yaa kuwaklajákch
        wé toowóo néekw.
Aadéi woosh goonée kuditeeyi yé.
Aadéi kwdayen yé.
Aaa, ách áwé yaakwnáx wudihaan.
Ch'a kaa sé duwa.áxch.   420
Ch'a kadusgáax.
Tle kaa wakshiyeex' áwé yóo kuwateek
yíndei nasxéex wé hít.

they just drifted.
While they were packing, I guess, this song kept
        flashing on the mind of Kaanaxduwóos'.
It kept flashing on his mind.
He knew too
when they went to get her.
My!
No, she didn't want to leave the house.   390

Only when they were drifting out
they saw.
The house was rolling over.
And it popped out of their mouths
"It's rolling over!"
It fell over sideways,
and she with the house.
Yes.
That's when her mother screamed.
She screamed.
Kaasteen's mother screamed.   400
Yes.
The other women also
screamed with her.
While they couldn't believe it, it was sliding downward,
the house she sat in,
downward.

Their voices
could be heard from far away,
crying.   410

They had no more strength.
Today
death is not like that.
It's like something dropping.
At that time though,
if anything happened to even an infant,
        the grief would leave us weak.
The way we didn't want to loose each other.
The way things were.
Yes, this was why he stood up in the canoe.
The voices were still loud.   420
They were still crying.

Aagáa áwé kéi akaawashée tle.   424

     First Song

Ahaa haa hei hei
ahaa haaa hei heiiiiy
ahaa haa hei heiiiiy
aa haa hei hei
ahaa haa hei hi.aa

Ishaan gushei hei
ax hidi hee
ishaan gushei hei
ax hidi hee
dinak yaa kxaagoot, aa
hee hee aahaaa
hee hee aaa
ahaa, haaa hei hei hi.aa haa

Repeat first verse and vocables

Ishaan gushei hei
ax aani hei
ishaan gushei hei
ax aani hei
dinak yaa kxaakoox aa
hee hee aahaaa
hee hee aaa
ahaa, haa, hei, hei, hi, aaa

Repeat second verse and vocables

hooooo, hoo, hoo.

Haa, aadéi yoo s kawdiyayi yé áyá.   425
Aadéi s wooteeyi ye áyá.
Haa.
Aagáa yéigaa shí áyá,
ya Kaasteen du nák yóot kuyawugoowú.
Yá hít du daakeidí yáx yan kawdiyáa,   430
yá Chookaneidí hídi.
Du een yá héen takaadéi nasxéex kaa wakkáax'.

She was dying before their eyes
as the house slid downward.
This was when he began singing, then. 424

   First Song

Ahaa haa hei hei
ahaa haaa hei heiiiiy
ahaa haa hei heiiiiy
aa haa hei hei
ahaa haa hei hi.aa

Won't my house
be pitiful
won't my house
be pitiful
when I leave on foot?
hee hee aahaaa
hee hee aaa
ahaa, haaa hei hei hi.aa haa

Repeat first verse and vocables

Won't my land
be pitiful
won't my land
be pitiful
when I leave by boat?
hee hee aahaaa
hee hee aaa
ahaa, haa, hei, hei, hi, aaa

Repeat second verse and vocables

hooooo, hoo, hoo.

Now this is what happened to them. 425
This is how they were.
Now.
This is the song from there.
when they left Kaasteen.
This house became like her coffin, 430

Ach áyá hítt ashoowatán,
shux'aanáx kei akashée,
yá shí.
"Isháan gushé ax hídi,"
yóo yaawakaa.
Aaa.
Du nák yóot yagóo ku.as, "ishaan gushei ax aani."
Aaa.   440
Tlél kwshá tle tléix' wóosht wul.aat
yá at wulyaakw.
Yá daatoowú yanéegu,
has du xooní,
yá shaawát,
has du wakshiyeex' yóo kootée,
aaa, hél tsu aadóo sá shí du tóo yéi wunei.
Ts'as akdudlixéitl' áyú.
Ch'as sh wuduwatáat áyú aadéi koogaganeixi yé yáx,
because tlax a yáanáx áyú yatee
        yú aan aadéi kawdzinéidi yé.   450
Tlél ch'a yángaa utí.
Ach ayú ldakát akdudlixéetl'.
Ch'a aan áyá yá shí du tóo yéi woonei.
Aaa.
Ach áyá for everlasting tsu ax eetéex yaa
        kana.éin aa.
Has du jiyís recorded-x yaa nxalayéx,
has axsakóowoot waa náx sá kuwusteeyí yá shí.
Tlél kwás káa du een
sh yawuskaa.
Ch'a yáa yeedat xángaa kwás yéi yaa kandunik káa. 460
No!
Tléik'!
Haa,
aadéi kakkwalanéek tsú
á ku.aa yáat'aa,
ách yéi kawduwaneegi át.
Aadáx áwé
Wanachích t'iká
yéi xwaajée.
A t'ikáa woogóo áwé   470
yaakwnáx wudihaan
aaa,
tsu haa xooní,

this Chookaneidí house.
It went with her to the bottom of the sea
        before their eyes.
This is why the words are of the house,
when he first sang
this song
"Pity my house,"
he said.
Yes.
And when they left her, "pity my land."
Yes.   440
I guess they didn't put the comparison together
at first.
When one who was precious,
their relative,
this woman,
died before their eyes,
yes, no one else thought of songs.
They were just afraid.
They just trembled to go where they could be saved
because it was too much
        the way the land was shaking.   450
It wasn't letting up.
This was why they were afraid.
Even with all this he thought of the song.
Yes.
This is the reason it's everlasting, also for
        the generations coming after me.
I'm recording for them
so that they will know why this song came into being.
But no man volunteered
to stay with her.
But recently someone said that one did.   460
No!
No!
Well,
I will come to it,
the part of the story
why people were saying this.
After this
I guess it was
out from Pleasant Island.
When they were passing it,   470

Chookaneidí,
Sdayáat.
Hú áwé tsu yéi yaawaḵaa
"Tleiyéix' s'é,
tleiyéix' s'é."

Ách áwé tle tliyéi yéi wootee wé yaa
        yanagwen yaakw; aaa.
"X̱át tsú,   480
ax̱ tundatáani
tlél aadéi
yóodei koonax̱diyaayi yé.
X̱át tsú ax̱ toowóo aadéi yateeyi yé
ax̱ x̱'éináx̱ yóot g̱as.aax̱."
Tle áwé awsigook̲; ldakát wé yaakwx' áwé awsigook̲.

Aag̱áa áwé du tóo yéi wooneiyi shí áwé tle
        kei akaawashée.

Aaa.   488

        Second Song

Ahaa haa aaa haa
hei hei aaa hei hei
ahaa haaa aaa haa
yei hei hayoo
aaa yei hei
aaa haa haa

Ax̱ aani hee
gushei hei aaa haa
ch'al guḵateen aa
shei aanaa haa hayoo
aahaa yei hei hei hayoo
aanaa aaa haa haa
haa haa yei hei hayoo
aahaa haa haa haa.

Repeat first verse and vocables

Ax̱ hidi hee
gushei ei aa haa

Sdayáat,
a Chookaneidí,
also our relative,
stood up in the canoe.
Yes.
He also repeated,
"Stop for a moment.
Stop for a moment."

That was why they held those moving
        canoes motionless; yes.
"I too
cannot let   480
what I'm thinking
pass.
Please listen
to the way I feel too."
They began drifting; all the canoes drifted.

This is when he sang the song
        that flashed on his mind.

Yes.
                                                                    488

  Second Song

Ahaa haa aaa haa
hei hei aaa hei hei
ahaa haaa aaa haa
yei hei hayoo
aaa yei hei
aaa haa haa

My land,
will I ever
see it again?
shei aanaa haa hayoo
aahaa yei hei hei hayoo
aanaa aaa haa haa
haa haa yei hei hayoo
aahaa haa haa haa.

ch'al gukateen aa
shei aanaa hayoo
aahaa yei hei hei hayoo
aahaa aaa haa

Repeat second verse and vocables

a haa haa haa
hooooo hoo hoo.

Haa, Sdayáat aayí áyá.
Aaa.   490
Yéi áyá dáxnáx áyá shí has awliyéx
yá at kandaxéel'.
Haa.
Hél ch'a koogéiyi a nák yaa s woonagwéin.
Haa,
tsu ch'a yá T'akdeintaan
tsu hél sh tóot has kuwdashí
ka yá Kaagwaantaan
ka yá Wooshkeetaan.
Ch'u tlei yéi yaa kuwanagwéin.   500
Ch'as hás áyá yá s du toowú néegu
        s du x'éinax kíndei yóo woonei.
Tlél ch'a koogéiyi a nák yóodei has yawugoo tle.
Haa.
Aagáa áyá tsá gunayéi yaawagóo.
Wooshkeetaan áwé
yá Excursion Inlet yóo duwasáakw yeedát,
aadéi áwé yan yaawagóo.
Kaagwaantaan ku.aa áwé s

yáa yá Ground Hog Bay,
Kax'noowú   510
yéi gíyá sh disáakw.
A áyá aadéi áyá yan yaawagóo
        hás ku.aa yá Kaagwaantaan aayí.
Uháan ku.aa wé tle tsú gunayéi
        haa yaawagóo s du dakádin.
Lakooxas't'aakhéen.
Yáadu á.
Yá at shasatéen; ch'u yeedát áwé á;

Repeat first verse and vocables

My house,
will I ever
see it again?
shei aanaa hayoo
aahaa yei hei hei hayoo
aahaa aaa haa

Repeat second verse and vocables

a haa haa haa
hooooo hoo hoo.

Now, this is Sdayáat's song.
Yes.   490
This is how the two of them composed songs
when trouble came.
Well,
they didn't just abandon her carelessly.
Now,
not even the T'akdeintaan
searched their minds,
or the Kaagwaantaan,
or the Wooshkeetaan.
They just left.   500
It was only these men who expressed their pain.
They didn't just leave her carelessly.
Now
only then they began leaving.
The Wooshkeetaan
went to the place
called Excursion Inlet today.
But the Kaagwaantaan

went to Ground Hog Bay.
I guess it's called   510
Grouse Fort.
This is where they went, the group of Kaagwaantaan.
As for us, we continued away from them.
There is
a river called Lakooxas't'aakhéen.

yá Frank Norten-ch aanx̱ wuliyex̱,
yá g̱eey yáx̱ yateeyi yé.
Tle á áyá, héeni wtuwa.aat.
Haa
lisaag̱ée x̱á yaakw yík.   520
Aag̱áa áyá áx' héeni aawa.aat; tle áyá tle
        chush ya.áak yéi wdudzinei tle,
Spasski.
Laḵoox̱as't'aakhéen yéi duwasáakw.
Tle á áyá tle áx' héeni has woo.aat.
Haa yax̱ at g̱wakú
adawóotl kayáx̱ at yatee.
Tlél daa sá ḵoostí.
Tle yéi áyá.

It flows there; it's still there today;
     where Frank Norten made his land,
a place like a cove.
It was there; we waded ashore.
Now
you know how tiring it is to be in a canoe.   520
It was then and there we waded ashore;
     this is where we prepared a place to live
at Spasski.
It's called La̲kooxas't'aakhéen.
It was there we waded ashore.
It was like
after a war.
There was nothing.
This is how it was.

Anóoshi
Yaaneekee x'éidáx sh kalneek

Nas'gadooshú jinkaat kaa nas'gadooshú áyá
      ax katáagu.
August
15th
dax áyá yé yakakgwagéi
ax katáagu.
Aagaa kuxdzitee.
S'iták
ax éeshch áa xat wusiwát.
Du hídi at al.aayéen ax éesh S'iták.
Ax' áyá kuxdzitee.   10
Atx áyá xat uwawát.
Ax éeshch aa xat wusiwát.
Aaa,
áa adáx áyá
yá Laaxaayík yóo duwasaagu yé at haawligás'
S'itákdáx.
Ayá áx' yei haa wootixwx'.
Aaa, yá L'uknax.ádi yóo haa duwasáakw.
Aaa, yá Lingit'aani tóox'
tlél tlax haa shayawdahaa.   20
Aaa,
L'uknax.ádi
átgaa tutí.
At has yawuguwún

First Russians
told by Charlie White

My age is 88.
On August
15th
that will be
my age.
That's how long I have lived.
Situk
is where my father raised me.
My father had his house there in Situk.
That's where I was born.
It's where I grew up.   10
My father raised me there.
Yes,
and from there
we moved to this place called Laax̱aayík
from Situk.
And that is where we lived.
Yes, we are called L'uknax̱.ádi.
In the world
there aren't many of us.
Yes,   20
L'uknax̱.ádi
were traders.
They travelled a lot
also to that side, the mouth of Copper River,

tsu héináx á Ikhéeni a wát,
átgaa tutí.
Aaa, áyá
yá Yakwdáatt has yawaagóo
jinkaat yaakw
yá at doogúgaa tutí.   30
Aaa,
kúxdei yaa has yakwdagoo áyá
has du kax' yaa kaawadaa
yú eey.
Waa sá akat xát seiwax'akw a saayí?

Aaa, Lituya Bay.
Ayá
ax' héent
wdzik'ít L'uknax.ádi,
jinkaat yaakw,   40
hóoch'
tlél tsu tleináx.
Kúxdei nú káx' has du een wulihaash
dáxnáx káa.
A tadáat kéen
dáxnáx.
X'aats'ák'u
yóo aa duwasáakw
ka
Xíxch'i Shaan.   50
Kúxdei nú káx' has du een wulihaash
yú yaakw a tadáat has kéen.
Woosh dayéen has dakeen akát.
Has du kaa yandéi yaa xiga.aat áyá
yá Xíxch'i Shaan yóo duwasáagu aa
xíxch' áyú a x'eitee.
Gwá-gwá-gwá-gwá.
Yá du dayéen aayí ku.aa áyú
sh wudligák yéil yáx áyú.
Sh dli.áxch,   60
gáa-gáa-gáa-gáa-gáa.
Dei yáa yeedát yáx has du kaa yándei yáa
        xeina.át.
Yaakw tadaat has kéen.
Hóoch'!
Hél has wuduskú waa sá has kawdayaayí.

trading.
Yes, now
these boats arrived at Yakutat,
ten boats
trading for furs.   30
Yes,
as they were voyaging back now
the tides
turned to rapids on them.
What is it? I forget the name of it.

Yes, Lituya Bay.
Now
this is where
the L'uknax̱.ádi capsized,
ten boats,   40
no more
there wasn't a single one left.
Two men
floated over to a back eddy.
Two
were straddling the overturned bottom.
One was called
X'aats'ák'u
and
Xíxch'i Shaan.   50
They were straddling the bottom of the
        overturned boat
that floated into a back eddy.
They were sitting facing each other.
As it was getting dark on them,
the one named Xíxch'i Shaan
was imitating a Frog.
G̱wá-g̱wá-g̱wá-g̱wá.
But the one facing him
was cawing like a Raven.
He made the sound   60
g̱áa-g̱áa-g̱áa-g̱áa.
It was getting dark on them, just like it is now.
They were straddling the bottom of the
        overturned boat.
No more!
No one knew what happened to them.

Has du kaa yan xeewa.at déi.
Wé has du een aa hás ku.aa hóoch'.
Kutx shuwaxeex.
Tle has du eetéex áyá keiwa.aa
yá yaakw tadaat has keeni.   70
Aaa,
anax áyá
yá
has awa.oowú
at doogú--
cháatl xáas'i gwéil, yáa yeedát
kudziteeyi aa
sél' gwéil yax gíyú utée,
tlél ulnaawún,
yú cháatl xáas'i gwéil yéi duwasáakw,   80
a toox' áwé yei duwa.óo wé at doogú,
yáxwch'
naagas'éi
ldakát át, k'óox'
k'óox' doogú
kóoshdaa
nukshayáan,
everything--
á áyá
Anóoshi aanídei akawahéit'.   90
Anax áyá
adaax' yana.áa
Anóoshi
áyá has koowashee
yá yan tl'átgi has a yungadláak.
Anax áyá
yan awlis'ís yá Lituya Bay
Anóoshi.
Anáx áyá yá yan tl'átgi has ayawadlaak
yú at doogú wé L'uknax.ádich aan too yei
        uwaháayi.   100
Atx has du aaní dei akawahéit'.
Anáx áyá yá tl'átk' has ayawadlaak Anóoshich.
Haaw!
Dei áyá yan kaxwliník.

Darkness now covered them.
The men with them were now gone.
They all died.
Daylight came without them
straddling the bottom of the overturned boat.   70
Yes,
through this
the
furs
that they bought--
in a halibut skin bag, like what we have
today,
it must have been like rubber bags,
they didn't leak,
they're called halibut skin bags,   80
this is what they had these furs in--
sea otter,
fox,
everything--marten,
marten furs,
land otter,
mink,
everything--
all this
the tide swept to Russia.   90
Through this,
when they discovered it,
the Russians
went searching
so they could find the mainland.
Through this
the Russians
sailed into Lituya Bay.
Through this they arrived at the mainland,
the furs that the L'uknax̱.ádi capsized with,   100
that were swept to their land.
Through this the Russians came upon this land.
So!
I have finished telling the story.

Yéil Yaagú
Jeenik x̱'éidáx̱ sh kalneek

Kulix̱éitl'shan wé eey.
Dax̱dahéen L'uknax̱.ádi ax̱' héent wudzik'ít'.

Wé Ltu.aa yaa kawudaayi a tóodei wookoox̱ú aa áwé.
Tlél tsú dleit ḵáa yá Alasgi awuskú.
Tlé yú gus' yát wulihásh
at doogú daa.aax̱w.
Tlé yá plástic gwéil ooyaa núch at naasi.
X̱óots naasi.
Tlé dulx̱áash tsú áwé s wóochdei dusḵáa.
At naasi   10
gwéil áwé wé at doogú; tlé yú gus' yat wulihásh
          Ltu.aa.
Wé héench aan yéi ḵuwsineeyi át.
Ach áyá yá Alasgi kaadéi
Anóoshi ḵuwashee.
Ayá a káx̱ ḵuwduwashee yá Alasgi kax̱' Lingít.
Has tsú tlél
tlél washéin has oo.oo, ch'a yéi
s'ís'aa een at has wulis'ées.
Ltu.aanáx̱ s'é kei aawlis'ís
Anóoshi yaagú.   20
Awé
Lingít l atyax̱ sh koolneek.
Yéil yaagú áyú.
Yóo áyú kdunéek wooch een,

Raven Boat
told by Jennie White

The rapids are very scary.
Twice the L'uknax̲.ádi capsized there.

This one boat travelled out of Lituya Bay
          when the tide had droppped.
No white man knew of Alaska.
The bundle of furs
floated out to the face of the clouds.
The intestines resembled a plastic bag.
Brown Bear intestines.
They are cut and sewn back together.
The intestinal   10
bag of furs floated to the face of the clouds
          from Lituya Bay,
the ones the people drowned with.
This is why
the Russians searched for Alaska.
That's how they found Tlingits in Alaska.
They didn't
have machines either they'd just
sail with canvas.
A Russian boat
first sailed into Lituya Bay.   20
And so
the Tlingits didn't tell it like it really was.
It was the Raven boat,

Yéil yaagú.
Yú Anóoshi áyú yéi yaa kanduník.
Wudusteení tle téix yoo kuguxsateek.
Ch'u yeedát yéi yatee yá Lingít.
Awé yóot'át
s'áxt'.   30
A tóonáx kukawduwatúl
ka
ketlháatl'i
gwéil yax wduwakáa ka yátx'i náa
atoo yéi wduwa.oo.
Tléi téix yoo kuguxsateek.
Yóo áwé Lingít aadéi yaa sh kagalnikch'i yé.
Wé s'íksh,
á ku.a áwé a toonáx kukawduwatúl,
k'ei tunaxkudutées' yáx.   40
A tóonáx áwé dultính
wé Ltu.aanáx kei klas'ées'.
Hél téix kuguxsatee aagáa.
Ketlháatl'i tsú kaa séix yawduwakáa.
S'áxt'
ku.a áwé yéi kwdagei
tsú a toonáx kukawduwatúl.
Káa yátx'i
séi yei duwa.óo.
Aadéi yóo at kaawaniyi yé shukát
        wé shgóona shudultee nóok.   50

was what they told one another,
the Raven boat.
That's what they were saying about the Russians.
If you looked directly at it you would turn to stone.
Even today the Tlingits are like that.
And that
devil's club.   30
They drilled holes in them
and
dog droppings
were sewn like bags
and put into their children's clothes.
You would turn to stone.
That's the way the Tlingits talked about this.
This blue hellebore
was hollowed through though,
let's see, like binoculars.   40
As it sailed into Lituya Bay
they looked at it through these.
Then they wouldn't turn to stone.
Dog droppings too were hung around children's
          necks.
But the larger
devil's club
had holes drilled through them too.
They were put on the necks
of their children.
That's the way things happened in the beginning
          when they awaited the schooner.   50

Gus'k'ikwáan
Asx'aak x'éidáx sh kalneek

This text was prepared and contributed by
Naatstláa (Constance Naish) and Shaachooká
(Gillian Story) as a memorial to Asx'aak
(George Betts) who gave so much help in their
early study of the Tlingit language upon
which the present system of writing Tlingit
is based.

Ltu.áa káa áwé duwa.óo,
ch'áaaaakw.
Atx'aan hítx'i ka ch'a yéi hítx' áa yéi dagaatee.
Yanshuká áwé yéi duwasáakw Ltu.áa,
        ch'u l dleit káa yan ulgáas'ji.
Wáa nanée sáwé tléix' ts'ootaat,
gáani yux aawagoot.
Awé dleit yáx yateeyi át áwé yú héen
        xukaadéi wududziteen, yú yax'áak;
kei latítch,
ka át wuliteet.
Wáa nanée sáwé tlax kaa xán yaa akanalséin.   10
"Daa sáyú?
Daa sáyú, daa sáyú?"
"Ch'a góot át áyú!"
"Ch'a góot át áyú!"

302

The Coming of the First White Man
told by George R. Betts

People lived in Lituya Bay
loooong ago.
Smoke houses and other houses were there.
There was a deserted place called Lituya Bay before
        the white man migrated in from the sea.
At one point one morning
a person went outside.
Then there was a white object that could be seen
        way out on the sea
bouncing on the waves
and rocked by the waves.
At one point it was coming closer to the people.   10
"What's that?
"What's that, what's that?"
"It's something different!"
"It's something different!"
"Is it Raven?"
"Maybe that's what it is."
"I think that's what it is--

"Yéil gwáa yóo gé?"
"Goodáx sá l yéi át áwé?"
"Yéi xwaajée yéi át áwé;
yá lingít'aaní alyéix yéil,
yéi sh kalneek tsu kúxdei guxdagóot."
Aatlein át áwé a yáx at yatee.   20
(Ch'u tle wé Ltu.áa,
áa yáx áwé déin.
Héen naadaa;
éil' áyú, a kaadéi naadaa daak gagadéinín.
Yeik gagaléinín ku.aas,
a kaadáx nadaa nooch.)
Ch'u tle a kaanáx áwé kei wshix'úl'.
Ch'u tle áwé aantkeení áwé at gutóot wudikél',
ch'a ldakát;
tle atyátx'i tsú,   30
at gutóodei kawduwajeil.
Yá at gutóodáx áwé, dultín.
Wáa nanée sáwé,
tle kasayedéin at wuduwa.áx.
Kach yóo shayéinaa áwé héent wududzigíx'.
"Tléil yilatíneek!"
atyátx'i yéi daayaduká.
"Tléil aadóo sá áx ulgeenéek.
Yilatín núkni, téix yee guxsatée.
Yéil áyú, haat oowakúx."   40
"Hé! A daat aawa.aat!"
A daat at kawdaxdiyaa.
Kach a tu.aasí daat áwé woo.aat, wé sailors.
Wáa nanée sáwé, ch'áaaakw dultínitx áwé,
s'íksh,
áwé wuduwal'íx',
s'íksh.
A tóonáx áwé kuyawduwawál,
áwé téix koonastéegaa áwé;
a tóonáx dultín.   50
Áwé a xoo aa áx algeenítx l téix koonastée áwé,
yéi kuyaawakaa,
"K'e aadéi daak yakwgwakooxú.
K'e aadéi daak yakwgwakoox."
"Daa sáyú?"
Áwé tle dáxnax yées káa áwé,
ch'a wé aasx' gutóodáx,

Raven who created the world.
He said he would come back again."
Some dangerous thing was happening.   20
(Lituya Bay
lay like a lake.
There was a current;
salt water flowed in when the tide was coming in.
But when the tide was going out
the sea water would also drain out.)
So the thing went right on in with the flood tide.
Then the people of the village ran scared right
        into the forest,
all of them;
the children too,   30
were taken to the forest.
They watched from the forest.
At one point
they heard strange sounds.
Actually it was the anchor that was thrown in
        the water.
"Don't look at it!"
they told the children.
"Don't anybody look at it.
If you look at it, you'll turn to stone.
That's Raven, he's come by boat."   40
"Oh! People are running around on it!"
Things are moving around on it.
Actually it was the sailors climbing around the
        mast.
At one point after they had watched for a
        loooong time,
they took blue hellebore
and broke the stalks,
blue hellebore.
They poked holes though them
so that they wouldn't turn to stone;
they watched through them.   50
When no one turned to stone while watching,
someone said,
"Let's go out there.
We'll go out there."
"What's that?"
Then there were two young men;

wé seet,
(yaakw áwé yéi duwasáakw seet)
yeik wuduwaxút'.   60
Ch'u tle a yíx aawa.aat.
Ch'u tle a daat has uwakúx; a daat has uwalít.
A daat has kóox áwé,
tíx' dzeit, yaa kawdudliyaa.
Ch'u tle a geidéi has duxoox,
kaa tl'eikch áwé s dusxoox,
kaa tl'eik.
Tle áa kei s uwa.át.
A daa s woos.éix;
        tléil tsu yéi s at gwasatínch.
Kach yú át wulis'eesi yaakw tlein áwé.   70
Ch'u tle yá a yeehídi yeedéi s du een ana.áat
        áwé,
has awsiteen --
ch'u tles has sh wudziteen.
Kach tunaxkaateen tlein áwé a yígu,
tunaxkaateen tlein.
Kaa yahaayí, a kaadéi duwatéeni át,
tle yóo s aawasáa.
Ch'u tle yá cook hídidéi s du een aawa.aat.
Ax' áwé s du x'éix at duteex.
Woon áwé has du x'eis wududzi.ée,   80
woon.
Has altín.
Dleit l'éiw tsú.
Dleit l'éiw,
has du x'ayee daak wududzi.ín.
Ch'u tle yá kóox xoodéi áwé has alxwénx',
        yá dleit l'éiw.
Kach yú shóogaa áwé.
Yá kóox áwé, woonx has oowajée.
Awé ch'a s altín.
Wáa nanée sáwé aa gawdudlixwéin.   90
"Ha! Gán!
K'e! X'éi yeedanú!"
"Yak'éi shákdéi."
Ach áwé aa gawdlixwéin.
Ch'u tle "Aak'é atxá áyá,
yá woon,
maggots,

from the woods
a canoe
(the kind of canoe called "seet")
was pulled down to the beach.   60
They quickly went aboard.
They quickly went out to it, paddled out to it.
When they got out to it,
a rope ladder was lowered.
Then they were beckoned to go aboard,
they were beckoned over by the crewmen's fingers,
the crewmen's fingers.
Then they went up there.
They examined it; they had not seen anything
        like it.
Actually it was a huge sail boat.   70
When the crew took them inside the cabin,
they saw--
they saw themselves.
Actually it was a huge mirror inside there,
a huge mirror.
They gave this name then,
to the thing an image of people could be seen on.
Then they were taken to the cook's galley.
There they were given food.
Worms were cooked for them,   80
worms.
They stared at it.
White sand also.
White sand
was put in front of them.
Then they spooned this white sand into the rice.
Actually it was sugar.
What they thought were worms, was rice.
This was what they had just been staring at.
At what point was it one of them took
        a spoonfull?
"Hey! Look!   90
Go ahead! Taste it!"
"It might be good."
So the other took a spoonful.
Just as he did, he said "This is good food,
these worms,
maggots,

aak'é atxá áyá."
Ldakát yéidei s du x'éi at dusxáa áwé,
tle náaw has du x'éi wududlináa,   100
náaw,
brandy gíyú.
Ch'u tle tlax kasayedéin yaa s sh nadanúk.
Tléil tsu ....
"Waa sáyá yéi yaa sh naxdanúk?
Gán! Kasayedéin yaa sh naxdanúk!"
Tle "Toowú sagú tsú ax tóox yei jikanaxíx"
yóo s x'ayaká.
Ldakát yéidei a yíkt has du een yoo akoo.áat
        áwé,
tsu a x'ayaaxt has du een aawa.át.   110
Has du jee yéi aa wduwa.oo.
Kóox
ka shóogaa
ka gáatl
ách has wududziwóo.
Has du een kadunéek, aadéi dus.ee yé.
Ha daat kát sá kwshé wé ágé wududzi.ée?
Tléil xá k'wátl kaa jee aagáa ....
Tléil a kát gadudzi.eeyi k'wátl.
Tle yan has kóox áwé,   120
koon has sh kalneek:
"Aantkeení áyú a yígu.
Kasiyéiyi át tsú a yígu.
Chush yahaayí daakeit,
yá looking glass,
chush yahaayí daakeit;
ch'u tle sh tudítéen.
Yáax' áwé,
haa x'eis wududzi.ée wé woon."
Ch'u tle ldakát has akanéek.   130
Aax áwé,
ldakát a daadéi daak kuyaawagóo.
Tlax shux'áa dleit káa yan wukooxú áyá,
Ltu.áa kaanáx;
Latooya Bay áyá yéi duwasáakw Ltu.áa,
yá Alasgi káx'.
Ha hóoch' áwé ax sh kalneegí.

this is good food."
After they were fed all kinds of food,
then they were given alcohol
alcohol   100
perhaps it was brandy.
Then they began to feel very strange.
Never before......
"Why am I beginning to feel this way?
Look! I'm beginning to feel strange!"
And "I'm beginning to feel happiness
          settling through my body too,"
they said.
After they had taken them through the whole ship,
they took them to the railing.   110
They gave them some things.
Rice
and sugar
and pilot bread
were given to them to take along.
They were told how to cook them.
Now I wonder what it was cooked on.
You know, people didn't have pots then....
There was no cooking pot for it.
When they got ashore   120
they told everyone:
"There are many people in there.
Strange things are in there too.
A box of our images,
this looking glass,
a box of our images;
we could just see ourselves.
Next
they cooked maggots for us to eat."
They told everything.   130
After that,
they all went out on their canoes.
This was the very first time the white man came
          ashore,
through Lituya Bay;
Ltu.áa is called Lituya Bay
in Alaska.
Well! This is all of my story.

NOTES

Basket Bay told by Robert Zuboff

Recorded by Constance Naish and Gillian
Story, Angoon, 1960's. Transcribed by Constance
Naish and Gillian Story. Translated by Nora
Dauenhauer

The transcription dates from the 1960's, and
was revised by Naish and Story in the early
1970's. The texts by George Betts and Robert
Zuboff transcribed by Naish and Story were to
have been published in Tlingit in the mid
1970's as part of the Tlingit Reader series,
but lack of time and funding delayed
publication. As a set, these narratives now
open and close the present volume, beginning
with the Tlingit migration to the Coast, and
ending with the arrival of the Europeans.
Work on the pair of transcriptions was taken
up again in the mid 1980's by the present
editors, in consultation with Constance Naish
and Gillian Story, who are now working on
Northern Athapaskan in the Canadian Northwest
Territories, at considerable geographic remove
both from Juneau and from their tapes and field
notes archived in Denver, and removed almost 15
years in time from their work in Tlingit.
Textual questions were minor, and revisions
were made as seemed appropriate.
As noted in the dedication, this text was
prepared and contributed by Constance Naish and
Gillian Story as a memorial and personal
tribute to Robert Zuboff, who spent many hours
with Naish and Story during their stay in
Angoon, helping them immensely in their early
study of Tlingit. The system of writing
Tlingit used in this book is based on the work
of Naish and Story and the help of Robert
Zuboff. See also the note and dedication to
George Betts' "Coming of the First White Man"
for acknowledgement of Betts' contribution to
the history of Tlingit literacy and linguistics.

This narrative deals with two themes, the unique life at Basket Bay in particular, and the more general history of how the Tlingit people migrated to and along the coast. The account of the ancestors coming down the Stikine River under the ice is often repeated by Tlingit elders. Anthropological and linguistic evidence and theory support certain aspects of the narrative, and question other parts as told here.

Linguistic evidence suggests and supports a Tlingit migration to the Southern coast, and then northward, as described in the narrative. The exact linguistic relationship of Tlingit to the Athapaskan family on the one hand, and to Haida on the other, remains the subject of much scholarly debate. The structures of Tlingit, Eyak, and Athapaskan are parallel, and some of the morphemes are recognizable, whereas the general vocabularies--especially the noun vocabularies--are not similar at all, and reconstructions a subject of dispute. If Tlingit and Haida are indeed related, the relationship seems very remote and unclear. All of this does suggest that the Tlingit split from an ancestral group in the interior, moved to the coast, and somehow along the way adapted a remarkably new vocabulary, while retaining the older grammatical structure. Perhaps the noun vocabulary comes in part from assimilation of an earlier coastal population. This is not uncommon in linguistic history. English, for example, retains its Germanic grammatical structure while absorbing a rich noun and verb vocabulary from languages around the world.

However, it is probably more likely that the present day Tlingit population of interior British Columbia and Yukon derives not from an original group that stayed behind, but from a coastal group that continued the migration back into the Interior at a much later date. The basis for this theory is primarily linguistic: there is very little difference

between Interior Tlingit and Central Coast
Tlingit, whereas if the Interior group had
stayed behind since time immemorial, and had
not shared in the migration to the coast, we
would expect major dialect variation--at least
as great as between Northern and Southern
Tlingit, and probably even greater than between
Tongass Tlingit and all other dialects.

3. K̲ák'w. Literally "Little Basket."
Basket Bay is located on Chichagof Island, on
the west side of Chatham Strait 11 miles north
of the entrance to Peril Strait.

8. Kasiyéiyi. This is a contracted form, a
shortening of the sequence of -i (attributive)
followed by yé followed by yáx̲. The underlying
full form is kasiyéiyi yéi yáx̲. Yé is usually
lengthened to yéi before yáx̲ as before suffixed
postpositions. Thus this is really a dropping
of -y y....

15. "In a grotto" is supplied in
translation. The people would use sapwood
(resin saturated wood) as torches. Keeping a
careful watch, they would hunt at low tide in
the grotto, then hurry out when the tide rose.

18. Kaak̲áakw. The name of the arch of the
natural grotto at Basket Bay, from which Robert
Zuboff's clan house derives its name.

33. We have inserted the k̲u.aa in the
Tlingit text to reflect his discourse
structure more closely. A line in which the
story teller corrects himself has been
deleted.

40. G̲adutéenín. Contingent. Note the
pattern of the -ín suffix, the progressive
stem, the aspect prefix -g̲a- and the conjugation prefix, which in this case is "zero."
The general translation of the contingent is
"whenever."

55, 56. The two -yéi yáx̲ sequences are the
same contractions as decribed in the note to
line 8: the sequence of -i (attributive)
followed by yé followed by yáx̲.

55. This line presents difficulties in
transcription and editing. The stem is
possibly -k̲'ét', -tl'ít', or -ts'ít'. The
dictionary forms are -k̲'eit' (to fall over,
like a ladder) -ts'eet' (to fill a container)
and -tl'eet' with the same meaning. Ts'eet'
seems to make the most sense.

86-90. Migration through the South...down
the Stikine River. Many elders recount the
prehistoric migration down the Stikine River,
under the glacial ice. Many Tlingit place
names and clan names document an arrival on the
southern coast and gradual migration northward
along the coast, arriving most recently in the
Yakutat and Copper River areas.

It is a general principle of linguistics
that older areas show more dialect variation
than more recently settled areas. The
southern dialects of Tlingit are more varied
than the central and northern. Tongass
dialect, now nearly extinct, differs radically
from the rest of Tlingit and is a "missing
link" between Tlingit, Eyak (nearly extinct),
and the Athapaskan languages.

107, 113. In Tlingit, there is grammatical
contrast between the verbs. In line 107, the
"non-zero" conjugation form woo.aat patterns
with kaadéi; in line 113, the "zero" conjugation
form uwa.át patterns with kát. Both mean "went
on it" or "went over it," but the "zero"
conjugation form kát....uwa.át conveys the
meaning of starting out.

115-132. The ones who went under the ice
went down the Sitkine; those who went over the
ice went down the Chilkat. The Deisheetaan and
K̲ak'weidí are historically related, which is
why Zuboff refers to himself here as
Deisheetaan. The K̲ak'weidí probably evolved
as a house group of the Deisheetaan. The
Dak̲l'aweidí are an Eagle moiety clan. The
killer whale is one of its major crests.
Robert Zuboff is a Child of Dak̲l'aweidí--
Dak̲l'aweidí yádi because his father is of that
clan.

119. Sit'ká. The name means "on the glacier," from sít' and -ká. This is not to be confused with the place name Sitka, which derives from Sheey at'iká, "On Outer Baranof Island," or "On the Outer Coast of Baranof Island."

136. Xutsnoowú. Tlingit place name for Angoon, meaning "Brown Bear Fort," often spelled Kootznoowoo or Kootznoohoo in English. This Tlingit place name is also used by the Russians in their histories of Russian America (Khlebnikov, for example.)

108, 112, 120, 132. These forms are nice examples of the use of the prefix ku- referring to action by or about people.

108.	kuwlihaash	they (people) floated
112.	wulhaash	"to float"
120.	kuduwasáakw	people are called
132.	kuwtuwashée	we began searching

143, 150. Tlingit. Dáak káx' is slower speech; dakkáx' is also common.

149. Shaadaax' is Robert Zuboff's Tlingit name. See notes to "Mosquito" for more on this.

153. Wusdaagéen. A decessive form, in the main verb (in contrast to the contingent form, which always has a short vowel in the suffix and is always in a subordinate clause.)

154. Nooch. Nooch is a helping , or auxiliary verb in Tlingit. Its stem is nook. Lines 151 and 154 provide a nice contrast of two interesting grammatical forms.

151. a daa yoo tuxatángi áyá
     what I'm thinking about
     (now; specific time)

154. yéi...a daa yoo tuxatángi nooch
     how I think (habitual, general,
     always, unspecified)

Mosquito told by Robert Zuboff, 79

Recorded by Nora Dauenhauer, Angoon, July 1971. Transcribed by Richard Dauenhauer. Translated by Nora and Richard Dauenhauer

   Publication History. The Tlingit text was first published August 1973 by Tlingit Readers, Inc. Copyright (c) 1973 by Tlingit Readers, Inc. Printed at Sheldon Jackson College by Andrew Hope III and Richard Dauenhauer, a production of Alaska Native Language Center. Publication of the original, now rare and out of print edition was a joint activity of Tlingit Readers, Inc., ANLC, and SJC. Typing of the original edition was by JoAnn George, cover artist for the present volume. The transcription was read back to Mr. Zuboff in May 1973, met with his approval, and was verified by him.
   Other versions. This story is very popular on the Northwest Coast, and exists in many published versions including the Boas/Shotridge edition of 1917, and Swanton (1909: No. 58.) It is sometimes known as "The Cannibal Giant." The motif of mosquito created from the ashes of a slain monster (Thompson A 2001) is also widespread in world folklore. The most generally available versions are in Keithahn (1963: 142-143) and Barbeau (1964: 378.) Barbeau (1964) also includes Siberian and other Northwest Coast versions. For a detailed study of 12 versions from Tlingit, Haida, Tsimshian, Bella Coola, and Kwakiutl, see Dauenhauer (1975: 103-122.) For an interesting Northern Athabaskan version in Chipewyan and facing English translation, see Li and Scollon (1976: 236-253) Story 9, "The Story of the Man Eater," collected by Fang Kuei Li in 1928.
   Robert Zuboff was a popular story teller in Tlingit and English, and "Mosquito" was one of his favorites. This story is "classic Robert Zuboff" in style, characterized by repetition,

terraces, code switching, sparsity of detail,
richness of action and dialog and the use of a
narrative frame in which he explains how he
relates to the story, which deals with his
Tlingit name, Shaadaax', and from the time when
the Tlingits lived in the Interior.

This is a deceptively simple story, and one
not to be used lightly, but treated with
respect, because it deals with very powerful
subject matter--ultimately the nature of evil.
Some Tlingit tradition bearers, such as Mr.
A.P. Johnson, view this story allegorically.
The Mosquito is the disease of alcoholism,
which is sucking the life blood of the Tlingit
people.

Shaadaax', on the other hand, insists on the
historicity of the story, connecting it with
the etymology of his Tlingit name and the
present Tlingit speaking communities of the
Yukon, Atlin, Teslin, and Carcross. Mr.
Zuboff reminds us that God loves the world,
and that creation was "good." Humans created
and create their own evil. In this story, the
mosquito originates from greed and the
obsession with revenge.

This story does not appear to be owned in
contemporary Tlingit oral tradition, and most
versions connect the story somehow with the
Interior or Migration. However, over 100 years
of published photographs and illustrations from
Klukwan such as Krause (1885, 1956) Keithahn
(1963) and Barbeau (1964) would seem to connect
the story to the Frog House of the Chilkat
Gannax̱.ádi of Klukwan, which owns the totem of
the Cannibal Giant Gooteel.

1, 6, 10. Awé. This is an example of the
Tlingit word áwé functioning as a phrase
marker, as described in the introduction.

9. Shaadaax'. Robert Zuboff's Tlingit name
translates as "On the Mountain" or "At Around
the Mountain." The analysis:

Shaa- daa- x'
Mt. around at/on.

This would be understood by a Tlingit
speaking audience, so it is assumed and not
explained by the story teller, although he
does often explain this when telling the story
in English. The name is important, because
this is the main reason the Tlingit Elder
Geetwéin tells the story to the young Zuboff,
and one important reason for Zuboff's strong
personal attachment to the story. His
namesake derives from the places and events
remembered in the story.

18, 19, 20. Tlingit. Notice how in the
original text the story teller switches
languages for emphasis. The technical term for
this is "code switching," as described in the
introduction.

27. Kúnáx̱. On the tape, this is ḵóonáx̱,
with emphasis and long vowel. We have
standardized the spelling here.

33, 34. For students of Tlingit, there is
a nice contrast of wooteex̱ and woot'éex'. Both
have the perfective prefix woo-. The first
verb is -tee, meaning "to be or live," with the
durative suffix -x̱ expressing action over a
long period of time. The second stem is -téex',
meaning "to be hard."

33. The Interior. The setting of the story
is the Interior, in contrast to the Coast;
specifically the southern Yukon Territory and
very northern tip of British Columbia. Until
the Alaska Highway reoriented traffic in the
area, it was common for Coast and Interior
Tlingits to travel and trade with each other
via the pass and river routes from the Chilkat
to the Taku. Trade between the Coast Tlingit
and Interior Athabaskan was conducted over an
even wider area, ranging from the Copper River
in the North to the Stikine and Nass Rivers in
the South. There are considerable differences
in material and social culture between the

Coast and Interior Tlingit, but the language is very similar. See the story by Tom Peters of Teslin for a sample of the Yukon dialect of Tlingit. Lines 32-54 make up a "frame within a frame" within which the background to the story itself is presented.

66, 98. Tlingit. The verbs are sequential mode, indicated by long, high vowel, the "A" form of the classifier (which for the "ya" classifier is "zero" and does not appear at all) and position in the subordinate clause. It means "when" or "as."

98. kei góot   when / as he came out

Compare line 65, a negative perfective main verb, and 66, with the sequential. This is also a nice example of terrace repetition.

65. Tléil yeik woogoot.
66. L yeik ugóot

65. He didn't come back.
66. When he didn't come back

76, 138. Examples of rapid speech.
96. He broke. In Tlingit this is imperfective--"he breaks." Such forms are more freely translated into English with past tense, as described in the introduction.
101-104. He struck it (again). In many Native American traditions four is the complete, ideal, or "magic" number, in contrast to the pattern of three in Indo-European and other traditions. The verb is also interesting. The nominal prefix -sha- specifies hitting on the head.
110. Naganeiyít. Purposive. Note the conjugation prefix na- and the aspect prefix -ga- patterning with the suffix -(y)ít. The general meaning of the purposive translates as "in order to."
138. Teslin is a major population center of

Inland Tlingit, located in southern Yukon.

140.   Tlingit. Aa Tlein. Literally "Big Lake." Atlin, B.C., an Inland Tlingit community in northernmost British Columbia.

142. Tlingit. Caribou Cross. Now known as Carcross, Yukon. An Inland Tlingit community located at what was traditionally a caribou crossing, later a railroad and now a highway crossing point at the end of Bennet Lake on the routes from Skagway to Whitehorse.

Kaax'achgóok told by A.P. Johnson, 74

Recorded by A. P. Johnson, Sitka, November
1972. Transcribed and translated by Nora
Dauenhauer

   Publication History. The original
transcription was a project of the Alaska
Native Language Center. The manuscript of the
transcription was approved by Mr. Johnson August
22, 1973. Tlingit text first published by
Tlingit Readers, Inc. 1979. Revision of the
Tlingit text and translation into English are
projects of the Sealaska Heritage Foundation.
   Other versions. Swanton (1909: Nos. 67 and
101, pp. 225 and 321 ff. See also the video
tape *Kaal.átk'* (Ostyn 1981) featuring
Charlie Joseph, produced by the Sitka Native
Education Program.
   Mr. Johnson recorded this story himself, and
gave the tape to Nora Dauenhauer to transcribe.
The tape includes a copy of an earlier tape
recording of the song, but this was edited out
of the transcription at the request of Mr.
Johnson, who dictated the alternate ending that
appears here. This is one of the many stories
of the Kiks.ádi clan, and is about one of their
most famous ancestors, Kaax'achgóok, who was
blown off course while hunting sea mammals in
the Sitka area.
   The delivery is generally even and uniformly
paced, with no long pauses between sentences.
At points of excitement and climax, the phrase
boundaries are "run on"--with a change to a new
topic and grammatical sentence within the
breath and phrase unit. This is noted in the
transcription by a long line with a period or
semi-colon between the sentences. This "run
on" style used here and by other narrators
conveys a sense of urgency to the story, an
increase of excitement.

1-29. The opening lines of this story
present a classic "narrative frame." The story
teller introduces himself through the pronoun
"us" as a member of the group he is telling
about, and continues to give his clan and
personal history, including his personal names
and those of some ancestors. He may be
emphasizing his paternal (Kaagwaantaan)
ancestors because his matrilineal identity as
Kiks.ádi is more obvious and less in need of
introduction. Most Tlingit narratives include
a narrative frame, and this is a splendid
example.

26. Wasdéik. A. P. Johnson's humor tends
to be dry and understated. This is the
English word "Mistake" pronounced with a
Tlingit accent.

27. Tlaakáak. This is a compound noun.
The orthographic convention is to write these
as a single word in cases where the tone is
"stolen" by one of the words; i.e. tláa káak
becomes lexically one word when the high tone
is "stolen" from tláa. Other compounds are not
often as clear and systematic; for example, we
have decided to write kaani yán, keilk'i hás,
and shatx'i yán as two words, although they are
also probably lexically one.

27-29. Here the story teller capsulizes the
narrative frame. This also specifically
indicates the traditional Tlingit line of
inheritance through the mother and mother's
brothers. Here the mother's maternal uncles
are his mother's mother's brothers.

30-36. Sitka...Gajaahéen. After summarizing
the detailed narrative frame in lines 27-29,
the story teller now turns to the setting. He
stresses that this did not happen in Sitka, but
in the place called "Old Sitka" in English and
Gajaahéen in Tlingit, after the river that
flows there. It is near the present site of
the Sitka ferry terminal.

40. We used to travel around in spring.
Reference is to spring subsistence hunting,

fishing, and gathering.

47. Fur seals would drift in on the tide.
The spring tides carry the sea mammals closer
to land to breed.

Some additional comment may be helpful at
this point. One aspect or function of oral
literature around the world is that it often
contains details on traditional technology and
survival skills. People can recall these
details from the stories as they are needed.
A. P. Johnson's narratives tend to be rich in
such detail, and many of the notes will
comment on these.

Sea mammals are important in this story, and
it may be useful to describe them here. Four
species are found in Southeast Alaska:

tsaa   harbor seal; hair seal (*Phoca vitulina*)
x'óon   fur seal (*Collorhinus ursinus*)
yáxwch'   sea otter (*Enhydra lutris*)
taan   sea lion (*Eumetopias jubatus*)

The harbor seal (tsaa) is the only common
seal found in Southeast Alaska, and the only
hair seal found in Southern Alaska. It ranges
from southern California to the Bering Sea to
China. It is sometimes also called the spotted
seal, but it is not the same as phoca largha,
also called spotted seal. Unlike the sea lion
or the fur seal, it cannot rotate its hind
flippers forward.

The fur seal (x'óon) is extremely rare in
Southeast Alaska today, but its range was
almost certainly wider in the precontact
period. When Nora Dauenhauer's grandmother was
a little girl they used to chase fur seals on
the outer coast in the spring. The fur seal is
primarily associated with the Pribilof Islands,
and it is a federally protected species
presently covered under international treaties
prohibiting pelagic harvesting (hunting on the
high seas.) The fur seal can rotate its hind
flippers forward. The fur seal is highly

valued for its pelt, and was hunted nearly to extinction in the 19th century.

The sea otter (yáxwch') is also rare in Southeast Alaska, a colony having been re-established near Sitka about ten years ago. It was widely hunted during the Russian period, when the colony's economy was based on the sea otter industry. Sea otters are not popular with fishermen because they consume large quantities of fish and shellfish.

The sea lion (taan) is so named because it resembles a lion. It is also called the Steller's or Northern sea lion. Unlike seals (other than the fur seal) they have external ears and rear flippers that turn forward.

There are many other species of seals found in the Eskimo and Aleut regions of Northern Alaska, but not found in Southeast Alaska. These include the spotted seal, ribbon seal, bearded seal (oogruk) and ringed seal (natchiq). For more information on seals and other species mentioned in the Tlingit narratives, we recommend the *Wildlife Notebook Series* published by the Alaska Department of Fish and Game. The fur seal is a "federal" animal and additional information may be available from appropriate federal agencies.

49. Tire out and kill. It is important in seal hunting to retrieve the animal before it sinks. Therefore the hunting techniques include harpoons with bouys, or, as described here, chasing the seals until they are tired or exhausted, and then spearing them.

50. Spear. The Tlingit term is woosáani, and refers to a particular kind of harpoon with a detachable point.

55. At s'aan.aaxw dzaas. This was a type of spear used when the seal was in a deep place. The thongs were designed to wrap the animal in a bundle, making it easier to retrieve.

57. Thongs that battered the head. The

thong attached to the spear point was rigged
with a club that would go into action after
the point hit the target, and would club the
seal's head as it swam or dived along.

59-62. Two wives. As most men of Tlingit
culture of his period, Kaax'achgóok practiced
plural marriage, having one older and one
younger wife. The older wife was probably
older than the husband, and the second wife
younger. This arrangement provided a
traditional "social security" as well as a
system for passing on knowledge and skills.

61. The Tlingit text has yanwát, as
pronounced on the tape recording; some
speakers pronounce the word yanwáat.

63. The Tlingit verb translated as
"hunting" is literally "to tire out."

73. He heard a voice. He heard a voice
among the seals warning the crying pup to keep
quiet.

78-80. He said to the maternal nephews.
Kaax'achgóok realized that the human voice he
heard among the seals was a bad omen.

85-87. Took them..broke them..threw them
into the sea. He is through with hunting.
Throwing his weapons away, Kaax'achgóok rejects
being a hunter, thus breaking a societal norm.

86. Tlingit: akal'íx't is a nice example of
what might be called a the durative suffix -t,
emphasizing that he is breaking them one by one,
or that he kept on breaking them, or broke them
continually. The grammatical pattern is
actually more complicated, as Naish and Story
(1973: 360-361) explain, and involves the
interaction of invariable stems and suffixes.

a -	ka -	l'íx'	- t
direct	round	breaks	suffix
object	thing		

96ff. Baskets. This is a description of
traditional cooking methods, using water-tight
baskets and heated stones to bring water to a
boil.

99. Boil. Tlingit uses two distinct verb
stems here, the underlying or dictionary forms
of which are:

shi-ootl   to boil salmon
si-taa   to boil meat (and other food)

The forms in the text are:

adush.utlxi nuch   they would boil salmon
dustéix   meat was boiled

103. "Couldn't you spoon some broth?" The
story teller's voice is soft and high here,
imitating the woman begging.
104. The woman goes against a societal norm
by begging, and is shunned. His wife's begging
and the rejection motivate Kaax'achgóok to
resume hunting fur seal which his younger wife
liked so much.
114. Tlingit: dagaak'éiyi aa; literally
"some very nice ones." This is a nice example
of the distributive prefix -dagaa-, which most
commonly appears as a prefix to the verb stem
"to be." Here it is used in an attributive
clause. The implication is that the very best
spears had been sorted out and were being
carried.

dagaa - k'éi - yi   aa
distribu-   to be   attri- ones
   tive   fine   butive

118. Fur seals. The noun is supplied in
translation.
129. Tup! As he speaks this sound-effect
word, the story teller claps his hands sharply
once.
132. "Be brave." The story teller's voice
here is chant-like, the phrase slightly sung.
167. Kaax'achgóok heard the noises. The
name is used in Tlingit. The Tlingit verb

incorporates the noun kayéik (noise.) The
abbreviation "cl" used here and elsewhere
stands for "classifier," one of the Tlingit and
Athabaskan grammatical prefix categories.

kayik –	.u –	wa	– .a<u>x</u>
noise	per-	cl	to hear
	fective		

176. Bamboo. Bamboo does not grow in
Alaska. The implication is that the men
crossed the Pacific to Hawaii or possibly the
Kuril Islands. The voyage of <u>Kaax</u>'achgóok
belongs in the annals of small craft navigation
such as Captain William Bligh's saving his crew
after the mutiny on the Bounty, the voyages of
the Vikings, the wanderings of Odysseus, and
the traditional chants of Polynesian
navigation.
193-194. "Remember to take good care of
your boat." These lines are another example
of the role of a maternal uncle toward his
sisters' sons. The maternal uncle is the
teacher and tradition bearer of the clan.
From here on, <u>Kaax</u>'achgóok will be instructing
his nephews on survival and on preparation for
the attempt to return home.
198. Fire rubbing sticks. Sticks used for
starting fire by friction. This can be done
in a variety of ways.
214-217. Tanning. These lines are
interesting because they show some of the uses
of the sea mammal pelts. Fur seal is
specified and sea otter implied for tanning for
furs. Sea lion is used for making raw hide.
218. Cut in a circular motion. This is
another reference to traditional technology.
By cutting in a continuous circular pattern,
one long strip of raw hide can be made, as
opposed to cutting many short strips the length
of the skin.
234. <u>Kaax</u>'achgóok. The name is supplied in
translation.

244ff. The stars. This passage is about knowledge of the stars and planets, and their relative positions as compared to their positions at home. This knowledge allows Kaax̲'achgóok to navigate home by the stars.

266-267. Perhaps Kaax̲'achgóok figured it out. From studying the stars he discovered where they were relative to home, and knew where to steer the canoe.

276. Under people's feet. Cushions, pillows, or kneeling pads were made from the bundles of sea lion whiskers.

295. They anchored. This passage describes the use of a sea anchor. See lines 268ff for the making of the sea anchor from bamboo poles and stomachs of fur seal filled with sand. In contrast, he specifies that the sea lion stomachs are used as water containers.

326. This is what they were calling a seagull. This line concludes a passage presenting a very nice image of snow capped Mt. Edgecumbe looking at a distance like a seagull floating on the waves.

327-328. They didn't want to call it by its name. They are avoiding direct reference in favor of indirectness.

341. They pulled some (kelp) on board. To anchor themselves, they grabbed some of the long kelp growing up from the bottom of the sea near land, and pulled them aboard. These can also be wrapped around a paddle then set in the bottom of the canoe or along the gunnel. Sea going Tlingit hunters may have learned this skill from observing sea otters or other marine mammals that anchor themselves in floating kelp when eating or sleeping.

347. Canoe rest. This is a translation of the place name mentioned in the Tlingit text: Yakwkalaséig̲ákw.

359-360. Kaax̲'achgóok carved a petroglyph which can still be seen today. In line 360 the story teller extends an invitation to go there and see it.

363-370. Near fall...food. In the fall
when the salmon are in the streams and rivers,
people would smoke and dry them to put up for
winter.

372-373. His wife had a husband. In
Tlingit tradition the widow was placed with a
relative of her husband to replace her
deceased mate.

375. Tlingit: galtíshch. This is a nice
example of the occasional, indicated by the
suffix -ch and the conjugation marker -ga-.

$$ga - l - tísh - ch$$
$$cl \quad to\ miss;$$
$$be\ lonely$$

378. She had already recovered. The young
woman had recovered from her grief.

380ff. The one who sailed away was still
lingering on her mind. The older woman is
still grieving. The recognition and
homecoming passage is very nicely done. It is
interesting to study the personalities of the
two wives and the story teller's attitude
toward the characters. The older wife is a
model of spiritual and social maturity.

399-400. It is interesting that she
recognizes him by his actions (rather than
having to rely on physical features.)

404-405ff. All his mannerisms were still on
her mind. The older wife had been mourning
for her husband so long she was near mental
breakdown, so her in-laws kidded her about it.

445ff. The distribution. Kaax'achgóok
handed out the valuable skins to those who
gave or might have given at his memorial
feast. (Thinking he was dead, his relatives
would have already hosted a memorial feast
for him.) The sea lion whiskers are also
valuable, and are used, among other things, in
traditional art such as decoration on dance
frontlets.

450ff. He spoke with his sister's son.

This is the nephew that took the bereaved wife
to replace his uncle. This brief speech by
Kaax'achgóok is a fine example of Tlingit
oratory in miniature, using politeness,
diplomacy, and metaphor. The young couple is
embarrassed (lines 427-430) and it now falls to
the uncle to resolve the complex situation.
He does this by giving his blessing to the
marriage and instructing the young couple to
care for each other.

453-454. You wiped the face of your
mother's maternal uncle. This is a metaphorical
expression thanking the nephew for helping wipe
away the tears of grief. The reference to
mother's maternal uncle rather than simply
"your maternal uncle" implies a greater age and
generation difference between the nephew and
Kaax'achgóok, who is probably the great uncle
of the nephew. It is entirely possible that the
"young man" she is placed with (line 377) is
younger than she is, so that the "younger wife"
in her first marriage will eventually become
the "older wife" of her second marriage.

459. You too. Having addressed the nephew,
he now addresses the young wife, and instructs
her to take good care of her husband.

466. Made up his mind. This is a
rhetorical question. He had composed a song
about what had happened to them, and is about
to sing it in public for the first time. Most
Tlingit stories about famous ancestors include
songs or have songs connected with them.

477-478. This is the only thing you won't
hear. The last five lines of the transcription
are an alternate ending dictated by Mr. Johnson
August 22, 1973. The tape recording includes
the Kaax'achgóok song played by Mr. Johnson
from an earlier tape recording. When the draft
transcription was read back to him for his
approval, he requested that the song text be
deleted and not included in the transcription.
He then dictated the last five lines as
transcribed and translated here as an

alternative ending. The tape and original
transcription also include comments on the
song, its Kiks.ádi clan ownership, and words of
appreciation to the transcriber and reading
audience. A very nice rendition of the song by
the Gajaa Héen Dancers is included on the video
tape (Ostyn 1981) entitled *K'aal.átk'*
featuring Mr. Charlie Joseph of Sitka, produced
in 1981 by the Sitka Native Education Program.
An older version of the song text is included
in Swanton (1909: 391, Song 5). As well as
artwork, stories and songs are clan owned
according to the Tlingit system of oral
copyright, but songs are more sensitive than
stories, which is why he requested that the
text not be included in print.

Naatsilanéi told by Willie Marks, 70

Recorded by Nora Dauenhauer at Marks Trail,
Juneau, October 4, 1972. Transcribed and
translated by Nora Dauenhauer.

Other versions: Swanton (1909: Nos. 4 and
71, pp 25ff and 230ff) Barbeau (1964: 290)
Garfield and Forrest (1961: 81-83, 123-125)
Olson (1967: 39-40, 28-29) and Velten (1944).
See also the version by J. B. Fawcett in this
volume. This story is sometimes called "Kéet"
or "The Origin of Killer Whale." A very nice
edition for children with an accompanying
teacher's guide was published by Henry and
Claribel Davis of Kake in 1973, but is now out
of print.
   The story appears to be very old, and is
identified with the southern Tlingit area.
Please see notes to the version by J. B.
Fawcett for more information on this, and on
the clans associated with the story.
   The oral delivery is characterized by marked
pauses after the end of most sentences (marked
with a period in the transcription.) Rather
than to note each of these pauses with extra
space between lines, we have marked only the
extra-long pauses--those lasting approximately
5 seconds or more.

   1. The transcription has been edited
slightly in this line at the request of the
tradition bearer.
   2. In addition to the pause between lines 1
and 2, there is some audience discussion,
after which the story teller continues.
   4-5. He would tell stories....about how
well he could use... crampon snowshoes.
Naatsilanéi seemes to have been bragging about
his ability to climb on rock with his crampon
snowshoes. Naatsilanéi's bragging sets the

dramatic action of the story in motion.
Perhaps to "get even" his brothers-in-law plot
to leave him stranded on a barren reef. The
brothers-in-law call his bluff, expecting him
to slip on the rocks and drown in the surf, but
Naatsilanéi is as good as he claims to be, and
does not slip, so they have to abandon him. All
versions of the story include the brothers-in-
law who are jealous of the hunting abilities
and other skills of Naatsilanéi. This version
is interesting in that it suggests that perhaps
Naatsilanéi was also socially out of line in
his boastfulness.

The story of Naatsilanéi is told to remind
people that when jealousy enters things can
turn really bad. The brothers-in-law are
driven by their jealousy to leave their
sister's husband on the island, without
considering the consequences. This is, of
course, in conflict with the demands and
traditions of Tlingit social structure. A
man's most valued kin is his brother-in-law
(his sister's husband.) A man will give gifts
to his brother-in-law. Contrary to this,
Naatsilanéi's brothers-in-law leave him
stranded on the barren rock to die. See also
the "Woman Who Married the Bear" for the
brother-in-law motif.

10. "...Let's let you...take me out!"
Naatsilanéi wanted to show off.

18-19. The waves reached high. The literal
translation of the Tlingit is also very
"poetic" and is a good illustration of Tlingit
grammatical structure.

Kei	ji-	la-	shát-	ch	wé	teet.
up	arm	cl	reach, grab	keep on	the	waves

The waves keep on reaching up snatching or
grabbing with their hands or arms.

22. He stuck to the spot. Without
slipping, Naatsilanéi was able to stick to the

place where he first landed.

24. Perhaps. Willie Marks uses the words
"perhaps" and "probably" (gwál) and "maybe"
(gíwé, gíyú) frequently in his story telling.
These are common devices in oral literature,
and should not suggest to us that the narrator
is unsure of his or her material. The device
works in at least four ways, creating:

a) limits of experience (he was not actually
there in person as an eye witness and does not
want to lie about the events)

b) reliability (this is how he heard it; he
is not making the story up)

c) aesthetic distance (as a narrator he can
remove himself from the events of the story)

d) closeness (at the same time he can create
an emotional closeness to the people and events
in the story by allowing us to get close to
them by asking and wondering what they were
really like.)

31. "Bring the boat over now!" In a
subdued voice, the story teller imitates a
shout here.

51. When he heard that thing. (Literally,
"aawa.axi át áwé" --"the thing that he
heard." For greater clarity in translation,
the order of the lines is different than in
Tlingit. At this point in the story,
Naatsilanéi first senses the approach of the
spirit helper, described several lines later
as a "huge man"-- káa tlein.

52. "I'm coming to get you." The story
teller's voice is raised slightly higher for
the dialog.

63. Naatsilanéi asked it. This is a place
where we have added the name for greater
clarity in translation, where the original
relies on the pronoun. Tlingit does not
distinguish "he," "she," and "it" in the
pronoun (although Tlingit does make other
pronoun distinctions not matched in English);

whereas this also gives some clarity in
English, it forces the translator to make a
choice between "he" and "it" when referring to
the helper.

65. Under this rock. Reference is to the
entire reef, or sea lion rock.

67. Lifted the edge of the sea like a
cloth. This is a very nice verb form in Tlingit
using the verb stem -.áax̲ meaning "to handle
cloth." "Edge" is conveyed by a nominal prefix.

73. He went there, down there. What
follows is an archetypical shaman voyage, an
out of life experience to the spirit world, the
result of which is a covenant with particular
animals and spirit helpers.

95. The Proverb..."he was like the man who
had a spear removed." Literally, "he became
like one from whom a spear point was removed."

Oo-	da<u>x</u>	kát		
It	from	spear	point	
ka-	w-	dzi-	tee-	yi
round	per-	cl	take	attributive
thing	fect.			
yá<u>x</u>	woo-	nei		
like	per-	become		
	fect.			

This proverb can be applied culturally to
someone who is feeling better after feeling ill.

98. That big balloon. The balloon was the
container for the Southwest wind.

99. A speed boat balloon. The story teller
is probably thinking of rubber-raft-type speed
boats.

102. "Don't think of this place again." The
Sea Lion People are telling Naatsilanéi not to
think about the island. This emphasizes the
importance in Tlingit traditional spirituality
of controlling not only one's physical actions
and speech, but one's very thoughts. See also

Tom Peters' story and J.B. Fawcett's "Kaats'"
where thoughts are visualized as beams of
light, and the point is made that animals have
the power to receive human thought. Therefore,
it is important to have good thoughts rather
than evil or counterproductive ones.

106-109. One, two, three, four. The story
teller counted this in Chinese (Cantonese--yet,
ngi, sam, si.) Note also that whereas three is
the "magic number" in English (and Indo-
European and Judeo-Christian tradition) four is
complete number in Tlingit (as well as
Athabaskan and many other Native American traditions.) He also counts in Chinese in line 165.

110. They tossed it in the air. This is a
nice verb in Tlingit, specifiying "to toss a
round object":

yóo	áwé	kei	ka-	w-	du-	wa-	g̲íx'
thus	it	up	round	per-	they	cl	toss
	was		thing	fect.			

117, 125. Probably it had a zipper....
Probably there was an automatic button.... The
tradition bearer said these lines jokingly, in
a deliberate anachronism, inserting
contemporary technology into the traditional
story. In Tlingit there is extra humor due to
the code switching.

> Gwál zipper áwé a x̲'atóowu á.
> Gwál wé automatic button g̲íwé áwu?

138. "Hey, honey!" Said jokingly.
Followed by audience laughter and comment
partly overlapping with the next line of the
narration.

146. Be sure lotsa rice. Again, jokingly,
and with code switching. Despite the surface
humor and detachment, the style of Willie
Marks shows his closeness to the characters.
Lines like "perhaps some food too" show that
he is asking himself, and raising the question

for the listener or reader, "what was it like
then? What was it like for Naatsilanéi?" The
humor also provides a bit of "comic relief" in
the midst of serious tragedy.

150. He adzed out those things. Students
of the language might be interested in the
phonetic contrast between

     axóot'   he adzed it
     a xoot   among them

151. Sea lions instructed him. Other story
tellers have told this with Naatsilanéi's
getting the idea of carving killer whales from
seeing killer whale designs on the walls of the
ill sea lion's house when he was down under the
sea. The idea of creating the killer whale was
given to Naatsilanéi as payment for helping
the wounded sea lion.

161. When the night turns over.... The
night is like a human sleeping. When it rolls
over, it is midnight. It is the traditional
belief that evil things happen about this time
of the night.

181. "The boat will come through here. / I
will tell you when to go for them."
Naatsilanéi is speaking to his carvings. He is
planning to have the Killer Whales kill his
brothers-in-law who left him on the reef.

194. Shhhhhh. Sound effects for the noise;
could also be translated as "swish" or "woosh", etc.

201, 203. The young boy. Notice the
different forms in Tlingit, one of which has a
long vowel, and one a short vowel. The long
vowel here is caused by the subject marker -ch
as a suffix.

     át k'átsk'ooch
     át k'átsk'u

This is not a phonemic distinction, but is
free or predictable variation and could be
standardized, and, in fact, is in the process

of being standardized in Tlingit spelling.
Both -oo- and -u- are heard with and without
the -ch suffix; both are "correct."
Technically, "real" lengthening occurs only
with stems ending in a short, high vowel.

215. That's why these things don't do any
harm to humans. This is the source of the
covenant between humans and Killer Whales, and
the source of the Killer Whale crest or at.óow.

218. Maybe to wherever he would die. This
is a powerful ending. Naatsilanéi gets his
revenge, but at the cost of alienation from the
community, and perhaps ultimately at the cost
of his own life, which, ironically, he loses as
a consequence of his own vengeance, rather than
through the treachery of his brothers-in-law.
Ironically, the theme of his own death closes
the story of his fight for life--which he
actually won! Naatsilanéi was a successful
man, good at whatever he did. The ending is
ambiguous: is he "throwing in the towel" and
expecting imminent death, or is he leaving the
community forever, to live out his life in
exile? Also, the "maybe" is typical of the
ambiguity of endings in much of Native American
oral tradition, where things are often left
open ended. On a technical note, the ending is
difficult to translate. As in much of translation, the choice involves editorial decision.
Of some possible choices, "to find a place to
die" is more active, and "to wherever he would
die" or "could die" is more passive.

Naatsilanéi told by J.B. Fawcett

Recorded by Nora Dauenhauer, Juneau, October
3, 1972. Transcribed and translated by Nora
Dauenhauer.

First transcribed October 3, 1972 as a project
of the Alaska Native Language Center; first
translated December 6, 1980 as a project of
National Endowment for the Arts Grant to Nora
Dauenhauer; transcription and translation
extensively revised as projects of the Sealaska
Heritage Foundation.

Please see the notes to the version by
Willie Marks for general commentary on the
story and for reference to other published
versions.

Most oral literature assumes that the
audience is already familiar with the story--
that the listener has heard it before. Because
of this assumption, J. B. Fawcett's style puts
more demands on the new reader. When the story
was told, Mr. Fawcett assumed the listener's
knowledge of the story, and therefore omitted
some details that, while minor, make the story
hang together. For example, jealousy is not
directly mentioned as the reason the brothers-
in-law decide to leave Naatsilanéi stranded to
die on the island. Also, many of the
transitions are not as clear for a person
unfamiliar with the story.

Therefore, we have arranged the version by
J. B. Fawcett second in the volume, after
Willie Marks, hoping that it will be easier
for the new reader to enjoy this version after
becoming familiar with the story by having
read it once before.

Otherwise, perhaps even still, appreciating
the story is like putting a puzzle together:
the picture is not complete until the last
piece is in place. J. B. Fawcett unfolds his
story gradually, a piece at a time, often

through "flashbacks." The story is not told
"in order."

J. B. was in poor health when he told the
story, and by this time was almost totally
deaf. Perhaps for these reasons, the delivery
is characterized by stuttering and many false
starts. These have been edited out by the
transcriber. His style is characterized by
rapid delivery of words within the line, but
generally clear pauses at phrase ends (marked
by line turnings and punctuation as described
in the introduction.)

4, 6. Taan...Klawock. On Prince of Wales
Island, west of Ketchikan. The narrator
identifies the story with the Southern part of
Tlingit territory, of more ancient settlement
than the north. (See the Basket Bay History
for more on migration and settlement.)

14. "Come here and get me, my brothers-in-
law." The brothers-in-law violate one of the
most traditional and valued relationships in
Tlingit social structure. Traditionally, a
man's most valued kin is his brother-in-law,
his sister's husband. Naatsilanéi appeals to
his brothers-in-law to come back for him, but
they leave him stranded on the island to die.

17. Our ancestors. The story teller is
establishing his relationship to the events
and persons in the story.

18. Tsaagweidí. Naatsilanéi was a man of
the Tsaagweidí, an Eagle moiety clan.

26. Someone talked to him.... Other
tradition bearers tell of how the person who
spoke to Naatsilanéi took him down under the
sea to see what was making the sea lion prince
ill. When he got there he saw the painting of
killer whales on the walls of the house they
took him to. In this version, Naatsilanéi
meets the Spirit Helper, but does not go on
the underwater journey.

29. A yát. On the tape, phonetically a
"gamma," a sonorant, an "unrounded w." Much

of J. B.'s pronunciation is very conservative.

41. The name Naatsilanéi is supplied in translation, but is not present in the original, which is more literally "he came to him." Tlingit has a "fourth person" pronoun which makes the pronoun object more specific than the English pronoun "him."

44. Get inside this.... Other tradition bearers explain this as the container of the southeast wind.

46, 48. Four times. Finally, on the fourth time. Here again is the pattern of four as the "magic number" or "complete number" in Tlingit culture, in contrast to, but serving the same function as three in Judeo-Christian and Indo-European culture.

50. It was a stomach. This is a large Sealion stomach, one and the same as the southeast wind container.

53. "Don't think back...." He was told to concentrate on his home village, to focus on his goal and not to worry about looking back. Again (as in the version by Willie Marks) the importance of correct thinking is emphasized.

59-74. This passage is unclear in Tlingit as well as in English. The "thing" is not specified by the story teller. We conclude that it is a tube-like object, perhaps kelp or Indian celery, or something similar that the helper gave him through which he would talk. In line 73, the stem -yísh refers to a long object.

80, 81. "Whatever you desire, just name it." The spirit helper is making the offer to Naatsilanéi.

85. These boats. Here Naatsilanéi encounters his second set of spirit helpers, explained more fully in line 119 as Brants. Here the small geese are seen as a fleet of boats, and appear human.

96. They didn't know. This is a transition, or flash, or change of scene to the wives and villagers. Here Naatsilanéi's

wives are introduced. The narrator is telling
how the brothers-in-law explained what
happened to their sisters, the widows.

103. "We don't know. A wave carried him
out...." As in other cultures, lies are
unforgivable in Tlingit tradition. It is
considered wrong to lie about a human or
anything. People could usually tell when a
lie is being told. Here the brothers-in-law
are telling lies about Naatsilanéi to their
sisters, the wives of Naatsilanéi.

108. That man. The spirit helper.

112. "That's your food." Nice use of
dialog here on the tape recording. The Spirit
Helper speaks in a lower tone of voice than
the narrator's voice or Naatsilanéi's.

119. Brant (a small goose.) The Brant
appeared to him like a human being, and spoke
to him in Tlingit. It is the Spirit coming to
help him (finally identified in the narration.)

122. Aagáa áwé in Tlingit. This is a
classic line and phrase turning in Tlingit
narrative discourse. The sentence ends with
falling pitch drop, followed by a very
significant pause, and picks up again with the
transition "aagáa."

123. Brant. The noun is supplied in
translation.

132ff. At one point. This is another
transition. The Spirit Helper is restoring
Naatsilanéi and his wife to each other.
Compare also the mention of midnight, as in
Willie Marks' narration.

143-153. This section is unclear. We
interpret the "thing" of line 143 to be the
tube-like object introduced in lines 59-74.
Naatsilanéi's wife is inside the house and he
is outside. They are talking through the tube,
much as Naatsilanéi and his helper used it to
talk through when he was in the bubble. The
verb stems -taan and -tsaak in lines 144 and
145 refer to long objects.

149, 151. "It's me." Names of the speakers

are supplied in translation. The Tlingit
performance uses different voices for the
narration, Naatsilanéi, and his wife.
Naatsilanéi's voice is very slow and
deliberate. The wife's voice is higher and
spoken in more rapid delivery. The speed is
reflected in the line turnings for one, and
run-on for the other.

154ff. His tools. The point being made is
of the great antiquity of Tlingit carving
technology.

168. "Let's look over there." A
transition. The brothers-in-law decide to go
hunting.

171. They were hunting.... "They" are the
brothers-in-law.

183. It was there he carved / the Killer
Whales. At this point Naatsilanéi carves the
killer whales to get even and take revenge on
his brothers-in-law.

198. In Tlingit, phonetically, "Shóo<u>x</u>
sitee." It's sure, i.e., certain, true. This
is "code switching" with the English word
"sure," with the r dropped.

200. This is not a story without value.
The narrator is emphasizing the value of the
story in Tlingit tradition. The story has
many values. One is that the Da<u>k</u>l'aweidí and
Tsaagweidí clans have names relating to Killer
Whale, and their emblem is the Killer Whale.
The passage also reiterates a theme common in
this collection--that these are true stories,
therefore of value. In folklore terms, these
are legends, not fictional folktales.

233-234 "...Don't do anything / to the
younger one." Naatsilanéi asked the killer
whales not to harm the younger brother. This
is probably the "man from whose lips this is
told" mentioned in the opening lines of the
story, the one who lived to tell about it.
Again, this version assumes that the listener
is familiar with the youngest brother-in-law's
compassion for Naatsilanéi, although the

incident is not included in this narration.
See next note.

244-245. The younger one had cried for him
/ on the island. Naatsilanéi knew the younger
brother-in-law was innocent and wanted to go
back for him.

257. Strands surfaced.... A group stemming
from the Tsaagweidí clan surfaced in Taku, the
Yanyeidí clan of the Eagle moiety. This story
and the Killer Whale crest are also identified
with the Dakl'aweidí clan. Because of the
recognized antiquity of the story, and because
younger clans evolve from parent clans, it is
understandable that more than one Eagle moiety
clan would have the story and crest in its
heritage. J. B. is emphasizing the lesser
known information here, probably assuming
audience knowledge of the Killer Whale as a
Dakl'aweidí at.óow.

258. Song. This is a typical pattern in
Tlingit oral literature, where a story, a
song, and an artistic design all refer to each
other in remembering the acquisition of a
shaman spirit by an ancestor. The song is
alluded to, but not sung in this narration.
Some story tellers sing the songs, others
mention them, but do not include them.

262, 265. Tlingit, ḵuwa.áxch. This is a
nice example of the use of the prefix ḵu-
indicating a human object or theme.

276. Their names.... Because of the great
antiquity of the story, all of the names are
no longer known to the narrator.

278. Our ancestors. The Tlingit text
includes one form of the word from which our
title derives: haa shagóonx'ich. The suffix
-x'- is plural, -i- is a "peg vowel" on which
the next suffix hangs, and -ch is a subject
marker.

280. Outer container. The term "outer
container" (in the text, has du daakeitx'í--
their outer containers) is usually applied to a
person's grandparents on both sides. The

narrator is explaining now that this is not
his story per se, that his clan was not in it,
but that his ancestors used to tell it because
it happened to "their outer containers"--their
grandparents on both sides. This is part of
the narrator's indirect "narrative frame."

   282. Tlingit, tlaagú. This word indicates
a very old or ancient story. In contrast, the
word "sh kalneek", used in lines 1 and 276 of
the story do not specify the age of the story.

   284. Deikee Lunaak.... The narrator is now
being even more specific regarding the
location of the island near the fort outside
of Klawock. Many Tlingit stories are very
specific about the places in which they
happened. Other published versions of the
story identify it with other places.

   The end. It is sometimes difficult to
determine where a "story" begins and ends. The
speaking on the tape begins with some
preliminary inquires about whether the tape
recorder is on, then the narrator says
something like "listen now," after which the
transcription picks up. At the end of the
story, where the transcription ends, after a
slight pause, the narrator continues to expound
on related points of concern. In particular,
he makes an appeal to document Tlingit history,
especially regarding the land. He expresses
concern with acculturation and loss of
knowledge of traditions, and comments "It's
only right that it be put on paper." Thus, the
"stories" are often set in a larger narrative
context, or may inspire the tradition bearers
to continue the narration on other topics.

Strong Man told by Frank Johnson, 77

Recorded by Nora Dauenhauer, Sitka, June 12,
1972. Transcribed and translated by Nora
Dauenhauer.

Publication history. The Tlingit text was
first transcribed as a production of Alaska
Native Language Center and first published
March, 1973, by Tlingit Readers, Inc. Copyright
(c) by Tlingit Readers, Inc. Publication of
this text inaugurated a series of traditional
Tlingit texts by various tradition bearers,
with covers designed by Tlingit artists. The
first edition, now rare and out of print,
featured a four color cover designed by Horace
Marks. It was printed at Sheldon Jackson
College by Andrew Hope III, Ed Schulz, and
Richard Dauenhauer. Typing for the original
version was by Vesta Dominicks.
    Other versions. Swanton 1909: Nos. 31 and
93, pp 145-150, 289-291) Garfield and Forrest
(1961: 73-77) De Laguna (1972: 890-892)
Keithahn (1963: 143-148) Barbeau 1964: 298ff).
    This story is told and written in the
southern dialect of Tlingit. Northern Tlingit
speakers describe the southern speech as "sing
song." Southern Tlingit is characterized by
different sentence intonation patterns than
Northern Tlingit, but these are not reflected
in the transcription system. However, another
feature of Southern Tlingit, which is easily
reflected in the popular writing system, is the
dropping of vowels in classifiers. For example:

Northern	Southern
akawlitéi̱x'	akawltéi̱x'
k̲usa.áat	k̲us.áat
yawsika̲a	yawska̲a
awusinei	awusnei
awsix'áa	awsx'áa

wusitee   wustee

When the vowels are dropped, some of the remaining consonants are no longer between vowels. Some of these consonants may change.

Northern   Southern

jiwdigút   jiwtgút
wooshdakán   wooshtkán
<u>k</u>udzitee   <u>k</u>utstee
awdli<u>g</u>ín   awtl<u>g</u>ín
ayawdudlitseen   ayawdutltseen
oowdlitsín   oowtltsín
kei wjik'én   kei wchk'én

These changes are very regular, and follow the same pattern as the alternations in noun and verb stems when suffixes are added or dropped.

Si	becomes	s			
li	"	l			
di	"	d	which becomes		t
dzi	"	dz	"	"	ts
dli	"	dl	"	"	tl
ji	"	j	"	"	ch

In this story, Mr. Johnson uses some northern forms as well as the southern forms. For example, where we might expect the southern "<u>k</u>uwtstee" we find the northern "<u>k</u>uwdzitee."

The narration is characterized by many false starts in some places, which have been edited out. Frank Johnson is remembered as a good story teller. He hadn't told this story for some time, but when he finds his pace, the delivery flows smoothly and without false starts.

Note the use of the narrative frame to open and close the story. In these frames, Tlingit story tellers usually identify specific personal, place, and clan names, thus

establishing the social context of the story.
They tell who the story belongs to, and what
their personal relationship is to the story.
Here Mr. Johnson identifies the story as
originating in the southernmost and most
ancient area of Tlingit settlement, called
Henyaa. The story belongs to the
Taakw.anneidí clan. At the end of his
narration, Mr. Johnson expresses his personal
connection to the story through his father's
people, the Shangukeidí.

   7. People trained for strength. This is a
reference to the tradition of the maternal
uncle's training his nephews by bathing in the
sea in winter. This training was to improve
self discipline and physical endurance.
   10. Sea lions. Sea lion meat was eaten as
subsistence food. The whiskers are used to
decorate hats and headdresses.
   1-16. Common in Tlingit story telling, the
composer is changing rapidly from topic to
topic in the opening of his story, thereby
introducing a number of main points he will
develop later. This technique is something
like a table of contents or an abstract in a
written presentation. By now we already know
that this is an ancient southern Tlingit story
that has something to do with ritual bathing
and hunting for sea lions, that Galwéit' is the
leader of the people, and that he has a nephew
who is a misfit despite his birth. Beginning
with line 17, he begins to expand on these
topics, and work them in to the weave of his
narration.
   16. Kuwudzitee. This is a northern form,
where one might expect the southern form
kuwtstee.
   18. Before daybreak...to the sea water. In
Tlingit tradition, the most important work is
to be done before daybreak "before the Raven
cries." They are going to the sea to bathe.
This is the Tlingit tradition of the maternal

uncle's training his nephews. Part of this
training involved strengthening through bathing
in the ocean before dawn.

21. Ulk'eiyéech. Whereas we have
standardized the spelling of single suffixes
short, we have not standardized for a series of
suffixes. Whereas single suffixes may be long
or short, depending on the speaker, there
appears to be automatic lengthing of first
suffixes when a second suffix follows.

22. He...went to the sea alone. The young
man goes to the sea alone because he is not
included in the ritual bathing; instead, he
bathes secretly at night while others sleep.

24, 25. Shall I tell it just the way they
tell it? This is an "aside" to the collector,
who replies, "yes." Here and other places in
the story, the narrator is aware of the
differing cultural attitudes toward mention of
body parts and functions. These are not
considered shocking in Tlingit, but may upset
some English speakers. Mr. Johnson asks this
question just before starting the sequence
where the young man emerges chilled from the
water and urinates on the warm coals of the
fire to create steam for warmth. This incident
is important and will be recalled much later
in the story when the nephew's name is discussed.

36. One of his mother's brother's wives.
Reference is to plural marriage, common in precontact and early contact times.

42. He would cry out in pain. This line
refers to how the men stayed in the sea, even
when the pain from the cold became unbearably
strong.

43. Kus.áat. The northern form would be
kusa.áat.

47. X'awduwatán. This is a northern form;
the expected southern form would be x'awtwatán.

54. Latseen / Strength. This is a
spiritual being who comes to help the nephew.
There is a strong Tlingit belief that if you
stay with something, it will be lucky for you.

From this there is also a proverb, "a káa
wdishúch--he bathed to get it." This is used
for someone who is really good at something.

61. Here and in subsequent lines, Tlingit
uses a pronoun, and we have supplied the noun
"Strength" in translation. Where Tlingit uses
such phrases as "he told him" we have
translated it as "Strength told him." This may
convey an allegorical flavor in translation not
present in the original, but otherwise the
pronouns can be confusing to the English reader.

63-68. This is a technically difficult
passage to translate, due to differing
concepts of anatomy. S'aak is "bone," and
x'áak is "between." Du s'aagix'áak is "his
joint" or, literally, the place between his
bones. But when the story teller refers to
the eight bones, he is presumably talking about
the place between the joints. The Spirit
Helper is giving the misfit nephew a rubdown.

64. La.ús'kw. This is a northern form,
where one might expect the southern la.ís'kw.

65. Yá, etc. This and other demonstratives
are pronounced long on the tape, but have been
normalized to the short form, following the
spelling convention.

66. Eight bones. This is, of course, based
on human anatomy, but may also be related to
the Tlingit "magic" or "complete" number being
4 or multiples of 4.

68. Al.ís'kw. This is the southern form,
in contrast to the northern form used in line 64.

70. Tsu héenx gagú. Go into the water
again. This is an imperative form and includes
the conjugation prefix -ga-. This form
contrasts with the imperative "gu" as in "haa
gú" (come here) or "neil gú" (come in.) This
form shows how the verb stem ya-goot can mean
go or come, indicating motion on foot to or
away from the speaker, and that the two Tlingit
verbs are in separate conjugation classes. The
imperative (or command) form is always the
clearest form for determining the conjugation

class of a Tlingit verb, because the conjugation marker (na, ga, g̲a, or "zero") is always present in the imperative.

76. The fourth time. This is another good example of how, in Tlingit tradition, "the fourth time's the charm." The nephew has now gained enough strength to throw or out wrestle his spirit mentor.

82. Tlingit. Yaa anasg̲úk is a plural stem; singular would be -hash. This is translated as "patches of frost."

93. It is called by another name. The other name is Aas Tl'íli, meaning "tree penis."

97. Immerse it in water. Other versions, perhaps more conservative and traditional, instruct the young man to urinate on the tree penis and put it back in the tree. Because it is winter, the branch freezes back in place.

99ff. Tlingit. The stem -x'áa, to twist a branch or root, appears in a variety of forms with both the s and y classifier. These may be of interest to students.

99.	gag̲isax'áa	imperative
101.	anasx'éin	progressive indicative
102.	awsx'áa	perfective
111.	anasx'eini	progressive particip.
117.	aawax'áa	perfective (y cl)

After much debate, we decided to translate the verb as "split" rather than "twist." The image is probably of twisting the tree until it split, then twisting it back together again so that it would appear normal.

109. He pulled it out. The uncle's pride does not let him see the truth.

112. But Strength had told the nephew. Nouns are supplied in translation. The Tlingit is an excellent example of the translation problem involved; literally "that man told/had told him." The pronoun "ash" indicates a 3rd party not included in what has just been talked about, not the "he" of the preceding passage

referring to the maternal uncle, but a
different "he." This "extra" pronoun in Tlingit
gives greater clarity in the Tlingit text than
in English, where pronoun antecedents can be
notoriously unclear. For clarity in English, we
have substituted nouns for pronouns.

113, 115. Tsu and tsú. Tsu (low tone)
means "again," and tsú (high tone) means
"also." Both words appear in these lines.
The distinctions made in Tlingit are difficult
to carry over into smooth English
translation. More literally, it runs "Put the
tree also back the way it was again."

113. Put the tree back the way it was.
Strength had instructed the nephew to restore
the tree to its original shape after splitting
it. This is an important detail, because the
maternal uncle, coming to the tree in the dark,
wrongly assumes that he has split it himself,
and thereby falsely assesses his own strength,
which will lead to his death. In actuality,
the nephew has already split the tree and
pressed it back together so that it froze
together again in the cold.

114. North wind. It is extremely cold
during the north wind. The narrator does not
state explicitly that the tree froze back
together (as did the tree branch the nephew had
pulled out), but this detail of the north wind
lets the listener or reader complete the
picture for him or herself.

115-117. The story teller reviews the main
point here: because the nephew had put the
tree back the way it was, the maternal uncle,
because it was still dark, thought that he
himself had split it. The maternal uncle is
also blinded by his arrogance.

120. Sea Lion Land. Here and for
approximately 10 lines the story teller
introduces and describes what is called a sea
lion "haul out." This is a place where sea
lions haul themselves out of the water and sit
on rocks. The sea lion (Eumetopias jubatus) is

so named because it resembles a lion. It is
also called Steller's or Northern Sea Lion.
Unlike seals (other than the fur seal) sea
lions have external ears and rear flippers that
turn forward. Please see the note to line 47
of the story by A. P. Johnson for a more
detailed description of various sea mammals.

The description is nicely "sandwiched"
between two phrases in lines 119 and 130--
"They began to get ready," and "when people
were preparing to go." The story teller first
describes where they are preparing to go, and
then describes the departure.

132-135. But he...etc. These lines
emphasize how pitifully poor the nephew was.
He is in rags and tatters during winter.

134. Gíwé...oonasgút. This is a good
example of the irrealis used in Tlingit
because the narrator is speculating "maybe"
rather than making a statement of absolute
fact.

136. Yawtwatsák. Northern would be
yawduwatsák. This is an interesting verb,
especially because it appears with a different
form and meaning in the following line. In the
first form it is to reject a person, to refuse
the company of, to socially push away. In the
second form it means to push a boat or canoe
along with a pole. The first form is a main
verb, the second in a dependent clause. Here
are the dictionary forms:

> ya-ya-tsaak   (tr)   to reject; refuse
>   company of
>   li-tsaak (tr)   to pole a boat;
>   push with pole

The underlying forms in the text are:

> ya-   wu-   du-   ya-   tsák
> face   per-   they   cl   push away
>   fect

```
du-    l-   tsaag-        ɬ
they   cl   push away     when
```

The contractions are too complicated to
explain here, but have to do with the number
of "allowable" open syllables before the
stem.   This pair of verbs provides a good
illustration of how the Tlingit verb system
operates, using a limited number of verb stems
arranged with an infinite combination of
prefixes and classifiers.   Stem tone and vowel
length are part of the system.

141.   There is a proverb.   "To go along as a
bailer" is a proverbial expression in Tlingit
that can appear in various forms: "I'll go
along as a bailer," "he can go along as a
bailer," "take me along as a bailer," etc.
This phrase is used by, for, or about someone
who is about to undertake an important task.
The idea is that anyone who bails a boat keeps
it from disaster, but there is even more
implied in the proverb.   Part of the message
is not to look down on or overlook the poor,
the different, or seemingly low.   Even a
person performing such a seemingly trivial
task as bailing the boat may, in fact, come to
the rescue.   Here the nephew does not go along
as the skipper, mate, or prestige crew, yet,
as the story evolves, he "saves the day." So,
there is a twofold message here: first, that
each person can play his or her part in a
task, however seemingly humble, and, second,
that things are not always as they seem, and
true power may come from places where we
overlook or least expect it.   As the story
unfolds from this point we see the pride and
arrogance of the uncle leading to his demise,
and the true inner strength of the nephew
manifesting itself.

151-152.   He was sure he could get the one
at the top.   This is the uncle's pride and
overconfidence.

161-164.   That's why...he stood up.   Only

now does the nephew stand up to be
recognized. It is significant that only now,
in line 162, is he identified by name by the
story teller. Up to this point he has
carefully been referred to by pronouns only.

162. Atkaháas'i. The name refers to
someone who smells of urine. The stem is
-háas', meaning puke or vomit; possibly this
name refers to a smell of urine strong enough
to make one gag or vomit. The name is used
because of how when he urinated on the ashes
the steam of the embers and urine surrounded
him and he began to smell like urine. People
assumed he was wetting his bed. (The Tlingit
term for a bed wetter is sh kadliháas'i.) This
name is considered derogatory, and some
tradition bearers object to Swanton's (1909:
289) use of it for a title. He is also referred
to as Dukt'ootl', which means "Dark Skin" and
refers to the soot. Most masks and carvings
depict him in brown or black paint. (See also
Swanton 1909: 146.) It is significant that in
lines 214 and 215 nobody knows his "real" name,
and he assumes his maternal uncle's name, along
with his widow and social position.

164. Wudiháan. This is a northern form.
The expected southern form would be wtháan.

165. They imitate him saying. The Tlingit
verb implies not only the nephew's speech of
the moment, but also the entire oral tradition
of story telling. This is one of the important
scenes relished by generations of tradition
bearers.

165-183. This is a marvellous passage in
which the nephew stands up, makes a speech
taking credit for his hitherto secret training
and deeds of strength, walks up through the
boat, not stepping over the thwarts but
breaking them with his shins, leaps ashore
without loosing his footing on the very
slippery seaweed, and punches out the young
sea lions.

171. Awé tle yaa nagúdi etc. The Tlingit

line has an exceptionally nice sentence
rhythm, playing on repetition of sounds and
verb stems. We have tried to convey a sense of
this in English.

184-190. The nephew now singles out the
large sea lion who killed his maternal uncle,
and rips it in half, avenging his uncle. This
motif is popular on totem poles, with the
"Strong Man" tearing the sea lion in two,
upside down, from the flippers downward. The
passage is an example of how nephews are
expected to come to the aid of their uncles in
all aspects of Tlingit social life.

187. Yax. Phonetically wax on tape. The y
becomes w under influence of the vowel in yóo.

191. Jiwtgút. This is an interesting verb
translated as "fighting his way through." The
northern form is jiwudigút.

```
ji-    wu-    di-   gút
hand   prf    cl    stem: go on foot
```

The whole complex conveys the sense of going
along fighting with the hands.

194-201. This one, etc. Reference is to
the older wife of the maternal uncle. She was
the only one who cared for him, who didn't
ostracize him. The moral is that we should
always respect a human being no matter what he
or she is or does or looks like. The wife had
given him an ermine, which he tied to his hair
going into battle, much like a medieval lady
giving a knight a kerchief. We can imagine
the contrast of the ermine and the nephew's
rags. This kind of hair decoration is called
ch'éen in Tlingit.

202. Soot. In Tlingit tradition, when you
are about to undertake a difficult task, you
put soot on your face.

206. The nephew married. Noun supplied in
translation. The following lines explain the
tradition that when a man's maternal uncle
dies, one of the nephews is expected to marry

the widow.

213. The young one. This refers to the younger wife. It is interesting to note that here, as in the narrative by A.P. Johnson, the older wife is admired for her compassion and other character traits, perhaps which develop with the maturity that the younger women lack.

215. His mother's brother's name. Following the death of a maternal uncle, the name is passed on to a deserving nephew. Because the "Strong Man" avenged his maternal uncle's death, he was given his uncle's name, Galwéit'.

216-227, 223. Seitéew. Frank Johnson is emphasizing the importance of the name here, and that many people have forgotten the name of the older wife. It was important to his father, because he was Shangukeidí, of the Eagle moiety, and the wife of Galwéit' was also Shangukeidí, therefore a relative and an ancestor of his father and of the story teller himself.

Some discussion (not included in the transcription) follows the story. In this, Frank Johnson identifies the story as belonging to the Taakw.aaneidí of Klawock. His personal connection to the story is not to the clan that owns it, but through his father's clan, the Shangukeidí.

Kaakex'wtí told by Willie Marks, 70

Recorded by Nora Dauenhauer, Juneau, October
5, 1972. Transcribed and translated by Nora
Dauenhauer

The manuscript was first transcribed October
1972, as a project of the Alaska Native
Language Center; revised and translated as a
project of Sealaska Heritage Foundation. The
story is sometimes known as "The Happy Wanderer,"
"The Man Who Killed His Sleep" (Sh yataayí
ashawdixichi káa) or "The Origin of Copper."
    Other versions: Swanton (1909: Nos. 32 and
104, pp 154 and 326 ff) De Laguna (1972: 270-
272) Olson (1967: 27-28).

    1. Kaakex'wtí was Chookaneidí, an Eagle
moiety clan of the Glacier Bay and Icy Strait
area. Because this information was known to
his immediate audience in the oral performance,
the story teller does not state it explicitly,
but assumes the shared knowledge. This assumed
and unstated information will become very
important later in the story, when Kaakex'wtí
returns to his people and is rejected, and sent
further down the bay to another Eagle moiety
clan, the Kaagwaantaan, who receive him and his
wealth. The story is important in the oral
literature of the Chookaneidí clan because it
is about the exploits of a famous ancestor who
brings copper to the people, and also because
it reminds the people how they lost this gift
through their inability to recognize it when
they saw it.
    2. Gathéeni. Literally, "Sockeye River."
There are two places by this name important in
Chookaneidí oral literature. In this story,
the narrator continues in his opening frame to
describe how this Gathéeni is located on the
outer coast near Cape Spencer, where its
inaccessibility made it a well protected

village site. This is where the story of
Ḵaakex'wtí begins. The other Gathéeni is near
the present day site of Bartlett Cove in
Glacier Bay, and is the setting for the events
recounted in the "Glacier Bay History".

17. How the...man was related. The
question is raised but not answered here. A
very common social as well as literary pattern
would be for the men to be the brothers-in-law
of Ḵaakex'wtí.

21. Perhaps. Willie Marks uses the words
"perhaps" and "probably" (gwál), and "maybe"
(gíwé, gíyú) frequently in his story telling.
See the note to line 24 of his telling of
Naatsilanéi.

24. What was it. The creature that flew
to his face was sleep.

28. It dropped. Ḵaakex'wtí killed sleep
when he killed the creature that was flying at
his face.

32. I have just been reprimanded recently.
This is some self deprecating humor, shared as
"in group" humor by those present at the oral
performance of the story. After having just
used the words "wé bird" the story teller
recalls and comments to the audience that he
has been reprimanded (by his wife, also present
during the story telling) for using English
words in his narratives.

34-39. This section describing the men
falling over dead is very much like the
passage in the story of Tuxstaa by George
Davis, forthcoming in this series.

35. Tlingit. This line has two Tlingit
"homonyms," and a word that is almost a
"homonym."

    a   he (special subject pronoun
            with verb of sitting)
  aa   the one
  aa   he/she/it sits

The various forms of the words a, á, aa and áa,

differing in vowel length and tone, can be very
confusing to students of Tlingit.

  a   possessive pronoun, 3rd singular,
      non-focal, inanimate (its)
  a   object pronoun, 3rd singular,
      non-focal, inanimate (it)
  a   object pronoun, 3rd singular,
      animate, especially human (him/her)
  a   subject pronoun, 3rd singular,
      used with verbs of sitting,
      standing, and motion (he/she/it)

Also, the form á can appear with its high tone
"stolen," so that it looks like the low tone a.
The following are easy to confuse:

  á   there
  á   he/she/it (3rd singular with focus)
  a   it/its/him/her/he/she (without focus)
  aa   one/someone
  aa   he/she/it is sitting
  aa-   combining form of á, with long vowel
        and low tone, as in aadéi (to there)
  áa   variation of áx' (there)
  áa   lake

    40. Kujákx. This is an interesting
expression in Tlingit, coincidentally moreso
in the context of this story. The idiom "to
fall asleep" in Tlingit, translated literally
into English, is "to be killed by sleep,"
whereas in English we literally "fall over
into sleep," whether we are standing, sitting,
or already lying down. In the story, of
course, the people are literally being killed
by sleep after Ḵaakex'wtí killed sleep.

táa – ch	ku –	ják–	x
sleep sub-	peo-	it	durative suffix
ject	ple	kills	continuing action

    41. Kuwanáakw. This is also interesting

for beginning students of Tlingit language.

ku - ya - náa - kw
peo-   cl   stem   durative
ple   die

63. Mount Fairweather. In Tlingit, Tsalxaan; the dominant mountain in the Fairweather Range north of Glacier Bay, important in the oral tradition of the Hoonah people. It is an at.óow of the T'akdeintaan.

71. Little deadfalls. Deadfalls are traps made for animals as small as ermine and as large as bear. They are constructed with a large perched or balanced log attached to bait. The log falls when the bait is taken. The trap takes one animal at a time.

75. Hooligan. In Tlingit, saak. Also spelled eulachen; a small fish, similar to smelt, rich in oil and traditionally burned in some places, so also sometimes called candlefish. The point here is that the technology of these people was limited to tiny deadfalls (usually associated with land animals) used to trap tiny hooligan, one at a time. Kaakex'wtí will introduce some fish trap technology as a gesture of friendship. The gesture is appreciated, and he is welcomed into the People.

74, 75. Satáan. This is an example of the "classificatory verb" widely discussed in the linguistic literature on Tlingit and Athabaskan. The combination of stem and classifier expresses the concept here of a long shaped object lying at rest.

76. Dagaatee. A good example of the "distributive" prefix, expressing that the footprints were distributed all around.

77, 78. These are interesting examples of different forms of the verb stem meaning to trap or kill by deadfall. Note the variation in the stem length and tone, and in the prefixes and suffixes.

77. dulx̱ést   are being trapped; they
    du-l-x̱és-t   are trapping
                      (imperfective; durative
                      suffix; may be trans-
                      lated as passive voice)

78. yeelxeisí   if you trap
    wu-i-l-xeis-í   (perfective conditional)
                      Note metathasis (switch-
                      ing) of the subject pro-
                      noun and aspect prefix
                      in the 2nd person per-
                      fective.

This is a hitherto unattested stem, not listed
in the Naish-Story dictionary. The dictionary
form is li-x̱és or li-xeis. The perfective
form (he trapped it) would be awdlix̱és. It
seems to be part of the invariable stem verbs
that pattern with a durative suffix in the
present. Note the contrast of this stem with
the verb in 114.

114. akawlix̱éis'i   the dumped things
     a-ka-wu-li-x̱éis'-i (attributive)

83a. Following line 83, a line has been
edited out of the transcription. Willie has
been gesturing in reference to the fish trap,
which he will name in the next phrase.
Referring to the tape recorder, he jokes, "A̱x
jín ágé atóodei duwateen? -- Can they see my
hand in that?"
84. T'éetx á. English 86, a trap, indeed.
T'éetx is a sock-like trap made out of spruce
branches and spruce roots, woven for strength
to hold the fish it has trapped in the water
until the fisherman comes to collect. It is
made to hook into the place in the stream
where the fish congregate. This kind of trap
is designed primarily for small fish such as
hooligan, but could also be used for larger

fish such as trout and salmon.

90, 92. Shahéek, shaawahík. Compare the
verb forms used in the main clause and in the
subordinate clause. These are marked in
English by syntax (word order) but not by
morphology (actual grammatical form.) In
Tlingit, the forms are different.

sha-héek   (when) it was full
                (sequential; sub. clause)

shaa-wa-hík   it was full
                (perfective; main clause)

The sequential is grammatically marked by its
position in the subordinate clause, the long high
stem, the "zero" classifier, and the conjugation
prefix (in this case also "zero".) The underlying
form for the perfective in the main clause is:

sha-wu-ya-hík

100. Weh-weh. The story teller is
imitating the sounds of the people talking in
a different language.

103. Gunanaa / Athabaskans. Most likely
Southern Tuchone.

108-111. Tsu and tsú. Tsu, "again;" with
high tone, tsú, "too" or "also," here
translated "finally."

114. Tlingit. The verb stem form here
looks similar to that in line 78, but is not
the same. The underlying form is ka-si-xaa,
meaning to pour out, dump out, or empty out in
mass by turning over a container. It appears in
lines 93 and 94 with the stem form -xéi- and
the durative suffix -x, and in line 114 as an
attributive perfective with the suffix -s'.

123. Tlingit. Kadukaa. The Tlingit stem
here is -kaa, meaning "to imitate," in
contrast to the stem -kaa, meaning "to tell,
speak, or say." The stem -kaa is not attested
in the Tlingit linguistic literature with this

combination of classifier and nominal prefix: ka-ya-kaa.

130. I forgot. The implication is that the story teller has forgotten some detail here from the way the story was told to him.

137. I told it wrong. The story teller is correcting himself here.

145. Lituya Bay. On the outer coast, about half way between Cape Spencer and Yakutat. He presumably came to Lituya Bay on his way home, and continued over to the west shore of Glacier Bay, according to tradition coming down at Berg Bay, Chookan Héeni, "Grassy River," where the village site was, and from which the Chookaneidí clan derives its name. See also Swanton (1908: 413) but keep in mind that the Chookaneidí do not share Swanton's informant's evaluation of the status of their clan. Swanton identifies Kaakex'wtí as being Kadakw.ádi, a part of the Chookaneidí from Glacier Bay.

149-160. Nagootk'í. Little Walker. The place gets its name because the rock looked like a human walking with a pack. Note also the relationship of the story to the land.

152. The song. Kaakex'wtí composed the song that the story teller mentions here. The song commemorates Nagootk'í, the tall rock Kaakex'wtí thought was a man coming toward him. Note also the relationship of song, story, and place. See also Swanton (1909: 390, Song 2) and de Laguna (1972: 1158) for versions of the song. See also de Laguna (1972: 271) where the L'uknax.ádi connection is explained. At that time, the L'uknax.ádi and Lukaax.ádi (two closely related Raven moiety clans were together in the Interior. Kaakex'wtí married a L'uknax.ádi woman named Kunuk' (or K'naak) and the song he composed was given to her.

161. It was given that name then. Kaakex'wtí was the one who named the rock.

166. Wé tináa / those coppers. It is unclear from the story whether Kaakex'wtí brought coppers to the coast in the form in

which they are associated with the Northern
Tlingit today, or whether he brought other
copper implements, or copper ore. The Southern
Tuchone had the easiest access to copper, and
may have kept their technology a trade secret,
as was evidently the case among the coastal
Tlingit. The most common Southern Tuchone
copper work seems to have been knives,
arrowheads, and ornaments for personal wear.
At any rate, he is credited with bringing
copper and the technology for working it to the
coast, where its most highly developed art form
is the "Copper" or tináa, a shield-like design
about two or three feet high, and separated in
the shape of a T by hammered ridges into three
sections, one at the top third, and the bottom
two-thirds divided vertically in half. One of
the few coppers remaining in clan ownership is
the "Daanawaak Tináa" of the Lukaax.ádi Raven
House in Haines, in the custodianship of Austin
Hammond. Mr. Johnny Frazer, a Southern Tuchone
elder from Champaign, Yukon, bore the Tlingit
name Tináa S'aatí (Copper Owner) and spoke
Tlingit fluently. See also McClellan (1975:
255-256) for more on copper among the Southern
Tuchone. The cover art for this book includes a
tináa.

174. T'aayx'aa / Dixon Harbor. One of the
large bays on the outer coast between Cape
Spencer and Lituya Bay.

184. Tl'anaxéedakw. There is a Tlingit
tradition that if you see Tl'anaxéedakw, you
will become rich. She is a woman who carries
an infant on her back. You can usually hear
her voice before you see her. The Kaagwaantaan
shaman accepts the appearance of Kaakex'wtí
as a good sign, thinking it is the spirit of
Tl'anaxéedakw. See Swanton (1909: No. 35, pp
173-175, and notes) for a version of the story.

186. Auke Bay. The story of Tl'anaxéedakw
is associated with the Auke People, originally
from Auke Bay, north of Juneau, and now of the
Juneau area.

195-196. "Hard case" Chookaneidí. The
story teller uses the English word in Tlingit--
Chookaneidí háatkées. Here and elsewhere it
is important to remember that the story teller
is also Chookaneidí, and is talking about his
own people--sometimes jokingly, sometimes
seriously.

197-201. The Chookaneidí man calls
Kaakex'wtí and his sons Kooshdaa káa--land
otter people, who appear in human form to lure
people away, after which they also become land
otter people. There is a "double insult,"
because he calls them "little land otter
people." He tells the strangers to keep
on going down the bay, and that the people who
are calling them live down the bay. "People
who cut tongues" refers to shaman practice. A
person who wanted spirit power would cut the
tongue of an animal and fast for the spirits
to come. In short--the Chookaneidí do not
recognize their clansman, fear him as an evil
spirit, and try to trick him into going away.
He keeps on going down the bay, where he is
received by the Kaagwaantaan clan, whose
shaman perceives him as a good spirit.

204,205. A proverb about "sending
Athabaskans down the opposite bay" is used for
someone who passes up a golden opportunity.

215. The people are the Kaagwaantaan.

The Woman Who Married the Bear
told by Tom Peters, 80

Recorded by Nora Dauenhauer, Teslin,
September 8, 1972 and August 29, 1973.
Transcribed and translated by Nora Dauenhauer.

Publication History. The Tlingit text was
first transcribed 1972-73 as a project of the
Alaska Native Language Center, and published
May 1973, by Tlingit Readers, Inc. The text
was first translated in 1980 as a project of an
NEH translation grant to Nora Dauenhauer. Text
and translation were revised extensively as
projects of SHF.

Other versions: Veniaminov (1840, 1984: 413-
415) Krause (1885, 1956: 185-186, from
Veniaminov) Barbeau (1964: 211ff, Tlingit, and
193, Tsimshian) de Laguna (1972: 880-883)
McClellan (1970) Sidney et al. (1977: 62-66).
See Emmons (1907: 329-330) for reference to a
similar motif. See also the version by Frank
Dick included in this volume. The story is
also known as "Bear Husband," and "The Girl
Who Married the Bear."

"The Woman Who Married the Bear" is one of
the most popular stories of the Inland
Tlingit. The story is told mainly to remind
people of how sensitive animals are, and, like
people, are not to be insulted. The woman
insults the bear, and later in the story the
brothers make fun of their sister because she
is different.

Most Coast Tlingit story tellers tell this
as an Athabaskan story, or otherwise identify
it with the Interior. Although it is
associated with the Interior Indians, it is
widely known and told on the coast. There is
a similar story that originates from the Coast
about a man who married a bear. See the story
of Kaats' told by J. B. Fawcett. The two
stories are often confused.

The most detailed study of this story is

"The Girl Who Married The Bear," by Catharine McClellan (McClellan 1970) in which she compares eleven versions of the story, of which version 2 is by Tom Peters. The monograph covers in detail all eleven versions she collected in Yukon, the lives of the tradition bearers, and the meaning of the story to Tlingit, Athabaskan, and Tagish Indians of the Yukon. It also comments on other versions from Eyak, Athabaskan, Coast Tlingit, Haida and Tsimshian oral literatures. Her focus throughout is on the dramatic tension of the story and the cultural context.

She writes, "what probably grips the story teller and the audience most strongly is the dreadful choice of loyalties that the characters have to make, as well as the pervasive underscoring of the delicate and awful balance between animals and humans, which has existed since the world began."

The loyalties are between blood and marriage. Should the woman side with her family or her husband? Should the bear kill his brothers-in-law or allow himself to be killed? The brother-in-law relationship is very important in Tlingit culture. It is a social link between opposite moieties, and in many places the social and economic unit is based on a man and his brothers-in-law. Does the woman's brother side with his sister or his older brothers? Do the nephews kill their maternal uncles?

The story is incredibly rich, with complex and subtle interplay of social and cultural conflict, culminating in the killing of in-laws, siblings, and kinspeople. This is tragedy of the first order, and, as McClellan observes, the girl's "loyalty to the lineage that should have been cherished has been in vain."

This story in particular is of interest for a number of reasons. As a work of oral literary art, each single version is valuable

and to be appreciated on its own merits. The
range of versions collected and published
offers opportunity for comparative study, and,
following the direction of Levi-Strauss, one
could study all versions to reconstruct the
"total myth." Also, any given version could be
approached, following the experiment of Elli
Kongas-Maranda (1973), by a combination of
critical theories.

The story is also about the relationship of
humans and animals, what Dr. McClellan calls
"the uneasy balance of harmony between animals
and humans." The action begins with the girl's
violation of taboo--insulting bears. The story
ends with directions for ritual observances for
corpses of bears. In traditional societies,
animals are considered to give themselves to
humans. To insure this relationship it is
important to remain on good spiritual terms
with animals. Humans receive, but must also
return, by proper handling of animal remains
and by maintaining a proper attitude of respect
for the physical environment and all things in
it.

This version by Tom Peters may be understood
as being in two parts. In Part One, the girl
insults the bear, is met by the bear and taken
off. She lives with him as a wife, has children,
and is rescued by her brothers who kill her bear
husband. This version, collected in Teslin,
Yukon September 8, 1972 and published May 1973,
ends here. Part Two was told by Tom Peters the
following summer, on August 29, 1973, after the
booklet version of his telling of Part One was
read back to him in Tlingit. It describes the
girl's re-entry into human society. This
continuation is also extremely powerful, and
deals with sibling relationships. On a mythic
level, it explores the themes of journey and re-
entry into society, and a society's ability to
handle differences. In short, "you can't go
home again." It is certainly one of the most
powerful and compelling stories in the book.

This story is told in the Yukon dialect of Tlingit. The most obvious difference from the coast speech is that Interior Tlingit often has m where coast has w.

        amsikóo = awsikóo
         máa sá = wáa sá

The m shows up especially in the perfective, which is marked by wu or w on the coast.

        yan kamdliyás′
        kei mshix̱′íl′
        tle mdudzikóo
            kamjix̱ín
            amsikóo
            amli.át
            amsinéi
            kamdligás′

Interestingly enough, the m never seems to appear in place of the w allomorph of the classifier -ya-. For example:

        akaawa.aak̲w
        daak̲ aawayísh
        x̲′amduwataan

The last form has both the -m- as a perfective aspect prefix and the -wa- as a variant (allomorph) of the -ya- classifier following the vowel u.

    The interior Tlingit pronunciation also has nasal vowels in some places. This also gives the effect of m. For example, the word haaw (log) sounds very much like haam, but is phonetically a long "nasal a" followed by "w."

    Another feature of Interior Tlingit is the use of yéi where the coast has yáa.

        yéi yageeyi = yáa yageeyi
        yéi yeedadi = yáa yeedadi

Also, the verb yéi yatee seems to be used where the coast has "-x̱ sitee."

2-7. These lines describe subsistence activity.

8-10. Berries. When a person goes for anything, the practice is that he or she doesn't go for that thing alone, but also has an alternative activity as a "contingency plan." Here the girls discover the berries and get them as well. Subsistence is carried out in this way. The overlap of the moose hunting and the berrying indicate that the setting of the story is fall. In the version by Frank Dick, in which they are gathering Indian Celery, the implied setting is spring, when the stalks of the plant are fresh and tender, before they turn woody.

24. Defecated. In Tlingit, gándei woodoogi yé, the place where he went outside. This is a euphemism similar to "going to the bathroom," and derives from the use of outhouses or simply going to the woods or beach for such activities.

27. What was it she said then. In Tlingit, aag̱áa áwé. This is an important transition in Tlingit, and difficult to translate. It means "that's when" or "Then it was" or "At that point," or "Then." This is also a pivotal point in the story--the moment of insult and the appearance of the bear.

Different story tellers handle this key passage in a variety of ways. It is the most important single passage in the story, because the girl's insult initiates the entire sequence of action that follows. Tom Peters leaves it for the listener or the reader to imagine the insult. Perhaps he is also being polite with a woman collector whom he has just met.

Other story tellers are more explicit, and delight in quoting the girl's insult. One story teller quotes her as saying, "They always shit right where people are going to step--those big ass holes." Frank Dick's

version also has some colorful language. One
Southern Tuchone version refers to "farting
bears."

According to Tlingit oral tradition, animals
of any kind can hear, and brown bear in
particular also are called by the euphemism or
circumlocution "Big Ears." This is why people
respect them. See the film on the Chilkoot
Tlingit *Haa Shagoon* (Kawagey 1981) for more
on this. Regardless of the precise words used,
the important message is that the girl
violates taboo by insulting the bear. This
point is totally missed by editors who "clean
up" such stories for young readers. To delete
this scene is to delete the main point of the
story. By whatever word or euphemism, the girl
steps in excrement and says something.
Although an unpleasant experience, there
is nothing wrong with stepping in excrement by
mistake. But serious wrongs may be committed
by lack of self control and failure to control
our thoughts and speech.

31. The man. The man is a brown bear who
looks like a man to the young woman. He has
transformed himself into a nice looking man.

33. Tlingit. Yéi yatee. Interior and
Coast usage differ on this verb; coastal
Tlingit speakers would tend to omit the verb
here.

39. Parents. In Tlingit (39-40) ax éesh
hás. Literally "my father plus plural
marker." It can mean "my fathers," including
all male paternal relatives, or it can mean "my
father and them," a conversational construction
common both in Tlingit and in Alaska Native
English, in which the rest of the group is not
defined but understood. Frank Dick, Sr. uses a
similar construction in ax tláa hás.

45. Tlingit. Stolen stress on yéi yateeyi
yéidei. The word yé is lengthened when it
combines with -dei.

49-51; 53-54. In both Tlingit and English
there is a nice repetition here, with the

second set of lines paralleling the first
set. "Hadn't gone" and "hadn't been going" are
translations of Tlingit wu.aadí and u.aatjí.
Both are participial forms, the first of which
is perfective and the second occasional,
contrasting one time action and action longer
in duration.

64–65. Don't look up at dawn. The bear-
husband doesn't want the girl to see them in
their natural state.

69. Why was he saying that. She is
beginning to get suspicious of why her husband
is telling her not to look.

103. Was...should be. In Tlingit nateech
yéi yatee. In Tlingit as in English there are
two forms of the verb "to be," one for a
shorter, specific instant, and one for a longer
duration of time. The Tlingit forms are
imperfective and occasional.

109. Then she knew. This is the "give
away." She knew from his instructions to pick
fallen spruce branches for their bed instead of
branches broken from a tree (the way human
beings would do.) Also, from the bear's point
of view, as we shall soon see, the freshly
broken branches would leave a clue for the
searchers. Tlingit makes a distinction between
tláxwch', fallen spruce branches without
needles, and haaw, spruce branches with
needles, whether fallen naturally or broken off.

114. She broke them from above. The girl's
motives are unclear here. Either she
consciously decided to let her family know
where she was by breaking branches from a tree
instead of picking up windfall from the ground,
or she just naturally took branches the way she
was accustomed to doing.

129–130. Footprints...that she had walked
with him. This is a dramatic clue, and is
also important in the story of Kaats'.

150. He knew. The bear knew that his
brothers-in-law were watching them.

151. Spring returned. Tlingit kundaháa.

Literally, it came back; more figuratively,
the season changed; more idiomatically, spring
returned.

154. Medicine leaves. In Tlingit (line
152) kayaanée. Certain leaves are used as
medicine for hunting.

159-171. This is partly dialog with the
collector on the nature of "medicine." The
passage is about using leaves to make medicine
to acquire certain things or power. In more
modern times, medicine was made to acquire
money. In the story, the brothers are making
medicine to acquire the spirit power to locate
their sister. Tom Peters talks about the
leaves being potentially dangerous to someone
who works with them. Strict rules of fasting
and self discipline are required. He says that
if you don't handle the leaves strictly
according to the rules you might go crazy. He
comments that he doesn't like to bother with
this kind of medicine.

174ff. Eight days. The passage refers to
the ritual of fasting and discipline that goes
along with making medicine.

186-188. Dogs. Dogs were trained with
certain medicine to be good at tracking.

187, 188. The Tlingit verbs are interesting
here. Both are decessive forms with the
"distributive" prefix. Here the actual verb
for "making magic" or "making medicine"
(héixwaa) is used, whereas in lines 172 and 173
the actual verb in Tlingit is more like "doing
the leaves" or "working on the leaves."

daxkustéeyin   ku-da-ga-   -s-tée-   yin
daxduhéixwayin   da-ga-du- -héixwa-yin

192-193. Just once. The brothers didn't
give up after just one try, but kept on
searching for their sister.

235. He already knew. Tlingit ch'u súgaa
dágáa yóo oowajée.

239. Roll...secretly. "Secretly" is

implied but not explicit in the Tlingit text.

240. After line 240 there is a question and answer set on the tape that is not included in the transcription. Tlingit pronouns do not specify gender. To clarify gender, the collector asked, "Wé du x̲úx̲ atx̲aayí ák.wé?--Was this her husband's food?" and the story teller replies "Aaa"--yes.

244. Animal of the forest. The implication is that wild animals can see and hear everything.

250-271. He couldn't find the den because of his thoughts. This scene in the story stresses the importance of right thinking as well as right speech and right action in relationship to the natural and spirit worlds. Human thoughts can be detected by bears, to whom they appear as beams of light.

254. Beam of light. In Tlingit, s'eenáa, meaning neither daylight, on the one hand, or fire or sunlight on the other, but any other beam, shaft, ray, or flash of light from an artificial source.

308. Ah hah! This is difficult to translate into English with the same meaning, function, and level of style. Other possibilities might be "Oh, no!" or "See?"

312. On the tape, an "aside" follows, that is not transcribed. Tom Peters asks the collector "Yisikóo gé daa sáwé tsaag̲ál?"--Do you know what a tsaag̲ál (bear hunting spear) is?

323, 347. "The bear" is added in translation.

330-341. The passage describes some of the technology of bear hunting. Typically the entrance to a bear den would face downhill, perhaps covered by an overhang or ledge. The best strategy for the hunter, giving him advantage over the bear, would be to approach from the uphill side. To lure the bear out, he tosses something into the den.

339. See. Tlingit ax̲satínch, an occasional form. The underlying form is a-g̲a-sa-tín-ch.

This is a nice image. The hunter only sees the powerful sweep of the paw, knocking his

mitten behind the bear, back inside, deeper
into the dark of the den. It seems to be part
of Tom Peters' style to focus on a few select
visual images as suggestive or representative
of the entire action or story--the dramatization
of a single vivid detail.

348. Tlingit. The form on the tape,
akaawadóok, is not used on the Coast. We assume
it corresponds to the Coast akaawlidóotl, to
trick, lure, entice, or tempt. As the hunter
is trying to lure the bear out, the bear is
trying to lure the hunter in.

357. That's why it's still done now. This
is a "classic" statement of the relationship
between the covenants established in the
stories of "ancestors" and correct human action
in the present. The oral literature explains
the "cosmic significance" of activities in
daily human life. In addition, the "story" is
connected to song, art, and genealogy--or, to
rephrase it, the "story" is told or recalled
or remembered in oral narrative, song, art,
and kinship.

373-374. Mouth get tired. Tom Peters'
voice on the tape imitates a faint and distant
calling. This recognition scene is also
similar to J. B. Fawcett's dramatic scene in
his telling of Kaats', where the long absent
human also announces his unseen presence in
the den through speaking to the dog.

386ff. The song. Because of language
complications in translation of the Tlingit
song texts, it was decided to include the song
in a note rather than in the narrative. Tom
Peters sings two songs with different
melodies, though with Nora Dauenhauer in 1972
as with Catharine McClellan in 1952, he refers
to the second song as the second "part."

The translation is problematic. The meaning
of the words as sung is not entirely clear. It
is ironic that McClellan in 1952 did not get a
Tlingit text, but did get a translation by Tom
Peters of the song he sang in Tlingit, and Nora

Dauenhauer twenty years later in 1972 got a
Tlingit text which poses problems in translation.
Now, in 1987, fifteen years after the Tlingit
collection and 35 years after the English
collection, we can put the verses together and
hope that they will eventually make sense.

Tom Peters, Song 1. August 1972.

> A xoox xagoot
> du shoodeek' ya yei s dixwaa
> yanyeidi yaat
> i, yaa, aa ee yaa ya
> ee yei nei hi yei
> ya hei ei, ei.

English translation, Summer 1952 (McClellan
1970: 27).

> I went through every one
>   of those young people
> and the last brother,
> I know he did the right thing.

Tom Peters, Song 2. August 1972.

> Xoox'ei yaanei
> ashookanax goodei ei
> ee i yaanei
> ee lingit'aani yeix
> aanjoon ee yaa ei.

English translation, Summer 1952

> I dreamed about it
> that they were going after him (? me?).

Tom Peters comments to McClellan that the
songs are sung when killing bears, so that the
bear feels good.
    391. Part Two. There is a break of about
one year between the end of Part One and the
beginning of Part Two. Tom Peters' telling of

Part Two was stimulated by Nora Dauenhauer's reading back to him, one year later, the published transcription of Part One. He could hardly believe that someone came back to him and read his own story back to him, in his own words, his own language, his own style. He was excited and enthusiastic, and commented something like "I haven't heard a story like that in a long time!" This comment gives us pause to reflect on how it must feel to BE the older story teller. Who is still alive to tell YOU stories? Excitedly, he said, "Let me tell you the rest of it!"

416-417. Pull on the skin. The image is a literal way of expressing shape shifting and metamorphosis. The woman moves between her human and bear natures, making the change by putting the skin on and off like a cape.

432-434. Mother..we want to play. The young woman must have been difficult for her brothers to take. All of them were master hunters who had made medicine to be great hunters. But she seemed to do just as well with her husband's skin on her back.

445. Her mind and body change when she transforms herself by putting on the bear skin.

508. He killed her. This is interesting when compared with the version by Tom Peters in the McClellan monograph. Here he actually kills her; in McClellan he doesn't kill her, but just hits her, and she goes off into the mountains with the children.

The Woman Who Married the Bear
told by Frank Dick, Sr., 85

Recorded in Juneau, April 3, 1984 by Fred
White. Transcribed and translated by Fred
White. Edited by N. and R. Dauenhauer.

Other versions: See the version by Tom
Peters in this book, and the notes to that
text.

The delivery of the performance is well
paced. The story teller had recently suffered
a minor stroke that affected some of the
muscles in his face, but he was generally in
good shape both mentally and physically at the
time the story was collected. The stroke
seems to have affected some of his pronunciation. For example, ch is often replaced with
t, and ch' by t'. Thus, in line 422 ach áwé is
phonetically at áwé on the tape, and hóoch' in
line 425 is phonetically hóot'. These have
been standardized. Likewise, there were many
false starts and stuttering throughout; these,
too, have been edited out by the transcriber.

This version by Frank Dick, Sr. is
strikingly different from the version by Tom
Peters, and from all the other published
versions of the story, especially at the end,
where he emphasizes the shunning of the girl,
the prohibition against eating brown bear
meat, and the introduction of black bear meat
as food.

Whether bear can be eaten seems in the final
analysis to be a family or even individual
matter, and there is wide variation on the
subject in Tlingit culture. There seems to be
a general preference for black bear meat over
brown bear meat, but no universal prohibition
against eating bear meat of any kind.

In McClellan's work (1975) one elder
comments that people don't eat brown bear
because grizzlies eat humans, and a Tagish
tradition bearer states that people don't eat

grizzly bear meat because grizzlies are half human.

Otherwise, bear meat may be avoided if a person is under some special personal bear meat taboo for physical, social, or spiritual reasons. But there is no universal Tlingit taboo against eating brown or black bear meat. One coast elder remarked that in time of need even wolves, eagles, and seagulls may be eaten.

1-18. Emphasis in the opening lines is on his retelling the story true to the oldest versions as first or originally told.

53-75. Frank Dick is especially colorful and vivid in the passage regarding the girl's language. Like Susie James in her version of the Glacier Bay History, Frank makes an editorial comment emphasizing the forthcoming disaster wrought by the careless words. This is an important passage in the story, because here the girl violates the Tlingit taboo against speaking badly of people and animals. It is important to note that many bowdlerized "retellings" of such passages in Native American literature omit what one such editor called "physiological functions." This is, of course, the main point of the story, and initiates all the tragedy and dramatic action.

62. Wé. Most of the demonstratives are phonetically long on the tape: wéi. The transcription standardizes short.

66-68. This is a proverb, used when something bad is going to happen.

70, 74. The Tlingit text has the verb for "tying" used in the occasional in line 70, and with the suffix -dáx̱, meaning "after" in 74.

adaa.us.áx̱wch
adaasa.áx̱wdáx̱

74, 75. The Tlingit verb is a sequential in line 74, in the conjunctive mode, and in the

subordinate clause. In line 75 the same stem
is perfective, in the indicative mode, the
main verb in the sentence, and in the main
clause.

74. g̲unéi góot   when she started to go
75. g̲unéi uwagút   she started to go

88ff. The sequence is a nice example of the
use of repetition in oral literature. Two
refrains are woven together, with slight
variation, in the Tlingit text--"she was all
right" and "he looked like a human to her."
"She was all right" can also mean "there was
nothing wrong" or "nothing special or unusual."
More literally, we have translated this as
"There wasn't anything different" and "she
didn't feel any different." Use of the refrain
builds up to the recognition scene soon to
follow. At the same time, Frank is emphasizing
that the girl is not being abused or mistreated
by the bear, and that the bear appears in human
form. This "shape shifting" is important in
this story and other stories of this kind.
89, 90. The word lingít (Tlingit) appears
three times in these two lines; we have
attempted to reflect its various meanings in
different English words.
113. The word "though" (k̲u.aa in Tlingit)
raises a problem in translation and
interpretation of the story. Translated as
"though," the word implies marriage as
punishment or teaching a lesson; if, on the
other hand, k̲u.aa is not translated, but
understood as introducing new information, it
would give a different meaning to the
passage. At any rate, there is an overall
pattern in Tlingit oral literature of the need
for a human being to share the life of the
animal spirits, to experience it, in order to
learn compassion and gain some level of
insight and wisdom.
122. They met up with the rest of the bear
people.

137-140. Wet wood, etc. The pattern in the
story is that things seem opposite in the land
of the bear. The Frank Dick version is
especially rich in detail regarding the
lifestyle of the bear people, and how it is
really the same as ours, but seems different
to us, and that we are not really capable of
seeing it at all. For example, they really do
smoke fish just like humans, but we perceive
them as eating fish raw from the streams.

As for the wet wood, not only in the land of
the Bear People, but in "reality" wet wood
does, in fact, burn better, once you get it
started. It lasts longer and gives nice coals.
Dry wood starts faster but also burns faster.

151, 156. In Tlingit, there are nice
examples of the verb "shake" in three different
forms within six lines:

151. kak̲kwakéek   (ka-u-ga-g̲a-ya-kéek) future
156. kawdukéegi   (ka-wu-du-kéek-i) participial
156. koodukíkch   (ka-u-du-kík-ch) occasional

178. The Tlingit verb stem -k'eet' implies
leaving, coming, or going as a group. It is
interesting to note the use of the prefix ku̲-,
usually referring to humans, in the expression.
This line also parallels and repeats line 144,
with slight variation.

180, 181. There is a nice phonetic contrast
on the tape in the words dux'áan and at x'áan.
Dux'áan is phonetically dux'wáan, with
automatic labialization of the x' following the
vowel u. At x'áan is as reflected in the
writing system, without the labialization.
Such automatic labialization is frequent in the
pronunciation of older and more conservative
speakers of Tlingit, and not as common among
younger speakers. At any rate, the automatic
labialization is predictable, not phonemic, and
therefore not reflected in the orthography. The
x̲' sounds following the word du in lines 421-

423 are also pronounced with the automatic
labialization. The verb stem means to dry
fish. The fish are hung either outdoors or in
a smokehouse, and smoke is applied as the fish
dry.

193, 198. The Tlingit verb in 193 has the
distributive prefix--many people were packing
up; 198 is without. Both are perfective.

$$da\underline{x}wuduwaxoon \quad (da\underline{g}a-wu-du-ya-xoon)$$
$$wuduwaxoon \quad (\quad wu-du-ya-xoon)$$

210. There is a contrast in Tlingit between
the word in this line, $\underline{x}'$éi$\underline{g}$aa (literally,
"for her mouth") and the word x'éi$\underline{g}$aa, meaning
"indeed" or "in truth" or "verily."

226, 228. Compare the two forms of the
verb. Both are perfective, but one is a main
verb and the other a dependent:

226. wujixíx   it ran   (indicative;
                               main clause)
228. wushxeexí   when it ran (participial;
                               subordinate clause)

231. Ch\underline{x}ánk' is a diminutive form of
dach\underline{x}án used in direct address. The fox is
addressing the brown bear as his grand-
child. The red fox is found on the mainland
and on some islands in Southeast Alaska, but
not on all of the islands. The fox is not a
culturally significant animal on the Coast--for
example, as a totemic figure.

The fox is not a common or widespread
character in Tlingit oral literature.
Certainly the wise or clever fox and the stupid
bear are not stock characters in Tlingit
folklore. The fox is listed among the animals
created in the Raven cycle, and de Laguna (1972)
has two short stories about Fox and Wolverine
and Fox and Crab from Yakutat. Fox as a
literary character seems more developed in
Tagish oral literature as described in

McClellan (1975). Other Coast elders whom we
have asked also recall incidents where fox and
weasel refer to others by kinship terms.
    249-254. This passage has four interesting
forms of the verb for calling or naming within
six lines:

249.	yéi duwasáagu	du-ya-sáa-kw-u	attributive
250.	yéi dusáagun	du- sáa-kw-un	decessive
252.	yóo duwasáakw	du-ya-sáa-kw	imperfective; habitual
254.	yéi wduwasáa	w-du-ya-sáa	perfective

    251, 252. Carry a dog. Two different forms
of the stem -nook are used:

251.	wu-du-dzi-nook	perfective
252.	ga-du-s -núk -ch	occasional

Literally, the stem -nook means "to carry like
a baby." The expression "to carry a dog" means
figuratively "to go hunting accompanied by a
dog" and is a euphemism for hunting, speaking
indirectly about the act.
    253. Dogs. The nouns are not always marked
for plural in the Tlingit text, but the sense
is plural, and in line 260 a plural possessive
pronoun is used, indicating more than one dog.
    253, 255. There are two interesting forms
of the stem -.aat:

253.	aawa.aat	they went
255.	woo.aat	they left

This may also be a euphemism or indirect
reference to hunting. See the notes to Kaats'
for more on this.
    257-267. This passage is a Tlingit example
of "Homeric simile."
    258. On the tape, yux is phonetically wux.

See also note to line 302.

259. Eyesight. In this story, the eyesight
of people and dogs shines into the den,
whereas in the Tom Peters version, it is the
thoughts that shine in.

272. This is a nice example of an occasional
form. The classifier and nominal prefixes
specify sharp objects like stakes or spears.

yakoolg̲eechch   ya-ka-u-l-g̲eech-ch

278. To the bear. The Tlingit text uses
the word yatseeneit. See the notes to Kaats'
for more detail on this euphemism.

288. Tlingit. The possessive suffix, which
we would normally expect, is not required in
this construction, which functions parallel to
the form x̲'awoolt two lines above.

302. In Tlingit, on the tape, du yádi is
phonetically du wádi. For many older speakers,
y and w are variants under certain conditions,
and are the modern sounds for an older Tlingit
"gamma"--a sonorant, an unrounded "w." Most
younger speakers have y everywhere, but some
conservative speakers retain w in the
environment of u, and y elsewhere.

ax̲ yéet   my child
du wéet   his/her child

Y and w routinely alternate in the Tlingit
classifier and possessive suffix systems.

307. This is an idiom in Tlingit. He
wasn't going to see things clearly, or look
where he was going; rather, just plunge in
carelessly, because he has already decided to
let himself be killed.

328. Tlingit. As.áa is an interesting use
of the classifier to make a verb causative or
transitive, as in the English contrast of sit
and set.

áa   he/she/it sits
as.áa   he/she sets him/her/it
            down; causes it to sit

333. Glove. This motif is usually used in
the story of Kaats', where the hunter is
tossed into the den by the male bear and the
woman bear hides him, telling her husband he
only threw the hunter's glove in.

355. Tlingit. Satéen is a "classic"
classificatory verb.

358. Tlingit. Tlél ix̱éix̱ik̲. Don't ever
eat that. Optative. The underlying stem -x̱aa,
to eat, appears here with the progressive stem,
the -x- suffix for habitual action, and the
optative suffix -ik̲. See the opening comments
to this set of notes for more on eating bear
meat.

364. My clothes. The motif of the girl
requesting her clothes is important in
comparative study of the story. Within the
story, it is important first step toward her re-
integration into the life of the family and
village.

374. Note, in Tlingit, the contrast:

yiyják̲   (wu-yi-ják̲)   you-all killed it
                          (perfective)
yiják̲   (yi-ják̲)   kill it
                          (imperative)

381. Tlingit. Du tláa hás. Literally "his
mother-plural." More loosely, his mothers, or
his mother and them; parents. See also the
note to line 39 of Tom Peters.

388. In this version, she leaves her bear
children; in other versions she takes them with
her to her village.

410. From here to the end, the version by
Frank Dick contains several motifs, sequences
and events unique to this version. Frank
Dick's focus is on the shunning of the girl and
the trouble caused by the prohibition against

eating the brown bear meat. The transformations
of smoke and the grouse to black bear are
unique here. One of the Interior versions in
McClellan (1970) has the smoke and tree, but no
black bear. It is unclear whether the black
bear already existed, and the girl is helping
people find it, or whether the story explains
the creation of black bear as an acceptable
food supply, in contrast to the brown bear
which is now a brother-in-law to the people.

414ff. There seems to be rivalry between
the girl and her older brother who is the
established leader.

Kaats' told by J. B. Fawcett, 83

Recorded by Nora Dauenhauer, Juneau, October
3, 1972. Transcribed and translated by Nora
Dauenhauer.

The text was first transcribed November 10,
1972 as a project of the Alaska Native Language
Center; first translated November 22, 1980 as
project of National Endowment for the Humanities
Translation Grant to Nora Dauenhauer; transcription and translation extensively revised as a
project of Sealaska Heritage Foundation.

This story is also known as "The Man Who
Married the Bear," and is sometimes confused
with the "Woman Who Married the Bear." Motifs
are sometimes interchanged by some tradition
bearers.

Other versions: Swanton (1909: Nos. 19 and
69; p 49ff, pp 228-229) Barbeau (1964: 215ff)
Keithahn (1963: 156) de Laguna (1972: 879-880)
Garfield and Forrest (1961: 29-37). The story
also has analogues in Sugpiaq (Chugach Eskimo)
and Central Yupik oral literature. See Nora
Dauenhauer et. al. (1986: 39-41).

The story teller's oral delivery is rapid,
with few pauses, and with very few false
starts (as compared to his performance of
Naatsilanéi, for example.) Parts of the story
were spoken in a whisper, and some lines are
totally inaudible on the tape, so that a few
lines have been "restored" by guesswork, and a
few lines have been lost. These lines are
indicated in the notes.

The rapid delivery presents technical
problems in punctuation in addition to those
discussed in general in the introduction. The
Tlingit and English punctuation differ in many
places in the text, especially where the Tlingit
has no punctuation at line turnings, and the
English has a comma. We have retained use of

the period in Tlingit to mark a sentence end
indicated by the end of a grammatical phrase or
unit, accompanied by falling pitch drop.

In many places, the narrator pauses long
enough for the pause to be indicated by a line
turning, but with no falling in pitch, although
it is the end of a grammatical unit. Where
this happens in mid-line, without a significant
pause, we have used the semi-colon to separate
the grammatical units. But where it happens at
line turnings, the Tlingit is either unmarked,
or marked sometimes with a comma. The English
is almost always marked with a comma.

By using a comma in English where we would
normally expect a period, we have attempted to
convey the sense of "pushing on," of a
continuing tone of voice. This may give the
English language reader the feeling of a
sequence of run-on sentences, but we hope with
this punctuation to convey the sense of rapid
delivery used in long sections of the text--a
sense which would be lost through the use of
periods. These sections contrast with the
sequences of lines that do end with longer
pauses and falling pitch drop, as indicated by
periods.

In addition to the special use of the comma
described above, the comma is also used as
normal in English to indicate appositions and
other phrases.

This story presents few problems to
understanding the basic plot outline. It is
an exciting story, well composed and delivered.
Most of the cultural notes supply additional
background on the relationship to bears in
Tlingit culture.

Because so few notes are required for basic
understanding of the story, we have devoted far
more notes for this story to grammatical forms
of interest to beginning and intermediate
students of the Tlingit language. Hopefully
learners of all ages and cultures will find in
these texts wonderful models of traditional

Tlingit literary language, and can use these
texts in conjunction with grammars and
dictionaries to savor the richness and
complexity of the language. Readers not
interested in Tlingit language study can skip
over these linguistic notes.

   Considering all aspects of content and
style, this is one of the finest stories in
the collection. One is inclined to agree with
the excitement and enthusiasm of the story
teller in his opening line. This is a
magnificent story.

   4.   Tlingit, al'óon. Many different words
are used in this text referring to hunting,
and types of hunting. These are:

      4.   al'óon
      5.   at gutóot aa wu.aadéen
      7.   at eenéen   (and line 8: at een)
      23. at natí

These are significant in Tlingit culture and
in the story, and should be noted.

   Al'óon conveys a sense of hunting with
weapons; it can also mean a technique of
stalking, sneaking up on, or spying on animals.

   The phrase at gutóot and some form of the
stem -.aat means to be walking in the woods.
This is the most indirect way of talking about
hunting, and is connected with the traditional
taboo of making direct statements about one's
intentions regarding animals. To make a direct
statement, especially about the future, is
considered bragging, or pushing your luck.
Tlingit tradition also holds that animals have
spirits that can hear you, and to talk about
them so bluntly might be considered arrogant
and drive them away. Thus one talks about
going for a walk in the woods or for a boat
ride, rather than about hunting or fishing.

   The stem -.een means to harvest or gather.

   The phrase at natí is very metaphorical,

indirect, and vague; it means "to do something."

This story is about the delicate relationship between bears and humans, and the vocabulary dealing with bears and hunting reflects the delicacy.

20. On the sea. Reference here and in the next line (reversed order in Tlingit and English) refer to subsistance hunting on land and sea.

22. Tlingit. This is a good example of the use of the conjunction ku.aa to change the subject and introduce new information.

25. Tlingit. koowóodáx. From the den. The second suffix, -dáx seems to cause elongation of the first suffix -ú-, normally written short, as in line 53, at koowú its den. This seems to be a phonetic and not a phonemic distinction, and will probably be standardized short in the popular orthography.

26, 27. The Tlingit text is again ambiguous and indirect, and uses the word át, meaning "thing." This is a euphemism for bear. The Tlingit word for brown bear, xóots, first appears in line 38. Later, in line 129 and elsewhere, another common euphemism or circumlocution is used--yatseeneit, meaning "living one," or "living creature." Bears are generally spoken of with considerable circumlocution in Tlingit, and when encountered directly in the forest, are most often addressed by kinship terms, depending on one's genealogical connection to the bear, which is generally either paternal uncle or aunt, or maternal uncle or aunt. In line 193, he refers to them as "noble children"--aan yátx'i.

28. Dogs. Reference is to hunting with trained dogs.

36, 37. Tlingit. Phonetically, on the tape, the pronunciations are ch'u weisú and áyú watee. Phonemically, y and w are allophones of each other, and reflexes of a "gamma" or voiced velar fricative retained in the speech of some older speakers, especially from Yakutat. Most younger speakers now use y

in all places, but older speakers such as J.
B. Fawcett regularly have w following u or oo,
and y in other places. This is normalized in
the popular phomemic spelling as y. See the
note to line 302 of Frank Dick's story for more
on this, and line 29 of J. B.'s Naatsilanéi,
where he retains the "gamma."

40. Ketchikan. The southern origin of the
story is also another suggestion as to its
antiquity.

43. Yes Bay. Located north of Ketchikan.

60. Private parts. The Tlingit text is
also a euphemism.

65. Kaats'. The name is also used in the
Tlingit text.

66. Confused. In Tlingit, x'óol' yáx̱, like
a whirlpool.

67, 68. Nice example of a "terrace" in the
oral style, where the narrator builds his
second phrase on the wording of the first.

69, 70. Along with the base form that
appears in line 24 and elsewhere in the story,
here are some nice examples for beginning
students of the range of forms for "dog."

24.	keitl	dog
70.	du keidlí	his dog
69.	du keitlx'í	his dogs.

The plural morpheme is -x'- (but is not
always required in suggesting plural); the
possessive suffix is -i; and the final
aspirated -tl becomes unaspirated -dl- when
between two vowels.

73. Tayee. This is a locative construction.

73. The context and meaning of the proverb
are not clear to the editors at this time.

74. Tlingit. The line contains a good
example of two forms of the same word:
yei.ádi, with the single, short suffix, and
yei.ádeex̱, with the sequence of two suffixes,
the possessive and the predicate nominative.

76. Tlingit. The stem -tsaaḵ is not

attested in any of the published literature on
Tlingit with this prefix. Most of the
meanings of the stem are with verbs of pushing,
poking, or connecting. See the Naish-Story
Tlingit Verb Dictionary for a some 16 other
meanings of the stem in combination with
various classifiers and nominal prefixes. The
dictionary form of this use of the verb is:

    lu-ya-tsaak̲ (int) to lie with the nose down.

The nominal prefix lu- refers to nose. The
image is of an animal lying face down, but on
its haunches, with its nose lower than its
rump. The verb may also be used of a baby
lying face down, but is generally not used of
a person lying face down with legs fully
extended.

    89. She put her paws... She is deceiving
her husband. A comparable proverbial phrase
in English might be "she pulled the wool over
his eyes."

    90. She felt something for him. In
Tlingit, the nominal prefix tu- , meaning
mind, implies that the feeling is spiritual and
emotional, and not purely physical. The
underlying form is tu-wu-di-tee. Wu is the
perfective aspect prefix, and -di- is the
classifier. The stem has many meanings in
Tlingit, mostly dealing with states of being.

    91. Tlingit. Jiwusk̲óox'ú. This is another
verb hitherto unattested in Tlingit linguistic
literature. The underlying text form is:

    ji-wu-si-k̲óox'-u

and is a participial perfective, the -u
suffix marking the verb in the subordinate
clause, and the -wu- marking the perfective
aspect. The classifier is -si-. The
dictionary form would be:

    ji-si-k̲oox'   (tr)

The verb has a range of meanings. The stem
with the -s-classifier refers to a long object
falling. With the nominal prefix ji- it means
to touch in passing with the hand, or the hand
falling on something in passing. In this case,
Kaats' touches the woman's genitals by accident
as he falls into the den.

96. Tlingit. Naxwudzigeedi. This is a
subjunctive form, the underlying form of which
is oo-na-ga-dzi-geet-i.

100. Nothing will happen. The female bear,
seeming like a human to him, instructs Kaats',
who has little choice but to trust and believe
in her. From here on there is no clue as to
what happened to the male bear, who disappears
from the story. One possibility is that
Kaats' and the female bear both killed the
male bear.

110. He had an accident. His relatives had
no idea where he was, and could only assume
that he had a hunting accident. Kaats' was
presumed dead.

119. Older brother. This is the older of
the remaining brothers, in contrast to the
reference in line 121 to Kaats' as the older
brother.

120, 121. The phrase is difficult to
translate, but is a nagging, taunting, or "put
down," implying "why not him?" or "what's
wrong with him?" People were using ridicule
and social pressure to urge the younger
brother into searching.

121. Tlingit. Yanduskéich. This form is
occasional, marked by the conjugation prefix
(in this verb -na-), and the suffix -ch. The
underlying form is:

       yéi   ya-na-du-s-kaa-ch

The dictionary form is

       ya-si-kaa (tr) to tell.

Various forms of this verb, usually in the
perfective, with different prefixes and
classifiers, are very common in narratives.
   122. Tlingit. K̲uk̲gwashée. This is a
future form. Futures in Tlingit are generally
complicated by contractions not immediately
obvious to beginning students. The underlying
form is k̲u-oo-ga-g̲a-shée.
   The order of prefixes is: human being,
irrealis, conjugation prefix, aspect prefix,
zero form of the classifier. As the vowels
drop according to the Tlingit rules for open
syllables, the g falls next to the g̲ and
becomes a k, and the irrealis prefix appears
as labialization or rounding of the g̲.
   124. Tlingit. Wududziteen. The text
offers beginning students a variety of forms
of the verb "see," listed here in their text
forms, underlying forms, and translation.

124.	wududziteen	they were seen
183.	iyatéen	do you see?
215.	aa x̲wsiteen	I saw some
245.	ayaawatín	he recognized him
249.	ash yalatín	he stared at him

124.		wu-du-dzi-teen
183.		i-ya -téen
215.	aa	wu-x̲a-si -teen
245.		a-ya-wu- -ya -tín
249.	ash ya-	-la -tín

   132. Taken by something. The Tlingit verb
stem -neix̲ is difficult to translate in this
context. It means generally to help, save,
heal, or rescue. Here it also means something
like enticed or enchanted, but both of those
English words imply a spell of some kind, and
none is really cast here. "Taken" is used as
a neutral English verb.
   143. Sunbeams. In Tlingit "legs of the
sun" or "sun legs." At this point we might also

comment on three motifs shared between this
story and the story of the Woman Who Married
the Bear. In both stories, the younger
brother is the successful searcher, footprints
play a role in the tracking, and the dogs'
thoughts are like sunbeams or beams of light to
the bears in their dens. Most tradition
bearers have the motif of the mittens used to
trick the spouse only in the story of Kaats' or
the Man Who Married the Bear, and not in the
story of the Woman Who Married the Bear,
although in the latter story the mittens are
dropped into the den by hunters to entice or
aggravate the bear.

145. Tlingit. Koodagánch is an occasional
form. Because it is a "zero" conjugation
verb, it has the irrealis prefix instead of a
conjugation marker. The ka- prefix designates
the round shape of the sunbeam streaming into
the den. The underlying form is ka-oo-da-gán-ch.

148. Tlingit. Kdahánch is an occasional
form. The underlying form is ga-da-hán-ch.

165. The dog's name translates as "Dry Fish
Dagger."

162. There is a possible contradiction or
confusion here.

170. The voice is very faint here on the
tape.

174. The nouns are supplied in translation.

178. To search. As noted earlier, it
is common in Tlingit tradition not to mention
or directly state intentions of hunting or
killing something. Such intentions were stated
indirectly, but in a way that people knew what
the activities were all about. Tlingit
tradition holds that the bears can hear and
understand people. Therefore the younger
brother keeps his real intentions secret from
the bear. His real agenda is not just to
search, but to find.

180. The angry men. The brothers of Kaats'
are becoming angry and frustrated because they
were convinced they could find him. Some

tradition bearers say that they didn't fast
properly and abstain from sexual relations as
they should have, whereas the younger brother
did.

185. Tlingit. The Tlingit verb wak̲kooká is
very interesting. It contains the nominal
prefix wak̲, meaning eye, and a second nominal
prefix, -ka- , designating a round object. The
verb stem is -k̲aa, meaning to say or tell.
The whole thing put together means "she told
him to use or do something with a round
object, namely, the eye." Eyes are round
objects. In short, she told him "Use your
eyes." The underlying form is ash
wak̲-ka-wu-k̲á.

189. It wasn't slowing down. The bear kept
rising to break, grab, or otherwise deflect
the sunbeams in order to slow the dogs, but it
didn't work.

190. Still doing this. Reaching for the
thoughts like sunbeams.

190, 202. Tlingit. Loowagúk̲ is an
interesting verb. The dictionary form is

   lu-ya-gook̲ (st) run

and means "plural subjects run." The verb
used with a singular subject is ji-xeex. It
contains the nominal prefix -lu-, meaning
nose, and evokes a picture of a pack of things
running with their noses outstretched. It is
hard to find an English verb that includes the
concepts of running and smelling at the same
time.

193. Noble children. A euphemism for bear.

203. Tlingit. The dictionary form is
ya-di-xoon, to peer or peep; also to point, as
a dog pointing with the face or nose extended.

213-226. This passage describes the
traditional technology of bows and arrows.

228a. Slap. This is a sound effect. The
story teller claps his hands once for effect.
Thus, he actually completes his sentence not

with a spoken word, but with a sound effect
indicating and emphasizing the shot or the
suddenness of the arrival.

230. The kinship term is supplied in
translation.

231–239. This passage is an "aside" to the
collector.

241. The name Kaats' is supplied in
translation.

243. Tlingit. Ix'adaxwétlx is an
interesting verb. The stem is -xwetl, meaning
to tire or be tired. The durative suffix -x
implies tiring over a long period of time, and
the nominal prefix x'a means mouth. Literally,
the verb means "your mouth is tired."

247. This line is whispered.

252. There is an inaudible line following
on the tape, but the story seems to move well
enough without it.

254, 255. Tlingit. Phonetically, on the
tape, xát is pronounced xwát, with automatic
labialization of the x after the vowel u.

257. Tlingit. Hóoch. The underlying form
is the pronoun hu followed by the subject
marking suffix -ch. This word provides a nice
contrast to the word hóoch', meaning "no more"
or "all gone," as used in line 109.

       hóoch   he (subject)   hú - ch
       hóoch'   no more

258. Tlingit. Keeneegéek. This is an
optative form, as indicated by the optative
suffix -eek and the irrealis prefix. It is
second person singular. The underlying form
is ka-oo-ee-neek-éek.

260. Tlingit. Kgeegóot. This is a future
form, second person singular. The underlying
form is oo-ga-ga-ee-góot.

267, 268. The story teller's tone of voice
changes here, becoming high, musical, and
playful, emphasizing the happiness of the
dogs.

270. Yo-ho-ho. The hyphens represent
glottal stops here. The vowel o is also
interesting here because it is "extra-systemic"
in Tlingit, appearing only in the word "ho",
as here and as in the expression "gunalchéesh,
hó hó," where the hó hó means "very much."

277-283. The younger brother told his wife
he had found his older brother Kaats'. He
didn't want to tell because he found Kaats'
living with an animal.

282. Tlingit. Kgwagóot. Future, third
person singular. The underlying form is
oo-ga-ga-góot.

283. Tlingit. Kukgwaháa. Future, third
person singular. The underlying form is
ku-oo-ga-ga-háa.

284. Messenger. The messenger is a slave.

294. Tlingit. Gaxtookóox. Future, first
person plural. The underlying form is
oo-ga-ga-too-kóox.

296. Tlingit. Gugagut yé. Future, third
person singular, in an attributive
construction. Vowel length as well as tone
appear to be "stolen" by yé. The underlying
form is oo-ga-ga-góot.

297. Teikweidí. A clan of the Eagle
moiety. The story teller now clearly
identifies the people who own the story because
of what happened to their ancestor.

306. X'ax'áan is a Teikweidí man's name.
It means, literally, "Angry Mouth."
X'ax'áan hás is literally "the X'ax'áan's."
The construction is often expressed in everyday
Tlingit-English as "X'ax'áan and them." This
is the particular group of Teikweidí to whom
the events happened.

308. Their ancestor became a thing of
value. Wé shukaadei káa áx' átx wusiteeyi yé
áwé. This is probably the single most
important cultural concept assumed in all of
the stories in this collection. Here, J. B.
makes it explicit. The ancestor (shuká) becomes
an at.óow. The phrase contains, in a different

grammatical form (literally, "the ancestralized person") the word from which the title of this collection comes. The Tlingit expression "átx̱ sitee" means literally "to be a thing." A thing of value is implied, but the word goes far beyond the literal translation. It is connected to the concept "at.óow," meaning, literally, an owned or purchased thing, as described in more detail in the Introduction. The thing is often purchased with a human life, as in the experience of Kaats'. In short, the "thing" is a clan crest. The story teller is explaining how at this time and place the experience of Kaats' took on this spiritual significance. The pattern is the same for many events in the lives of the ancestors of various clans: 1) an event happens in the life of an ancestor or progenitor; 2) some aspect of the event becomes a "crest" or at.óow--the ancestor, the animal, etc.; 3) the land where it happened is also important in the spiritual life of the people.

314, 320. Tlingit. Du yátx'i. Phonetically du wátx'i on the tape, with w conditioned by the preceding u.

318. Solid rib cage. Solid rib cage bears are those known to have no space between their ribs. The ribs are, or are like one piece of bone. Therefore they are not easily killed. This detail also appears in other stories.

323. "They are bears," supplied in English translation. The Tlingit text leaves the conclusion for the listener to complete.

324. Tlingit. Ugootch. This is a clear example of the occasional, with the -ch suffix and the irrealis prefix u- used with the zero conjugation verb.

326a. A whispered, inaudible line is omitted here.

333-335. Spoken in a very rapid whisper, with excitement, but difficult to hear.

336. In contrast, this line is spoken loud and clear.

339-342. This passage is characterized by stuttering, and false starts, and is partly reconstructed.

349, 351. The repetition here is a nice example of oral style, used for emphasis and as a compositional device, not to be confused with false starts or stuttering.

352. Tlingit. X'eetaanéek. Optative, second person singular. The underlying form is x'a-oo-ee-taan-eek.

359a. The slap or clap here is one of satisfaction by the story teller.

363. Joy, etc. This is an interesting passage. It would seem difficult for a bear to kill a seal. Hence the excitement of the bear children when Kaats' supplies them with the seals. For those interested in structural theories of literature, anthropology, and folklore, this story seems rich in structural polarities discussed by Levi Strauss and other structuralists; for example, land vs. sea, sea vs. shore, shore vs. inland, land mammals vs. marine mammals, etc. It is interesting that Kaats', the human, is a mediator among these polarities, and that since his time bears are part human, thus mediating the polarity of human vs. bear.

367. This line is spoken in a whisper.

374-380. This passage is one of many in the story wherein the narrator meditates on the relationship between humans and bears, and how much the bears understand us, have compassion, and are like us, but that humans historically have been unable to reciprocate. The relationship is now delicate and often ambiguous.

381. Tlingit. Yóo yagútk is phonetically yóo wagútk on the tape. This is an imperfective form with a durative suffix.

382-387. Spoken in a rapid whisper. Line 388 Awé héen / it was water spoken in a strong, loud voice.

393. Kaats' had been missing for some time,

and was presumed lost. Somehow, perhaps
through the wife of the younger brother, the
wife of Kaats' discovers that he has been
living alone in the woods--or worse yet, as
rumor and gossip about the footprints would
have it, that he has been living with an
animal. The phrase ux̱ kéi uwatee has a range
of meanings and is difficult to translate.
Among the meanings are: trouble, death, an
accident, a mechanical breakdown, to get sick,
an incident, and an experience.

394-397. The motif of plural marriage is
common in the stories, but the general pattern
is for the younger wife to make cultural
mistakes, not the older.

398-406. A number of cultural things are
happening in this comment by the story teller
to the collector. First, aware of the
different politeness styles in traditional
Tlingit and contemporary European-American
culture, the Tlingit elder is apologizing,
lest he embarrass a younger Tlingit woman who
may possibly be influenced by non Tlingit
standards. He is preparing her for what the
wife of Kaats' says about the bear.

Second, as an older Eagle moiety man, the
story teller addresses the younger Raven woman
as his daughter. He continues, telling her
that although she is Raven (Lukaax̱.ádi; child
of Chookaneidí), she has genealogical
connections to the Teik̲weidí clan that owns
the story. He states explicitly how good it is
that she is asking about it, and implies here
and in other references to the Teik̲weidí that
he encourages verification of the story by
Teik̲weidí elders.

412. The Tlingit text uses the word
yatseeneit, one of the circumlocutions for
bear. The narrator is being extremely
indirect here, in contrast to the words of the
wife he is building up to introduce.

417. Hey there. The story teller's voice
is in a very high pitch here, imitating a

woman's voice.

419. The comment by the wife is the turning
point of the story. She is being nasty,
sarcastic, and "catty" to Kaats', and she is
breaking a strong Tlingit cultural taboo by
speaking badly of animals. Her actual comment
is ambiguous, but is a thinly veiled reference
to the genitals of the female bear.

The construction translates more literally
as a "tiny faced thing with hair on it" or a
"tiny faced haired thing." The insertion of
the diminutive -k'- in the verb complex is very
rare in Tlingit. The nominal prefix ya- refers
to face, and yak' would be "little face." This
example suggests that the set of nominal
prefixes may be further modified by diminutives.
The entire verb is an attributive construction.
The underlying form is ya-k'-wu-dzi-x̲aaw-u.

424. This line is whispered.

425. Kaats' now breaks his agreement with
the bear wife by speaking to the human wife.
This is also an interesting construction. In
Tlingit as well as in English, the entire
first subordinate phrase is the subject of the
sentence. The word yéich derives from the word
yé and the subject marker -ch.

427. This is difficult to translate. We
have used "you," but the Tlingit text is more
literally "this one." It is as if he is
talking about her, even though she can hear,
saying something like "What has she done now?"

443. The songs. These are the dirges,
lamentations, or cries that the bear wife will
sing over the body of her husband. Note as
elsewhere in these stories the pattern of a
story, song, and artistic design all
containing and referencing each other.

444. Outer containers. This term may also
be translated as "our makers," or "our containers"
and refers to grandparents, ancestors, and
relatives of past generations. See also the note
to line 280 of J. B.'s Naatsilanéi.

449-454. This is a difficult passage in

Tlingit, where both singular and plural forms
appear. Two persons are watching: one, a
coward; the other, a slave, who is also a
messenger.

455. Note the "shape shifting" here, where
the bear appears in human form to the
witnesses.

460. Reference is to ceremonial face paint.

Glacier Bay History
Told by Susie James, 82

Recorded by Nora Dauenhauer, Sitka, June
1972. Transcribed and translated by Nora
Dauenhauer.

Publication History. The text was
transcribed as a production of the Alaska
Native Language Center. The Tlingit text was
first published August 1973 by Tlingit Readers,
Inc., copyright (c) 1973 by Tlingit Readers,
Inc., printed at Sheldon Jackson College by
Andrew Hope III and Richard Dauenhauer. The
first edition featured a four color totemic
design of the Woman in the Ice by John Marks.
Revised and translated as a project of the
Sealaska Heritage Foundation.
    Other Versions. Boehm (1975: 48) Bohn
(1967: 39). See also the version by Amy Marvin
in this collection.
    The Glacier Bay History told by Susie James
is an excellent example of traditional world
view--the cosmic significance of human
behavior in relationship to "eternal return" of
resources. If people live correctly--by right
thought, right speech, right action, things
will go well. Above all, humans must respect
the world of spirits--the spirits of animals
and other forms of life and energy in the
world. If these spirits are respected, the
life in which they are embodied will continue
to return to the people, sustaining human life.
    A number of literary, social and spiritual
themes are presented, including individual and
social responsibility within the family and
community at large, both at a given point in
time and for all future time; blood guilt and
redemption; puberty; and the relationship of
people, animals, and the land.
    The history is a powerful account of the

spiritual significance of Glacier Bay to the
Chookaneidí people. The style is very "baroque"
in that the composer introduces many themes
into her narration immediately--almost one per
line or phrase--and then continues to develop
and weave them. The story concludes with two
of the most sacred Chookaneidí songs--lamenta-
tions for the land and houses of Glacier Bay.

Two highly developed narrative traditions
exist for the Glacier Bay History. Each is
powerful. We do not argue that one is better,
more accurate or more correct than the other,
or that either is wrong. The versions are
simply different. Such differences are common
in oral literature. Each has its emphasis and
tragic focus and impact. We invite readers to
enjoy both.

In version one the grandmother, Shaawatséek'
stays behind in place of the young
granddaughter, Kaasteen. The woman in the ice
is the older woman, Shaawatséek'. Emphasis
here is on the sacrifice of the grandmother,
on the Tlingit tradition of "standing in," and
accepting the responsibility not only for one's
own actions, but the actions of others. One's
actions impact not only the individual, but his
or her entire community, and not only now, but
for generations to come. The young woman makes
a mistake, but the older woman takes action to
redeem her family and people. The grandmother
comments specifically that many children will
be born of the young woman, and therefore the
young woman should survive. The young woman
will guarantee the biological survival of the
people, but the old woman will guarantee the
spiritual and social survival of the people.
This is the version told by Susie James. This
would seem to be an older version, but this is
impossible to prove.

In version two the young woman, Kaasteen,
herself stays behind with the houses to redeem
her people. The Woman in the Ice is Kaasteen,
the younger woman. The tragedy in this version

focuses on the immediate loss not only of the
young woman, but the grandchildren never to be
born. The young woman accepts responsibility
for her actions, and takes appropriate steps to
redeem herself, her family, and her people. The
sense of sacrifice is extremely powerful
because it is the life of a woman of child
bearing age. This version is more common in
Hoonah today. This narrative tradition is
represented in this volume by Amy Marvin.

In this volume, both versions are told by
respected tradition bearers of the Chookaneidí
clan. The versions differ only in which woman
stays behind. The versions agree on the names
(Kaasteen the granddaughter, and Shaawatséek'
the grandmother). Most important, the versions
agree that this is a Chookaneidí story, that
the land of Glacier Bay is sacred because it
was purchased with the blood of the people, and
that the spirit of the woman remains in the
ice. They also agree on the songs attached to
the history. Throughout each story, we can see
and appreciate and enjoy the personal styles of
the two elders. Each has her own way of
envisioning and recreating the specific details
of the story, and relationship of events--for
example, the details of the seclusion during
the puberty rites, the details of how the
little sister relates Kaasteen's calling the
glacier, etc.

Susie James is a speaker of a now almost
extinct dialect or speaking style of Tlingit
associated with the "old timers." It is
characterized by replacing "n" with voiced "l",
(like the English L) . For example, héen
(water) is héel (with a voiced l.) The reverse
process sometimes happens in the English of the
very "old timers", who sometimes say "hoten"
for "hotel", and "model skills" for "marten
skins," etc. In the narrative, Susie uses the
"standard Tlingit" n, but in the first song,
she uses the voiced l throughout--a<u>x</u> aalí for
a<u>x</u> aaní (my land). Where the letter l appears

in the vocables, it is always voiced, never
voiceless. In texts where the voiced l sound
is significantly frequent, we normally write it
with an underlined l, to distinguish it from
the "regular l," which is voiceless in
Tlingit. In texts in which it is rare, as in
this volume, we indicate the voiced l in the
notes. The voiced and voiceless l never
contrast in Tlingit; the voiceless l, where it
occurs, is always a variant of n.

Susie James' style is characterized by very
rapid delivery within the line, creating an
overall impression of speed. She delivers her
narrative in a soft, high voice, and has a
range of voices for her characters, as
indicated in the notes.

Title. A literal translation of the title
is "(When) the Glacier Comes Down on the People."
    1. Gathéeni. "Sockeye (Red Salmon) River."
This is on the site of present day Bartlett Cove.
    4. Glacier Bay. The name "Glacier Bay" was
not traditionally applied to the area, but its
name was S'é Shúyi, "The Edge of the Clay," so
named because the entire bay was a valley of
clay with grass growing in it. After the glacier
came down and had receded, it became Sít' Eeti
Geey, "The Bay where the Glacier Was." Then it
also became Xaatl Tú, "Among the Icebergs."
    1-6. Note how the story teller is
presenting many themes one after the other,
without developing them. Once the themes are
presented, she will begin to tie them together,
connecting the land, the salmon, the people,
the ice, and various traditions.
    11. Houses stood. In English, "stood," but
in Tlingit, literally, "sit." Two Tlingit verb
stems are used. Here, the plural stem -keen,
and, as in line 126, the singular stem -.aa.
    14-16. Susie is naming the house groups at
Glacier Bay who were part of a then still
undivided Chookaneidí clan, but separated into
house groups. Subsequent to the events

recorded in the story, the Kaagwaantaan and
Wooshkeetaan evolved into separate clans. As
far as is known the Eechhittaan did not take on
a separate identity as a clan. This is a
natural process in the evolution of Tlingit
social structure, as a group of people
literally outgrows one house and builds
another. Eventually the house groups take on
status as separate, but closely related
clans. Lines 126–136 include two more houses,
Naanaa Hít and Xinaa Hít.

At the time when Kaasteen violated the
taboo, the Chookaneidí clan consisted of 5
houses: Kaawagaani Hít, Woosh Keek Hít, Eech
Hít, Naanaa Hít, and Xinaa Hít. After the
events in the story, they evolved into three
distinct clans.

The etymology of Kaagwaantaan derives from
Kaawagaani Hít Taan, "The House that Burned."
There was also a Kaawagaani Hít in Hoonah
before the fire of 1944. The name Wooshkeetaan
derives possibly from Woosh Kik Hít Taan,
"Half of a House." The name Chookaneidí means
"People of the Grass" and is related to
chookán, "grass." The clan is named after
Chookan Héeni, "Grassy River," that flows in
Berg Bay in Glacier Bay, on the opposite shore
from <u>G</u>athéeni, Bartlett Cove.

Another group of Chookaneidí not mentioned
in the text was also at Glacier Bay, although
their relationship to the other groups is not
completely understood. The name of this group
is Kadakw.ádi, and the name is sometimes heard
as an alternative to the name Chookaneidí.

The point emphasized here (both in the text
and the note) is that at the time of the story,
the Chookaneidí, Kaagwaantaan, and Wooshkeetaan
were all house groups of the same clan, and
subsequently evolved into three distinct but
closely related "brother" or "sister" Eagle
moiety clans sharing a common heritage. The
three clans are often grandparents of each
other. As Ray Nielsen, Susie James' grandson

commented in reference to annotating this
story, "Don't forget to mention our brothers,
the Kaagwaantaan and Wooshkeetaan."

23. At the start.... The Tlingit term
wooweit refers to the time during which
biological changes take place and the female
child becomes a woman, with her first
menstruation. The Tlingit word is related to
the word for "enrichment." This is a difficult
passage to translate, and could be "At the
start of her enrichment," or "At the start of
puberty," or "At the start of her puberty
rite," or "At the start of her seclusion."

23. She was curtained off. A girl was
curtained off or otherwise isolated during
this time. This was a strict training period
for life skills, adult thinking, and self
discipline. There were things she couldn't do,
foods she couldn't eat, etc. Training included
sewing, arts, crafts, and traditional technology.

25-30. There were very many of us. This
line suggests that there aren't as many
Tlingits any more, that there are many who
were adopted out or otherwise "lost" to the
community. It also suggests an important
point for the story teller--a cosmic
connection between proper training and behavior
and the well being of the people, including
fertility of the land, animals, and people.
This holistic world view is common in
traditional societies, where spirituality,
wellbeing, and environmental protection are
united, and directly connected to human
behavior. At the end of this training period
and ritual isolation, the young woman would be
considered mature, and a marriage would be
arranged for her, very often as the junior
wife in a plural marriage.

30. Tlingit. The tape has jidusnéiyeen,
with the s classifier.

32. Tlingit. The tape has nalé, without
the normally expected irrealis prefix u-. This
is an accepted grammatical variant.

30-40. This passage links up with the
foreshadowing in line 21, "what was she
thinking?" The dramatic emphasis here is
that the training was almost over, but things
are about to go wrong. The salmon and
seclusion themes are being worked together.
Notice the very long lines from 25 to 37, as
the story teller speed increases with the
dramatic tension.

42. Extension. A special room extending
from the main house was constructed of cedar
bark so that Kaasteen could live there alone.

58. Tlingit. The tape has keitl jiyáx̲. The
nominal prefix has been edited out.

68-69. The lines between 68 and 90 are
delivered in a range of dramatic voices.
Beginning with Atlée / Mother! a change is
made from the normal narrative voice to the
other voices. The little girl speaks in a
very soft and high voice.

70. The mother's voice is a conspiratorial
whisper.

72. Girls don't bring news from back
rooms. This is a proverb, the cultural
equivalent of which is probably something like
"People shouldn't tell tales out of school."

73-81. Now the young girl speaks in a
whisper too, her voice gradually vocalized
toward the end of the passage.

82-89. Whispered; again, the mother speaking.

89. Tlingit. The line contains two forms
of the stem -kaa, an indicative and an optative.

90. Susie James' regular narrative voice
resumes here.

91. Tlingit. The verb yanagwéich is
interesting. It is an occasional form, with
the -ch suffix and the conjugation prefix -na-.
It also has the nominal prefix ya-, meaning
"face." The verb presents images of the face
or head of boats in a fleet going up to the
face of the glacier to hunt seals.

93, 96. Tlingit. Kana.éin and akunalséin
appear here with their progressive stems.

In some grammatical forms, these verbs look
very much alike, although their underlying
forms are quite different. The dictionary
stems are -sei, "to be near; come close," and
-.aa, "to grow; cause to grow."

126-136. In addition to the Kaagwaantaan,
Wooshkeetaan, and Eechhittaan mentioned in
lines 14-16, two other houses are now
mentioned: Naanaa Hít, meaning "House up the
River," and Xinaa Hít, meaning "House down the
River." The names derive from locative bases
meaning "further up" and "further down."

By mentioning Kaaxwaan, Mrs. J. C. Johnson,
Susie's contemporary in Hoonah and a paternal
aunt of the collector, the story teller is
inviting and encouraging verification of the
house name. Kaaxwaan was from Naanaa Hít, as is
Amy Marvin. Susie James is a descendant of
the Xinaa Hít. Both are house groups of the
Chookaneidí clan.

137-138. Many other houses. The
traditional pattern is that every other
generation either rebuilds a clan house, or
builds a new one, usually the same house, and.
of the biological paternal grandfathers. In
other cases, people divide into another house
group due to the expanding population. For
example, Naanaa Hít was rebuilt in Hoonah.
The number of houses indicates that the people
had been in Glacier Bay for many generations.

139. Row of houses. In addition to the
five houses mentioned by name, there was a
second row of houses in back of these. It is
important to remember that the community would
have included houses of Raven moiety groups,
although these are not mentioned by name in
the story. These Raven clans would have been
the marriage partners of the Eagle clans. It
is also important to remember that although a
house is considered belonging to one clan, it
would be occupied by people of both moieties,
because a husband and wife would be of
different moieties according to the

traditional marriage patterns. One of the
Raven moiety clans that would have been part
of the community is the T'akdeintaan.

152, 153. "Her mother" here is the mother's
mother, Shaawatséek', the grandmother of
Kaasteen.

155, 156. Just prepare. These two lines
show that Shaawatséek' had already removed
herself from the rest of the family and had
already made her decision to stay.

163. Uncles' house. Tlingit possession is
always difficult to convey in English.
Reference is to a singular house possessed by
plural maternal uncles. Sometimes the Tlingit
noun plurals are ambiguous. She is actually
staying with all the houses, even though
physically she can only be in one.

168. Children will be born. Shaawatséek'
gives the main reason she will stay with the
houses, as opposed to Kaasteen's staying. She
will save not only the life of her
granddaughter, but the unborn children she will
bring into the world, who in turn will bring
more children into the world. These
grandchildren are recognized in two ways: 1)
descendants through the female line,
grandchildren who are members by birth of the
Chookaneidí clan; and 2) descendants through
the male line, who are by birth members of
Raven moiety clans (following the mother's
line) but whose fathers and grandparents are
Chookaneidí. The Tlingit term for this is
Chookaneidí dachxán—grandchild of Chookaneidí.

173. Tlingit. Tlingit has a range of
variations on the stem -kaa, meaning to say,
tell, reply, etc. Many of these forms are
found between lines 173 and 217:

        173. yéi adaayaká
        173. x'ayeeká
        181. yóo x'ayaká
        192. yéi yawakaa
        203. yéi ayawsikaa

213. yóo yaawaḵaa
217. yóo ash yawsiḵaa

We have translated most of these simply as
"he said" or "she said," but the rich
combinations of prefixes in Tlingit convey
different shades of meaning.

184. Switched. Susie James is emphasizing
here that the granddaughter Kaasteen goes
aboard the evacuating boats, and does not stay
behind. This is the only major point on which
the two narrative traditions disagree. On the
tape there follow 3 lines which have been
edited out, an "aside" within an "aside." The
narrator asks the collector, again inviting
verification,

> Did your paternal aunt
> Kaaxwaan
> tell it to you?

> We i aat
> gwál tlél i een yóo akoonik̇k
> wé Kaaxwaan?

185-190. This is the way I know the
story.... My maternal grandfathers. Susie
James is identifying her line of transmission,
who passed the tradition on to her.

191ff. The speed of the story slows at this
point, as reflected in the short lines
indicating more pauses.

196. The maternal uncle. The great uncle
was composing a song to commemorate their
evacuation from Glacier Bay.

198-209. Tlingit. Four forms of the verb
"to make" or "compose" are contained in these
lines.

198. alyéix   he is making (indicative)
200. alyéixi   (trying) to make (participial)
207. xalayéix   I am making (indicative)
209. ilayéxni   if you make (conditional)

221, 229, 230. Tlingit. There are three
different forms of the stem -chaak, to pack.

221. kaydachák   pack (imperative)
229. has kawdichák they packed
230. kducháak   they packed (indefinite)

240, 241. Nice example of a "terrace" in
oral style.

240. yaa kunanein they were getting ready
main clause, indicative mood, progressive

241. yan kunéi when they were ready; subordinate clause, conjunctive mood, sequential

250. The song from Naanaa Hít. Reference is
to the song "Ishaan gushéi," which is used by
the Chookaneidí during the cry for the dead.
The two songs with which Susie James concludes
her narrative are among the most serious and
sacred of the Chookaneidí clan. They are sung
on very solemn occasions, especially during
the feasts for the removal of grief. Susie
accompanies herself with a drum. For complete
discussion of variant verses, see the notes to
the story by Amy Marvin. Song lines are not
numbered. Also, since the melody overrides
the Tlingit tone system, tone is not marked.
As in most Native American music, the song
consists not only of its text, which contains
the poetic images and meaning, but sets of
vocables or "burden syllables" such as "ee,"
"aa," "ei," "haa," etc. that have no meaning
but serve to establish the melody.
As mentioned in the general discussion at
the beginning of these notes, the letter l in
the vocables and text of this song indicates a
voiced rather than a voiceless l. This voiced
l is a variant of n, substituting for n, but
never contrasting with it. It is in free
variation with n, and in the second song,

Susie James uses the n and not the voiced l.

Between the first and second songs, Susie whispers, "<u>X</u>'eit shután! <u>X</u>'eit shután!" asking the collector to turn off the tape recorder.

Glacier Bay History told by Amy Marvin

Recorded by Nora Dauenhauer, Juneau, May 31,
1984. Transcribed and translated by Nora
Dauenhauer.

For other versions, please see the story by
Susie James in this collection and the notes to
it, which also include details not repeated
here on Glacier Bay, world view, and the clans
mentioned in the story.

Amy Marvin is one of the eminent Chookaneidí
tradition bearers in Hoonah today, and is a
direct descendant of the ancestors mentioned in
the Glacier Bay History. She was requested to
tell this story so that both traditions would
be represented in this collection. Her version
is very rich in details, and provides historical
perspective on many of the cultural institutions
of Tlingit heritage, such as feasting for the
removal of grief in memory of the departed.

Amy Marvin sets her central narrative of the
events at Glacier Bay in the context of a
larger history. She begins with the story of
the girl who raised the bird at Glacier Bay,
then turns to the events that destroyed the
idyllic life there. Her history then
continues to the founding of Hoonah. The
transcription presented here concludes with the
very beginning of the last part of Amy's
history, with the refugees from Glacier Bay
landing at Spasski and having to start over
again with almost nothing.

Although the two stories are different in
style and detail, with each story teller
selecting different features to emphasize and
develop, the two stories actually disagree on
only one important point. In the tradition
represented by Susie James, the older woman,
Shaawatséek', stays behind; in the tradition
represented by Amy Marvin, the younger woman,
Kaasteen, stays behind.

Amy Marvin's delivery in the "narrative frame" or first part of the story is very rapid, with very slight pauses between sentences. When she reaches the "story proper" the speed decreases in general, and there are more pauses. A general pattern is for the phrase or section of lines to begin with a loud, firm voice, then gradually diminish in volume to an almost whispered "yes," and then begin the pattern again. Some examples of this are indicated in the notes.

1-55. Amy Marvin, as Susie James, opens her narrative with a description of life in harmony with nature. The immediate story is set in the context of an earlier story about the girl who raised the bird whose call imitates the name of the clan.

5-7. In Tlingit, the verbs are different and the adverbs the same; because we had to use the same verb in English, we have made the adverbs different.

14. This line is an "aside."

15, 16. Ts'ítskw is the contracted form and is the normal generic term for any small song bird in Northern Tlingit. The longer form, ts'ats'ée, is used in the South.

24. Tlingit. Yéi ayanaskéich. Occasional. The stem is -kaa.

25, 26. Tlingit. Gútgook. Optative. Here, the optative suffix -ook is added to the durative suffix -k-, which becomes -g-. "Do not go repeatedly or habitually."

31. Tlingit. Stuck in the mind, neil yaawdigích (perfective: yaa-w-di-gích) it found a home, went inside a home. The stem ya-da-geech refers to a sharp object entering, going into, or piercing; neil is the nominal or thematic prefix referring to home.

36, 38. Tlingit. The stem -xeet, multiply:

36. aa-w-dzi-xeet	perfective
38. yaa ga-s-xít-ch	occasional

41. Choo-kaneidí. The bird is imitating or
repeating the clan name, and the story teller
is imitating the bird call of the Chickadee.

59, 60. Tlingit uses the same word, yées,
as the adjective "young" and the adverb "newly"
or "recently."

61. Tlingit. Dus.áa has the s classifier,
making the verb causative. They caused her to
sit; they had her sitting.

72. Someone in this condition. This is one
of the great miracles and mysteries of life,
and in many traditional societies women were
and are considered to have great power,
especially at this time. The power can also be
unconscious and dangerous, and many ritual
taboos often apply. In traditional societies,
the onset of menstruation is also one of the
great rites of passage in a woman's life, and
in the life of the community.

76, 77, 79. Feast. The Tlingit stem -eex'
is used in verb and noun form, and is very
important. In English, the event is popularly
called "potlatch" or sometimes "party." The
Tlingit term is based on the stem -eex', which
means "to invite," as to a banquet or feast.
Amy Marvin will explain this in detail later in
lines 307-330. The main concept is to feast,
not with one's "enemies," (as is popular in the
anthropological literature on the subject) but
in sharing food and gifts with the opposite
moiety, and, through them, with the departed.
Thus there is no relationship to the spirits of
the departed except though sharing with the
living. This concept is central in Tlingit
tradition, and in this, Tlingit tradition may
well differ substantially from the potlatch
tradition described for the southern Northwest
Coast.

The term is difficult to translate. We have
avoided using the word "potlatch," and have
used something on the theme of "feast." The
stem is used as a verb in lines 76 and 77: the

prefix ku- refers to action involving people, and the subject pronoun -du- is a 4th person pronoun generally translated as "they" or by using the English passive voice.

ku-w-du-wa-.éex'   there was a feast;
                     people were invited;
                     people had been invited;
                     they invited people.

The noun phrase in line 79

ku.éex'-dei   to the feast (feast-to)

reduces the components to their simplist form, ku.éex'--"people-invitation." The feast in these lines is not for Kaasteen, but is coincidentally at the same time.

84. Little girl. Presumably the younger sister of Kaasteen.

104. Lifted the edge. The wall was made of bark, and could be lifted in sheets.

131, 132. Witness. In Tlingit, witless, with a voiced l that patterns as a dialect variation of n.

146-161. Emphasis here is that the glacier did not advance along the surface of the land or water, but from underground, upsetting the surface layers of soil and trees, and, of course, the village. A glacier is like a river of ice, and it is not uncommon for soil and vegetation to collect on top of the ice.

177-180. She named the glacier. Here and in lines 180-191 there is reference to the power of names and naming things. She not only called it, but called it by name. There is twofold violation of cultural taboos here; first, proper protocol would be to refer to the ice and the spirits of the ice indirectly, not addressing it directly by name; second, this is violation of the self control expected during her training. Her violation of taboo was not a malicious or evil act, committed in knowledge,

but an accident, committed in ignorance. Even
though accidental, the consequences were
disastrous.

207. Tlingit. Yándei is phonetically
wándei on the tape.

213, 214. Tlingit uses two different forms
of the stem sheet'.

ku-ka-na-shít'   pushing people along;
    (with y classifier and ku- prefix;
    stative verb; to crowd out; progressive)

akanalshít'   pushing it along;
    (with l classifier; transitive verb;
    to push out; progressive)

217, 219. Tlingit uses two forms of the
stem gaas', to move a household with future
plans unspecified:

ga-x-la-gáas'-i   subjunctive; let's move
ga-x-la-gáas'   future; we will move

231. The saying, "They had her sitting as
seed." A young woman of child bearing age
would be the wealth and seed of the people,
their hope and guarantee of the continuing
survival of the group.

245. Double quotes. This is ambiguous, but
we take the entire line to be gossip or hearsay,
within which the girl is quoted.

248. Opposite groups. The clans of the
opposite moiety, in this case presumably the
T'akdeintaan, who would have been the
predominant Raven moiety clan of the area. The
Tlingit term is guneitkanaayí, based on the
stem naa, group of people, also used in lines
217 and 219. The following lines specify a
paternal aunt, in Tlingit, aat, which we have
translated variously as paternal aunt and
father's sister in lines 249 and 250. Kaasteen
as Choonkaneidí and Eagle moiety would have an
Eagle mother and a Raven father; the father's

sister would also be Raven moiety.

254. The storm we just had. Amy is referring to a recent storm in SE Alaska.

271. She didn't deny it. This line is spoken emphatically. The dialog following is soft and whispered. The entire passage is delivered very rapidly. Acceptance of blame and even blood guilt is very important in the story. She realizes and repeats in lines 269–274, "What I said will stain my face forever." Her actions have ruined the physical village in the present, and will ruin the reputation of her people forever. She can redeem herself and future generations of her people only by a conscious act of courage to balance the unconscious act of whimsey that brought on the disaster. This version is very powerful because Kaasteen takes the step herself, transforming herself from a dangerous and immature girl to a courageous woman whose act is the redemption of her people. With reference to line 231, "for seed," the choice is a great sacrifice, not only of her own life, but of the lives of children never to be born.

287–288. "Us" refers to the Chookaneidí. "All of them" refers to the women of the Raven moiety clans; "all of us" to the Chookaneidí and Eagle moiety. The entire community is now expressing its support for Kaasteen's decision.

299–303. The rhythm here is of alternating loud and soft voice. The voices in parentheses are softer. The story teller is imitating a person announcing at a feast, and the cry being repeated or echoed by the "naa káani," the in-law serving as a coordinator or "emcee" at the request and direction of the hosts. The two phrases are those used during the distribution of food and material goods at a memorial feast—"x'éidei" for food and "kaadéi" for dry goods and money—when these are dedicated to the spirits of the departed, and the names of the departed are called out.

296, 309. In Tlingit the stem jaak, to

kill, is used grammatically in two ways:

296. dujákxi   attributive; whatever was
                killed
309. dujákx   main verb; they killed.

Also, the verb is used metaphorically in line
309, where the meaning is to "kill" or "cut off"
ownership. This is an expression used for
materials set aside for distribution at a
feast. The -x is a durative suffix.

306-330. These lines are the most succinct
explanation of Tlingit feasting that we have
recorded to date by a Tlingit tradition bearer.
Here Amy Marvin explains the spiritual purpose
of the ritual distribution of food and goods at
a memorial feast. As explained in the notes to
lines 76, 77, and 79, the Tlingit word for
"potlatch" is literally "an invitation."
Although domestic and community tensions can
and do arise, as with the organizing and
sponsoring of any large family or community
affair, emphasis from the Tlingit point of view
is not on rivalry or hostility as suggested by
such titles as "Fighting with Property," or
"Feasting With Mine Enemy," but rather on
actions and "Words That Heal." (See Kan 1983,
1986.) It is significant here that access to
spirits of the departed is through sharing
expressions of love with the living. All are
members of the same community--hosts and
guests, Eagles and Ravens, physical and
spiritual, living and departed.

311. Tlingit kuwaakéik is a durative form
from ya-kaa; people say (more than once.)

315. Tlingit. Asinéegu. Some speakers use
an alternate form with the stem -nook.

319. Tlingit. Kei xtudateeyít is a nice
example of the purposive, with the conjugation
prefix kei, the aspect prefix -ga- (which
becomes -x- according to regular rules for
contractions and closed syllables) and the
suffix -yít. The purposive means "in order to."

346. Aaa / yes is whispered.

347. "Am I going to bring" / "Yee eetídei."
Spoken in a loud voice. This and the following
lines emphasize the impact of the story--the
sacrifice not of the older woman but of the
young woman of child bearing age with her whole
life ahead of her. The grandmother is willing
to sacrifice her life in place of her granddaughter for the good of the family, clan and
community.

349, 350. Gaysagú. Plural imperative.

359. I will not go aboard. Tlél yaax yéi
kkwagoot. This line is spoken firmly, with
great determination--a very heavily accented,
trochaic line. The following line is more
relaxed, then line 361 firm again, with extra
stress on yáa, equivalent to stress on "here"
in English.

372. It measured up. The Tlingit in lines
317 and 372 is difficult to translate. The
idea is "there is a saying" and that what was
done measured up to or was acceptable or not
found wanting or lacking according to expected
norms.

376. Mother's people. The Tlingit (tlaa
hás) could also be translated "her mothers" or
"her parents." Because the lines just before
emphasize the paternal aunts and uncles, we
take the intent of this line to include those
of the mother's clan.

374-382. The lines from 374 (Du aat has /
from her paternal aunts) to line 381 (aaa / yes)
are spoken diminishing in volume. Line 381 is
whispered. Then, line 382 (They didn't paddle
/ Tléil tle yóot) is in a loud, firm voice.
This is a frequent pattern of Amy's delivery.
See also the notes to 346 and 347 for example.

393-396. Tlingit. The stem -xeex appears 4
times in these 4 lines, in 3 different forms:
wusixíx, wsixíx, and uwaxíx--all perfectives.
This is a good example of how Tlingit stems are
used with different prefixes and classifiers to
express different meanings. With the classifier

s, it refers to the falling or dropping of a
large or complex object (such as a house falling
over) and with the y classifier, a small object
(such as a word) falling or dropping.

399-401, 404, 421. Tlingit. The stem -g̲aax̲
is used in a variety of forms. With the d
classifier it means to scream or cry out in
pain. With the s classfier the verb is more
causative or passive.

399.		ka-da-g̲áax̲	imperfective
400, 401.		ka-w-di-g̲aax̲	perfective
404.		ka-w-dzi-g̲aax̲	perfective
421.		ka-du-s-g̲áax̲	imperfective

For more on the classifier system, see the
Grammar Sketch in the Naish-Story Dictionary.

424. The first song follows. Song lines
are not numbered. The first song was composed
by K̲aanax̲duwóos'. Amy Marvin sings this as a
dirge, very, very slowly, compared to Susie
James, who sings it considerably faster. Amy
accompanies herself on a drum. Songs present
different problems of translation. For
example, the vocables or burden syllables of
the opening lines repeat the last syllable of
the text word: ishaan gushei-ei, hidee-ee.
The translation could be pity-ee and hou-ou-
ouse, extending the text word over 3 syllables.
See also the note comparing 3 versions of this
song at the end of the notes to this story.
2nd verse: dinak̲ = du nak̲.

425-462. In this passage, Amy explicates
the song, beginning with the very powerful
comparision of the clan house becoming like a
coffin for Kaasteen.

441. Comparision. This is an ambiguous
passage, and could mean "joining them together"
and / or "comparision." It is unclear whether
reference is to joining the two verses together
into one song, or making the thematic connection
between the loss of the girl on one hand, and
the loss of the house and land on the other.

455-457. Everlasting...recording. Amy is concerned with passing the tradition along to coming generations. This has been difficult in an age characterized by extreme generation gaps created in large part by the impact of schools. The 2nd and 3rd quarters of the 20th century have seen widespread abandonment of Tlingit language and world view, combined with the introduction of technology such as radio and television, that seem to be the death knell of oral tradition around the world. Like many other elders, Amy is involved in using the new technology to help keep the memory of old ways and values alive. She is concerned not only that the song survive, but its meaning as well.

458-462. No man. Amy is emphatically repeating that Kaasteen and Kaasteen alone died with the houses. No male was there.

470. Between 469 and 470, there is dialog on the tape that has been edited out.

> AM. Ch'a yeisú ax yéetk'ich xaan
>   uwasáa Dleit Káa x'éináx.   Tle
>   akát xat seiwax'ákw.
> ND. Pleasant Island.
> AM. Aaa. Uh huh. A áwé.
>
> AM. My son just gave me the name in
>   English, but I forgot it.
> ND. Pleasant Island.
> AM. Yes. Uh huh. That's it.

488. The second song follows. This was composed by Sdayáat.

496-500. Amy is emphasizing that only the Chookaneidí have songs to commemorate this event, even though other clans are part of the history.

500. These men. The Chookaneidí men, because the girl was their close blood relative. She was related in a different sense to the Raven and other Eagle moiety clans.

505-528. After evacuating Glacier Bay, the

people moved eastward along the north shore of
Icy Strait. Excursion Inlet is now the site of
a cannery and was a camp for German POW's
during WW II. Many Hoonah people spend summers
at Excursion Inlet. The Grouse Fort / Ground
Hog Bay site is farther east along the shore,
toward Swanson Harbor and Point Couverden.
Amy's group landed on the south shore of Icy
Strait, on the north shore of Chichagof Island,
at the place called Spasski in English,
opposite The Sisters Islands. All of the
groups eventually settled in present day Hoonah.

528. The transcription ends with Amy's
powerful description of the evacuation of
Glacier Bay and how the people started over
again with nothing. However, the recording
session and narrative continue, and Amy
continues on other topics not included here.

Song Versions. As shown in well known
studies of European and American ballads and
other folk music around the world, personal and
local variation are to be expected in most song
traditions. Such variation exists in the
versions of the Glacier Bay songs with which we
are familiar. Most differences are relatively
minor. The patterns are the same, but specific
words may be in different places. For example,
Susie James and Amy Marvin sing the verses to
"Ishan gushei" in a different order. Amy has
ax̱ hídi first, and ax̱ aaní second; Susie has ax̱
aaní first and ax̱ hídi second. They also use
the two verb stems differently. Susie uses the
stem -goot, "to go on foot" with land, and the
stem -k̲oox̱, "to go by boat" with house. Amy
does the reverse, using -goot with house, and
-k̲oox̱ with land. Also, where Amy Marvin sings
the songs in the body of the story, and
includes exegesis, Susie sings them at the end
of her story, and in a different order, singing
"Ishaan gushei" second, where Amy sings it
first.

"Ishaan gushei" is sometimes heard with an

additional verse not sung by either Susie James
or Amy Marvin. In 1969, at the request of
Willie Marks, J. B. Fawcett recorded the song.
The order of verses is the same as Susie (land,
then house) but he uses the stem -goot with
both of these, reserving the stem -koox for the
third image--my river. The third verse is:

> Ishaan gushei, ax héeni,
> Ishaan gushei, ax héeni,
> dinak yaa kxakoox.

> Pity my river, / pity my river,
> when I leave it by boat.

A version of the song recorded at the memorial
feast for Jim Marks in Hoonah, October 1968,
sung by the group of Chookaneidí hosts with
David McKinley as song leader is same as the
version by Amy Marvin.

Susie's version of Sdayáat's song (Ax aaní
gushei) raises an interesting problem because it
is a fragment. For one reason or another, she
does not sing the "third line," ch'al gookateen
/ will I never see it again. The full pattern is

> Ax aani   (ax hidi)
> gushei
> ch'al gookateen?

Susie replaces the text line with vocables.
There are 2 explanations. She may have been
deliberately abbreviating the song--just
"quoting" from it, or alluding to the full text
she assumes the collector knows. Or, on the
other hand, she may have forgotten the words,
or have gotten confused. We will never know.

The performance of a song varies according
to the setting or context. A tape recording
session is not the same as a memorial feast.
In the above comparison we have not examined
the vocables at all, because to do so without
the music is relatively meaningless. The full

pattern for singing a Tlingit song is:

Vocables twice
First verse twice
Vocables twice
Second verse twice

If the song is sung as a cry at a memorial, the "Hoooo ending" is added, signifying a cry of pain.

As in most Native American music, the song consists not only of its text, which contains the poetic images and meaning, but sets of vocables or "burden syllables" such as "ee, aa, ei, haa, hee, hei," that have no meaning, but serve to establish the melody. Although it is sometimes hard to define a "line," most images and singing patterns are in multiples of two or four.

As a final comment, it is important to emphasize that these are among the most sacred of the Chookaneidí songs. Each clan has its serious and sacred songs, along with many that are more secular or light hearted, often called "love songs." It both angers and grieves Tlingit people to hear their songs recorded and used without permission, most often as background music in inappropriate places such as children's television, commercials, or as in a recent movie where a well known "star" playing an Indian woman walks across the plains to the music of a Tlingit canoe song. In other words, where these songs have been reproduced without permission and consultation it has always been where the text and context are totally out of place for what is being depicted by film makers who want "something Indian" as background. The Glacier Bay songs are an excellent example of how serious songs are in Tlingit tradition, and how they fit into the history, ceremonial life, and oral literature of the Tlingit people.

The First Russians told by Charlie White

Recorded by George Ramos, Yakutat, 1962.
Transcribed and translated by Fred White.
Edited by N. and R. Dauenhauer.

   This story may be taken as a prelude to the
accounts which follow, or as "Part One" of a
"Lituya Bay Trilogy." The following two
accounts treat the first encounters with the
Russians and French at Lituya Bay. In this
account, Charlie White offers a Yakutat
tradition about the motives of the Russians for
exploration--a wealth of furs that drifted to
Russia from a fleet of capsized Tlingit
canoes. More detailed historical notes
accompany the story by Jenny White which gives
the Tlingit account of the arrival of the first
Russians. Even though the French arrived at
Lituya Bay two years earlier than the Russians,
we have grouped the stories by Charlie White
and Jenny White together and placed them first,
and conclude the volume with the history by
George Betts.

   1. Age 88. There is some conflict in the
data here. De Laguna (1972) has 1879-1964 as
the dates for Charlie White. Our sources give
1880-1964. In either case, he would not be 88
at the time of recording, but would have died
at the age of 84 or 85. It may also be that
both 1879 and 1880 are incorrect birth dates.
   15. Laaxaayík. A village site very close to
Yakutat.
   32. Voyaging back. The implication is that
the traders were from Lituya Bay or south of it
and had travelled north, perhaps beyond Yakutat
and as far as Copper River, had returned as far
as Yakutat, and were in the home stretch heading
toward or into Lituya Bay when they capsized.
See de Laguna (1972: 937, plate 20) for an

areal view of Lituya Bay. Plates 34-39 are of
interesting old engravings by Europeans of
their experiences at Lituya Bay. Bohn (1967)
also has photographs and old engravings.
    56, 59. These are interesting verbs in Tlingit.

   <u>x</u>'eitee   to imitate by mouth; to be
                         a certain way with the mouth

   sh wudli<u>g</u>ák   to imitate a raven (to make
                         the sound "<u>g</u>á")

Another similar and interesting verb, not in
the text, is

   akaawa<u>g</u>ées   to imitate an eagle (to make
                         the sound "<u>g</u>ée")

    78. Utée. Note the irrealis prefix
expressing uncertainty--"it must have been
like...." The irrealis is also used with a
definite negdative, as in line 79.
    82. Yáxwch'. Pronounced yúxwch' on the
tape. Such assimilation is common in Yakutat
pronunciation. An a or aa changes to u or oo
under the influence of a following labialized
velar, in this case the xw.

Raven Boat told by Jenny White, 81

Recorded by Fred White, Juneau, 1984.
Transcribed and translated by Fred White.
Edited by N. and R. Dauenhauer.

Jenny White begins her narrative by
emphasizing the dangerous entrance to Lituya
Bay, and by reviewing the history of the
capsized canoes with their lost furs that lured
the Russians to Alaska. She then moves to the
actual arrival of the Russians at Lituya Bay.

The first encounters between Europeans and
Tlingits at Lituya Bay are interesting because
they are recorded both in written and oral
traditions.

The more familiar written tradition consists
of the log books of La Pérouse published in
English in 1799 and a well known article by Lt.
G. T. Emmons published in 1911. The lesser
known written account is of the log books of
Izmailov and Bocharov published in Russian in
1791, but in English translation only in
1981. La Pérouse sailed into Lituya Bay on
July 2, 1786; the Russians arrived two years
later, almost to the day, on July 3, 1788.

The oral tradition seems received in two
general versions--those which specify the
Whites as Russians, and those which do not.
It is possible that the Tlingit oral accounts
record two separate historical meetings--one
with the French and one with the Russians,
although motifs from the two histories are
shared. Both traditions are represented here.

The accounts by Charlie White and Jenny
White of Yakutat, whose ancestries are from
Lituya Bay and the Lituya Bay area, identify
the Europeans as Russians, and emphasize the
motif of the capsized canoes and lost furs
drifting seaward to entice the Russians to the
source. For further discussion of the Yakutat
tradition, see de Laguna (1972: 258-259).

The account by George Betts, who also lived at Lituya Bay as a young man, does not specify the Europeans as either Russians or French and does not include the lost fur motif. It is more similar to Emmons (1911) and suggests a southern or Juneau-Sitka tradition.

The account published by Emmons (1911) was collected by him in 1886, one hundred years after La Pérouse, from Cowee, the well known leader of the Auke people living in Juneau (referred to by Emmons by its Tlingit name, Dzantik'i Héeni, which he spells Sinta-ka-heenee.) In the Cowee version, a group of L'uknax̱.ádi men from Grouse Fort (K'ax'noowú, "Kook-noo-ow on Icy Straits") capsize at Lituya Bay enroute to Yakutat. While they camp at Lituya Bay mourning their dead, the Europeans arrive. The Tlingits wonder if this is White Raven (the sails being huge white wings), roll skunk cabbage as telescopes for protection against being turned to stone, send an old man out to make contact, and conclude the encounter with friendly and successful trade. The Cowee version recalls that the Europeans also lost men to drowning in the treacherous entrance to Lituya Bay. A parallel tradition of uncertain origin appears in the *Alaska magazine* (Vol. 1, No. 3, March 1927, 151-153) and is in turn quoted verbatim by Bohn (1967: 24-25).

Because the history of Tlingit contact with Europeans, especially Russians, is not widely known, it may be interesting to review some of the highlights here.

1741. In July 1741 the Russians under command of Chirikov sighted land in Southeast Alaska. In this famous first encounter with the Tlingits near Sitka, Chirikov sent one boat and crew ashore, and they did not return. A second boat was sent, and also did not return. The following day, two Tlingit canoes appeared. From Bancroft's account (1886, 1970: 67-71) it appears that the Tlingits and Russians were mutually astonished, and that the Tlingits

paddled shoreward, shouting "Agai", which may
possibly be Tlingit ("ay x̲áa!") for "Paddle!"
Chirikov returned to Russia.

1786. July 2, 1786, La Pérouse sails into
Lituya Bay and makes peaceful contact with the
Tlingit. He describes the great risk entering
the Bay, and notes that on July 13, 21 of his
men were lost at the mouth of the Bay when
their boat capsized. Cenotaph Island in
Lituya Bay is named for a monument erected in
their memory. He stayed 26 days, recording
his interesting observations.

1787. Dixon makes contact.

1788. Douglas makes contact.

1788. July 3, 1788. The first documented
Russian contact by Izmailov and Bocharov at
Lituya Bay. More information below.

1791. Malaspina makes contact.

1791. Shelikhov's *Voyage to America 1783-
1786* is published in Russian. Chapter Three
is the voyage of Izmailov and Bocharov.

1796-1805. The Russians establish a fort
called Novorossissk near Yakutat, destroyed by
the Tlingits in 1805.

1799-1802; 1804. The Russians establish a
settlement near Sitka in 1799, which is
destroyed by the Tlingits in 1802. In 1804
the Russians return in force, win the Battle of
Sitka, and reestablish the settlement on the
present townsite of Sitka.

1799. Jean La Pérouse voyage report is
translated from French and published in two
volumes in London: *La Pérouse voyage around
the world performed in the years 1785-1788*.
See Vol. 1, pp 364-411.

1911. Lt. G. T. Emmons publishes an article
in *American Anthropologist* 13 (1911) 294-
298, entitled "An account of the meeting
between La Pérouse and the Tlingit," in which
he compares a Tlingit oral account by Chief
Cowee of 1886 with the events recorded in the
La Pérouse logs.

1981. Shelikhov's *Voyage to America 1783-*

1786 published in English translation by Limestone Press, edited by Richard Pierce. It is interesting to note that whereas the La Pérouse report was published in English almost immediately, the Russian report was not published in English for 190 years!

Because the history of Russian exploration of Izmailov and Bocharov in Lituya Bay is less known in the west than the encounter with La Pérouse, one's first reaction may be to assume that the Tlingit oral tradition has simply confused the French and the Russians. Certainly the same motifs (the coming of Raven, the use of plants for binoculars, etc.) appear in both traditions. However, there is no reason to doubt that the Tlingits encountered both French and Russian explorers at Lituya Bay, although it may be difficult or impossible to assign or restrict motifs of oral literature to one encounter or the other. Again, because the Russian historical evidence is less well known, it is interesting to review some of the highlights here.

The galiot "Three Saints" sailed from Three Saints Bay on Kodiak Island on April 30, 1788, with orders to explore the American mainland. Under command of navigators Izmailov and Bocharov, the ship explored Prince William Sound, and reached Icy Bay at the terminus of the Malaspina Glacier on June 4. On June 10 they sighted Yakutat Bay, and were met by Tlingits (whom they refer to as Koliuzh) wearing European clothing the Russians surmise they had traded from foreign vessels.

They anchored in Yakutat Bay June 11, and spent some time meeting and trading with the Tlingit. The journals contain interesting ethnography, describing houses, clothing, customs, and Tlingit names as perceived by the Russians. The Tlingit also describe the lands to the south--Lituya Bay and the Chilkat area.

The Russians received two slaves from the Yakutat Tlingit. One was a young Kodiak boy

who had been captured by the Kenaitze, traded
to the Chugach Eskimos, then to the Eyaks, then
to the Tlingits. Another boy was from east of
Yakutat, identified as Chich'khan (possibly
Tsimshian?) Both were valuable as interpreters
and guides.

The logs record interesting conversations
with the leader (toion) named Ilkhaku
(possibly Yéil X̱aagú? a Raven name from
Chilkat, where the leader told the Russians he
was from.) They gave him a Russian copper
amulet, and a portrait of Crown Prince Paul
with inscription in Russian and German.

On June 18 they placed a copper possession
plate at Yakutat Bay, and on June 21 set sail,
exploring the Yakutat area, and listing a
number of rivers by their Tlingit names,
including Antlin, Kalkho, and Kakan-in.
Antlin is Aan Tlein in modern orthography,
Ahrnklin on most maps; Kalkho is probably
X̱eilx̱wáa, the Italio River, named after Frank
Italio, Shangukeidí, maternal grandfather of
Emma Marks, widow of Willie Marks; Kakan-in,
which the Russians translate as "Muddy Creek,"
we cannot reconstruct at present, other than
the -in, which is héen, meaning river or
water. The k's could be any combination of
the k, x, or g sounds.

On July 3 they leave Kakan-in and 17 miles
south arrive at Lituya Bay. The journals
discuss in great detail the complex navigation
into the bay. They encounter the Tlingit, but
it is too late in the day to trade.

On July 4 the Russians re-anchor. The
leader Taik-nukh-takhtuiakh is welcomed on
board and into the cabin with two elders.
There is detailed description of the
conversation and trade encounter.

July 5. One of the translators reports that
three summers earlier a large vessel had been
there and had left a broken anchor, which the
Tlingits had dug out at low tide and carried
into the woods. The Russians located it and

traded for it. (1788 would be the third summer, counting 1786, 1787, and 1788, after the arrival of La Pérouse.)

Also on July 5 the Russians bury a copper possession plate. The log contains a detailed description of its location. Again, the journal contains interesting ethnographic observations. The Russians understand Lituya Bay to be a summer camp, and that the people are "subject to" the chief they had met in Yakutat.

On July 9 the Russians sailed out. The major problems were difficulty in finding a good anchorage, and scurvy appearing among the hunters because of an unchanging diet of salted food. (The Russians do catch halibut and pick salmon berries and/or raspberries, according to the log. It is unclear how much of the sea mammal meat they consume.)

Navigating across the gulf of Alaska, the ship reached harbor at Kodiak on July 15. The following year, from April 28 to August 6, 1789, Bocharov sailed back to Okhotsk, where he delivered the maps and journals.

1. Reference is to the entrance of Lituya Bay. It is crucial to catch the tide and currents just right when entering and leaving.

18. Wulis'ées. On tape, the story teller first says wuligáas', then corrects herself, changing to wulis'ées. The stem -gáas' means "to migrate," whereas the stem -s'ées means "to sail," and is related to the word s'ís'aa earlier in the same line, meaning "canvas" or "sail."

19. Ltu.aanáx. Literally through, not into, the Bay. Tlingit focus is on sailing through the entrance to the Bay; English focus is on sailing into the Bay.

19. On the tape, there is a brief exchange with the collector here, which is not transcribed. He asks, "Anóoshi?" ("Russian?") and she replies, "Anóoshi yaagú xaa," ("a Russian boat indeed") after which the

narrative continues.

25. Raven Boat. The white sails were perceived by the people as wings of the White Raven (from mythical times, before he turned black.)

27, 36. Kuguxsateek. Future durative.

The Coming of the First White Man
told by George Betts

Recorded by Constance Naish and Gillian
Story, Angoon, 1960's. Transcribed by
·Constance Naish and Gillian Story. Translated
by Nora Dauenhauer.

As noted in its dedication, this text was
prepared and contributed by Constance Naish and
Gillian Story as a memorial and personal
tribute to George Betts, who spent many hours
with Naish and Story during their stay in
Angoon, helping them immensely in their early
study of Tlingit. As noted elsewhere, the
system of writing Tlingit used in this book is
based on the work of Naish and Story and the
help of George Betts.

The George Betts and Robert Zuboff transcriptions were prepared and contributed as
a set by Constance Naish and Gillian Story, and
we have tried to arrange them as a set in this
volume, opening with the Zuboff account of the
migration to the coast, and closing with the
Betts account of the arrival of the Europeans.
Please see the notes to the Basket Bay story
told by Robert Zuboff for background on this
text.

Also, please see the notes to the Charlie
White and Jenny White narratives for more
information on Tlingit and European encounters
at Lituya Bay, including a review of other
published versions. The most accessible of
these is Bohn (1967: 24-25) which has a very
detailed account based in turn on Emmons (1911)
and which quotes verbatim an article from the
Alaska Magazine (Vol. 1, No. 3, March 1927
151-153). This latter account is of dubious
provenience and has many editorial trappings of
Christian piety (such as Raven as the
"principal divinity of Tlingit mythology" and
the "second coming of Raven.") Such cultural

stereotypes are noticeably absent from the
narrative by George Betts, a good stylist and
an ordained minister well versed in traditional
Tlingit spirituality as well as Christian
spirituality.

Title. The Tlingit title, Gus'k'ikwáan,
means "People from Under the Clouds."
21-28. On the tape, the intonation here
suggests the parenthetical nature of the
information.
30. Atyátx'i. The story teller actually
pronounces the word adátx'i on the tape, but we
have used a more standard spelling here and in
line 37.
35. Ḵach. This is a nice little particle,
and can be translated a variety of ways: "It
turned out to be...", "Here it was....", or
"Actually it was...."
85. The pronunciation on the tape is
x'eiyee.
103. Tlingit. Tlaẖ. Daẖ-, contracted from
daga- is also a possible reading here, with a
slight change in meaning: daẖkasayedéin. "They
began to feel strange," as opposed to "...began
to feel very strange."
105. Tlingit. The first word is the
English Lituya, pronounced with voiced l and
the vowel "a".

BIOGRAPHIES

George Betts / Asx̱'aak
(September 15, 1891 – August 19, 1966)
Kaagwaantaan; Ḵook Hít Taan

George and Katie Betts, late 1950's. Photo
courtesy of Frances Cropley and family

George Richard Betts was born in Sitka,
September 15, 1891. His Tlingit name was
Asx'aak, meaning "Among the Trees." He was
Eagle moiety, of the Kaagwaantaan clan, and of
the Box House (Kook Hit Taan). His mother's
name was Ts'ayís--Fanny Lee in English. She
was from Haines.

George's father was a miner, and the family
followed the mines, so he grew up with first
hand experience of the Gold Rush era in
Juneau, Haines, and Skagway.

From an early age, George had a passion for
learning. At the age of 12 he welcomed the
opportunity to attend the Sitka Training
School, later known as Sheldon Jackson
School. His achievement there qualified him
for scholarships and opportunity to continue
his education "outside."

But George experienced what would be the
first of many conflicts in his life that would
require making tough decisions between modern
and traditional values. In this case, steamer
ticket in hand, he bowed to the desires of his
clan and family leadership, who wanted him to
stay in Alaska and prepare to be a leader in
the Tlingit tradition.

George stayed in Alaska. At the age of 15
he was forced to leave Sheldon Jackson School
and become the family breadwinner.

He went to work in the mines. This was a
drudgery beyond description for a young man
equally excited by books and boat decks. He
soon quit the mines, and moved to Lituya Bay,
where he lived for two years, speaking only
Tlingit and following a very traditional life
style. He was later to comment that this
experience came at a crucial point in his life,
after the years at Sheldon Jackson School,
where Tlingit language and customs were
strictly forbidden.

He then moved to Douglas to work for the
Ready Bullion mine, the largest of all mines
in the Treadwell area. In Douglas, at the age

of 18, he met Katie Brown, a Salvation Army
worker from Killisnoo. It was love at first
sight, and George and Katie were married
November 25, 1909. The marriage lasted just
short of half a century, until Katie's death
by cancer on December 31, 1958.

After their marriage, the young couple went
to visit the bride's home in Killisnoo, and
ended up staying several years. George worked
in logging, and skippered his own logging boat,
called the *Famous*. From this period date
many of his fascinating experiences with his
father-in-law, who was a traditional Tlingit
i̱xt'--a shaman. The Betts family made their
home in Killisnoo until fire levelled the
village in 1928. They then moved to Angoon,
where he built a house for his family in two
months.

George was described as a man who "liked the
feel of a boat deck under his feet." He was a
very successful fisherman. He had two seine
boats, and then his most well known boat, the
St. Nicholas. He fished for Hood Bay and
Chatham Canneries. His life style had been to
devote most of the fall, winter, and spring
months to church work, and the summer to
fishing. Gradually, he came to make one of
the greatest decisions and sacrifices of his
life. He gave up fishing for full time church
work.

Religion was important throughout George's
life. His father was Methodist, and his mother
Salvation Army. His wife was also Salvation
Army, but gradually George was drawn to the
Presbyterian Church, and he and his wife both
became Presbyterian. Eventually, he desired to
become an ordained minister.

To study for his ordination, George returned
to Sheldon Jackson School, along with his
daughter Frances. He finished his course work,
and continued his studies by correspondence.
The family spent 1939-1940 in Angoon, and the
War years 1940-1945 in Petersburg.

In was in Petersburg that George and Katie Betts became involved in one of the most controversial experiences in his ministry-- what would today be called a "street mission." George joined the Longshoreman's Union, and worked with the "man in the street"--and the woman in the street as well, helping many persons physically and spiritually survive the discourging war years in Southeast Alaska.

George Betts was ordained in Juneau April 4, 1943, and spent the next thirteen years in Hoonah. He retired on December 31, 1957, and moved to Angoon. He remained active in church work, making many sound recordings of scripture and devotional messages.

After his retirement he also ran the *Princeton Hall* for many years, both as minister and skipper, until the vessel was retired and replaced by the *Anna Jackman.*

After the death of his wife in December 1958, George devoted many hours to the work of Bible translation. In this effort, he worked with the English team of Constance Naish and Gillian Story, linguists with the Summer Institute of Linguistics / Wycliffe Bible Translators, assisting them in their grammatical analysis of Tlingit, and in the translation effort. This work laid the foundation of all subsequent Tlingit language work in the 1960's, 1970's and 1980's. (See the introduction to this book for a more detailed description of the work of Naish and Story, and its importance for Tlingit language and cultural studies.) The story by George Betts in this book is transcribed by Naish and Story, and is submitted here as an expression of their gratitude to Mr. Betts for his contribution to the history of Tlingit scholarship.

George Betts received many honors during his lifetime, among them the Sheldon Jackson Christian Citizenship award in 1961.

He is remembered as a good story teller,

with a large repertorie from the episodes of
his rich life and wide travels in Alaska and
the Lower 48. He is also remembered as a
musician. He was photographed with the "old
time" Juneau-Douglas Indian Band, and played
trumpet with the Hoonah Salvation Army Band.

He died August 19, 1966 and is buried in
Evergreen cemetery in Juneau.

His family includes his daughter Frances
Cropley, and her children Sally Millholland
(Juneau), William Betts Phillips (Petersburg),
Les Charles Phillips (Juneau), Elvera Louise
Moeller (Los Angeles) Kathy Jo Cooper (Juneau)
and Jesy Edward Phillips (Anchorage).

This biographical sketch is based on a
longer biography of George Betts written by
Genevieve Mayberry, and on other material
graciously supplied by his daughter, Frances
Cropley, to whom the editors express their
gratitude.

Frank Dick, Sr. / Naakal.aan
Born: August 20, 1899
L'uknax̱.ádi; Kaagwaantaan yádi

Frank Dick, Sr. was born in Sitka on August
20, 1899. He is of the Raven moiety and the
L'uknax̱.ádi clan of Dry Bay. His Tlingit name
is Naakal.aan. He is the last living historian
of the L'uknax̱.ádi of Dry Bay and the Diginaa
Hít Taan. His father, Kashkéin, was
Kaagwaantaan from Sitka of the Ḵook Hít (Box
House.) His mother was Xéetl'i, a L'uknax̱ sháa
of the Diginaa Hít Taan from Dry Bay.
    Frank was a commercial setnet fisherman,
first in Dry Bay and later, for most of his
life, in the Situk and Anklin Rivers (S'itáḵ
and Aan Tlein.) He was skilled in carpentry and
boat building. He built his own skiffs for
fishing and has built several for other
fisherman. He retired from fishing when he was
79 years old. Since he retired he has been
making model skiffs, bentwood boxes, drums and
halibut hooks. He also carves Tlingit canoes.
    When he was seventeen he was a guide for two
white men on the Alsek River in Dry Bay. They
took the journey from Yakutat in a canoe. They
pulled the canoe with their supplies up the
Alsek River to the lake that feeds the river
near Whitehorse. From Whitehorse he took the
train to Skagway and caught a steamer to

Frank Dick, Sr. in his home in Juneau, 1985,
standing with some of his artwork. Clockwise
from top: dance paddles, raven drum, dogsled,
frog drum, Yakutat canoes (with extended keels
for paddling in areas with icebergs) and
(center) model of skiff; bentwood boxes on the
floor. Photo by Fred White

Yakutat, arriving there on the fourth of July.
The trip took them two months.

He has been a member of the ANB in Yakutat
since 1939. He also served in the Home Guard.

Frank never received a formal education.
His father died when he was very young in
Sitka, and from there his uncles took him to
Dry Bay, where he was raised and taught by his
uncles traditionally in the Tlingit ways.

--Biography researched and written
by Fred White

J. B. Fawcett / Tseexwáa
(June 12, 1889 - October 3, 1983)
Wooshkeetaan; T'akdeintaan yádi

Stone lithograph of J. B. Fawcett, "Tseexwáa,"
by R. T. Wallen, Juneau, November 1972.
Reproduced courtesy of R. T. Wallen

J. B. (John Bruce) Fawcett was born in
Juneau on June 12, 1889. His main Tlingit
name was Tseexwáa, but he was also called
Tlaak'wátch. He was of the Wooshkeetaan clan of
the Eagle moiety, and of the Thunderbird House
in the Juneau Village. The Thunderbird House
Screen now in the State Museum in Juneau, on
the ramp leading to the upper level, is from
this clan house. J. B. was a child of the
T'akdeintaan.

He was married twice, first to a Lukaax.ádi
woman, then to Tooléich of Hoonah, and had two
sons, John Fawcett (Sgeinyaa) and William
Fawcett.

His brother was Charlie Fawcett, who was a
reader in the St. Nicholas Orthodox Church in
Hoonah, and who is remembered for his reading
of prayers in Tlingit. J. B. was also related
to Maggie Anderson of Juneau, who raised his
son John Fawcett when his wife died.

"He was a dresser," recalls his clan
brother-in-law Joe Moses. He wore a three
piece brown suit, and always wore his gold
watch with a gold chain. He wore a Stetson hat,
but kept on losing them. "He'd put one down
and lose it. The only thing he didn't lose
were his eye glasses."

As a young man, J. B. was active in sports.
He won a race up Star Hill in Juneau on the
board walks in 1928 or 29, and when he was
older he could "still beat young fellows in the
100 yard dash." Joe recalls how some of the
others had track shoes and shorts, but all J.
B. took off was his coat and tie, and away
he'd go. He was also a player and manager for
a Hoonah baseball team called the "Alaskans,"
and a contemporary of other locally well known
Tlingit baseball players such as Joe White, who
played for the Hoonah Packing Company.

J. B. was a strong man, but not a fighter.
Once a man broke into his house. J. B.
watched him coming in through the window.
When he was finally inside, J. B. asked him,

"Why didn't you come in through the door? The door is right there." He grabbed the intruder and threw him back out through the window.

He was a fisherman and a hunter. Though born and raised in Juneau, he lived much of his life in Hoonah. He ran one boat for a cannery and later got his own purse seiner named *Bruce.* He fished for Icy Straits, Excursion Inlet Packing, and Hoonah Packing. He fished Point Adolphus, Tenakee, Salisbury Sound, and in the Craig, Klawock, and Ketchikan areas. In addition to his commercial fishing, he also lived a subsistence lifestyle with his wife Tooléich.

He liked hunting, and had various adventures. Once on a trip to Marble Island in Glacier Bay his motor broke down and he had to row his rowboat all the way from Berg Bay to Hoonah to get help for his seine boat.

It was also on a hunting trip that he damaged his hearing. He slipped crossing a log and his rifle went off, wounding him in the head. Though bleeding through the nose and mouth, he managed to tear up his shirt, bandage his head, and walk home. He suffered increasing hearing loss for the rest of his life. There are numerous anecdotes about J. B.'s endless loss of hearing aids and batteries. For the last 12 or more years of his life he was totally deaf and unable to discuss the texts included here, but he was still able to tell stories and enjoyed doing so.

J. B. was highly regarded as a tradition bearer. He knew a lot of songs, and was well known for his singing and drumming, and especially for his talent in performing the Halibut Spirit Dance (Cháatl ḵuyéik) a yeikutee or ermine headdress dance usually danced behind a blanket or robe at a feast. He was also a ǥuwakaan (peace maker) and was also known for dancing with a cedar rope around his neck. At one point the dancer tosses the coil

into the air, and it lands either on his or on
a second dancer's neck.

J. B. was dedicated to keeping his ancestral
house alive and occupied. Even when no longer
able to keep it in repair, he continued to
live in the Thunderbird House as long as he was
physically able to do so. His clan brother-in-
law Joe Moses built him a special room in the
Thunderbird House so he wouldn't get cold.
Joe's wife Esther was J. B.'s niece; Joe and
his wife took care of J. B. during these
years. As a final gift to her, J. B. gave
Esther Moses a moose hide robe with a
Thunderbird figure on it. Joe recalls, "He
was a nice man. Very kind. He was a gentle
man."

J. B. sang bass in the Orthodox church
choir, and served as church elder (starosta)
for several years. Although he spoke and
understood English well, he could not read or
write, and signed his name with a co-signer.

He lived the last years of his life with his
cousin George Jim of Angoon, and spent the
last year of his life in the Pioneer Home in
Sitka, where he passed away on October 3,
1983. He is buried in Angoon.

J. B. is the subject of one of the prints in
R. T. Wallen's series of lithographs on Tlingit
elders, Tseexwáa, reproduced here through the
courtesy of the artist.

The editors thank Joe Moses, brother-in-law
of J. B. Fawcett, and Ms. Ruth Lokke for their
help in researching this biographical sketch.

Susie James / Kaasgéiy
(August 10, 1890 – November 3, 1980)
Chookan sháa; T'akdeintaan yádi

   Susie James was born August 10, 1890, in
Hoonah, the daughter of Percy and Lilly
Jackson. She was of the Eagle moiety,
Chookaneidí clan, and Xinaa Hít (House Down the
River) mentioned in the Glacier Bay History.
She grew up in Hoonah, and after moving to
Sitka as a young woman she married James Bailey
Howard, who died in 1953. In 1959 she married
Scotty James, who died in 1961.
   Susie raised her family subsistence style in
the Coho House in Sitka. Along with raising
her family, Susie worked in the Todd and
Chatham canneries. During the Depression years
and when her husband was out fishing, she
supported her family by selling her handmade
moccasins, dolls and beadwork on Main St. She
continued making moccasins, much sought after
by buyers, until very late in life.
   Susie is also remembered as making excellent
bread and dry fish. For many seasons 5 to 7
of the family members lived at Ashgú Geey
(Oosgoo Bay) drying fish.
   She was a member of the St. Michael's
Orthodox Cathedral Choir in Sitka, and helped
organize the St. Mary's Sisterhood, of which

she served as treasurer. Susie felt a very
strong committment to the Church, and her
stewardship took her far beyond local and
family bounds to Hoonah, Angoon, and Juneau to
work in behalf of the Church. She helped
construct the first Orthodox church in Angoon.

Susie James, 1975. Photo courtesy of
Patricia Pelayo Helle

    She was also a lifetime member of the
Alaska Native Sisterhood, joining it in 1920.
She was an honorary member of the Salvation
Army Home League, and in 1962 was made an
honorary member of the Sitka Historical
Society. The members of the Pioneer Home
elected her as Mother of the Year in 1979.

Pat Helle remembers her grandmother "as a very active, self disciplined person, always working with her hands. Anything worth doing was worth doing well. We remember her for her deeply held religious beliefs. All family gatherings were preceded with prayers. She was a unifying force in the family."

Of all the tradition bearers in this collection, Susie was probably the most monolingual in Tlingit. Her English was very limited. Although physically tiny—so short that when she sat in a chair her feet wouldn't touch the floor—Susie was a woman of great stature. She became a midwife at the age of 16 and was active in this profession for over 50 years. She delivered at least 1,000 babies, and received an award from President Truman in recognition for her work.

She delivered babies in canneries, fish camps, and other remote communities. The weather in Southeast Alaska often renders travel unreliable, but even moreso in Territorial days through the late 1950's transportation was irregular and difficult, and often by mail boat or fishing boat. She was a skilled midwife working under adverse conditions. When her great grandson was being born breech birth, she managed to turn the baby around for normal delivery. Many members of her immediate and extended family, as well as children of friends and the community at large were helped into the world by Susie.

Many of her years as a wife and widow were spent in extended family situations. Susie lived for many years with her daughter and son-in-law Mary and Nick Pelayo, who were well known chefs and restaurant operators; it was in this house that most of the fieldwork with Susie was conducted. She also lived with her granddaughter Betty George and her family. She moved to the Pioneer Home in 1975, where she died on November 3, 1980, at the age of 90.

Although she became physically impaired in

the last years of her life, she remained
mentally alert to the end, and was able to
describe her sense of impending death in
powerful and poetic images as a rising tide
gently lapping at her feet.

   She was preceded in death by her children
Betty Howard, Louise Howard, Dora Nelson, Eli
Howard, and Mary Pelayo, but was survived by
her children Pauline Poquiz and Joseph Howard
of Sitka, and Lillian Bombard of Worcester,
Mass. She is also survived by 32 grandchildren,
61 great grandchildren, 32 great-great
grandchildren, and many nieces and nephews.

   The editors thank Ms. Esther Clark and
the children and grandchildren of Susie James,
especially Patricia Pelayo Helle, for their
help in researching this biography.

Susie James, Robert Zuboff, and Nora Marks
Dauenhauer in Sitka, August 1973. Photo by R.
Dauenhauer

Andrew P. Johnson / Ixt'ik' Eesh
(May 31, 1898 – January 8, 1986)
Kiks.ádi; Kaagwaantaan yádi

A. P. (Andrew Peter) Johnson, a prominent
member of the Kiks.ádi clan and a child of the
Kaagwaantaan clan, was one of Alaska's most
distinguished Native scholars. He served his
people with faithful dedication for more than
half a century.

Andrew P. Johnson was born in Sitka, Alaska
on May 31, 1898. He was born into the Kiks.ádi
clan of the Raven moiety, the son of Peter and
Bessie Johnson. His ancestors have been traced
back to before the Russian occupation of Sitka.
Raised as a traditional Tlingit, he was
educated in the old ways. He received
instruction in clan history from many of his
distinguished forebears.

As a boy of thirteen, Andrew lost his
father, an uncle, and two cousins who drowned
at sea while hunting fur seals. Not many months
after, his mother died also. His grandparents
were gone. He was all alone.

He was placed in the Russian Orphanage for a
short time because he had no place to go. When
he was about fourteen years of age, Andrew came
to Sheldon Jackson School. For many years this
was the only home that the orphaned boy knew.

When he walked into the superintendent's

A. P. Johnson at the Sheldon Jackson College
Museum, Sitka, September 1983, demonstrating
replicas of traditional Tlingit tools and
weapons that he researched and made. He is
wearing a frog shirt of red felt with
predominantly green beadwork. Photo by R.
Dauenhauer

office, the superintendent asked what he
wanted. Andrew replied, "An education!" (His
father had served in the United States Navy so
the boy could speak English.)

The superintendent said, "No Room! Go home
to your parents."

Andrew replied, "What home? What parents?"

"What grade are you in?" asked the
superintendent.

"I am not in any grade," Andrew answered.

The superintendent asked Andrew to wait in
his office. He left and returned a short while
later. "Come with me," he said to Andrew.

At this point Andrew was placed in Fraser
Dormitory with the small boys. He had his
first class around the middle of February,
placed with small children. During class the
teacher pointed to the picture of a dog and
asked, "What is this?" Andrew answered, "A
dog." (Although he could not read, he could
speak English.) Because he was taller than
other members of the class, the students
laughed and humiliated him when he was asked
to stand up.

Andrew used every available moment to study
on his own. At the end of each school year he
would spend the summer fishing, but before he
left on the boat, he would demand the next
year's books and study while aboard the fishing
vessel.

Andrew advanced through the eighth grade in
four-and-one-half years. During this period,
the school needed a shop teacher and asked
Andrew to teach. He taught and earned tuition,
room and board. He later became assistant boys'
advisor and while still a student was called,
"Mr. Johnson."

Andrew was the valedictorian of the first
Sheldon Jackson High School graduating class in
the spring of 1921. He attended Park College in
Missouri for two years, 1921 to 1923. Under the
auspices of the Presbyterian Church, he studied
for the ministry and was ordained as a field

evangelist by the Presbytery of Northern
Arizona. He worked on the Navajo Reservation as
an evangelist from 1925 to 1936. For his work
in this capacity, he received the gift of an
automobile but never *really* received it. It
was used by other mission personnel. He
received $35 a month clear for his work.

While Andrew was in attendance at Park
College, he became very ill and spent two-and-
one-half months in Kansas City hospital, with
severe chest pains. He was advised by his
physicians to move to a warmer climate. During
this time, Johnson recalls he was Presbyterian
but not a Christian. He classified the Bible
along with the great mythologies of the world.
While in the hospital he had heard the surgeon
pray. . . asking God to direct his hand and the
work he would do.

Andrew says he accepted the Lord many years
ago, when a friend visited him in his room in
Albuquerque, New Mexico, and talked to him
about salvation. He took a long walk out in
the desert and sat down. While he was out
there, he came face to face with eternity, and
for the first time prayed, "My Lord, My god, I
have accepted you as my own personal Savior.
If you will add a few more days to my life, I
will not be ashamed to testify."

Andrew says of his ordination as a field
evangelist, "I was working in a Catholic
field, I was working for God, not preaching
denominationalism. My message to the people was
that Christ died for them."

On June 1, 1925, Andrew married Rose
Peshlakai. Her father was one of the first
head chiefs of the Navajos, and one of the
first to do metal silver work with the Navajo
people.

Three sons were born to Andrew and Rose:
Elliott Peter, Steve Peshlakai, and Sterling
Philip. The Johnson family eventually grew to
include three daughters-in-law, four
grandchildren and five great grandchildren.

Andrew worked in the United States Civil
Service for thirty-two years. He went to Fort
Wingate to work with the Bureau of Indian
Affairs as head of the leather craft department
(1936-1947).

Then after twenty-six years outside, he had
the opportunity to return to Alaska, to work at
Mt. Edgecumbe High School, across the channel
from his native home of Sitka. He and Mrs.
Johnson talked it over and prayed about the
situation. Mrs. Johnson concluded: "I know what
kind of man you are...you will never be happy
making a lot of money...I can always patch the
children's clothes."

In 1947 the Johnsons returned to Alaska, and
Andrew worked in the crafts department at Mt.
Edgecumbe High School from 1947 to 1968. Upon
his retirement he was given the Master Teacher
Award and a medal for commendable service by
the Department of the Interior. In making the
presentation, Charles Richmond, the Area
Director for the Bureau of Indian Affairs
wrote:

> Mr. Johnson has been an
> inspiration to all the Native boys
> over the years of his faithful
> service. He has been a hard working,
> sincere employee who has given
> unselfishly of his time and talents
> to better his contributions to the
> education and knowledge of his
> students, and to help the people of
> his race to live better and more
> satisfying lives. In recognition of
> this service and for his
> contributions to the educational
> program of the Bureau of Indian
> Affairs, Mr. Johnson is granted the
> commendable Service Award of the
> Department of the Interior.

Andrew Johnson served his people as

minister, teacher, and officer in Native
organizations. He served as President of the
Sitka Alaska Native Brotherhood, Grand Vice
President of the Grand Camp ANB, President of
the Tlingit-Haida Association, and member of
the Tlingit-Haida Central Council.

From 1968 to 1971, he was director of the
Alaska Native Brotherhood Center at the
Visitor's Center. He was on the staff of
Sheldon Jackson College from 1968. For two
years, 1971 to 1973, he worked at Sheldon
Jackson under a grant from the Danforth
Foundation to develop a set of cassette tapes
on Tlingit culture and a program to teach the
Tlingit language. He taught courses in Tlingit
language and culture at the College, and was
involved from the very beginning with the
Tlingit Language Workshops held annually on
the Sheldon Jackson Campus in the early
1970's.

In 1976 he was commissioned by the Sheldon
Jackson Museum to prepare exhibits of replicas
of early Tlingit weapons as part of the
museum's Bicentennial display.

As a member of the Kiks.ádi clan he was an
expert in Tlingit tribal songs, dances and
customs, and skilled teacher. In addition to
his work with religious activites, he served as
interpreter, spokesman, and narrator for his
people.

Andrew Johnson was well qualified as a
scholar in both the traditional Tlingit sense
and the western academic sense. He was a
master teacher and a master craftsman. He had
to his credit many drawings, works in silver
and gold jewelry, and many works in metal,
such as the tináa at the Sitka Visitor Center,
and the medallion designed for the golden
anniversary of the Alaska Native Brotherhood.

For many years he conducted morning
devotions over a local radio station broadcast
to neighboring villages. He also translated the
Bible into Tlingit on a series of tapes to be

shared with the people in the villages. Mr.
Johnson was gifted with the ability to stand
with an English Bible in his hand, and compose
oral translations of scripture into eloquent
and articulate Tlingit.

In addition, he taped the history of the
Tlingit people on both audio and video tape.
Notable is the legend of the Cannibal Giant,
now available from Tlantech Ltd., a family
corporation named after Mr. Johnson's maternal
uncle (L.aanteech; see the text, lines 11-13.)

In May 1971, Sheldon Jackson College honored
Andrew Johnson with a certificate in
commemoration of the fiftieth anniversary of
the graduation class of 1921. He received many
other awards during his lifetime, including the
Christian Citizenship Award from Sheldon
Jackson College (May 11, 1979), the Master
Teacher Award, and a Commendable Service
Award. He was listed in the 1986 *Who's Who in
the West*.

A. P. Johnson had many students during his
lifetime. He was not an "easy" teacher. He
was a generous, but exacting mentor to the
younger generations. Perhaps the teaching he
repeated most often was his insistance on three
elements as the basis of understanding and
working within traditional Tlingit culture:
belief in God and respect for spiritual things;
understanding of the Tlingit clan system
(social structure); ability to appreciate and
use diplomacy and protocol.

Most students recall his mixture of
austerity and humor. The austerity was
imposing, sometimes temperamental; the humor
was most often understated and ironic, perhaps
best described as sardonic. At any gathering
of his former students, people enjoy recalling
the memories of the "one liners" or "put-downs"
with which the teacher often brought his
message home, sometimes in reponse to a
student's lack of knowledge, but most often in
response to a student's lack of judgement, or

protocol. Here is an example told by one
former student now a prominent figure in
corporate politics:

One day in shop, a student, having
reassembled an engine, had one piece left
over. Running to his teacher, he excitedly
asked, "Mr. Johnson, Mr. Johnson! What should
I do with this." To which A. P. Johnson
calmly replied, "Oh, I don't know. Just hang
it on the motor somewhere."

As in much traditional teaching, the
instruction here was not technical information
about the location of an extra part, it was
about something else.

The Johnson's marriage of 55 years ended
with the death of Rose Edith Johnson on
December 25, 1980. On February 20, 1982 A. P.
Johnson married Etta P. Dalton.

As his own end drew near, he prepared for
death with the dignity of a traditional elder.
In his last days he sang for his assembled
family one of the spiritual songs he called the
"National Anthem" of his clan and house group.
He then retired to his bed, where he passed
away on Wednesday, January 8, 1986, at the age
of 87.

This biographical sketch is based on the
biography of A. P. Johnson entitled *A Master:
In Service to the Master: The Story of Andrew
Peter Johnson* written by Evelyn Bonner,
Director of Library Services, Sheldon Jackson
College, for the occasion of Mr. Johnson's being
awarded the Christian Citizenship Award, May
11, 1979; on information contained in the
obituary for A. P. Johnson written by his son,
Steve Johnson, and published in the *Daily
Sitka Sentinal*, Friday, January 10, 1986;
and on additional personal information supplied
by Steve Johnson. The editors thank Ms. Bonner
and Mr. Johnson for their help and contributions.

Frank G. Johnson / Taakw K'wát'i
(Dec. 15, 1894 - May 2, 1982)
Su_ktineidí; Shangukeidí yádi

The long and active life of Frank Johnson
presents a cultural biography of one of the
prime movers in the social and intellectual
history of Tlingit people in the twentieth
century. His life embraced a wide range of
activities: fisherman, educator, mechanic,
labor organizer, cultural leader, statesman,
and writer.

Frank Glonnee Johnson was born December 15,
1894, in a camp about 40 miles south of Kake.
His Tlingit name was Taakw K'wát'i, meaning
"Winter Egg" and referring to the winter
nesting season of ravens. He was Raven moiety,
of the Su_ktineidí clan, and child of
Shangukeidí.

The family lived and worked in Shakan, which
had a sawmill and a box factory. At the age of
12, Frank worked 10 hours a day in the box
factory, earning 5 cents an hour. At that
time, women earned a dollar and a half a day
for sliming, and the going wages for men were
three dollars a day.

Frank attended Sheldon Jackson Training
School in Sitka, and Chemawa Indian School in
Salem, Oregon. He graduated from Salem High

School in 1917.   In 1927 he received his
Bachelor of Science degree from the University
of Oregon.
    Back in Alaska, he became active in the
Alaska Native Brotherhood, establishing a
lifelong record of service. He served as
Grand Secretary, Vice President, and in 1931
was named Grand President. At the time of his
death he was past Grand President Emeritus of
ANB. He was also active in Tlingit and Haida
Central Council.

Frank Johnson on the Sheldon Jackson
College Campus, Sitka, June 1972,
during the second Tlingit Language
Workshop, at the time of his recording
of "Strong Man." Photo by R. Dauenhauer

    For many years Frank Johnson alternated
between the sea and the school house. He
taught and fished in Kake and Klawock. He was
partners with his brother in a seine boat.
Frank recalled, "The best fishing year we had

in our boat the *Helen J.* was her first year out, in 1917, when we came in third for the season with 225,000 fish. The high boat had 250,000."

Frank taught school for several years in Kake. He is warmly and enthusiastically remembered by his students. Gordon Jackson recalls, "He was my 5th grade teacher." Gordon described how "liberal" and humane Frank was because he taught Tlingit traditions in school, much to the pride and delight of the youngsters--but often to the consternation of the parent generation who shared with non-Native educators of that era an insistance on "English only" and total exclusion of Tlingit culture from the schools. "The kids loved him," Gordon recalls. "We used to row for Frank Johnson," he said, describing how the 5th graders would row their boats all over the area, catching fish to fill their favorite teacher's smokehouse.

Frank was active in the organization of unions for cannery workers and gillnetters. He served as Secretary-Treasurer of the Alaska Purse Seiners Union and Alaska Marine Workers Union. He was instrumental in the passage of the Alaska Native Claims Settlement Act of 1971. He lobbied for ANCSA, using his own money.

In 1947 Frank Johnson was elected to the Territorial House of Representatives on the Republican ticket. He served in the legislature for 10 years, during which time he was sent to Washington, DC to attend hearings. He was named chairman of the Ways and Means Committee for the Territory, and is listed in *Who's Who in Alaska Politics.* When he retired from politics, he returned to teaching and fishing. He moved to Ketchikan in 1970.

During the last years of his life, Frank was actively involved with the Indian Education Program of the Ketchikan Indian Corporation.

From 1976–1978 he wrote down many personal remembrances of early Tlingit lifestyle. He was also active in Tlingit literacy activities, and attended Tlingit language workshops at Sheldon Jackson College in the early 1970's. It was during such a workshop in June 1972 that he worked with Nora Dauenhauer to record his narration of the "Strong Man," which was transcribed by Nora Dauenhauer in Frank's Southern Tlingit dialect, and published by Tlingit Readers, Inc. in March 1973. This book inaugurated a new series of traditional Tlingit texts by various tradition bearers.

Frank G. Johnson died in Ketchikan on May 2, 1982, at the age of 87, and is buried at Bayview Cemetery. He was married three times. Though he had no children of his own, he is survived by many nieces and nephews, including Ed Thomas and Stella Martin.

This biography is based on materials researched by the Indian Education Program of the Ketchikan Indian Corporation, to whom the editors express their gratitude.

Willie Marks / Kéet Yaanaayí
(July 4, 1902 – August 7, 1981)
Chookaneidí; Lukaax̱.ádi yádi

Willie Marks, Juneau, May 1976,
on his 50th wedding anniversary.
Photo by R. Dauenhauer

Willie Marks came into the world at Marks
Trail on Douglas Island across from Juneau on
July 4, 1902, to the accompaniment of fireworks
display. His Tlingit names were Kéet Yanaayí,
Tl'óon, Yaduxwéi, and Wáank'. He was of the
Eagle moiety and the Chookaneidí clan. He was
the survivor of two houses, the Brown Bear Den
and Brown Bear House of Hoonah. His father
Jakwteen was Lukaax̱.ádi from Yandeist'akyé in
Chilkat. His mother's name was Tl'óon Tláa, a
Chookan sháa from Hoonah. He was the youngest
of six children.

Willie was baptized Russian Orthodox early
in his life. His mother, father, three
brothers and one sister were also communicants
of the Russian Orthodox Church. Before the
Juneau Douglas Bridge was built they would
cross the Gastineau Channel to Juneau by row
boat to St. Nicholas Church on Sundays.

When he was seventeen he and his brother
Peter signed up to go to Chemawa Indian School
in Portland, Oregon. He recalled the food as
being terrible, mostly potatoes, and not
enough. The boys would steal potatoes, sneak
them raw into bed at night, and slip them from
bunk to bunk for boys who didn't have any.
They got so hungry for boiled salmon that,
when they talked about it, they would imitate
the sounds of the boiling pot. He also told
stories of extreme punishment of students for
speaking their native languages.

After an unhappy period at this school
Willie and Peter ran away and found their way
to a coastal Indian village where the Indians
helped them. They sent home for help. His
mother and father sent their fare to come home
through the law enforcement which was the
Federal law at the time. When asked for their
identification they had none except their names
which were monogrammed inside their suit coats.
They used these to prove they were Willie Marks
and Peter Marks. They got back home this way.
They were lucky to reach home, because other

The old smoke house at Marks Trail, on Douglas
Island, May 1977, Nora Marks Dauenhauer
emerging. The photograph is representative of
much of Tlingit traditional village life style
in the contemporary world. Note the TV
antenna, skiffs, and driftwood. Named for the
logging trail Willie's father, Jim Nagatáak'w
made and used in the late 19th century, this
has been the home of the Marks family for five
generations. The stories by Willie Marks were
recorded in the house at the right. Houses of
the extended family in the background. Photo by
R. Dauenhauer

students who ran away from the school were
never heard of again.

From the time he was born, Willie and his
family lived a subsistence lifestyle, following
the seasons of the resources. The family
maintained conservative traditions at a time
when traditional ways of living were
discouraged by missionaries and government
institutions. They wintered on the outer coast
past Cape Spencer at Lituya Bay, Dixon Harbor,
or Graves Harbor, where they built permanent
tent sites. In some seasons and places, the
boats would be run up on the beach on an
exceptionally high tide, and propped up for the
winter. At other times they would stay at
anchor.

Willie and his family built smoke houses at
Idaho Inlet, Elfin Cove, and Swanson Harbor for
putting up fish from various rivers in the
areas. King salmon was salted for winter use.

As a young man, Willie continued this
tradition with his own family until the
outbreak of World War II. The extended family
consisted of three families and their boats:
Willie and his family on the *New Anny;* his
brother Jim Marks and his family on the
Kingfisher and later the *Tennessee;* and his
brother John Marks and his family on the
Bernice. Willie's family consisted of him, his
wife Emma, his father Jim Naṉatáak'w, his
mother Eliza Marks, his older sister Anny
Marks, and the oldest of the children--Nora,
Alex, Raymond, Peter, and Katherine.

The Jim Marks family consisted of Jim Marks,
his wife Jenny Marks, and the children Austin
Hammond and Horace Marks. The John Marks
family consisted of John and Mary Marks and
their daughter Betty Govina.

The site was a small "tent city" with three
or four living tents, a carpentry shop, and
even a sauna. The older children of the family
recall celebrating Russian Christmas with
treats of carefully preserved apples (by

Anny Marks (sister of Willie) and Emma Marks
skinning seals on the back deck of the *New Anny*
at Glacier Bay, 1943 or 1944. Photo courtesy
of Emma Marks

Christmas well frozen) and by carolling from
tent to tent, and with candy canes that Aunty
Anny had taken along and saved for the
children.

When World War II prevented the family from
going out to the Cape Fairweather area, they
began going to such places as Sumdum Bay,
Snettisham and Tracy Arm.

Such a life always taxed the imagination and
survival skills of the family. One winter
when they were leaving to return to Juneau,
the manifold of the engine cracked from icy
slush pumped up into it, but Willie mananged
to bring the family and boat back with a home-
made "patch-job" weld. One of the children
recalls, "Our work day consisted of just staying
alive."

Not everybody stayed alive. The baby
Katherine died of whooping cough, and Willie's
father died of old age. When Willie's father
died on the outer coast, the family carried the
body back to Hoonah, where he is buried under
the little grave house in the small cemetery
near the ferry terminal. Willie cared for his
mother until she died at Marks Trail in Juneau
in the 1940's; she is buried beside her husband
in Hoonah. He also cared for his sister Anny
Marks, one of the major story tellers and
tradition bearers in the family, until her
death; she is buried in Evergreen Cemetery in
Juneau. The family held feasts in memory of
their deceased relatives, according to Tlingit
tradition.

Willie is remembered by his sons and others
as an excellent hunter. He loved to hunt deer,
seal, bear and mountain goat. Most of the
winters they lived out in camps he supplied the
family with fresh meat: deer and mountain goat
in the fall, seal in the winter and bear in the
spring. Periodically he killed sea lion for
food. In the spring they picked seaweed and
seagull eggs.

He was also, of course, a fisherman. Most

The *New Anny* at Glacier Bay, crew rowing ashore for
subsistence gathering, May 1961. One Hoonah elder
commented, "Glacier Bay was our refrigerator."
Photo by Alex Marks

of the fish consumed at the family dinner table were what Willie caught in the winter. They knew of places where they could fish for king salmon in the winter.

Willie was a fisherman all of his life. He purse seined on the *Anny* which was his mother and father's first seine boat. While his older brother Jim skippered the *New Anny* before he acquired his own fishing boat, Willie was a crew member and engineer of the *Anny.* When his father sold the *Anny* they got the boat *New Anny* which his brother Jim captained and Willie engineered.

While his mother and father were still alive they fished for a cannery in Petersburg, and later located to Port Althorp near Elfin Cove until a fire at Port Althorp destroyed the main cannery buildings. They then relocated to Icy Straits Salmon Packing Co. where he seined for the company during World War II. He later began fishing for Excursion Inlet Packing Co. Around the later 30's he and his older brother put a hook-off at North Pass near Inian Islands which they both used to fish from when they seined. This was near the site where Willie's grandmother, the mother of Tl'óon Tláa, capsized and drowned on a neigoon berry picking excursion.

Willie fished with his brother Jimmy on the *New Anny* until Jimmy acquired his own seine boat, at which time Willie became the skipper of the *New Anny.* Willie skippered the *New Anny* while he seined for Icy Strait Salmon Packing Co. and later Excursion Inlet Packing Co.

He did halibut fishing in the spring and sold his catch for many years at the Juneau Cold Storage. In the summer he converted his boat for seining. After seining he converted for trolling. He power trolled at Cape Cross, Soapstone Harbor, Elfin Cove and many other places in the Icy Strait area. As a young man he also hand trolled around Sitka, Biorka

Loading halibut into the hatch of *New Anny,*
September 1963. Willie Marks operates the
winch, his son Paul at the right. Photo by
Alex Marks

Island, and Icy Strait. While Willie trolled on
the New Anny with his wife and younger
children, the rest of the family--his mother,
sister, daughter, and two sons--hand-trolled
in their own rowboats and dinghies.

Willie was a boat builder. The hull of the
second boat by the name of *New Anny* was built
in Juneau in 1939. Willie finished the deck,
cabin and all the finishing work. In his
lifetime he rebuilt the *North Pass* and
Tennessee, both his brother Jim's boats. As
a young man he built himself a boat by the name
of *Nora* which he eventually sold to a man in
Elfin Cove. Willie had hunted and trolled in
it until the family grew too large for it.
Being small, it could go places the New Anny
couldn't. He built and rebuilt numerous row
boats for members of his family. He began
building another boat toward the end of his
life, but didn't finish it due to ill health.

Willie Marks was very eclectic. For
example, he was one of the first fishermen to
install a machine in his power skiff for
seining, converting from hand power. Although
he was raised on Tlingit foods and ate them all
his life, he also loved Chinese food, which he
learned to eat in cannery oriental kitchens.
He enjoyed eating with chopsticks. As a young
man Willie learned how to roller skate and ice
skate. He went over to the city of Douglas to
roller skate at the roller rink.

He also learned to play steel guitar from a
Hawaiian by the name of Sam Stone who came and
lived in Juneau. Each time Willie and his
family came to Juneau, Willie and his brother
Peter spent all of their free time learning how
to play steel guitar from Sam. Willie and his
nephews David Williams and Willie Williams
played guitars every chance they had. They
attracted a lot of attention each time they
tied up at Hoonah, Elfin Cove or Juneau when
they played guitar. Willie learned to dance
Hawaiian Hula which he taught to his sister

The *New Anny,* Willie Marks' fishing boat at
Harris Harbor, Juneau, 1972, rigged for halibut
fishing with bouys, chute for lines at stern.
Willie's parents purchased the hull and Willie
finished building the boat. This photo also
captures some of the flavor of Southeast Alaska
with its sea-oriented towns and villages on the
shorelines of fiords, characterized by small
boat harbors. Photo by R. Dauenhauer

Anny and niece Mary Johnson so they could
perform during the happy part of a memorial
feast given in Hoonah for his brother Peter
Marks, because in his life Peter loved
Hawaiian music so very much.

Willie was trained from childhood to be a
ceremonial leader and shakee.át dancer. In
almost all of the memorial feasts hosted by his
family an ermine headdress was put on him to
dance behind a blanket the dance called Yeik
utee. This type of dance was done prior to the
distribution of the money brought out in the
feast.

Willie Marks carving a dance staff in
the living room of his house at Marks
Trail, Juneau, 1969 or 1970. Photo by
Alex Marks, courtesy of Le Florendo

Willie was a ceremonial leader of the Brown
Bear House and the Brown Bear Nest House of the
Hoonah Chookaneidí. His oldest brother
inherited the position of "Lingít tlein" or
"hít s'aatí" of Brown Bear House. During Jim
Marks' leadership, Willie assisted him in the
ceremonies he gave. In 1968 when Jim Marks
died, Willie inherited his brother's position
as house leader. Willie gave the memorial
feast for Jim Marks in Hoonah in October 1968,
at which time he became steward for the clan
at.óow.

Willie was a well known carver. He came
from a long line of carvers; his namesakes were
carvers in the Snail House and Brown Bear Den
House. He carved many totem poles for tourist
shops. He carved many masks and totem poles
for the Anac Cache based in Juneau, Alaska. He
was commissioned to carve traditional pieces
Shaatukwáan Keidlí and Shaatukwáan Sháawu or
better known as Tsalxaan s'áaxw for the
T'akdeintaan of Hoonah. He also made pieces
for Austin Hammond, Lillian Hammond, Nora
Dauenhauer, Rosita Worl, Ethel Montgomery, and
many others.

He taught his nephews David Williams,
Willie Williams, and Horace Marks to carve, as
well as all eight of his sons, five of whom are
alive and still carving and doing silver
smithing or design: Peter, Jim, John, Leo, and
Paul.

Willie was a member of the Alaska Native
Brotherhood, and with his brother Jim Marks
was involved in fund raising for the old ANB
hall in Juneau. He and Jim Marks brought out
their at.óow and then brought out money in
memory of the former owners. This was
contributed as the seed money in the building
account.

During the early years of the Juneau Indian
Studies program, Willie taught carving to the
elementary grades, and was a story teller.
While he was still teaching, the Postmaster

General of the United States visited Juneau,
and while he was being officially received in
Juneau, Willie adopted him into his clan with
the name of Ch'eetk'. The Postmaster General
gave him a special set of commemorative stamps.

Willie travelled widely in his retirement
years, invited as a carver and dancer with the
Marks Trail Dancers and Geisan Dancers of
Haines to places as distant from Juneau as the
Boston Fine Arts Museum and Harvard
University. At Salem he gave considerable
thought and a few spoken words to the treatment
of witches and Native Americans by the Founding
Fathers. At Salem he also commmented, "Is that
the Atlantic Ocean? Holy smokes! So this is
Salem, Massachussetts. I was in Salem, Oregon
50 years ago." At Salem Willie also visited
Plymoth Rock, which he regarded with
considerable displeasure, no doubt because he
had spent much of his life trying to protect
the family land from encroachment by the
growing White population of Juneau.

To Willie as the most educated of the
children fell the task of dealing with new laws
alien to Tlingit tradition. He was able to
protect some of the land his father Jim
Naǥataak'w had used and occupied on Douglas
Island. Of the original Marks Trail, named for
the logging trail up the mountain, 2.61 acres
were salvaged, after mining and homestead
claims took the rest.

Unfortunately, the Indian Allotment
Legislation providing for Indian title to land
occupied and in use by Native Americans, was
passed long after the legislation which allowed
White newcomers to Alaska to gain title to land
through mining or homestead claims, despite
Native use and occupancy, and in violation of
the terms of the Treaty of Purchase from
Russia.

Willie married Emma Frances of Yakutat in
1926 in the Juneau court house. Their witness
was a Tlingit man by the name of Hopkins. Emma

Willie Marks at Marks Trail, 1950's, posing
with a log for a totem carving commissioned by
a Seattle store. Photo courtesy of Emma Marks

was 16 years old at the time, and Willie 24.
She was the step daughter of Willie's maternal
uncle. The couple celebrated their Golden
Anniversary in Juneau in 1976, with all eight
living children present, grandchildren,
relatives and friends. The couple raised a
family of 16 children during their marriage of
56 years, which ended with the death of Willie
on August 7, 1981. He is survived by his wife
Emma, and 8 of their 16 children. He is buried
in the Alaska Memorial Park in Juneau.

Willie and Emma Marks, Juneau, May 1976, at
their 50th wedding anniversary. Photo by
Richard Dauenhauer

Amy Marvin / K̲ooteen
Born: May 16, 1912
Chookan sháa; T'ak̲deintaan yádi

Amy Marvin was born on May 16, 1912 at the
place on Icy Strait called "Ducks' Point" in
Tlingit. Her given name in Tlingit is K̲ooteen.
She was born into the Eagle moiety and Chookaneidí clan. Her mother was living on their
traditionally owned land in the Ducks' Point
area, and her father was helping build the
first company owned building at the Icy Straits
Salmon Cannery when she was born.

Her mother's name was Sx̲einda.át. Her
father's name was Shx̲'éik'--Pete Fawcett in
English. He was of the Yéilkudei Hít (Raven
Nest House) of the T'ak̲deintaan clan of Hoonah,
making Amy T'ak̲deintaan yádi. Amy's mother
married twice. Her first husband was G̲anéil,
and her second husband Shx̲'éik'. Amy is the
youngest of 14 children of the two marriages.

Amy is of the Naanaa Hít, the Upper Inlet
House, one of the houses in Hoonah named for
the house in the Glacier Bay History. Amy
Marvin is a direct descendant of Kaasteen and
Shaawatséek'.

Amy grew up in Hoonah and has spent most of
her life in the village. She remembers the old
Hoonah where she was raised, and when some of

the churches and missionaries began to
undermine the traditional culture by teaching
that the old Tlingit beliefs were not good.

As a traditionally raised Tlingit, Amy
Marvin shares the feeling of most of her
generation that the land is the true spiritual
and economic base of the Tlingit people, not
cash and profit. As her recounting of the
Glacier Bay History illustrates, the land is
the spiritual history of the people, and the
history is the land. It both angers and
saddens Amy to witness the continuing loss of
lands, and the unwillingness or ineffectiveness
of the various agencies, institutions, and
corporations to help prevent the loss.

Amy Marvin at the Memorial Feast for Willie Marks,
Hoonah, October 1981. She is drumming on the Brown
Bear Drum, an at.óow of the Brown Bear House. The
Drum was commissioned by Jim Marks. After his death
it passed to the stewardship of Willie Marks, and
since Willie's death is in the stewardship of Mary
Johnson. Photo by R. Dauenhauer

For example, Amy talked about their clan
owned land at one of the cannery sites. She
said a superintendent once asked if he could
move the graves of her family's relatives so
that the cannery could build houses on the
land. They promised to make it nice, so the
family would feel good about it. "'No!' said
my father. 'We've already lost too much
there. I don't want you to move them.'"

Amy explains how another superintendent
recently put his survey markers on Amy's
mother's land. She asks, "Why did he do that?
The land is not his. It's not his business.
He hasn't bought it. If only someone could
help us prove the land is ours and not his."

Another example is the lake behind one of
the canneries. The story of this lake records
the history of how a Chookaneidí shaman named
Shaxóo caught a halibut for his curious father.
Amy comments, "It would be good if the
Corporation would help us reclaim it again."
Such experiences are not unique to Amy Marvin
and her people, but are common throughout
Southeast Alaska. As shown in the Glacier Bay
History, the land is important not only
because the ancestors of the people used it,
but because they shed their blood on it and
for it.

Amy has been active all her life. She
began cannery work in Port Althorp in 1924,
when she was 12 years old. She was so young
she didn't even know how much they paid her.
She later worked at P.A.F. cannery, up the bay
from Excursion Inlet, and after that at
Excursion Inlet Packing. She worked for years
at the filler machine, and later at the patch
table. Amy is presently a senior companion to
the senior citizens who are shut in. She went
to school in Juneau to train for the job, and
visits her clients daily after lunching at the
Hoonah Senior Citizens' Center.

Amy is active in the Orthodox Church and
remembers when the Tlingit translations of

Orthodox prayers were being taught to the choir
at St. Nicholas Church in Hoonah. She said the
songs were introduced by a man named Yeika,
David Davis of Sitka. Amy is still part of
this choir, singing alto, and travelled to
Sitka with other members of the Hoonah choir in
1980 to join with the combined Orthodox choirs
of Southeast Alaska in recording liturgical
music in Tlingit.

Amy is one of the most talented tradition
bearers alive today. She learned to make
baskets when she was very young. While her
mother was working in the cannery, Amy would
get into her mother's nicest materials, take
the best grass, and play at weaving baskets.
She learned to do beadwork at the same time.

Amy is an excellent story teller among
her people. She is the family historian,
keeping the history, names, and music alive.
She is also noted as an orator, and has never
failed to give a speech in a feast.

She is also a song leader and a drummer. Amy
is a lead drummer in the Mt. Fairweather
Dancers in Hoonah. She has been asked to lead
in ceremonial dances in K̲oo.éex' (feasts) by
different clans of Hoonah. She knows the songs
of her clan, many of those of the other clans
of Hoonah and other communities in Southeast
Alaska. When asked how she learned to drum, she
answered, "When my father's feasts took place,
I listened for the dignified sections and I
lived by them."

Amy's eldest brother died early. Her
brother John Fawcett was the second oldest in
her family. John was her half-brother; after
his father died of a gunshot wound, his
maternal grandmother raised him. He was the
leader of the Hoonah Alaska Native Brotherhood
band. Amy's younger sister Mary is remembered
as having a lyric soprano voice and for her
singing in the Hoonah Orthodox Church.

Amy was married twice, first to Sam Knudson,
then to Harry Marvin. She has six children--

Tlingit Cannery workers, Hoonah, 1946. Photo
courtesy of Emma Marks

five boys and one girl. When asked how many
grandchildren she had, she slapped her hands
together and laughed, "Too many! And some are
still in the making!"

Tom Peters / Yeilnaawú
(July 1, 1892 – April 20, 1984)
Tuk.weidí; Yanyeidí yádi

Tom Peters was an inland Tlingit, with
relationships to the Pelly River Athapaskans.
The son of Sam and Mollie Peters, he was born
on July 1, 1892, at the head of the Taku River,
and lived most of his life in Teslin.

Tom Peters in Teslin, Yukon, August 1973 at the
time of his recording of Part Two of "The Woman
Who Married the Bear." Photo by R. Dauenhauer

His Tlingit name was Yeilnaawú, and he also
had a name from his grandfather's slave,
Koolch'ál'ee--his father's father's slave from
the Coast.

He was Raven moiety, of the Tuk.weidí clan,
an offshoot of the Deisheetaan. His mother's
name was Xwaansán, of the Tuk.weidí. Her
mother's name was La.oos (Tuk.weidí) and her
father's name was Sht'aawkéit (Yanyeidí).

His mother's older sister was named
Kaax'einshí. Although his maternal uncle had
two names, Yeildoogú and Sháanak'w, Tom had
only one maternal uncle, who was responsible
for his upbringing. His mother's family
consisted just of the three of them--Tom's
mother, his maternal aunt, and his maternal
uncle.

His father's names were Naagéi and Ichdaa.
He was of the T'aakú kwáan (Taku people) from
Atlin, and of the Yanyeidí clan, an offshoot of
the Dakl'aweidí, that used the bear as one of
its crests. Tom was too young to remember when
his father died, but he recalled "There used to
be many of my uncles on my father's side." His
father had both younger and older brothers. The
Tlingit name of Sam Peters' mother was
Shuwuteen; the Tlingit name of his father (Tom
Peters' paternal grandfather) is not available.

Tom worked as a trapper and fishing guide at
Teslin. He had contact with the White world
beginning mainly with the building of the
Alaska Highway during World War II. In 1951 he
worked with Catharine McClellan, and, among
other things, told a version of the "Woman Who
Married the Bear" that is analyzed in detail
in McClellan's monograph of 1970. (See notes
for more information on this.) In 1952 he also
guided McClellan on an archeological survey,
and taped more songs and stories.

As he grew older, Tom Peters became
increasingly interested in his group's ties to
the coastal Tlingit. He eventually became
head of the Tuk.weidí, inheriting Jake

Jackson's ceremonial dress.

As a tradition bearer he was very humble and quiet, and very knowledgeable. He enjoyed having his story read back to him, and others in Teslin (such as Virginia Smarch) enjoy telling the story of his experiencing the story read back to him.

Tom was married twice. The name of his first wife is not available at present; his second wife's name was Alice Sidney Peters, in Tlingit K̲aashdáx̲ Tláa, a woman of the Yanyeidí clan. Her mother was Marie Sidney, in Tlingit Skaaydu.oo, and her father was Edgar Sidney, in Tlingit Neildayéen. She died on August 20, 1970.

There are eight children: Mary ("Graffie"), Skaaydu.oo, married to Charlie Jule, Tsít'as, a Kaska man from Ross River; Florence, Wooshtudeidu.oo, married to Jack Smarch, Keix̲'anal.át of the Deisheetaan clan; Albert, At.shukáx̲, not married; Ida, Lugóon married to Ray Douville; Sadie, Kax̲duhoon, married to Harry Morris, Shk'inéil' of the Ishkeetaan (a house group of the Gaanax̲.ádi); Frank, Aasgán Eesh, not married; Theresa, K̲aaganéi, married to Tom Dixon, and John, Shgoonaak̲, married to Annie, K̲'ayaadéi, a woman of the Kook̲ Hit Taan, which Tom Peters identified as being one with the Gaanax̲.ádi.

(This Kook̲ Hit Taan, with the "second k" "back in the mouth" and spelled with the underline translates as "Pit House" and is different from the Sitka K̲ook Hit Taan with the FIRST K pronounced "back in the mouth" and underlined, which translates as "Box House" and is, for example, the house group of George Betts.)

Tom commented on the tape that there used to be many clan children. He was very proud of the size of the family, commenting that "My grandchildren are just as many as the dust-- how many there are of them."

When asked about the sad things in his life,

he said the worst experience was losing his
wife. "No matter what you do, you can't
forget the one you got good treatment from.
It's difficult."

Tom Peters lived a long and active life.
His relative, Elizabeth Nyman of Atlin, whose
maternal uncle was Tom Peters' father,
commented, "He walked straight and packed his
water two buckets at a time." Then suddenly,
he had a stroke, lingered a while in the
hospital, and died on April 20, 1984, about two
months short of his 92nd birthday.

The editors thank the Yukon Native Languages
Centre in Whitehorse for help in researching
the Tlingit personal and clan names in this
biographical sketch.

Charlie White / Yaaneekee
(August 15, 1880 - 1964)
L'uknax.ádi; Teikweidée Yádi

Charlie White was born at Situk near
Yakutat, Alaska on August 15, 1880. His Tlingit
names were Yaaneekee and X'ajawsaa Eesh. He
was Raven moiety and L'uknax.ádi from the Situk
river, and belonged to Diginaa Hít Taan house
group. His father, Gadaneik, was Teikweidée and
the chief of the Situk River. His mother was a
L'uknax sháa from Gus'éix in Aakwéi (between
Dry Bay and the Italio River.)
    Charlie White built the last L'uknax.ádi
Eech Hít in the old Village of Yakutat. He was
the city Marshall of Yakutat before WW II, and
during the war he served in the Home Guard.
    He was an active member of the Alaska Native
Brotherhood in Yakutat since it was established
there, serving as Sergeant at Arms during the
1931 convention in Yakutat, and for two years
after.
    He fished in the Johnson Slough and Anklin
River (Aan Tlein) as a commercial fisherman up
until his death at the age of 84. The Johnson
Slough was the traditional land of his
forefathers.
    Charlie never received a formal education,
but was traditionally raised and taught by his
uncles. In 1904 he was naa káani for the

Charlie White posing in traditional dress, Yakutat
1949. Notice the seal skin drying on the frame
(t'éesh.) Photo by Frederica de Laguna

Teikweidée at the Sitka Potlatch. He was a song leader with Olaf Abraham in Yakutat for many years, and their dance group later became the Mt. Saint Elias Dancers.

Charlie was married to Jenny White and they had two daughters, Ethel Henry and Maggie Francis. He is survived by four grandchildren and eleven great grandchildren.

--Biography researched and written
   by Fred White

Jennie White / Jeeník
Born: June 20,1903
Shanguka sháa; X'atka.aayí yádi

Jennie White was born in Dry Bay on June 20,
1903. Her Tlingit names are Jeeník,
Shtukáalgeis', Sx'andu.oo Tláa, and
Yaxyaakandusxút'. She is of the Eagle moiety,
the Shangukeidí clan, and the Thunderbird House
of Dry Bay. Her mother's name was Kaax'eiti.
She is X'atka.aayí yádi. Her father's name was
Geisteen, a X'atka.aayí from Lituya Bay. Her
father's English name was Lituya Bay George. He
used to walk the mail for the miners from
Lituya Bay to Yakutat before the whole family
moved to Dry Bay. She had three brothers and
three sisters. She is the last living historian
of the Shangukeidí from Dry Bay.

She started working at the cannery in Dry
Bay when she was very young, and remembers
working for thirty five cents a day. After
that, she did commercial fishing by setnet in
Yakutat from 1932 till 1966.

When she was sixteen she went to Sheldon
Jackson Vocational School for two years, but
finally left because of the conditions there,
one of which was being forbidden to speak her
own language, Tlingit.

She has been beading Tlingit dance regalia
all her life. She has also made sealskin
moccasins, beaded blankets and tunics. She is
also well known for her knitting. As one
grandchild put it, "Every christmas you were
sure to get a pair of knitted socks."

Jennie White, Juneau, September 1986.
Photo by M. Bryan Thompson

She was married to Charlie White, who died in 1964. She is now married to Frank Dick, Sr.

In her lifetime she raised many youngsters from Yakutat when they lost their families due to illness. The last person she raised was Fred White, whom she takes pride in today for speaking the Tlingit language fluently and working with it to pass it on to future generations.

--Biography researched and written by
Fred White

Robert Zuboff / Shaadaax'
(October 14, 1893 - April 19, 1974)
Kak'weidí; Dakl'aweidí yádi

Robert Zuboff was born on October 14, 1893
in Killisnoo, and lived there until the village
was destroyed by fire in June 1928, after which
he relocated in Angoon.

He was Raven of the Kak'weidí clan,
popularly called the Basket Bay People in
English, and child of Dakl'aweidí. His clan
house was Kaakáakw Hít, named for the arch in
Basket Bay--the arch of the natural grotto
described in his story. Upon the death of his
cousin Peter Dick (Kaatéenaa), Robert Zuboff
became the leader of the Kak'weidí.

As with many other Tlingit elders, he was
steeped in the history of his people, and the
two stories told by him in this volume are
directly linked to the history of his personal
name and of Basket Bay. Another of his favorite
stories, but not included here, is of the
person who raised the pet beaver that destroyed
the village of Basket Bay. (See Swanton 1909:
No. 68 and de Laguna 1960: 136-137 for more on
this.) The Beaver slapped its tail and turned
the village upside down. Typical of his
style, Bob Zuboff would comment on the story,
"That Beaver dropped the first atomic bomb!"

A commercial fisherman most of his economic

life, Robert Zuboff owned two boats.   The
first was named the *Louise*, and the second,
which he gave to his son when he retired, and
which he mentions in his story, was named
Guide.   He fished for New England Cannery.

He was active in community life, and was at
one time the mayor of Angoon.   At one time he
also owned a small share in the Hood Bay
Cannery.

Robert Zuboff was married twice.   His first
wife died in the late 1930's.   The couple had

Robert Zuboff, Angoon, July 1971 telling
"Mosquito." Photo by Duncan Fowler

three daughters and one son. Bob felt great
loss after the death of his wife, and
eventually married Tilly Wells of Sitka, who
died in the early 1970's.

As his wife Tilly developed arthritis and
became more invalid, Bob took care of her and
did much of the domestic work. He enjoyed
gardening and grew rhubarb in his yard and
jarred it. He loved to cook, especially what
his nephew Cyril George calls "real camp
style" and is remembered for his pies with
thick and tasty crusts. His more exotic
recipes include boiled halibut stomach (dip it
in boiling water, slice it and fry it) and a
combination of navy beans and salt-deer meat.

He was also quite a hunter, and taught his
nephews special techniques for removing deer
vertebrae to displace the weight and make the
deer easier to pack out of the woods.

Once, while guiding a man for trout fishing,
he had an encounter with a bear that left him
scarred for life. They were hiking to one of
the lakes near Angoon. Hearing a noise, Bob
turned, making a wisecrack to and about the
man he thought was behind him, but found
himself face to face with a charging brown
bear.

Bob had a lever action rifle, but no bullet
chambered. The charging bear bit the rifle.
Bob, pushing the bear away with the rifle,
pushed it into the bear's mouth up to the
stock, and his hand along with it. The bear
bit into his hand and the rifle stock, and
tossed him like a rag doll, beating him
between two trees on either side of the trail.

Finally, his hand tore free. He chambered a
round and fired. The shot entered the bear
through the shoulder and came out through the
hip. The bear turned and bit its own hip. Bob
chambered another round and took the clear head
shot now offered, killing the bear.

The encounter left him with scars on his
hands, arms, and body. His rifle bore the teeth

marks on the stock, and Bob would bring it out
and show it when he told the story.

Above all, Bob Zuboff is remembered as a
story teller. He loved to tell stories, and
was a fine oral stylist in English as well as
in Tlingit. His stories are characterized by
colorful language, action, and vivid dialog.
He was invited to different universities to
tell stories, but he especially loved children,
and in addition to story telling, he taught
many young people of Angoon the traditional
songs and dances, explaining also the history
and meaning of each. The group that he
instructed is still active in Angoon.

Not only was Robert Zuboff a story teller in
the tradition of a Tlingit elder, but he was
also a great humorist, and left a rich legacy
of jokes and anecdotes which continue to
circulate, and to which are added new stories
and memories about him. Many examples of this
type of Tlingit oral literature rely on puns in
Tlingit or English, or on the contrast of
different or inappropriate levels of style.

For example, when most of the fishing
industry was changing over to the new nylon
nets, he was reluctant to switch. When asked
why, Bob joked, "Nylon net always reminds me of
women's panties."

His nephew Cyril George tells this one about
him: many years ago, a new type of seiner,
very large, with deep, wide nets arrived in
Alaskan waters. They were outlawed in Alaska
after a year or so because they could clean
out an entire bay in one set. Because the net
was wound on a large drum, the boats were
called "drum seiners." When Cyril was a young
boy fishing with his father, one day on a
slack tide near Tenakee, young Cyril looked
out of the front hatch of his father's boat to
see his maternal uncle Bob Zuboff passing
slowly by on the *Guide.* On the front deck
were two "old timers", Tom Jimmy and Jim Fox,
singing traditional Tlingit songs, and

accompanying themselves on a Tlingit drum.
Young Cyril called to his father, "Hey, Dad,
there's a real drum seiner going by!"

Robert Zuboff spent much time with Constance
Naish and Gillian Story of the Summer Institute
of Linguistics / Wycliffe Bible Translators,
helping them in their study of Tlingit and in
their efforts at Bible translation. (See the
Introduction for more on this.) The
transcription by Naish and Story of Robert
Zuboff's Basket Bay History is submitted here
as an expression of their gratitude to him for
his contribution to the history of Tlingit
scholarship.

Despite the seriousness of the translation
work, and his dedication to it, Bob's humor,
joy of life, and love of language itself show
through in some of his anecdotes about the
project. Much of this humor, of course, is
untranslatable, but one example comes close.
The way Bob told it, they were working on the
marvellous passage in Matthew 14: 22-34 where
Jesus walks on water. Stylist that he was, Bob
in his telling of the story would capitalize
on the dramatic action of the passage--the
storm, the fear of the disciples, and the
approach of what they saw as a ghost walking
on the water. But at the critical moment, Peter
says, "Hey Man, is that you?"

Robert Zuboff was a life long member of the
Orthodox Church. He sang a powerful bass in the
choir and in later years was head of the
church committee for St. John the Baptist
Orthodox Church in Angoon. Although he was a
staunch Orthodox, he also enjoyed singing with
the Salvation Army, and could sing the
"choruses" in Tlingit by the hour. As a
secular musical activity, he played bass drum
in the town and Salvation Army Band. His
cousin Peter Dick was band leader.

Robert Zuboff died on Easter 1974--in
Orthodox tradition a wonderful day to die in
that one rises with Christ on His day of

resurrection, the day without night, the death
of death itself.

He was succeeded in his position as leader
of the Basket Bay people by his nephew Cyril
George, who is now the steward and custodian
of the clan at.óow, some of which is in his
personal possession in Juneau, and others in
the possession of clan members in Angoon.

The editors thank Cyril George and John
Lyman for their help in this biography.

Robert Zuboff and Susie James at the Sheldon
Jackson College Print Shop, Sitka, August
1973, watching the first edition of the
Tlingit language texts of their stories coming
off the press, 8 months before Zuboff's death.
Photo by R. Dauenhauer

REFERENCES

This bibliography lists the important references
mentioned in this book. No attempt is made at
a complete listing of works in anthropology,
folklore, or linguistics. The bibliographies
of the most recent works that are listed here
provide a good starting place for further study.

Bancroft, H. H. (1886) 1970. *History of Alaska
    1730-1885*. Hafner. Darien, CT.
Barbeau, M. 1964. *Totem Poles*. 2nd ed. National
    Museum of Canada. Ottawa.
Beekman, J., and John Callow. 1974. *Translating
    the Word of God*. Zondervan. Grand Rapids.
Boas, F. 1917. *Grammatical Notes on the Language
    of the Tlingit Indians*. University of
    Pennsylvania Museum. Philadelphia.
Boehm, W. D. 1975. *Glacier Bay*. Alaska Northwest
    Publishing Company. Anchorage.
Bohn, D. 1967. *Glacier Bay: The Land and the
    Silence*. Sierra Club. Ballantine Books.
    New York.
Dauenhauer, N., and R. Dauenhauer. 1976. *Beginning
    Tlingit*. Tlingit Readers, Inc. Distributed
    by Sealaska Heritage Foundation. Juneau.
_____. 1984. *Tlingit Spelling Book*. 3rd ed.
    Sealaska Heritage Foundation. Juneau.
_____. 1984b. Audio Casette Tape for *Tlingit*

Spelling Book. Sealaska Heritage Foundation. Juneau.

Dauenhauer, N., R. Dauenhauer, and G. Holthaus, eds. 1986. *Alaska Native Writers, Storytellers, and Orators*. Special issue of *Alaska Quarterly Review*. Vol. 4, Nos. 3 and 4 (Spring and Summer 1986). University of Alaska-Anchorage.

Dauenhauer, R. 1975. "Text and Context of Tlingit Oral Tradition." Ph.D. dissertation. Department of Comparative Literature. University of Wisconsin-Madison.

de Laguna, F. 1960. *The Story of a Tlingit Community*. Smithsonian Institution. Bureau of American Ethnology Bulletin 172. United States Government Printing Office. Washington, D.C.

_____. 1972. *Under Mount Saint Elias*. Smithsonian Contributions to Anthropology. Vol. 7. (In Three Parts.) Smithsonian Institution Press. Washington, D.C.

Emmons, G. 1907. *The Chilkat Blanket*. With notes on the blanket designs by Franz Boas. Memoirs of the American Museum of Natural History. Vol. 3, Part 4 (329-401). American Museum of Natural History. New York.

_____. 1911. "Native Account of the Meeting Between La Pérouse and the Tlingit." *American Anthropologist*. New Series. Vol. 13 (294-298).

Garfield, V., and L. Forrest. (1948) 1961. *The Wolf and the Raven*. Univ. of Washington Press. Seattle.

Hymes, D. 1981. *"In Vain I Tried to Tell You"*: *Essays in Native American Ethnopoetics*. Univ. of Pennsylvania Press. Philadelphia.

Kan, S. 1983. "Words That Heal the Soul: Analysis of the Tlingit Potlatch Oratory." *Arctic Anthropology*. Vol. 20, No. 2 (47-59).

_____. 1986. "The 19th-Century Tlingit Potlatch: A New Perspective." *American Ethnologist*. Vol. 13, No. 2 (May 1986) 191-212.

Kawagey, J. (Producer) 1981. *Haa Shagóon*. Film. 16mm. 29 min. Distributed by Chilkat Indian Association. Haines, AK. Also available in

VHS cassette from the Alaska State Film
Library, Juneau.

Keithahn, E. 1963. *Monuments in Cedar.* Superior
Publishing Company. Seattle.

Krause, A. (1885) 1956. *The Tlingit Indians.*
Trans. by Erna Gunther. Univ. of Washington
Press. Seattle.

Krauss, M. 1980. *Alaska Native Languages: Past,
Present, and Future.* Alaska Native Language
Center Research Papers, No. 4. Alaska Native
Language Center. Univ. of Alaska-Fairbanks.

Krauss, M. and M.J. McGary. 1980. *Alaska Native
Languages: A Bibliographical Catalogue. Part
One: Indian Languages.* Alaska Native Language
Center Research Papers, No. 3. Alaska Native
Language Center. Univ. of Alaska-Fairbanks.

Leer, J. ed. 1978. *Tongass Texts.* Alaska Native
Language Center. Univ. of Alaska-Fairbanks.

Li, Fang Kuei and Ronald Scollon. 1976. *Chipewyan
Texts.* Institute of History and Philology
Academia Sinica, Special Publications No. 71.
Nankang. Taipei. Taiwan.

McClellan, C. 1970. *The Girl Who Married the Bear:
A Masterpiece of Indian Oral Tradition.*
National Museums of Canada. National Musuem
of Man. Publications in Ethnology, No. 2.
Ottawa.

_____. 1975. *My Old People Say: An Ethnographic
Survey of Southern Yukon Territory.* National
Museums of Canada. National Museum of Man.
Publications in Ethnology, No. 6. Ottawa.

Maranda, E. 1973. "Five Interpretations of a Mel-
anesian Myth." *Journal of American Folklore.*
339: 3-13.

Nida, E. 1964. *Toward a Science of Translating.*
E. J. Brill. Leiden.

Olson, R. 1967. *Social Structure and Social Life
of the Tlingit in Alaska.* Univ. of California
Anthropological Records. Vol. 26. Univ. of
California Press. Berkeley.

Ostyn, C. (Producer) 1981. *Kaal.átk'.* Video tape.
Sitka Native Education Program. Sitka.

Shelikhov, G. (1791) 1981. *A Voyage to America*

1783-1786. Trans. by M. Ramsay. Ed. by R. Pierce. The Limestone Press. Kingston, Ont.

Sidney, A., K. Smith, and R. Dawson. 1977. *My Stories Are My Wealth.* Council for Yukon Indians. Whitehorse.

Story, G. and C. Naish. 1973. *Tlingit Verb Dictionary.* Alaska Native Language Center. University of Alaska-Fairbanks.

_____. 1976. *Tlingit Noun Dictionary.* 2nd. Ed. Revised and expanded by Henry Davis and Jeff Leer. Sheldon Jackson College. Sitka.

Swanton, J. (1908) 1970. *Social Conditions, Beliefs, and Linguistic Relationship of the Tlingit Indians.* Johnson Reprint Corporation. New York.

_____. (1909) 1970. *Tlingit Myths and Texts.* Johnson Reprint Corporation.

Tedlock, D. 1983. *The Spoken Word and the Work of Interpretation.* Univ. of Pennsylvania Press. Philadelphia.

Velten, H. 1944. "Three Tlingit Stories." *International Journal of American Linguistics.* 10: 168-180.

Veniaminov, I. (1840) 1984. *Notes on the Islands of the Unalashka District.* Trans. by Lydia Black and R. H. Geoghegan. Ed. by R. Pierce. The Limestone Press. Kingston, Ont.